CHARLES CRISMIER

SEDUCTION OF THE SAINTS

Staying Pure In A World Of Deception

elijah Books
Richmond, Virginia

All Scripture quotations are taken from the King James Version of the Bible. The choice of the King James Version was based upon its continued prominence as the most quoted, read, remembered and published version in the historical life of the Western Church. Emphasis is indicated by bold-faced type to highlight portions of the text for particular focus throughout.

Seduction of the Saints
Copyright ©2009 Charles Crismier
All rights reserved

Published by Elijah Books
P.O. Box 70879
Richmond, VA 23255

Cover Design by David Eaton
Interior Design by Pine Hill Graphics

Publisher's Cataloging-in-Publication Data
(Provided by Cassidy Cataloguing Services, Inc.)

Crismier, Charles.

    Seduction of the saints : staying pure in a world of deception /
    Charles Crismier. -- 1st ed. -- Richmond, VA : Elijah Books, 2009.

       p. ; cm.

     ISBN: 978-0-9718428-4-7
     Includes bibliographical references.

      1. Temptation--Religious aspects--Christianity. 2. Christian life.
   3. Eschatology. 4. Judgment day. I. Title.

BV4625 .C75 2009
241.3--dc22   0903

Printed in the United States of America.

Contents

Part V:
False Gospels for Synthetic Times

Part VI:
Seducing Spirits and Doctrines

A Preface and a Plea

NEAR THE END of the 20th century, I became strongly impressed to warn God's people of the difficult and challenging times coming upon the earth. Of particular concern were my American countrymen who profess the name of Christ in a nation proudly religious yet profoundly undiscipled.

As founder of Save America Ministries in 1992 and as host of *VIEWPOINT*, a daily, issues-oriented radio broadcast since 1995, a deep sense of concern about the spiritual condition of my brothers and sisters in Christ increasingly threatened to overwhelm me. The weight of the burden began to take its toll in my own physical health. Over a period of three to four years, as health deteriorated with the mounting stress from the developing picture of a spiritually back-slidden nation, I came face to face with the reality that, despite daily reasoning, wooing and warning by radio, I could not change the heart of those who claim the name of Christ. Only God, by His Spirit, can change a man or woman's heart. I was a mere messenger.

During the last fourteen years, I have been privileged to interview over 2000 Christian leaders, authors and broadcasters on *VIEWPOINT*. Since I often frame daily issues confronting our hearts and homes in the context of rapidly developing end-time events, I have explored with a number of guests their own viewpoint on the preparedness of professing Christians in America for Christ's Second Coming.

I have inquired of pastoral and para-church leaders what percentage of those professing to be Christians in our country they believe to be prepared for our Lord's return. Shockingly, the average response has been only 10 percent. The responses have ranged from 5% to 15%. How does this strike you? To me it is frightening!

According to the most recent Gallup Poll, 45% of Americans claim to be either born-again or evangelical Christians, yet our spiritual leaders find only 5 to 15 percent of these are living lives ready to face Christ at His return. The potential consequences are staggering. Terrifying!!

We are being set up for massive deception, giving all new meaning to Jesus' words, "Strait is the gate, and narrow is the way, which leadeth to life, and **few there be that find it**" (Matt. 7:14). Yet the prevailing message by pastor and para-church leader across the land is an ear-tickling message of the moment, pandering to self interest while bowing to the shrine of the Market. We are not, by and large, discipling God's people for eternal destiny, but instead are engaged in a temporal do-ci-do with the culture.

It is in this context I write with a passion born of urgency. Time is running out. For several years I have labored with the growing conviction that God's people desperately need to be warned of the massive and multiplied deceptions beginning to sweep the earth. The time is now!

To write about deception is a daunting task, for the breadth of the problem is vast and the scope of potential permutations and combinations of deceptions is enormous. To attempt to identify and articulate all is impossible. The best that can be done is to present an orderly and principled framework for identifying various forms of deception and their delivery systems and to prepare the mind and heart of the reader to identify falsehood and embrace truth. Realizing I most likely will fall short in the estimation of some, I nevertheless trust that by this book many will be spared an undesired eternal destiny.

It is said that fools rush in where angels fear to tread. That is particularly true when areas of potential deception cross over into or invade realms of doctrine. I acknowledge that I approach those discussions with considerable trepidation, yet I am trusting that you will not "throw out the baby with the bathwater" should we venture into thoughts that may step on some tender toes. The doctrines and traditions we hold sometimes have unintended or unconsidered consequences that may lead people into deception or into a false sense of security, deterring them from shoring up already weakened walls of spiritual defense. I ask for God's grace and your mercy as we continuously pick our way through some of these ministry minefields.

Read the pages that follow prayerfully. Be open to the Holy Spirit's tug on your own heart and mind. Remember, we are dealing with matters of destiny… eternal destiny. Let us prepare the way of the Lord together, preventing the *Seduction of the Saints.*

Yours for a Revived Church,
and a Prepared Bride,

Charles Crismier

PART I

The *Nature* of *Seduction*

Who can be seduced?
What is the nature of seduction?
Why would God allow people to be seduced?
Where do we find seduction in the Scriptures?
When does seduction take place?

Seduction in the spiritual realm closely parallels seduction in the fleshly realm. Just as all those created in God's image are prone to sexual seduction, so are we prone to spiritual seduction.

In the chapters following, we will explore the nature of seduction from God's viewpoint, particularly in light of the unique historical and prophetic times in which we live.

Chapter One

Titanic Deception

*"A tale of haunting deception hovering
over history's most remembered disaster."*

THE LIGHTS FLICKERED OUT, and in a thunderous roar, everything on the super-ship seemed to break loose. Beds and boilers lurched as the black hull of the *RMS Titanic* tilted perpendicularly; its three great propellers reared against the heavens. And then it was gone, and 1522 souls with it.

There had been no sense of urgency when the *Titanic* first struck an iceberg in the North Atlantic at about 11:40PM on April 14, 1912. When Edith Brown Haisman last saw her daddy, he was standing on deck, smoking a cigar and smiling at his wife and daughter. "I'll see you in New York," he said confidently, as his family was bundled into Lifeboat No. 14. "Everyone kept saying, 'She's unsinkable,'" recalled Haisman.[1] But the *unthinkable* happened to the "unsinkable." Emerging from the depths of the sea and lifeboat survivors is a tale of haunting deception hovering over history's most remembered disaster.

"A Night to Remember"

It was "A Night to Remember" said Walter Lord in his classic 1955 best seller. But the *Titanic* was by no means the largest disaster in modern history. Unlike the *Lusitania* and the *Hindenburg*, it had virtually no political import. "Yet it remains the only disaster that people generally care about." Stephen Cox, author of *The Titanic Story*, asks, "What is there about the Titanic story that keeps us coming back to it? What is the significance of this story?" "You can have a real story without risks, but the best stories are those that ask the riskiest questions about good and bad. When we try to answer them, we recover our sense of dignity of human life.... That's why we keep coming back to the *Titanic* story – because it makes us think about the things that matter."[2]

It is little wonder, then, that historian Steven Biel in his reminiscing cultural history of the disaster, *Down With the Old Canoe*, speculates that "The three most written-about subjects of all-time" may be "Jesus, the Civil War, and the *Titanic*."[3]

"Buried 12,000 feet beneath the sea in total darkness, gone from a world it momentarily defined, the *Titanic* refuses to die." "It's a morality play...," observed *Newsweek*, "a biblical warning to those who would dare to challenge the Almighty...."[4]

"We're All On The Titanic"

It remains a night to forget for those who were on board, but a night to remember for the world. It is an irresistible tale of tragedy and truth. "Seventeen movies, eighteen documentaries and at least 130 books have attempted to reveal the moral and spiritual mysteries played out in the drama of deception played out before the world on the decks of the *Titanic*."

"It's a moment in time that encapsulates what life is all about," said Tullock, of RMS Titanic, Inc.[5] The Titanic wasn't annihilated in an instant. It took two hours and forty minutes to sink, during which people – rich and poor, young and old – had to make choices. "It is an interesting fact that newspaper reports, magazine articles and books published shortly after the *Titanic's* sinking referred to eternal truths," wrote Bob Garner, senior producer for Focus on the Family. Yet "most of these were secular publications," he noted. Garner had been a working associate of Dr. Robert Ballard, who first discovered the remains of the great ship in 1985, resting two miles down on the ocean floor in the cold, pitch–blackness of the North Atlantic.[6]

There are pivotal points in our lives when we are brought face-to-face with the things in life that matter most. At those junctures are choices that must be made, choices that inevitably determine the course of destiny. Deception often delivers us to the brink of destiny. "It's a metaphor" for life, observed James Cameron, director of the extravaganza film production in 1996. In a very real sense, "We're all on the "*Titanic*."[7]

The "Unsinkable"

The *Titanic* was large even by today's standards. This was the grandest of the grand, "representing all the power, wealth, luxury and arrogance of its age." "The *Titanic* was built at the height of the Industrial Age, a time when technology ruled as a 'god'." She was promoted as "unsinkable," with her 16 watertight compartments. Several passengers wrote in their diaries that they overheard people claim, "even God couldn't sink this ship."[8]

Yet the *unthinkable* happened to the "unsinkable." One deception led to another. Passengers boarded, brashly confident in their safety. The ill-fated Capt. Edward J. Smith was also boldly confident, cranking up the speed to set a new trans-Atlantic speed record, even as the regal vessel approached the well-known North Atlantic ice fields. No safety drills had been conducted.

The wireless operators ignored or made light of repeated warnings of icebergs ahead. Even the captain seemed complacent. At about 11PM, when the ship's crew spotted "iceberg ahead," frantic orders were given to turn the massive liner. There are few more dramatic or spine-tingling lines in the history of cinema than those of the *Titanic* captain in an earlier film when, upon news of "iceberg dead ahead," he cries pleadingly to his ship, "turn," "Turn," "TURN!" exclaiming, "Dearest God!" "And upon news of having struck the berg, he utters softly, "Impossible!"

Yet the deception continued. Even though a three-hundred foot slice a little over a quarter-inch wide was scraped by the ice through the hull, nothing was detectible by anyone on board. But the "unsinkable" ship had been mortally wounded.

Still, nothing was detected by the passengers on board, even as the "watertight" compartments filled with water. Few had any clue what was happening. Many joked even when ordered to begin boarding lifeboats. Not until the "unsinkable" began listing and tilting did passengers realize they were in trouble.

"It was dreadful," remembered Eva Hart, a 7 year old survivor who, with her mother, was put on a lifeboat as her father was left behind. She could hear the screams echoing across the freezing waters as the huge ship rose, and suddenly slipped below, and all was darkness. "It was absolutely dreadful," she lamented.[9]

And so it will be when the consequences of creeping spiritual deception become manifested in our lives as we approach the end of the age. Pomp, pride, power, perks and position keep our spirits falsely afloat while this great "unsinkable" ship of earth takes on water, ready to plunge into the abyss where time and eternity meet. The overwhelming majority will be deceived. Their destiny will be determined. Their mournful cries will be deafening. The *unthinkable* will happen to the *unsinkable*. It will be dreadful. Absolutely dreadful. Yet there is a key... a missing key.

The Missing Key

"It looked for all the world like an ordinary key, but this unremarkable piece of metal could have saved the *Titanic* from disaster." Such were the opening words in a heart-rending report of remorse in the *Telegraph* online paper published in the United Kingdom August 30, 2007.[10]

Catastrophically for the *Titanic* and her 1522 passengers that lost their lives, the key's owner, Second Officer David Blair, was removed from the crew at the last minute, and in his haste, forgot to hand it to his replacement. The key is thought to have fitted the locker that contained the crow's nest binoculars, vital to detecting lurking threats to the liner in pre-sonar days. Without the glasses, lookouts in the crow's nest had to rely upon their own eyes, which were unable to perceive the disaster lying ahead until it was too late.

A survivor, Fred Fleet, was called by Congress to testify. When asked by the chairing U.S. Senator how much sooner the binoculars would have made the looming iceberg visible, he answered, "Enough to get out of the way."

Ninety-five years later, the key and its significance has truly come to light and was put up for auction. Alan Aldridge, auctioneer, said, "We think this key is one of the most important artifacts from the *Titanic* to come to light." "It is the key that had the potential to save the *Titanic*."

The Significance of Perceived Insignificance

For want of a key, the *Titanic* sank. For lack of a seemingly insignificant piece of metal, the world's greatest luxury liner and most of those who trusted in her safety met their demise. Dreadful! The *unthinkable* happened to the *unsinkable*.

And so it will be as the great ship of this world plunges at breakneck speed, setting new global and economic records, into the freezing and darkening waters of end-time deception. For most, it is not what we know but what we don't know that will define a destiny of destruction, both temporally and eternally. Yet we plunge proudly ahead, thinking we are "unsinkable." This is true for both professing believers and unbelievers. Both went down with the *Titanic* for lack of a key.

The key was not truly seen as significant until after the disaster. Yet it was this seemingly insignificant key that would have provided the clarity of vision and depth of understanding to avoid the deceptively dangerous iceberg that lay ahead.

At this remarkable and unprecedented moment in human history, the greatest and most significant key to avoid personal and collective shipwreck is ignored or deemed relatively insignificant. The Bible, the very inspired Word of God himself, has become either disregarded or disdained. Yet it alone, insignificant as it may seem in light of mans' titanic achievements, provides the key to life, revealing the dangers lurking not only in the swirling waters around us but in the dark and turbulent waters ahead.

We are on a collision course with destiny. Destruction for most lies ahead. Our vision is clouded. Our perspective is limited to our personal or collective earth-bound thoughts, yet the Creator, the Lord of history, knows what lies ahead. The Bible is our binocular. It is the "key" that opens our vision, our hearts and our understanding to see beyond our naked human visual limitations. Yet we must value the key enough to get out the "binocular" that will enable us to see the dastardly deceptions ahead that wait privily to destroy the unwary.

Pastor and people, presidents, potentates and the poor are all on board mans' prideful ship, churning headlong into the darkness of deception. Never in human history have the forces of deception combined with the Devil's demonic host into such a formidable agent of destruction to lead you into perdition. The greatest warnings to you and me come from our Lord himself and from His disciples. The telegraphed warnings are principally to the church, to those who profess to be followers of Christ.

Most will not heed the warnings. The apostle Paul warned that they will be gripped by "strong delusion" and that they will "believe a lie" (II Thess. 2:9-12). Some pastors, through proud and neglectful delay, will, like the Captain of the *Titanic* in a last desperate moment, cry, "Turn," "TURN," **"TURN!"** But it will be too late. They will wince silently in eternal remorse, "Dearest God." "Impossible!"

Most will simply plunge blindly ahead, deceptively convinced of the unsinkability of their ship in which they have idolatrously placed their trust. Hordes will trust the counterfeit Christ for a last great fling on the titanic of earth, spurning the hope and direction promised by Christ, the "Captain of their salvation" (Heb. 2:10), and His seemingly insignificant key. The carnage will be dreadful. Absolutely dreadful!

Don't let it happen to you!

Your Key to Avoid Deception

The Scriptures, known as the Bible or "God's Word," provide the "key" to avoid end-time deception. Our problem is not that we do not have the key but that we do not truly and seriously put it to use so that we can be guided in our lives to avoid the icebergs of life and the massive deception that now threatens to destroy us.

This book is an effort to take out the "binocular" of God's Word so as to give a more distant and distinct view of the deception now surrounding us and of the profound danger that lies ahead if we do not make timely course correction. Destiny will be determined by the value we place upon God's "key."

Remember, the *Titanic* is a metaphor for life. In a significant sense, "We're all on the *Titanic*" together. We may just want to replace the earthly captains in whom we trust with Yeshua, the Messiah, the Christ, who alone is the true "Captain" of our salvation and who alone can guide us in this particularly desperate moment of history through the multiplied icebergs of deception that threaten shipwreck to our lives.

Bon Voyage!

Chapter One

Daring Thoughts
for *Deceptive Times*

1. Do you agree that we have entered a time of unprecedented deception? What proofs point to such a conclusion?

2. What thoughts are prompted to your mind by the story of the *Titanic*? Why do you think it is history's most remembered disaster?

3. Do you agree that, in many respects, the *Titanic* is a metaphor for life… that in a very real sense "We're all on the Titanic together? How might that be true?

4. Why do you think the captain of the Titanic was so careless and the passengers so cavalier, even in the face of treacherous waters and known danger?

5. Do you think there is any greater desire to avoid deception today than there was to avoid danger on the Titanic? Why, or why not?

6. What is the current status of your mind and heart as it relates to spiritual deception? Do you think you are unsinkable? Do you believe you have any vulnerability to being spiritually seduced?

Beware of Deception

"Take heed that no man deceive you" (Matt. 24:4).

ETERNAL DESTINY IS AT STAKE! Any discussion of spiritual deception demands a level of soberness of mind and heart seldom sought and even less seldom taught in an age in which men and women are intent on seeking "their best life now" rather than preparing mind and heart for the soon return of Christ.

A meaningful and life-changing look at our life and times in the light of God's Word of wooing and warning will have profound significance for the way we think and live. At times, it will be provocative... and occasionally it may even pierce to discern the thoughts and intents of our hearts. Any attempt to deal with deception that does not woo and warn, and that is not profoundly provocative and piercing would be ear-ticklingly deceptive. This our Lord well understood as He addressed his disciples privately just before his crucifixion.

Deception is Dangerous

Jesus knew his time was near. He had just departed with his disciples from his final visit to the "temple made with hands" (Matt. 24:1-2), warning of its destruction. Our Lord knew that one day "soon" he would return for a bride "without spot, wrinkle, or any such thing" (Eph. 5:25-27). He was gripped with the warning of the prophets that precious few would truly "abide the day of his coming" and be able to "stand when he appeareth" (Mal. 3:2). Since the creator of all things (Col. 1:16) knew that "the Most High dwelleth not in temples made with hands" (Acts 7:48) and that men and women made in God's own image (Gen. 1:26-27) would be and truly are "the temple of God" (I Cor. 3:16), the prophet of Nazareth (Matt. 21:11) knew also that "If any man defile the temple of God, him shall God destroy" (I Cor. 3:16).

So Jesus had wept over Jerusalem which had rejected the prophets and now would reject God's final word of wooing and warning through Him, the only begotten Son of God, as well (Matt. 23:34-37). He warned of the destruction of the earthly temple by the world-dominating Romans that would come to assault the covenant people and destroy many (Matt. 24:1-2). The warning words of the prophet Daniel echoed in Jesus' mind of a final world-wide "beast" empire that would serve as Satan's final engine of destruction against the saints, to "make war with the saints," to "speak great things against the Most High," "to wear out the saints," and to even "prevail against them" (Dan. 7:7-25).

The words of the prophets were woven into the very fabric of the Master's mind as He sat with the disciples whom He had chosen to "be with Him" during his earthly ministry. He loved them. He had given himself to them, and soon he would give his very life for them. He was concerned about the things that mattered most. Their fleshly temptations and trials he well knew, for he had triumphed over them (Heb. 4:15) and would soon "resist unto blood, striving against sin" (Heb. 12:4). Knowing their weaknesses in the flesh and the determination of the Deceiver to destroy the disciples' souls and consign them to eternal perdition, Jesus took his final intimate moments on the Mount of Olives to warn them, and those who would hear them, of the unprecedented outpouring of deception and destruction that would define the end of the age.

God's Wooing

His discipling ministry was now complete. Jesus knew, as foretold by the prophets, that death and resurrection would be His crowning glory and culminate his mission. The Father had revealed all through His servants the prophets.

Yet another event lay ahead, of which the prophets also foretold. Most referred to it as "the Day of the Lord." Joel exhorted, "Blow the trumpet in Zion, and sound the alarm on my holy mountain: let all the inhabitants of the earth tremble." Why? Because "the day of the Lord cometh, for it is nigh at hand" (Joel 2:1). Joel then prophetically inquired, "The day of the Lord is great and very terrible; and who can abide it?" (Joel 2:11). Amos joined the prophetic choir, crying, "Prepare to meet thy God" (Amos 4:12).

But it was Malachi, the prophet of transition awaiting the first coming of the promised Messiah, who served as God's final prophetic old-covenant voice. He lamented the spiritual corruption of the covenant people. He warned of their selective obedience to God's Word and ways (Mal. 2:7-8). He excoriated their "treacherous" divorce practices, their gross self-centeredness and greed for personal gain on the near edge of the first-coming of the long-awaited "Anointed One" (Mal. 2-3).

"Ye have wearied the Lord with your words," warned Malachi. You pretend that God is not a God of judgment (Mal. 2:17). In spite of your tears, God "regardeth not the offering any more nor receiveth it with good will at your hand" (Mal. 2:13). "Take heed to your spirit," he pleaded. And then came wooing words: "Return unto Me, and I will return unto you" (Mal. 3:7). But wooing was not enough. They were deceived. While claiming to be the sons of Abraham by faith and lineage according to God's promise, they, like the religious leaders of Jesus' day, lived as if "Ye are of your father the devil" who "from the beginning abode not in the truth" (John 8:44). They, like us, needed a grave warning to shake them from the deception that had enveloped their words and ways.

Jesus' Warning

"The Lord, whom you seek, shall suddenly come to His temple," warned Malachi. "But who may abide the day of His coming? And who shall stand when He appeareth?" queried the prophet. The implied and lamentable answer was "FEW."

As Jesus concluded his famous "Sermon on the Mount," opening his earthly ministry, he warned those who would follow Him of the narrow way he defined for a life pleasing to the Father. He warned that **few** would "abide" it.

> *For wide is the gate, and broad the way, that leadeth to*
> *destruction, and many there be that go in thereat: [But] strait*
> *is the gate, and narrow the way, which leadeth unto life, and*
> *few there be that find it (Matt. 7:13-14).*

"Beware of false prophets," Jesus warned as he began his ministry. "They come to you in sheep's clothing…" (Matt. 7:15). The Master even described ways to identify "false prophets" (Matt. 7:16-20), concluding his Sermon on the Mount with a further warning against deception.

> *Not everyone that saith unto me, Lord, Lord, shall enter into*
> *the kingdom of heaven: but he that doeth the will of my Father*
> *which is in heaven.*
> *Many will say unto me in that day, Lord, Lord… but I will*
> *profess unto them, I never knew you: depart from me, ye that*
> *work iniquity (lawlessness) (Matt. 7:21-22).*

From Jesus' viewpoint, the most serious issue regarding deception was not what a person says he or she believes, but whether both the **belief** and the **life** line up with the will and ways of the Father (Matt. 7:21). It is little wonder, then, that Jesus warned those who had followed him for three and a half years of the profoundly deceptive times that would intensify as the earth and its kingdoms convulse in their inexorable thrust toward history's final hour.

The Deceiver and his demonic minions will be intent on taking hordes of persons created in God's image to eternal destruction and damnation. False prophets and counterfeit christs will arise and "shall deceive many." Because of the prevailing lawless spirit, "the love of many shall wax cold" (Matt. 24:5-12).

Jesus, as he awaited the prophesied events that would lead shortly to his crucifixion, spent his final precious hours before they would share their last supper together, giving a detailed description of what would happen just before his Second Coming. He wanted them and their followers to be ready.

When asked, "what shall be the sign of thy coming, and of the end of the world," Jesus answered and said, "TAKE HEED THAT NO MAN DECEIVE YOU" (Matt. 24:4). He that shall endure to the end, the same shall be saved" (Matt. 24:13).

Will Deception Determine Your Destiny?

Will deceptive teachings, cultural mandates, political promises, demonic devices, fear of man, fleshly lusts, religious systems, pursuit of world peace and a host of other end-time events, practices and purposes deprive you or me of our eternal destiny with Jesus Christ? The answer to the question is itself deceptively difficult.

If we simply deny the possibility of our own deception, believing it could only happen to others or to unbelievers or disbelievers, we may have very well confirmed we are already operating in the most dangerous of all deceptions… the prideful conviction that you or I could not be deceived. Since all warnings of the massive and unprecedented deception that will be characteristic of the end of the age ushering in Christ's Second Coming were made to believers in Christ, we should appropriately be concerned that both Jesus and the Apostles who warn us had an understanding and viewpoint of the end times that differs from that of modern "disciples" on the near edge of Christ's return.

Can saints be seduced? Can believers in Christ become so deceived that it will deprive them of true saving faith? Do not answer too quickly with blithe theological mantras, for eternal destiny is at stake. We must therefore explore in detail what the Scriptures truly say about *the SEDUCTION of the Saints.*

Are these the end times? Are we already seeing the unfolding of the deception foretold by the apostles and prophets, including Christ? We are warned by the beloved Apostle Paul that "ye are not in darkness, that that day should overtake you as a thief." "Therefore… let us watch and

23

be sober" (I Thess. 5:4-7). We must therefore explore the end times and our times.

To even purport to discuss deception in a manner that does not itself prove to be deceptive is a daunting task. The desperate need for this discussion has been incubating for years as I awaited permission from the Holy Spirit to proceed. I am convinced that the time is ripe and that the moment all history has awaited is upon us.

Therefore, let us prayerfully and humbly embark upon this open conversation together. What forms does deception take? What are the agents of deception? Is there an environment that leads to deception? Is it possible for a professing Christian to become an active participant... even leader... in deception? How can a person identify deception before becoming hopelessly entangled? Is it possible to be delivered from deception once a person is deceived? Is there any deception from which there is no deliverance?

All these questions and many more we will grapple with from God's viewpoint as disclosed in and through the Scriptures. But it is important to remember throughout our conversation that there are no neutral viewpoints. All of our ideas and conclusions have consequences. And many of those consequences are eternal. So let us begin, realizing ultimately that it is God's truth, and only HIS truth, that will both make us free and keep us free. VIEWPOINT always determines DESTINY!

We are the **temple** of the Holy Spirit (I Cor. 6:19). Four hundred years before Messiah's first coming, Malachi warned concerning Messiah's Second Coming: "... the Lord, whom ye seek, shall suddenly come to his temple..." (Mal. 3:1). There is no longer a temple made with hands. Christ is coming to your temple and to mine. But will our "temple" truly be his temple? Or will we be given over to deception and destruction as was Israel, the "elect" of God (Isa. 45:4).

Malachi poses a most profound question for our moment in history as we prepare to usher in the glorious appearing of our Lord and Savior Jesus Christ. "But who may abide the day of his coming? And who shall stand when he appeareth" (Mal. 3:2)? Will you? Or will deception deprive you of your destiny? "Take heed that no man deceive you" (Matt. 24:4).

Chapter Two

Daring Thoughts
for *Deceptive Times*

1. Why do you think both Jesus and His apostles gave dire warnings to the saints concerning deception?

2. Why do you think the prophets asked, "Who may abide the day of his coming? and "Who shall stand when he appeareth?"

3. Have you ever noticed that all of the warnings of the Bible concerning deception are addressed to professing believers, the saints?

4. Can saints be seduced? If not, why are they warned?

5. Who will abide the day of Christ's coming?

6. Have you been acutely aware of the deception sweeping across our world and even through the church? What have you witnessed? Have you been swayed by it?

Chapter Three

End Times and Our Time

"This know… that in the last days perilous times shall come"
(II Tim. 3:1).

PERILOUS TIMES ARE PROMISED for that era of human history often referred to as "the last days" or the "end times." The "end of the age" or "the day of the Lord" are also biblical expressions portraying that decisive period of God's final work among His creation leading to the culminating event known as "the Second Coming" of our Lord and Savior, Jesus Christ.

Are These the "Last Days?"

Are these the "last days?" Are the *last days* here… again? The Apostle Peter announced after Jesus' crucifixion and resurrection, "The end of all things is at hand," exhorting believers to exercise "hospitality without grudging" to prepare the way of the Lord (I Pet. 4:7-8). Paul, the great Jewish apostle to the Gentiles, warned, "The day of Christ is at hand" (II Thess. 2:2). The beloved disciple, John, announced, "It is the last time" (I Jn. 2:18). And the prophet Joel, around 800 BC, declared, "… the day of the Lord is at hand" (Joel 1:15). What, then, are the "last days?" Is this the appropriate moment in history to warn specifically of *last days* deception?

What Are The "Last Days?"

If the apostles from the time of Christ and the prophets predating Christ by 800 years warned of the *last days* and even spoke of them being, "at hand," how are we today to understand this term? Is it possible to frame the last days with accurate scriptural perspective?

The Apostle John records Jesus' final words on the cross, completing the Savior's earthly ministry. "It is finished," cried Jesus. What was it that was "finished?" Certainly Jesus had finished his life and ministry. He had fulfilled the "work" of salvation, obeying the Father even unto death (Phil. 2:8). He had become, as the "Lamb of God," the final sacrifice for sin (Heb. 10:10-14) to those who would receive him (John 1:12), purging our conscience from dead works to serve the living God (Heb. 9:14).

Fulfilling Jeremiah's prophesy and the Father's original intent, Jesus made effective God's covenant to write "my laws into their hearts, and in their minds" (Heb. 10:15-16; Jer. 31:31-34; Deut. 30:6, 14; 6:6). And, through the "veil" of his flesh (Heb. 10:20), Christ allowed us, as "priests of the Lord," "Ministers of our God" (Isa. 61:6) to enter into the Holy of Holies with true hearts "in full assurance of faith" (Heb. 10:21-22).

The "middle wall of partition" between Jew and Gentile was broken. Uncircumcised Gentiles, "aliens from the commonwealth of Israel, and strangers from the covenants of promise" were now, through circumcised hearts, "made nigh by the blood of Christ," joined with faithful Israel as "one new man," "no more strangers and foreigners, but fellow citizens with the saints…" (Eph. 2:12-14). Paul, a Jew, would become "the apostle of the Gentiles" (Rom. 11:13) to provoke unbelieving Jews to jealousy (Rom. 11:11) "until the fulness of the Gentiles be come in" (Rom. 11:25), so "all Israel," believing Jews and Gentiles, "shall be saved" (Rom. 11:26).

Has "the fulness of the Gentiles" come in (Rom. 11:25)? It has been nearly 2,000 years since Paul wrote these words. Jesus had declared just before his crucifixion, "And this gospel of the kingdom shall be preached in all the world for a witness unto all nations; and then shall the end come" (Matt. 24:14). Wycliff Bible Translators, dedicated to the mission of translating the scriptures into every language on earth, has now established the year 2025 as their date to complete this work. Is this the generation that will usher in "that blessed hope, and the glorious appearing of the great God and our Savior Jesus Christ" (Titus 2:13)?

The renowned Bishop Ussher, observing God's divine pattern in creation and in history, noted that God worked six days, and on the seventh day He rested. Ussher, based upon the Creation account coupled with biblical genealogical history, observed that God's work among men, created in His image, would follow the same pattern. His study lead him to believe that Creation occurred in the year 4004 BC, according to our current Gregorian calendar. Since prophetic scriptures generally see that "one day is with the Lord as a thousand years" (II Pet. 3:8), man's allotted work would conclude 6,000 years after Creation or in the year 2004 BC, after which would occur the "Sabbath" millennium, a final period of 1,000 years commonly referred to as the "Millennial Reign of Christ." Ussher's analysis places us clearly in that generation.

The **last days,** according to Scripture, began with the finished work of Christ on the cross and the outpouring of the Holy Spirit upon all flesh who would receive "the promise of the Father" (Acts 1:4-8). It began first with the Jewish believers gathered in Jerusalem from around the world on the day of Pentecost, the Jewish "Feast of First Fruits" or Shavuot (Acts 2:1-13). Peter, addressing the Jewish brethren experiencing the amazing "wonderful works of God" as the "promise of the Father" was poured out, recalled the prophesy of Joel 800 years earlier, declaring, "this is that which was spoken of by the prophet Joel," saying, "in the **last days**, saith God, I will pour out my spirit upon all flesh…" (Acts 2:14-47). The spirit-empowered Jewish believers, receiving the "promise of the Father" and looking to Christ, the crucified and resurrected one, as the long-awaited Messiah, quickly spread the message, first in Jerusalem, then in Judea, then in Samaria and throughout the Gentile world (Acts 1:8). By the year 2030 AD., 2000 years will have passed for the "fulness of the Gentiles" to be completed since the inception of the **last days.**

Jesus, opening his heart to his disciples on the Mount of Olives just before he was to die for the sins of the people, described the events that would precede his Second Coming and "the end of the world" (Matt. 24:3). In the midst of his discourse, the Lord noted: "This generation shall not pass, till all these things be fulfilled" (Matt. 24:34). Of what generation did he speak? While some believe he spoke only of that current generation, the weight of scholarly conviction would indicate Jesus meant "that generation in which the final described events occurred." We must therefore ask, "Is that our generation?"

Scoffers are aplenty. Many belittle those who bring focus to the Second Coming as using "fear" tactics. Others are saying that ever since the resurrection of Christ men have expected Christ's soon return; that for 2,000 years Christians have speculated or believed that their generation was *THE* generation. The mocking title of a recent book by a well-published evangelical author reveals much of the attitude of the church today, particularly in America: "ARE THE LAST DAYS HERE AGAIN?"

The Apostle Peter warned of this spiritually paralyzing attitude that, itself, would lead to dulling complacency. "Knowing this first," he said, "that there shall come in the last days scoffers… saying, Where is the promise of his coming? For… all things continue as they were from the beginning of the creation" (II Pet. 3:3-4). Peter declared such people are "willingly ignorant" (II Pet. 3:5). They are dangerously deceptive, keeping people from preparing the way of the Lord in their lives. And so Peter urges us to "be diligent that ye may be found of him in peace, without spot, and blameless" (II Pet. 3:14).

The Final Prophetic Countdown

Should true believers be anticipating the soon return of Christ? If so, how soon? We are well admonished by our Lord that "of that day and hour knoweth no man, no, not the angels of heaven, but my Father only" (Matt. 24:36). But Paul warned that while "the day of the Lord so cometh as a thief in the night" and will take most people by complete surprise, that "ye, brethren, are not in darkness, that that day should overtake you as a thief." We may not know the *day* or the *hour*, but we must know the *season*. "Therefore let us not sleep, as do others; but let us watch and be sober [serious minded] (I Thess. 5:1-6).

Is this the **season** for Christ's return? Are we in the final prophetic countdown to the end of the age? What are the key prophesied events that should grab the attention of anyone who is not asleep? Consider just a few that fall broadly within our generation.

1. The Rebirth of Israel

The rebirth of the nation of Israel is considered by most scholars to signal the final prophetic countdown to the "day of the Lord." "Shall a nation be made to bring forth in one day? Or shall a nation be born at once?", asked the prophet Isaiah rhetorically (Isa. 66:8). Isaiah then describes in poignant summary the world events that will follow that rebirth (Isa. 66:9-24). Read... and consider.

Never in world history has a nation that was destroyed, dismembered and dispersed throughout the face of the earth been reborn. Yet on May 14, 1948, the state of Israel was reborn, rejected as prophesied, never to be truly reckoned among the nations (Num. 23:9), while yearning for worldly favor. It was truly a miracle of biblical proportions. But that which has followed has rivaled the historic and prophetic significance of rebirth.

2. The Return of the Jews

"The Lord will... yet choose Israel, and set them in their own land" prophesied Isaiah (Isa. 14:1) around 712 BC. Jeremiah echoed the hope around 601 BC.

> *Behold, the days come, saith the Lord, that it shall no more be said, The Lord liveth, that brought up the children of Israel out of the land of Egypt; But, The Lord liveth that brought up the children of Israel from the land of the north, and from all the lands whither he had driven them: and I will bring them again into their land that I gave unto their fathers" (Jer. 16:14-15).*

Yahweh had warned His betrothed, Israel, through Moses, that if they refused to obey His voice as they entered the earthly "Promised Land," God would "scatter thee among all peoples, from one end of the earth even unto the other" (Deut. 28:64). It would be a lengthy and horrific experience because of the betrothed's adulterous behavior toward the Lord (Jer. 23:9-40). Both the ten northern tribes (Ephraim) and the two southern tribes (Judah) would apostasize. But God would woo back "the remnant" (Jer. 23:3).

> *Behold, I will bring them from the north country, and gather them from the coasts of the earth saith the Lord. Hear the word of the Lord, O ye nations and declare it… He that scattered Israel will gather him, and keep him, as a shepherd does his flock" (Jer. 31:8-10).*

Since the rebirth of the State of Israel, a most astounding thing has happened. A people scattered throughout the world have been returning to the land eternally deeded by God to Abraham, Isaac and Jacob, whose name was changed to "Israel." Just as the prophets foretold, they came first and largely from the north. The collapse of the Soviet Union aided the escape of huge numbers of Jews both from Russia and from former Soviet satellite nations.

God means business. The Lord had forewarned the nations, "I will say to the north, Give up, and to the south, Keep not back: bring my sons from afar, and my daughters from the ends of the earth" (Isa. 43:6). Israel has come from the north. Jews have come from the south. Ethiopia has "given them up." India is "giving them up" from the east.

"Behold, I will save my people from the east country, and from the west country; and I will bring them, and they shall dwell in the midst of Jerusalem: and they shall be my people, and I will be their God, in truth and righteousness" (Zech. 8:7-8). Until the year 2006, more Jews resided outside Israel than inside the "Promised Land." As of 2006, for the first time in modern history, more Jews resided in Israel than in America, the great Gentile refuge. The Jewish poet, Emma Lazarus, had written, "Give me your huddled masses, yearning to breathe free: I lift my lamp beside the golden door." But the golden door is now closing, even in the West. Anti-Semitism is now rampant in Western Europe, especially in France and Britain, and is exploding even in America. The dramatic discomfort is driving the Jews home.

In 2006, more Jews made aliyah (return) to the land of Israel from North America than ever before in history. God said, "I will hiss for them, and gather them; for I have redeemed them" (Zech. 10:8). "I will send for many fishers… and they shall fish them; and after will I send for many hunters and they shall hunt them…" (Jer. 16:16). It is all happening in this generation, just as God said. The global financial debacle is now driving the Jews to return from the West.

The Jew will soon find no safe harbor, even in historically hospitable western countries, as economic upheavals, dramatic population shifts and global politics again make the Jews the scapegoats for the world's problems and the objects of scathing scorn. The horrors of the holocaust will pale in the face of the hate-filled anti-Semitic sentiment soon to be unleashed worldwide, resulting in annihilation of two-thirds of the then-living descendants of Jacob (Zech. 13:8-9).

3. The Rejection by the Nations

Even as the Jewish people are rejected and ostracized globally, so too will be the nation of Israel. From the moment of her rebirth in 1948, the nations considered her an "untouchable." As a leprous person is a social outcast, so Israel was an outcast among the nations. Betrayal seems to have been her birthright, even by the best of "friends," Britain and America.

From ancient times, Israel longed to be like the nations around her. She wanted a king just like them, rejecting the Lord as her king. God gave her the desire of her heart, but sent leanness into her soul. Yahweh betrothed Israel as His "elect" among the nations, but she fornicated with them, lusting to be like them. Israel never comprehended God's husbandly jealousy to protect her as a virgin bride for Himself, chaste, unadulterated by the ways of the world.

The prophet Balaam had made clear from the days of the Exodus that "the people shall dwell alone, and shall not be reckoned among the nations" (Num. 23:9). But to this day, even after her divinely directed rebirth, Israel still craves to be cordially embraced by and numbered among the nations, just as followers of Christ crave to be embraced by and accepted by the surrounding worldly culture.

National Israel is now being rejected openly and nationally by the nations of the earth just as prophesied. Even as God again chooses Jerusalem (Zech. 1:17, 8:2-3), the nations reject Jerusalem. Since the early 1990's, the United States Congress voted to place America's embassy in Jerusalem, but both Republican and Democratic presidents have repeatedly refused to do so. The U.S. Federal Court refused to correct an American citizen's birth certificate from "Jerusalem" to "Jerusalem, Israel." The only two remaining nations with embassies in Jerusalem, Costa Rica and El Salvador, chose to remove them from Jerusalem in 2006 AD, our generation, so as to come into "politically-correct" alignment with all other nations in their attitudes toward Israel and her "eternal capital," Jerusalem.

Zechariah made it abundantly clear in 520 BC that Jerusalem would become "a cup of trembling" and "a burdensome stone" for all peoples and nations (Zech. 12:2-3). Implicit in the prophet's warning is that all nations will ultimately come against Jerusalem as Israel's capital. God is on record: "I will seek to destroy all the nations that come against Jerusalem" (Zech. 12:8-9).

The pattern is clear. The presidents, potentates and parliaments of earth have and are rejecting Israel. Furthermore, the world's foremost power brokers are conspiring together to compel Israel to offer up her God-deeded land on the profane altar of world peace. This is not prophetic speculation. It is profound reality… in our time… in this generation.

4. The Fulness of the Gentiles

Paul, the Jewish apostle to the Gentiles, warned Gentile followers of Christ not to be proud, thinking that somehow they were better than, or perhaps even replaced, the Jews as the "chosen" ones (Rom. 11:1-32). In his lengthy discourse, Paul spoke of a period of time allotted to the Gentiles. Follow his words closely.

> *I would not, brethren, that ye should be ignorant of this mystery, lest ye should be wise in your own conceits; that blindness in part is happened to Israel, until the fulness of the Gentiles be come in (Rom. 11:25).*

As we did in Chapter 1 we must again ask, has "the fulness of the Gentiles come in"? The period from the first Adam to Abraham, the physical father of Israel and the Jews, and the father of our faith as Gentile believers in Yeshua, was approximately 2000 years. The era of Israel and the Jews, from Abraham to Christ, the "last Adam," was likewise approximately 2000 years. The era of the Gentiles since the crucifixion and resurrection of Christ and birth of the Church is nearly 2000 years.

Since the days of William Blackstone and Theodor Herzl in the late 1800's, whose visions gave ultimate conception to the reborn nation of Israel in 1948, the focus and locus of history and prophecy have shifted increasingly from the Gentile world toward Israel. It is now an inescapable fact: the nations of the earth are now focused intensely on Israel. Jerusalem has increasingly become the prophesied "burdensome stone" (Zech 12:3).

The great political and religious power brokers of earth view Israel as both the prize and preventer of world peace. And Jerusalem has become the "apple of their eye" as they all seek, in their own convincing ways, to become king of the holy mountain. Without question, the season of the Gentiles is rapidly fading into the pages of history while Israel emerges as the center of the world. The rapid crescendo of conflict and conquest surrounding Israel seems to lead inexorably to culmination in our generation.

Where Do We Fit in History?

The tributaries of history and prophecy are now converging as never before into a surging maelstrom, rushing inexorably toward the final events of history as foretold by the ancient prophets, the apostles, and our Lord. Conditions on earth have been carefully described so that you and I would not miss the season of our Lord's return as Israel did at Jesus' first coming. Let it not be said of us that we "knew not the time" of his visitation (Luke 19:44).

1. Historical Conditions Reported

- *Days of Noah*

"As it was in the days of Noah," warned Jesus, "so shall it be also in the days of the Son of Man" (Luke 17:26). What were the moral and spiritual conditions in the days of Noah? We are not left to wonder. A quick inspection of Genesis 6:5-13 reveals:

Corruption was the norm.
Violence was pervasive.
Wickedness was great.
Minds and hearts were evil.
Judgment came "suddenly," after lengthy warning.

- Days of Lot

"Likewise also as it was in the days of Lot... even thus it shall be when the Son of Man is revealed," said Jesus (Luke 17:28-33). What characterized the days of Lot that should capture our attention today? Several passages give us clear insight (Gen. 18:20-33, 19:1-28, Ezek. 16:49-50):

Sin was grievous.
Sodomy was scandalously practiced.
Cultural influences defined passions.
Pride abounded.
Prosperity was worshiped.
Time was squandered.
The poor and needy were ignored in an orgy of greed.
Abominations became the norm.

2. Behavioral and Attitudinal Conditions

Paul, apostle to the Gentiles, wrote to his ministry protégé, Timothy, describing the "perilous" nature of the "last days." His behavioral portrait perfectly describes our times. "For men shall be...

Lovers of their own selves, covetous, boasters, proud, blasphemers, disobedient to parents, unthankful, unholy. Without natural affection, truce breakers, false accusers, fierce, despisers of those that are good, traitors, heady, high minded, lovers of pleasures more than lovers of God; having a form of godliness... led away with divers lusts, ever learning, and never able to come to the knowledge of the truth" (II Tim. 3:1-7).

3. Spiritual Conditions

The attitudes and behaviors that Paul describes as defining the **last days** are a reflection of and issue from the scandalous spiritual conditions. These conditions prevail due to unfettered lust, resistance to truth, corruption of mind and reprobation concerning faith, resulting in unprecedented "learning" but inability to "come to the knowledge of the truth" (II Tim. 3:6-8). In this spiritual environment, "evil men and seducers shall wax worse and worse, deceiving and being deceived" (II Tim. 3:13).

"The time will come," warns Paul, "when they will not endure sound doctrine; but after their own Lust shall they heap to themselves teachers, having itching ears; and they shall turn away their ears from the truth…" (II Tim. 4:3-4).

Are the "Last Days" Our Days?

The evidence confirming the matching of mankind, the world, human society and religious thinking to that described as characteristic of and defining the last days is overwhelming and shockingly descriptive. We see a reflection of ourselves, our culture, society and the world in a biblical "mirror" that ought to cause us to shrink in horror. Our magazines, newspapers, televisions and Internet exploration have blatantly and progressively blared the moral and spiritual realities of our times for an entire generation, leaving us without excuse if we had "an ear to hear" and "eyes to see."

But attitudes, behaviors and spiritual conditions are not our only reference points. Prophetic fulfillment is accelerating at breathtaking speed. Never in history has such a confluence of precise and profound moral and spiritual conditions, prophetic happenings and horrors occurred with the technological capacity of fulfillment. Mankind is on notice. We would be well advised to prepare the way of the Lord in our lives for history's final hour.

How Should We Respond?

1. We must respond in faith!

Without faith, we cannot please God (Heb. 11:6). Faith is the victory that will enable us to overcome in the evil day (I Jn. 5:4). Faith is not passive but active. It leads us to trust God in the midst of great trials such as the Scriptures warn are coming. And trust is always and first reflected in absolute loving obedience to God's Word and ways (Jer. 14:15-24, I Jn. 2:3-6, I Jn. 5:2-4).

If we respond in genuine faith demonstrated in genuine trust and obedience, we will not be taken by surprise by the dramatic events soon to unfold before the eyes of an unprepared world (I Thess. 5:1-4). If we are true disciples of Christ,

- We must be sober-minded and vigilantly-watchful, refusing to drift into passive spiritual sleep (I Thess. 5:5-7);
- We must put on the whole armor of God and the protective breast-plate of righteousness born of faith that worketh by love, and for an helmet, the hope of salvation (I Thess. 5:8; Eph. 6:10-17);
- We must prepare to meet our God (Amos 4:12), and We must prepare the way of the Lord, making straight paths of righteous living in a worldly wilderness (Isa. 40:3).

2. We must not fear man!

God has not given you the spirit of fear, but of power, love and a sound mind (II Tim. 1:7). The wicked flee in the face of man's rejection, reaction and resistence, but "the righteous are bold as a lion" (Prov. 28:1). The fear of man is a snare (Prov. 29:25), and it will lead you to deception and destruction.

"Be strong in the Lord and in the power of His might" (Eph. 6:10). Strengthen your heart in advance with the "word of faith." Be strong and of a good courage; be not afraid, neither be thou dismayed: for the Lord God is with thee…" (Josh. 1:9). Remember…

1. Do not fear those who can only do bodily harm (Lk. 12:4);
2. Do not fear persecution. It will come if you are living a godly life (Matt. 10:21-26, Jn. 16:2); and
3. Do not fear what man can do to you (Heb. 13:6).

3. We must fear God, and Satan's deception!

"The secret of the Lord is with them that fear him" (Ps. 25:14). The fear of the Lord is the beginning of wisdom (Ps. 111:10). Fear

God! Maintain an awesome respect for Him and His authority in your life, in the Church and in the world. The fear of the Lord and your great love for Him are your greatest defenses against deception.

Over and over God tells His servants to "fear not" powers, persons, and prevailing circumstances. There is one exception, however. Jesus explicitly warns us to "fear him that is able to destroy both soul and body in hell" (Matt. 10:28). Deception is dangerous. It can destroy both soul and body in hell if gone unchecked and unrepented. For this reason, we must diligently explore the nature of deception and how to identify and avoid it. Satan's greatest glee is in the *Seduction of the Saints.*

Chapter Three

Daring Thoughts for *Deceptive Times*

1. Do you believe we are in "the last days?" Why?

2. Why has Israel been described as God's "prophetic time-clock?"

3. Does it appear to you that the world's focus is being re-directed toward Israel and Jerusalem? Why?

4. Does our world resemble the "Days of Noah" and the "Days of Lot?" In what ways?

5. Do these appear to be "perilous times?"

6. How should true believers respond and live if we really believe Jesus is coming soon?

Can Saints Be Seduced?

"… in the latter times, some shall depart from the faith, giving heed to seducing spirits…" (I Tim. 4:1).

WHOM DOES GOD WARN? Are the warnings of Scripture primarily to the unregenerate or to those who claim the name of the God of Abraham, Isaac and Jacob, or who profess Jesus as Lord? What group of people are presumed to read and study the Word of God? Are they saints… or sinners? The apostle Paul declared, "the natural man receiveth not the things of the Spirit of God." Why is that? Paul states, "They are foolishness unto him: neither can he know them, because they are spiritually discerned" (I Cor. 2:14). If we are to be concerned about seduction, it is critical to understand to whom the warnings against seduction are directed. In this chapter we explore that threshold issue.

Seduction

The words *seduce, seduction,* and *seducers* or derivations of these are used nine times in the Bible. They appear four times in the Old Testament and five times in the New Testament.

To **seduce** means "to deceive; to cause to wander from truth, virtue or safety; to cause to err or go astray." Scriptural warnings against seduction, therefore, are warnings against deception. They seek to prevent us from wandering from "the faith which was once delivered unto the saints" (Jude 30b).

The prophets, apostles and our Lord were concerned that the saints be protected from the love of the world, from the lust of the flesh and from the lure of the devil. Sinners were already trapped by the ungodly trinity of the world, the flesh and the devil. But saints were to be new creatures in Christ. Old things were to have passed away. All things were to have become new (II Cor. 5:17). They were no longer known as **sinners** but as **saints**.

Who Are The Saints?

The prophet Daniel warned that a "little horn," commonly believed to refer to an end-time man who will incarnate Satan as a counterfeit Christ, "shall wear out the saints of the most High" (Dan. 7:25). Paul exhorted believers in Christ that they should live "as becometh saints" (Eph. 5:3). We are "called to be saints," writes Paul, and "the saints shall judge the world" (Rom. 1:7, I Cor. 6:2).

In the world of pop culture and common parlance, a **saint** is deemed to be one whose life reveals a higher level of moral virtue than the average person. Sometimes a person is described as a **saint** who performs a particularly virtuous or worthy act, usually without any apparent or direct benefit to himself. People commonly shy away from being called a **saint** because they feel it separates them from the common society and may result in subtle rejection, being seen as better than others.

Interestingly, God expects that those who call themselves by the name of His Son, Jesus, and who claim to be His disciples be separated from the world and its ways. "Wherefore come out from among them, and be ye separate saith the Lord... and I will be a Father unto you, and ye shall be my sons and daughters" (II Cor. 6:17).

We, in our flesh, experience a continual tension between our Scriptural identity as **saints** and our fleshly identity as **sinners**. This is why, while professing to yearn to be like Christ in our hearts, we, in reality, seek in our fleshly minds to be like the world. This was Israel's continual struggle, and it is ours today. We really don't much want to be known as saints, do we? We are unwilling to be truly separated unto the Lord who has betrothed us. We are "two-souled." And as James, our Lord's brother warned, "A double-minded man is unstable in all his ways" (Jam. 1:8). We are prime candidates for seduction and deception.

The word **saints** appears 95 times in Scripture, 35 times in the Old Testament and 60 times in the New Testament. Almost every time the word appears, it is in plural form. The Old Covenant concept of **saint** was to be hallowed, holy and godly. The New Covenant conveys similar meaning, including a person who is sacred, set apart, pure, morally blameless and holy. A saint, then, would be one who is godly, walking in holiness, morally pure and blameless, having sins cleansed by the blood of Christ.

Does this describe you? Does it describe your family or your congregation? If not, you are probably already and unwittingly caught up in seductive deception. Seducers always seek to undermine sainthood. Through partial truth, twisted truth and misapplied truth catering to the love of the world, the lust of the flesh and the lure of the devil, many a saint is seduced. So who are those who seduce? The Bible gives us some vivid pictures, and they are not pretty.

Who Are the Seducers?

Paul warned Timothy that "evil men and seducers shall wax worse and worse, deceiving and being deceived" (II Tim. 3:13). Are all seducers "evil men?" Certainly Paul seems to lump them together. But if the life, ways and message of all seducers are openly and notoriously "evil," how then are the people seduced? Are people so inherently evil, as a whole, as to willingly be deceived by openly evil persons?

OLD TESTAMENT DECEIVERS

The Bible gives us some helpful clues, but even God's viewpoint on this issue is increasingly rejected by most, including professing Christians. The prophet Jeremiah revealed, "The heart of man is deceitful... and desperately wicked: who can know it?" (Jer. 17:9). Jesus foretold that the end-time spiritual environment will look like "the days of Noah" when men's hearts were "evil continually" (Lk. 17:26, Gen. 6:5). But perhaps most importantly, Paul made expressly clear that in the season of the **last days**, professing believers in Christ will not be willing to put up with "sound doctrine" consisting of the full counsel of God, "but after their own lusts shall heap to themselves teachers, having itching ears" (II Tim. 4:3).

The general tenor of the minds of men and women, yes even those who profess Christ as savior, will be to hear only what they want to hear... what is pleasing, what makes them feel good, what seems to go along with the trends, what seems generally acceptable, what markets well and seems "successful." The clear trend will be, and now is, to "turn away their ears from the truth" (II Tim. 4:4). In such an environment, anyone who participates in the seduction from the truth is, by nature, a seducer and "evil" in God's eyes, for God always sees that which differs from His clear truth, refusing to agree with Him on any issue, as "evil" (See Num. 13-14, especially ch. 13:32, 14:35).

In such perilous times, when people "resist the truth" and become of "corrupt minds," even "reprobate" or perverted in their faith (II Tim. 3:8), "seducers shall wax worse and worse," multiplying so that deception actually becomes the norm, "deceiving and being deceived" (II Tim. 3:13). Times are truly perilous when the majority not only want to be deceived but become complicit themselves in propagating deception. Because such people "received not the love of the truth," "God shall send them strong delusions, that they should believe a lie: that they all might be damned who believed not the truth but had pleasure in unrighteousness" (II Thess. 2:10-12).

The spiritual history of Israel and Judah reveals this perilous phenomenon in part, but it will be amplified to an art form in these end times. After the reign of Solomon, Jeroboam, son of Nebat, became king over the ten northern tribes. Because they had no access to the temple at Jerusalem, Jeroboam took counsel and made two golden calves which he placed in Bethel and Dan, declaring, "behold thy gods, O Israel...." He set up a counterfeit priesthood to lead his alternative worship system, and "this thing became an sin: for the people went to worship" before these calves (I Kings 12:25-33). Notice! Jeroboam seduced the people with his rationalizations, but the people participated in and propagated the deception.

A similar thing happened in Judah. Manasseh, the son of the godly king, Hezekiah, reigned 55 years in Jerusalem. He built the high places, reared up altars for Baal, worshiped the stars and built altars for their worship in the temple courts. He set up graven images, led the people in dealing with the occult, and "wrought much wickedness...." The people refused to follow the known will of God, choosing rather to follow Manasseh's leadership. God said, "Manasseh **seduced** them to do more evil than did the nations whom the Lord destroyed..." (II Kings 21).

Consider the source of the seduction. As with Israel. So with Judah. It was "an inside job." The people had a will to be deceived and the seducers were their own leaders, not outsiders.

The Lord ordered Ezekiel to prophesy against the prophets of Israel, their own premier spiritual leaders, who purported to be the mouthpieces for God. "Prophesy against the prophets of Israel," God thundered, to those who "prophesy out of their own hearts." "Woe unto the foolish prophets, that follow their own spirit, and have seen nothing... they have seen vanity and lying divination... a vain vision." "They have **seduced** my people, saying, Peace; when there was no peace" (Ezek. 13:1-10). The prophets were the seducers, but the people were willingly "seduced" because they were of a mind and heart to be seduced.

NEW TESTAMENT DECEIVERS

The New Testament reveals and warns of seducers in the Body of Christ. Peter warned of "false prophets" and "false teachers." He said, "many shall follow their pernicious ways," and "through covetousness shall they with feigned words make merchandise of you" (II Pet. 2:1-3). The "merchandising" of God's people has never been greater than it is today. Truth is defined, and re-defined, according to whatever producers, publishers, pastors and prophets deem the market will bear.

The prevailing question driving modern "ministry" today is not, "What hath God said?," but rather, "What do the people want to hear... and, of course, pay for?" What sells? When the market defines ministry, truth is always a casualty. The door to deception is flung wide open, and the dollar reigns supreme. Such is modern ministry... and itching ears love it. Burger King defined ministry's modern mantra well, "Gotta give the people what they want." "Have it your way."

"In the latter times," Paul foretold, people "shall depart from the faith, giving heed to seducing spirits..." (I Tim. 4:1). A *seducing* spirit, in order to seduce, masquerades as a purveyor of truth. Most deception, therefore, wraps itself around a nugget of truth so as to have the aura of biblical support, but always tweaks the truth so as to either *misrepresent* it in substance or *misapply* it in practice.

For this reason only, Paul's admonition to Timothy to "Study to show thyself approved unto God" should become every believer's mandate so that we might "rightly divide the word of truth" (II Tim. 2:15). Beware! **Seducing spirits** are carried through the mouths of men who are not necessarily small-time cult leaders but who, more frequently, become bigtime and popular voices, gaining prominence largely by means of their pleasingly seductive messages. People want to believe what they want to believe. That is human nature referred to in the Scriptures as the sin nature or carnal nature, which is "enmity against God" (Rom. 8:6-8).

Jesus minced no words. Expanding on this warning, "Take heed that no man deceive you" (Mk. 13:5), He declared, "false Christs and false prophets shall arise... to seduce, if it were possible, even the elect: (Mk. 13:22). Jesus hammers the warning home, saying, "But take ye heed: behold, I have foretold you all things" (Mk. 13:23).

If these seducers and deceivers are not dangerous to the saints, then why do Jesus and His apostles direct their warnings to believers? Unbelievers are deceived and condemned already, aren't they (Jn. 3:18)? Clearly, it is professing believers that concern Jesus, John, Peter and Paul in their warnings.

"But," you say, "didn't Jesus say that seducers would deceive the elect "if it were possible" (Mk. 13:22)? The thought of most readers, then, is to conclude, *I'm a believer, and if I'm a professing believer, I'm also one of the **elect**, therefore I can't be seduced or deceived.* Yet such a conclusion makes a mockery of the repeated severe and specific warnings to followers of Christ to beware of deception, deceivers, seducers and deceiving spirits. Something is both spiritually and logically fallacious... yes deceptive... about such an interpretation. So the haunting question remains... "Can the saints be deceived?"

Can the Saints Be Deceived?

If we conclude, at the outset, that the saints cannot be deceived, there is clearly no further need or biblical foundation for a book titled *SEDUCTION of the Saints.* Neither do the repeated warnings of our Lord and his apostles have relevance. Yet huge numbers of pastors and their parishioners do not believe professing Christians (the saints) can be deceived. Why have they formed this belief that renders repeated scriptural warnings moot? The obvious answer is that their theology has been formulated in such a way as to foreclose the applicability of the Bible's serious warnings to the church about deception and spiritual seduction.

Consider for a moment. If you were Satan, the arch deceiver, and you wanted to invent or style a deceptive technique that would frustrate any effort that God might make to protect and warn His professing sheep against the whiley craftiness of the demonic wolves seeking to devour their souls, what would you do? The answer is simple. Convince the sheep that "they," individually, are under no threat from the spiritual wolves. Convince them that by virtue of them being "sheep," they are immune from wolf attack and destruction. "And how," you say, "might Satan ensure this deception has maximum effect and is easily received?" The answer, again, is simple. Lead the people to misapply and misinterpret God's own Word so as to render God's own warnings to the sheep inapplicable to them, while claiming Biblical authority for their belief. If Satan could use this technique effectively to deceive Adam and Eve (Gen. 3:1-6) and bring about the fall of man created in God's image, why should it not be effective to bring about the fall of men and women re-created in His spiritual image called "followers of the way," "believers," "disciples," or "Christians"? If the Deceiver would use this technique in his effort to deceive and destroy Jesus in His wilderness temptations (Matt. 4:1-10), why should he hesitate to employ it to deceive and destroy those who call themselves by His name?

We must all come to admit and recognize that the most effective deception ever devised is the use of Scriptural authority to support ideas, attitudes and behaviors that are contrary to God's will, or that differ from God's intended purposes as disclosed in the whole of His Word. We must also admit and recognize that our fleshly natures are not only prone to participate in and embrace such seemingly desirable misapplications and interpretations of Scripture but, in a perverse sort of way, take delight in doing so if it seems to provide a more pleasant or palatable understanding of portions of the Bible we do not like.

For this reason, the apostle Paul warned us to "rightly divide the word of truth" (I Tim. 2:15). Why the warning? Because you and I have a dangerous propensity and weakness to *wrongly* "divide," interpret or apply God's word of truth. Wrong interpretations or wrong application leads to seductive deception. These are seductive precisely because such interpretations and applications are often rooted in what our natural man finds most desirable to believe and in desired results that are most accommodating to our flesh.

Since the misquoting and misapplication of God's own Word is Satan's threshold and most effective method of seduction and deception, it should be obvious that it is not unbelievers but professing believers who are the objects of his craftiness. We must also remember Paul's warning to the church not to marvel, "for Satan himself is transformed into an angel of light" (II Cor. 11:14). As an "angel of light," the Deceiver seeks to mislead, disarm and destroy unsuspecting believers, using their willing or negligent ignorance of God's Word against them, convincing them to quote chapter and verse to support the very deception that threatens their souls and eternal destiny. Pastor, priest and people are all open game and are increasingly capitulating to Satan's classic ploy.

It is therefore impossible to seriously and with integrity discuss the seduction of the saints without entering a theological minefield strewn with common and popular beliefs about God, salvation, Christian living, heaven, hell and eternal destiny and destruction. Contrary to common belief, the most potentially dangerous to the broader cross-section of believers are not the more blatant and obvious errors of cults but rather the less obvious and more pervasive theological beliefs and systems that often, unintentionally and unwittingly, leave millions of unsuspecting believers open to Satan's nefarious deceptions. Perhaps the most common and popular such idea is that saints cannot be deceived… and certainly not me.

Why are so many professing Christian believers convinced that they cannot be deceived? Why do they often vehemently maintain that the warnings of Jesus, Paul, Peter and John do not pertain to them individually? The answers are rooted in the theological systems and teachings to which they have been exposed and which they have chosen to embrace.

These systems and teachings are the expressions of specific viewpoints that seem to carry a measure of, or even substantial, biblical support and therefore become convincing to those who choose to embrace them. The problem is that these theological systems, often described by the names of the men or groups that devise them, inevitably skirt or ignore significant portions of Scripture that cannot be conveniently squeezed into the mold of the system.

The deceptive problem for believers is not just in what is said, but in what is NOT said, thus leaving those who embrace these systems vulnerable to deceptions they do not know, or have been told do not exist. Pastor and people alike are caught up in these systems, preaching them as if they were the "gospel" truth, leading to faulty and even deceptively dangerous beliefs, attitudes and behaviors, potentially jeopardizing their own lives, those of their families, and even the destiny of those who hear them.

All viewpoints determine destiny. There are no neutral viewpoints. All viewpoints, including theological viewpoints, have consequences. And those consequences are often unintended, but are nevertheless real, and potentially pernicious to our souls. As a point of simple, but perhaps profound, recommendation, it might behoove us who profess Christ's name in these last days to set aside our allegiances to these systems and to explore afresh the entire Word of God. God has promised to watch over His Word and His Word alone to perform it. He has made no commitment to bless, endorse or enforce any of our man-made systems of theology or denominational dogmas, no matter how sincere or well-intended they may be. Allegiance to man's theological systems will carry no weight when we stand before the Lord of Glory on the Day of Judgment.

What then are the leading reasons why multitudes of professing believers are convinced they are exempt from deception and therefore need not actively seek to avoid Satan's wiley ways?

HAPPINESS versus HOLINESS

Since 1960, the attitudes and teachings of professing Christians and their pastors, together with radio and television ministers, have changed dramatically, particularly in the western nations. These changed attitudes, teachings and drifts in emphasis have been exported around the globe and now have infected and affected fundamental convictions of the church worldwide.

The driving engine of these changes is best described as "the pursuit of happiness." Jefferson's words memorialized in America's *Declaration of Independence*... "life, liberty and the pursuit of happiness" have become engraved in the hearts and minds of American Christians as if describing God's fundamental design and goal for our lives. The result, after decades of spiritual drift, is a "gospel" preached from our pulpits that does not call people to be saved from sin but to be saved from unhappiness. New "believers" are not called to repent but to be healed. The hope of our calling is no longer *holiness* but *happiness*.

Psychology has, in effect, become a surrogate savior. "Believers" are unrepentant, yet in hot pursuit of happiness through a mixture of therapy, self-help, positive thinking and a few favorite Bible verses. The very concept of spiritual deception or seduction in such an environment is vague, at best, and for most just does not register as relevant. The very idea of holiness is now nothing more than a theological abstraction. God says, "Be ye holy" (I Pet. 1:15-16), but the pursuit of happiness has seduced us so that the very idea of deception must necessarily apply only to those "pagans" who have not embraced the hope of happiness in Christ.

The collective effect of the exchange of *holiness* for the pursuit of *happiness* is vast and its implications great. The initial impact is to lure professing believers into a state of mind and heart rendering deception or seduction almost meaningless. That is dangerous, but is not as pernicious as the next reasons why so many believers believe they are impervious to deception.

ELECTION versus DEFECTION

Beware when the *Word* of God is raised as a standard to insulate professing Christians from the *warnings* of God! Yet that is precisely what we professing believers are prone to do, almost unconsciously. Since our flesh or soulish man is constantly at war with our spirit, our flesh or carnal nature constantly demands its feelings to be salved and satisfied. Fundamentally, our flesh revels in God's mercy, love and promises but recoils at God's truth, judgment and warnings. Frankly, we just really don't much want to hear God's warnings, preferring always His wooings.

Thus, even as "believers," we set ourselves up for self-deception by our very propensity to embrace "truth" that makes us feel good but reject "truth" that does not make us feel good or that does not tell us what we want to hear. Our fleshly or carnal nature, at enmity with God (Rom. 8:5-8), screams at us to choose interpretations of scripture that satisfy the flesh. When a number of scriptural passages might be interpreted as opposing each other, our flesh requires that we decide in favor of the interpretation that pleases our flesh and reject the interpretation, or even a vast array of other passages, that do not seem to say what we want to hear.

For this reason, our study of the Bible on issues that potentially conflict with our flesh requires a level of spiritual integrity that is increasingly rare because the spirit of deception has become the prevailing spirit here at the end of the age. With this caveat in mind, we briefly explore two doctrinal issues that are, alone, responsible for huge numbers of professing believers having the opinion that they, individually, cannot be deceived. The first is the doctrine or teaching on "election."

Jesus, in addressing his disciples on the sign of his coming and of the end of the age, began, saying, "Take heed that no man deceive you" (Matt. 24:4). Later on in this "Olivet Discourse," Jesus stated:

> ...for there shall arise false christs, and false prophets, and shall shew great signs and wonders; insomuch that, if it were possible, they shall deceive the very elect (Matt. 24:24).

Many believers respond to this passage with this line of reasoning:

1. I am part of the "elect;"
2. It is not possible to deceive the elect;
3. Therefore, it is not possible for me to be deceived.

That might seem to be a reasonable and logical deduction based upon a single verse. But consider... why would Jesus and the apostles Paul, John and Peter warn the saints about deception if the saints could not be deceived? Are the *saints* the *"elect"*? If the *saints* are also the elect, should we not have concern that notwithstanding our fleshly desire to believe that we cannot be deceived, that there is perhaps substantial reason to believe that such interpretation is neither correct nor in accordance with the rest of scripture?

The words translated "the elect" from both the New and Old Testaments come from root words meaning "select or chosen." We are reminded of the words of Jesus that many would seek to gain entrance to the great wedding of Christ and His church but would be rejected, not having a proper wedding garment, because "many are called, but few are chosen" (Matt. 22:14). But who are the *chosen*? When are they chosen? Who determines whether they are chosen? What does it really mean to be of the *elect*? And when are the elect finally determined? The answer to these questions may not be as simple as many choose to believe.

We have neither space nor time in this book to give an exhaustive treatment of these questions, but, instead, we will attempt to at least present the issues of concern, presenting scripture that casts a much different light on election than that embraced by large numbers of western professing Christians. Viewpoint always determines destiny. Therefore, our viewpoint on this subject is critical. The context for discussion is not just the New Testament or Pauline epistles but the entire Bible.

The word *elect* occurs 17 times in scripture, with four of those being in the Old Testament book of Isaiah. Interestingly, Isaiah declares **Israel** to be God's elect, not the church. Read carefully...

> *For Jacob my servant's sake, and* Israel mine elect, *I have even called thee by thy name: I have surnamed thee... (Isa. 45:4).*

This may come as a shock to many. Israel is God's *elect*. You may be thinking, "But isn't the Church God's elect?" The simple answer is, "yes." Both Israel and the Church are elect of God. But then you may be wondering, "Wasn't Israel, including Judah, rejected by God for her rebellion and disobedience? Didn't God make the Church the object of His election? Didn't Jesus say, "Ye have not chosen me, but I have chosen you, and ordained you... (John 15:16)?"

The problems in our understanding as Gentile, western Christians now begin to emerge. Jesus, in John 15:16, was addressing Jewish disciples whom He had chosen. Paul, a Jew, addressing the church at Rome, asked, "Hath God cast away His people [Israel]? God forbid (Rom. 11:1)." "God hath not cast away His people [Israel] which he foreknew," declared Paul (Rom. 11:2). "Even so then at this present time also there is a remnant according to the election of grace (Rom. 11:5). Note! Paul here is speaking of Israel, NOT the Church.

So where does that leave the Gentile Church? Paul speaks with great particularity to this concern. He states, "… through their [Israel's] fall salvation is come unto the Gentiles, for to provoke them [Israel] to jealousy (Rom. 11:11). Paul then warns Gentile believers, referring to Israel as the original olive tree of God's elect or chosen purpose, that Gentile believers should not become proud as if they are more chosen. In fact, says Paul, you Gentiles are the fruit of the root, and the root is Israel. The only hope of Gentiles is to be grafted into the original or chosen olive tree, Israel, through the promises made to Abraham, "That the blessing of Abraham might come on the Gentiles through Jesus Christ; that we might receive the promise of the Spirit through faith (Gal. 3:14).

Paul, warning professing Gentile believers that the same fate can happen to them that happened to Israel, makes a bold proclamation that huge numbers of professing Gentile believers and their pastors who hang their hats on a misunderstanding of election never seem to find time to read or include in their teaching. Here is Paul's warning. Read it… and take heed.

> *For if God spared not the natural branches, take heed lest he also spare not thee.*
> *Behold therefore the goodness and severity of God: on them which fell, severity; but toward thee, goodness, **if** thou continue in his goodness: otherwise thou also shalt be cut off (Rom. 11:21-22).*

The apostle Paul then goes on to say, "… they also [Israel], if they abide not still in unbelief, shall be grafted in: for God is able to graft them in again (Rom. 11:23).

From these passages we learn many truths about *election*. We also learn things that rather significantly differ from much common belief and teaching about *election* and the *elect*.

1. The word *elect* refers primarily to a community of people chosen by God, not to individuals.
2. Israel is the elect, chosen by God.
3. The Gentile church, as an ekklesia (the Body of Christ), is elect only as grafted in to the "olive tree" of Israel so as to inherit the promises through Abraham.
4. The majority of those constituting Israel were "broken off" from the community of the elect, and "spared not" by God.
5. Gentiles also can be broken off by God from the community of the elect or chosen (the Church).
6. Repentance by those individuals broken off or cast off from the elect or chosen community will allow them, by God's goodness, to be grafted back in, becoming again part of the *elect*.

We then find the clincher that helps to complete what the Bible really teaches about election; causing all other passages through the scriptures to come into alignment. Here it is…

> … *There is a remnant according to the election of grace*
> *(Rom. 11:5).*

To understand and rightly divide the Word of God, all passages dealing with an issue or subject must be interpreted together so that there is no confusion between them. God is not schizophrenic or a multiple personality. Neither is He confused, nor does His memory fail from one passage to another that might be interpreted differently. The problem of interpretation is ours. We tend to choose interpretations that we like, that are convenient and comfortable, or that suit our man- made theological systems. But as the apostle Peter made clear, "… no prophecy of the scripture is of any private interpretation" (II Pet. 1:20).

We now have good, sound, and biblical understanding of chosenness, election, and the elect that binds the whole of God's Word together and will help to clear up many misunderstandings and their possibly dire consequences.

1. The word *elect* refers primarily to a community of people rather than to individuals
2. Israel is God's elect.
3. The Gentile Church, consisting of individual believers in Christ, becomes part of the election by being grafted into Israel through the promises made to and through Abraham.
4. The majority of individual Israelites became un-elected from the elect group because "… they are not all Israel, which are of Israel" (Rom. 9:4-8, Rom. 2:28-29). They were "cut off."
5. Individual professing Gentile Christians can also be "cut off" from the community of the *elect* as were the Israelites.
6. Genuine repentance, according to the goodness of God, will allow either Jews or Gentiles to be re-grafted into the community of the elect.
7. Only a comparatively small portion (remnant) of both Israel and the Gentile Church will ultimately be considered by God as part of the *elect*, and even those will remain only by God's extraordinary loving grace (His favor and enabling power) (Rom. 11:5, Matt. 7:13-14).
8. It is this remnant which is ultimately "chosen in him before the foundation of the world" to be "holy and without blame," "predestinated" unto adoption (Eph. 1:4-5).

Now we have the rest of the story. We can see, now, why Jesus declared that if it were possible, these very elect, a small remnant of Jew and Gentile believers, should even be deceived. All true Israel [this remnant elect] shall be saved (Rom. 11:26). These are those who "endure to the end," said Jesus, because "the love of many shall wax cold" (Matt. 24:12-13). For this reason, Jesus gravely warned early in His ministry:

> *Enter ye in at the strait gate: for wide is the gate, and broad is the way, that leadeth to destruction; and many there be which go in thereat: Because strait is the gate, and narrow is the way, which leadeth unto life, and **few there be that find it** (Matt. 7:13-14).*

Undoubtedly the reason that "few there be that find" the strait gate to life is because the majority who even embark in that direction become deceived so as to head in the direction of broader ways.

SECURITY vs. APOSTASY

Can a professing believer be both absolutely secure in Christ and yet apostasize from the faith? Is it possible that one who embraces Christ as Savior can fall away and either passively or openly reject Christ? If a person "falls away" and never repents, will Christ embrace him or her as "without spot, and blameless," "holy," and "without spot or wrinkle" in the day of the Lord (II Pet. 3:14, Eph. 5:27, I Cor. 1:8)? If such a person enjoys perpetual "security" in Christ, why the multitude of warnings to professing believers against deception and seduction?

Why did Jesus declare in His final warning to the twelve who had followed him closely, "He that shall endure unto the end, the same shall be saved" (Matt. 24:13)? Why did Paul, the apostle from whom many claim a doctrine of "eternal security," warn the professing Christians in the church at Thessalonica concerning the revealed identity of the antichrist, saying:

Let no man deceive you [Christians] by any means: for that
day shall not come unless there come a falling away first...
(II Thess. 2:3)?

It should be apparent to any reasonably-minded person not otherwise pre-committed to a theological camp that one cannot "fall away" from a place he or she has never been. Paul repeats the same theme to his ministry disciple, Timothy, warning...

...in the latter times some shall depart from the faith, giving
heed to seducing spirits... (I Tim. 4:1).

Again Paul drives the same understanding home that once sincere believers can apostasize. Describing that "in the last days perilous times shall come" (II Tim. 3:1), he laments:

For the time will come when they [professing believers] will not
endure sound doctrine; but after their own lusts shall they heap

to themselves teachers, having itching ears; And they shall turn away their ears from the truth… (II Tim. 4:3-4).

The Apostle Peter also warned that many believers would follow the "pernicious ways" of deceivers who would "make merchandise" of the people in the final years of history (II Pet. 2:1-22). The warnings against "falling away" are numerous and serious. It therefore takes little imagination to see the spiritually deadly consequences of the belief embraced by so many that all who once embrace Christ are "eternally" and perpetually secure, no matter what their life ways are following a one-time confession of faith. This becomes nothing short of masterful deception.

It is little wonder, then, that Paul yet again warned that Christ has reconciled "to present you holy and unblameable and unreproveable in his sight:

> **If ye continue in the faith grounded** *and settled, and be not moved away from the hope of the gospel… (Col. 1:21-23).*

DEFECTION and DECEPTION

Jesus and his apostles make clear: deception leads to defection from the faith. If defection from the faith had no eternal consequences, the dire and direct warnings against deception would not be threaded throughout the New Testament. All warnings against deception are addressed to the saints.

Recognizing the grave realities, Paul warned the Corinthian church that what happened to the Israelites coming out of Egypt, preventing them from entry to the Promised Land, happened to them "for examples; and they are written for our admonition unto whom the ends of the world are come" (I Cor. 10:11). He then gave you and me a warning to be taken seriously:

> *Wherefore let him that thinketh he standeth* **take heed lest he fall** *(I Cor. 10:12).*

Paul enjoins us… you and me… in this dramatic moment of human history as the final events of the prophetic countdown to our Lord's

Second Coming unfold daily before our eyes. Paul pleads, "… let him that thinketh he standeth take heed lest he fall." We ignore such a warning at our personal peril.

Jude Does Not Jest

There is hope! Many will fall as the seduction of deception becomes more and more deceptive. Yet those who "endure unto the end, the same shall be saved" (Matt. 24:13). A remnant shall endure to the end, and I want to be among that remnant "elect," don't you?

Jude did not jest as he wrapped up the New Testament message leading into the Revelation. He concludes his rather severe statement of woes and warnings with words of hope that must hover over our hearts as we look further into the devastating and deceptive war of seduction being waged against the saints.

> *But ye, beloved, building up yourselves on your most holy faith,*
> *praying in the Holy Ghost, Keep yourselves in the love of God,*
> *looking for the mercy of our Lord Jesus Christ unto eternal life"*
> *(Jude vs. 20-21).*

Note, then, Jude's wonderful benediction to each of us. He reminds us that in the midst of the horrors of end-time deception, God is able to keep us from falling… if we truly want to be kept. Jude would never have given such gracious words if it were not possible for us to fall, would he? Meditate now. Memorize and remember these words.

> *Now unto him who is **able to keep you from falling**, and*
> *to present you faultless before the presence of his glory with*
> *exceeding joy, To the only wise God our Savior, be glory and*
> *majesty, dominion and power, both now and ever. Amen*
> *(Jude vs. 24-25).*

And all the saints echo… AMEN!

Chapter Four

Daring Thoughts
for *Deceptive Times*

1. Are the warnings of Scripture regarding deception and seduction addressed to saints… or sinners? Why?

2. Who are the saints? Are you a saint as described in Scripture?

3. Can saints defect or fall away from faith in Christ? If your answer is "No," how do you explain the numerous Bible passages warning about believers "falling away" or "departing from the faith?"

4. Why did Jesus, John, Peter and Paul all deliver dire warnings to believers regarding deception and seduction?

5. Are there ways in which you have found yourself drifting away from God and His commands through deception or seduction? Why have you been vulnerable?

PART II

The *Truth* about
Deception

Why is deception deceptive?
Who are those who will be deceived?
What part do I play in being deceived?
What does deception reveal about my life?
Where is deception most likely to enter my life?
Why is it so easy to be deceived?
When does deception begin… and end?

If deception is truly deceptive, we should well expect that there are nuances about deception that make it deceptive. We should also expect that there are aspects about ourselves and our lives that render us more ready to be deceived than we would like to think.

In the following chapters, we will discover truths about deception, causing us to think soberly about our own propensity to be deceived.

Chapter Five

The Truth about Deception
Part 1

"The thief cometh not, but to steal to kill and to destroy…"
(Jn. 10:10)

DIRECTION DETERMINES DESTINY. Most people have experienced the frustration of having embarked upon a journey toward a destination only to discover that somewhere along the way they have veered off course. It takes little imagination to comprehend the range of emotional reaction and response upon discovery that one is truly off course, not headed for the desired destination.

Frustration and exasperation might be expected as normal response for the time and money wasted in pursuing a wrong direction. A person might well be angry for having been given wrong directions or for having misunderstood directions. Intended purposes and schedules may have been thwarted or even aborted. Precious time and opportunities have been lost. Just imagine the anguish of heart for those who missed that once-in-a-lifetime experience, all because of a wrong direction. Destiny may well have been determined just by a seemingly simple misdirection.

And consider. People never intentionally set out to misdirect themselves. Most folk giving directions do not deviously, or even mischievously, set out to provide wrong information to others seeking directions. Motivation or intention becomes irrelevant when it comes to giving or receiving directions. Destiny is all that matters.

Timing can be as critical as directions. The right information received at the wrong time can be heartbreaking. A man boarding a plane to rendevous with his wife for the birth of their first child winces with agony when he discovers he somehow got on the wrong flight. A beloved pastor, rushing to Richmond to perform a wedding for dear friends, discovers mid-flight he is heading for Richmond, Indiana instead of Richmond, Virginia, and there is no possibility he can make the wedding. Destiny has been determined. The opportunity of a lifetime is lost.

So it is spiritually. As with the natural, so with the supernatural. Wrong directions can be devastating. Timing can be troublingly crucial. Good intentions are irrelevant. Truth alone triumphs. Direction determines destiny. It has been aptly said, "The road to hell is paved with good intentions." The longer one remains on the wrong course, the greater the difficulty in making timely course correction. This is the gut-wrenching, heart-rending reality of spiritual deception. Yet unlike most travel misdirections, spiritual misdirection is seductive... alluring... because while we do not want to miss God's Promised Land, our flesh would often not want to travel the narrow path to get there. It is important, therefore, that we take a closer look at THE TRUTH ABOUT DECEPTION.

Deception is Deceptive

Deception is DECEPTIVE!!! Repeat that to yourself. Deception... is... deceptive. This is a very simple, yet profound, truth. The profound implications of this simple truth will determine the eternal destiny of untold millions of citizens of planet earth, yes even of many professing Christians whose lives have been misdirected or who have drifted off course. Remember, the saints can be seduced. And remember also the warning words of Christ, "... strait is the gate, and narrow is the way, which leadeth to life, and few there be that find it" (Matt. 7:14).

If deception were not deceptive, there would be no deception. And that is precisely why deception is so dangerous to your eternal destiny. It might be a fair statement that no deceived person ever believes he or she is deceived unless and until the deception is revealed, and even then most still refuse to believe they are deceived. That is why the scriptures deliver such dire warnings to the saints about deception.

Our times are enshrouded in deception spiritually, politically, economically, militarily… even emotionally. There is a dramatically decreasing desire for truth at any and every level of society. The apostle Paul put it this way: "But evil men and seducers shall wax worse and worse, deceiving, and being deceived" (II Tim. 3:13). "Many shall follow their pernicious ways," declared Peter (II Pet. 2:1-3). People will be "Ever learning, and never able to come to the knowledge of the truth." Why? Because they "… resist the truth," they are "of corrupt minds," and they are "reprobate concerning the faith" (II Tim. 3:7-8).

Deception Dominates End Times

Shortly before His crucifixion, Jesus, gathering with His disciples on the Mount of Olives, warned them four times concerning the massive spiritual deception that would seduce those who professed to be His followers. "Take heed that no man deceive you," he warned. "Many shall come in my name," he said, "and shall deceive many." "Many false prophets shall arise, and shall deceive many." "For there shall arise false Christs, and false prophets, and shall show great signs and wonders…" (Matt. 24:4, 5, 11, 24).

The entire world will ultimately be engulfed in Satan's final effort to compel counterfeit worship of his counterfeit Christ by a comprehensive confederation of a global government and global economy undergirded by a global religion forcing every man, woman and child to receive "the mark of the beast." All who receive the mark on their hand or forehead will "drink of the wine of the wrath of God" and suffer eternal damnation, being "tormented with fire and brimstone," and "the smoke of their torment ascendeth for ever and ever" (Rev. 13:11-18, 14:9-11). Only those who "keep the commandments" and "the faith of Jesus" will endure this deception (Rev. 14:12).

Deception Dances With Sin

Deception takes many forms, comes through a multitude of sources and presents itself through a myriad of facts. Though often hidden, deception weaves its way, linking them all. Deception always dances with sin. In fact, deception is the consequence of our adulterous dalliances with sin. Sinful choices and attitudes, by themselves, provide the entré for more full-blown deception. They are the threshold over which deception is invited into our lives. Perhaps this is why we are told, "There is a way which seemeth right unto a man, but the end thereof are the ways of death" (Prov. 14:12).

Solomon provides a classic example. It was said, "God gave Solomon wisdom and understanding exceeding much, and largeness of heart." "He was wiser than all men…" (I Kings 4:29-31). God told him, "Let your heart be perfect with the Lord… to walk in his statutes, and to keep his commandments…" (I Kings 8:61). "But King Solomon loved many strange women" (I Kings 11:1), "… and his wives turned away his heart," "and his heart was not perfect with the Lord" (I Kings 11:3-4).

How about your heart? Have you, like Solomon, toyed with sin? Anger, unforgiveness, pride, rebellion, adultery, fornication… ask God to reveal your heart. "It is the little foxes that spoil the vine" (Song of Solomon 2:15). Have you, through the deceitfulness of sin, hardened your heart, opening the door to the inexorable progression of deception (Heb. 3:13)? Sin, however seemingly small, is insidious, and further deception crouches at the door, asking, "Will you dance?"

Deception Occurs Often By Degree

Just as deception gains entrance into your life through sin, so it marches confidently to take residence in every room of your life through failure to repent, thus facilitating persistence in sin.

Sin morphs into forms that satisfy your flesh. It conforms to the weaknesses of your personality and background. It advances to fill every space left void as you nudge out the Holy Spirit, who, through His still small voice, seeks to bring conviction, restoring your soul. Deception follows on the heels of rejection of the spirit of repentance. Deception gains dominion by degrees, at first seemingly imperceptible until it has you firmly in its seductive grasp. Do not let it happen to you!

Deception Seems Desirable

Deception gains instant traction in our lives because it is packaged attractively. It markets well to our carnal nature. This is how false teachers gain such prominence quickly, drawing substantial followings. "They with feigned words make merchandise of you…" (II Pet. 2:3). They scratch your "itching ears," telling you what you want to hear rather than what God wants you to hear (II Tim. 4:3).

This is how Satan captured Eve in the Garden of Eden. He caused her to question what God had actually said, luring her to substitute her own reason over God's wisdom. Once she entertained the sinful thought of substituting her thinking for God's thoughts, she was easy prey to rely upon the testimony of her own senses. Eve was seduced by the serpent because what he offered was desirable. "When the woman saw… that the tree was pleasant to the eyes, and a tree to be desired to make one wise, she took of the fruit…" (Gen. 3:6).

Even prophets and pastors can be and frequently are seduced through fleshly desire. Balaam was bought through the lure of desire, causing him to be willing to treacherously betray Israel. The promise of power, perks and position, luxurious garments and a pocket full of extra shekels by the ungodly king of Moab captured his heart with covetousness. Desire opened the gate of deception, and God had to speak to him through the mouth of a donkey to get his attention. Carnal desire was so strong that God's prophet tried five times to pray himself out from under the known will of God to obtain that which his flesh craved (Num. 22-24).

Our natural tendency is to see these biblical accounts as "things I would never do," deceiving ourselves in the process. Yet these forms of deception are so rampant among the saints as to be tacitly justified as "normal" and "acceptable."

Consider the matter of divorce and re-marriage which have, since the early church, been historically taboo among the saints. It was well understood that God hates divorce and considers it treachery (Mal. 2:13-17). The words of Jesus were unequivocal: "Whosoever shall put away his wife, except it be for fornication [sexual sin before marriage], and shall marry another, committeh adultery, and whoso marrieth her which is put away doth commit adultery" (Matt. 19:9). Paul confirmed it all with clarity, declaring, "The wife is bound by the law as long as her husband liveth; but if her husband be dead, she is at liberty to be married to whom she will; only in the Lord" (I Cor. 7:39; Rom. 7:2).

How, then, over the years since the pagan "sexual revolution," has the church, both pastor and people, overturned wholesale the clear commands and heart of our Lord to take the lead with a higher divorce rate in the church than among the nation as a whole? How has the divorce rate in the Bible Belt of America exceeded the nation as a whole by fifty percent since 1997? How has the divorce rate among our pastors now become the second highest of all professions, equal to that of their parishioners? Why did the world's fastest growing Protestant evangelical denomination recently change its historical position to allow divorce and remarriage when one's spouse is still living?

Eve and Balaam can tell us how. It looked good to the eyes. It was desirable to the flesh. And most of all, what God had said just no longer seemed reasonable to our minds in light of the new cultural mores and the craving covetousness of our carnal natures. We have been dramatically deceived, hypocrisy supplanted holiness, and desire defiled destiny. We have been seduced.

Deception Requires Decision

No man is deceived against his will. Every man and woman is ultimately deceived by choice. And this should be at once both consoling and terrifying. Deception requires decision. You cannot be deceived against your will. If you could be deceived against your will, God could not hold you responsible.

Decision determines destiny. Every decision we make is important. Seemingly small choices lead progressively to a series of further choices which determine the direction of our thinking. As a man thinks in his heart, so he is and becomes (Prov. 23:7).

Jesus declared, "…no man is able to pluck them [or you] out of my Father's hand" (Jn. 10:29). Yet immediately preceding this statement,

Jesus noted: "My sheep hear my voice, and I know them, and they follow me" (Jn. 10:27). What happens if I listen to and follow the seductive tones of other voices, even those purporting to speak on behalf of or in the name of our Lord but who twist or tweak the truth or its proper application? Will I continue to be our Lord's "sheep"?

It is indeed true that no one can pluck you or me out of the Father's hand, but we can do so ourselves by our choices. To believe otherwise is itself deception, making a mockery of the love of God, turning God into nothing more than a heavenly puppeteer, making puppets of those created in His image with whom God can have no more relationship than a child with her doll or teddy bear.

This was the precise purpose of the spiritual drama enacted with eternal consequences in the Garden of Eden. A loving God presented a choice to His son Adam, and through Adam to Eve. Eve was deceived through the lust of the eyes and chose to ignore Adam's clear instruction concerning what God had said. Adam then decided to adopt Eve's decision, born of deception, for himself. God cast them both from the Garden, decision had determined destiny, and the entire human race died in Adam (I Cor. 15:21-22). Only Christ's decision to obey, as the last "Adam," enabled mankind with the hope of resurrection, if we truly "believe," following Christ in obedience through His grace (I Cor. 15:13-22; Jn. 3:16; Eph. 2:8-9; I Jn. 5:3-4).

Decision always determines destiny. The final test of true worship will be defined by decision. It will be a decision that will determine eternal destiny. A choice to trust the anti-Christ system by receiving the "mark of the beast," revealing true worship, will consign the recipients to the torment of eternal damnation and the outpouring of the wrath of God (Rev. 14:9-12).

It would be only natural to wonder, in the abstract, how people seemingly walking with Christ and at least moderately knowledgeable in God's Word would make, or even consider making, decisions leading to deception potentially culminating in eternal damnation. The apostle Peter, who three times denied Christ contrary to his own covenant promise to the Master with whom he had sojourned for three years, tells us how such decision for deception happens. He tells us that in the last days "they willingly are ignorant" (II Pet. 3:3-5). A man is "drawn away of his own lust and enticed" (Jam. 1:12-15). The flesh is allowed to overpower faith. The creeping character of the carnal nature insidiously consumes the defenses of biblical resistence, leaving our minds vulnerable to the Deceiver.

Give no place to the devil, we are warned (Eph. 4:27). We must continuously and purposely "bring every thought into captivity to the obedience of Christ." We must cast down and take dominion over "every thought that exalteth itself against the knowledge of God" (II Cor. 10:3-5). These are true weapons of our warfare against deception. God's grace is sufficient for us in our weakness to enable us to be victorious over deception (II Cor. 12:9). It is unfortunate, however, that most will yield to the seductive wooing of the destroyer of their souls (Matt. 7:13-14). Their foolish hearts and minds will become darkened (Rom. 1:21). And their destiny will be determined. Do not let it happen to you. Flee every temptation. Remember, deception requires your decision.

Deception is Seldom Direct

Deception is deceptive precisely because it *is* deceptive. Few are deceived by direct, frontal attacks against their souls and their faith. No, deception comes in more subtly. It often comes gradually rather than suddenly. Just as our faith is built "line upon line, precept upon precept," so is deception.

Deception is usually wrapped around a nugget of truth, giving us a rationale to justify it. Deception is often wrapped in religious robes, giving it an aura of rightness. For this reason we must study to show ourselves approved unto God, "rightly dividing the word of truth" (II Tim. 2:15).

Eve's deception in the Garden of Eden involved the very Word of God. Satan, the serpent, quoted Scripture. But he put a spin on it. He marketed the Word to Eve's flesh. He gave Eve a desirable excuse to rationalize what God had said, to her own destruction. How many of us who adamantly profess to be "Christians" today, yield frequently to thoughts and corresponding actions that equivocate with what God has clearly said in His Word? Why do we do it? We see it more subtly. The truth becomes nuanced, taking on progressive shades of "gray." We actually become agents in our own deception, don't we?

Prophets, pastors and presidents are no exception. They, like we, find ways to wrap a religious robe around carnal motivations, making us all complicit in our own deception. As we have discussed, the ancient prophet Balaam was quite adept at such self-deception. He knew precisely the blessed role of Israel in God's eyes. Yet he was willing to betray Israel to the king of Moab for the lure of power, perks and position. How could he justify such egregious betrayal? It was easy. He wrapped his carnal desires in prayer. Five times he attempted to pray out from under the known will of God (Numb. 22-24).

Christians and their pastors have developed such religiously-wrapped deception into veritable art forms on the near edge of Christ's Second Coming. Have you? It has become, as declared by the prophets, "like people, like priest" (Hos. 4:9, Isa. 24:2). Be careful! Deception walks softly.

Deception Lies Dormant
Pending Decisive Moments

Deception is always pending. It is always lurking in life's shadows. It is doubtful that Judas ever believed he would betray Christ. In fact, Scripture seems to indicate that Judas did not really intend to bring Christ to the cross, and that upon discovery of the deadly results of his betrayal to the Master, he hung himself in despair (Matt. 27:3-5). Rather, deception lay dormant until opportunity knocked. Judas, along with the other disciples, was greatly distressed over the costly breaking of the alabaster ointment over Jesus. After all, "this ointment might have been sold for much, and given to the poor." "To what purpose this waste?" asked the disciples (Matt. 26:7-13).

Note! "Then one of the twelve, called Judas Iscariot, went unto the chief priests… and from that time he sought opportunity to betray him" (Matt. 26:14-16). Deception lurks in the corners of our lives pending decisive moments when our flesh is weak or our carnal nature is allowed to rage, undisciplined by our spirit. In such moments, the Deceiver strikes, and our responsive decisions may well set the direction and determine the destiny of both our natural and spiritual life.

As with carnal Cain, sin "lieth at the door" (Gen. 4:7). Since deception dances with sin, the stage is set, the person is primed to act in deception. Just ask the apostle Peter. "The fear of a man is a snare" (Prov. 29:25). The psalmist had declared, "The Lord is on my side. What can man do unto me?" (Ps. 118:6). Yet Peter's fear of man led him to deny his Lord not once… not twice… but three times. He feared man rather than God. Sin crouched at his door. Peter's agony of despair could not undo the deception leading to denial.

What decisive moment in your life has brought you to effectively "deny" your Lord through deception? What would it take? A lie to protect against the potential of a lost business deal? Cheating on your income taxes to "save kingdom dollars"? Receiving the "mark of the beast" so that your children can eat or to preserve the temporal life of a loved one who is otherwise facing the guillotine because of your faith or theirs? Decisive moments often determine spiritual destiny.

Deception Reveals Darkened Character

It has been said that a man's character is revealed not so much by how he acts in good times but by how he acts under stress. Stress brings into the open things that were otherwise hidden. So it is with deception.

True spiritual substance is not always manifested by superficial observation or appearances. Things in our lives are not always as they appear to be. "Man looketh on the outward appearance, but the Lord looketh on the heart" (I Sam. 16:7). For this reason, the apostle Paul said, "I judge not my own self" (I Cor. 4:3). He warned:

> *Judge nothing before the time, until the Lord come, who both will bring to light the hidden things of darkness, and will make manifest the counsels of the hearts… (I Cor. 4:5).*

It is clearly a breach of integrity when what I say I believe is not displayed in the way I live, in my choices, attitudes, and actions. When the *fruit* of my life does not reveal the professed *root*, my faith is outwardly suspect, open for all to evaluate without ultimate condemnation. The deceptiveness of sin pulls back the shades from the windows of my life, "bringing to light the hidden things of darkness" (I Cor. 4:5).

These "hidden things of darkness" were revealed in the lives of many biblical personages, each in a different way, such as Jacob (the supplanter) and Jonah (a prophet running from God). In the New Testament, Ananias and Saphira looked great on the outside but were seduced by a lying spirit, and it cost them their lives. Judgment from God was immediate as a warning to the early church that the Kingdom of God is serious business not to be treated with hypocrisy. But the Old Testament provides another example that should truly capture our attention. It is pregnant with illustrative principle for these end times.

Lot was the nephew of Abraham, the father of the faith, to whom God imputed righteousness because he believed and acted accordingly (Rom. 4:3, Jam. 2:14-16). Comparatively speaking, Lot was a "righteous" man (II Pet. 2:8). Yet given the opportunity, the scripture says he "pitched his tent toward Sodom" (Gen. 13:1-15). Lot, like many Christians today, was infatuated with popular culture. He loved the world and was seduced by its pleasures and promises. While he deplored the abominations of Sodom and the extreme wickedness of Gomorrah, he nevertheless intentionally chose to raise his family there. And it was not until Abraham separated himself from Lot and his compromised or darkened character that God pronounced His great blessing on Abraham (Gen. 13:14-15).

The glittering ways of the world are compromising many a professing believer's relationship with God. The lure of popular culture, its siren call, and its appearance of success have invaded the entire church, even our evangelical and "fundamental" churches. While deploring with Lot the abominable practice of homosexuality, we have been seduced by the *spirit* of Sodom. The saints have been seduced from pulpit to pew.

As God judged the salacious spirit of Sodom, Lot's sons-in-law mocked his warnings and were destroyed. Lot lost his wife as well. She longed for what she had left, and turning back, she became a pillar of salt, an eternal testimony to the danger of dancing with deception. Lot lost his wife as a result of his darkened character. What are you prepared to lose?

Chapter Five

Daring Thoughts for Deceptive Times

1. How does our *direction* determine our *destiny*?

2. Since deception, by its very nature, is deceptive, how can we identify it?

3. Can you see ways in which "deception dances with sin" in your own life? Take a few moments and reminisce on your past, even your immediate past.

4. Why does deception appear desirable?

5. Can you, in the honesty of your heart, imagine any deception that did not or would not require your own decision for it to become dominate in your life?

6. What decisive moments in your life have opened your mind and heart to the seductive power of deception?

7. Does your character most resemble that of Abraham or of Lot?

Chapter Six

Further Truth about Deception
Part 2

"… seducers shall wax worse and worse,
deceiving, and being deceived" (II Tim. 3:13).

GOD'S WISDOM CONFOUNDS THE WISE of this world. Man inevitably seeks to exalt his feelings and flesh over God's truth, the foundation and fulness of our faith. When man seeks to wrap his flesh and feelings in an aura of faith, deception crouches at the door.

Deception Progressively Dominates

Mankind seems to specialize in this subtle striving for godhood. We continue to elevate our own ideas and thoughts as equal to or superior to God's viewpoint, despite all the biblical warnings and historical displays of the horrendous consequences of such arrogance portrayed in scripture. Perhaps this is why God enjoined:

Let the wicked forsake his way, and the unrighteous man his
thoughts; and let him return unto the Lord…

> *For my thoughts are not your thoughts, neither are your ways*
> *my ways, saith the Lord (Isa. 55:7-8).*

Paul put it differently, stating, "But God hath chosen the foolish things of the world to confound the wise; and God hath chosen the weak things of the world to confound the things that are mighty." Why did God do this? "That no flesh should glory in his presence." The result, contrary to general opinion even among many professing Christians, is that "not many wise men after the flesh, not many mighty, not many noble, are called" (I Cor. 1:26-29).

When the word "faith" is conscripted to authenticate man's thoughts and worldly wisdom that contravene God's Word, seduction leads to spiritual adultery or "fornication" with the world. Fornication with the world produces bastard sons, who present a pretense of godliness in a variety of religious practices but who lack purity of heart. They have "uncircumcised hearts." Jesus spoke pointedly to this problem: "Ye hypocrites… this people draweth nigh unto me with their mouth, and honoureth me with their lips; but their heart is far from me. In vain they do worship me, teaching for doctrines the commandments of men" (Matt. 15:7-9).

Deception progressively dominates, using the very language of faith. Historically, discussions of the world's religions used the word "religion." During the latter half of the 20th century, world religions were increasingly referred to as "faiths." *Faith* was a word that Christians understood clearly to apply to their relationship with Christ alone. Now, common parlance worldwide is of "my faith" and "your faith." Folks of whatever religious persuasion have become "people of faith." Political correctness has captured the hearts and minds of Christian believers, compelling them into the world of generic, man-made faith… a "faith" that pleases all and offends none. The *power of the cross* has been supplanted by the seductive power of *political correctness*.

The collective effect of this progressive deception has been devastating. We, as believers, have adopted "line upon line" the precepts, wisdom and ways of the world, purporting even to use them to "evangelize" people to Christ. Our love for Christ and the purity of His kingdom has been supplanted by the lure of the world and its wisdom. How is it happening? We have wrapped deception in religious or spiritual robes to hide the nakedness of our seduction. The dangers ahead for professing believers in such an environment are incalculable.

Deception is Always Dangerous

Deception is never innocent because it demands that we make a choice. Therefore, we are held accountable before the God who gave us freedom to choose. Because we are held accountable for our choices, however innocuous or innocent we may pretend them to be, deception is decidedly dangerous to our destiny, both in this life and in the life to come.

Scripture paints numerous classic portraits of deception's dangers in both Old and New Testaments.

REMEMBER LOT'S WIFE

Lot was the nephew of Abraham, father of the faith and through whom both Jew and Gentile have hope through the covenants of promise through faith (Gal. 3:13-14). Each sojourned toward Canaan, the land of promise, but Lot became sidetracked toward that which seemed more appealing. Although generally a "righteous" man by comparison (II Pet. 2:6-8), Lot "pitched his tent toward Sodom" (Gen. 13:12), subjecting both he and his family to the most alluringly dangerous spiritual environment of the day, a symbol of debauchery and prosperous debasement to all future generations (Jude vs. 7).

God could not find even ten righteous in all of Sodom and Gomorrah (Gen. 18:32) and therefore determined to destroy these wicked cities that incarnated the pomp, power and pride of man's wisdom displayed in unfettered prosperity and perversion (Ezek. 16:48-50). He therefore dispatched two angels to destroy the place and to warn Lot to flee with his family. But the family lingered. They were infatuated with the spirit of Sodom, just as the majority of professing believers today are increasingly lusting after the ways of the world.

The angels grabbed Lot, his wife and their daughters by the hand, and had to forcibly lead them out to pry their hearts loose from their love of the world. And angels warned them, "look not behind thee," "but his wife looked back…" and "she became a pillar of salt" (Gen. 19:12-26).

Jesus, looking prophetically toward the days immediately preceding His Second Coming, described a time of massive worldly deception. He said it would be "as it was in the days of Lot" (Lk. 17:28). And to all who would purport to follow Him, he warned, "Remember Lot's wife" (Lk. 17:32). The deceptive allure of the spirit of this age is deadly. Remember Lot's wife.

PROPHET OF GOD

Prophets are not exempt from deception. Furthermore, the danger of deception to a prophet may be greater than the danger to others. To whom much is given, much is required (Luke 12:48). Furthermore, when one who is called as a prophet fails to accurately deliver God's Word, seeking to please the people, or fails to obey the Word delivered, the consequences can be deadly.

Just ask the prophet from Judah (I Kings 13). He faithfully and powerfully cried out, warning of God's impending judgment upon King Jeroboam, and even performing two miracles to confirm the warning. The king offered hospitality, begging the prophet to refresh himself in the king's house. But the prophet refused, saying, "It was charged me by the word of the Lord, saying, Eat no bread, nor drink water, nor turn again by the same way that thou camest" (vs. 9). So the prophet returned another way.

Now here is where it gets messy. You are about to see why few, if any, American pastors will preach from this passage.

Now there dwelt an old prophet in Bethel, and his sons reported all that the man of God from Judah had done that day. It resonated well with the old prophet, so he sent his sons to find and fetch the man, inviting him in for some good hospitality. The old prophet yearned for prophetic fellowship. But the young prophet from Judah responded, "I may not return with thee… nor eat bread nor drink water with thee in this place: for it was said to me by the word of the Lord, Thou shalt eat no bread nor drink water there, nor turn again to go by the way that thou camest" (vs. 16-17).

The old prophet, speaking with seemingly prophetic authority, said, "I am a prophet also as thou art, and an angel spoke unto me by the word of the Lord. Bring him back with thee into thine house… but he lied unto him" (vs. 18).

Now read carefully with all your heart! The young prophet, heeding the voice of the older prophet, went back with him to his house. "And it came to pass, as they sat at the table, that the word of the Lord came unto the prophet that brought him back: And he cried unto the man of God that came from Judah, saying, Thus saith the Lord, Forasmuch as thou hast disobeyed the mouth of the Lord and hast not kept the commandment... But camest back... thy carcass shall not come unto the sepulcher of thy fathers" (vs. 19-22).

The rest of the story is not pleasant. As soon as the prophet from Judah departed, "a lion met him by the way, and slew him...." "And when the prophet that brought him back... heard thereof, he said, It is the man of God who was disobedient unto the word of the Lord" (vs. 24-26).

Disobedience to the word of the Lord is dangerous! It is always birthed in deception. All disobedience begins with deceptive thinking that usually includes some, or all, of these ideas...

- But that doesn't seem right (Prov. 14:12).
- But that isn't what most are saying or doing (Matt. 7:13-14).
- But my pastor or that prophet said... (Matt. 7:15).
- But you don't understand my circumstances (Isa. 55:7-9).
- But I prayed about it (Num. 22-24).
- But God wants me happy (I Pet. 1:13-16).
- But I'll miss out on this opportunity (Prov. 3:5-6).
- But I read in several books that... (II Cor. 10:3-5).
- But it doesn't fit with our modern culture (I Cor. 1:18-20).
- But I just can't do it (Phil. 4:13).
- But could God possibly mean that (Prov. 30:5-6)?

To play fast and loose with God's Word is to dance with deception and death. That is true for prophet, pastor and people alike. Test all things against what God has said. Resist the temptation to rationalize. Resist the fleshly propensity to "forum shop," looking for some other scripture, some other interpretation, some other pastor or prophet, some other church that will tell you what you want to hear (II Thess. 4:3-4). It may feel good today, but it will destroy you tomorrow.

Remember! The Holy Spirit is present to teach and to guide you. He is "the Spirit of truth," and "He will guide you into all truth" (John 16:13). The Holy Spirit is NOT your feelings but is there to quicken your faith.

God does NOT change (Mal. 3:6). We are the ones who change. God's Spirit will never lead you to believe or act contrary to His written Word. And be comforted with this: God's Spirit and Word will never lead you where His grace cannot keep you.

Deception is dangerous!

Deception Defines Dominion

We become the servant of that to which we yield. When we obey, we are servants of God. When we disobey, we serve Satan and his kingdom, giving him dominion. Sin leads to death; obedience leads to righteousness (Rom. 6:16).

It becomes clear why the Apostle Paul warns, "Let not sin reign in your mortal body, that ye should obey the lusts thereof. Neither yield ye your members as instruments of unrighteousness unto sin: but yield yourselves unto God…" (Rom. 6:12-13). Yielding to deception leads to sin, gradually shifting our life's dominion from Christ to Satan. This is why James urges: "Submit yourselves therefore to God. Resist the devil, and he will flee from you" (James 4:7).

"Submitting to God" means agreeing with what God has said in His Word and choosing to conduct my life accordingly. When I choose otherwise, I have submitted to Satan to that extent. Deception sets in, leading me to increasingly choose contrary to what God has said, leading me unwittingly down the primrose path to destruction.

Joshua declared, "Choose you this day whom you will serve" (Josh. 24:15). We must make the choice for dominion daily, sometimes multiple times during a day. Israel vowed, "God forbid that we should forsake the Lord… nay, but we will serve the Lord. His voice will we obey" (Josh. 24:16-24). But they did not obey God. They corrupted themselves through progressive deception and "ceased not from their own doings, nor from their stubborn way" (Judg. 2:19). In fact, "they turned quickly out of the way" and did not obey the commandments of the Lord (Judg. 2:17).

Jesus warned, "He that shall endure unto the end, the same shall be saved" (Matt. 24:13). Will you endure the incessant deception that seeks to captivate the allegiance of your soul into Satan's dominion? Are you truly delighting "in the law of God after the inward man" (Rom. 7:22)? Or are you submitting to "another law" warring against your mind, bringing you "into captivity to the law of sin" (Rom. 7:23)?

Remember, "the carnal mind is enmity against God: for it is not subject to the law of God, neither indeed can be" (Rom. 8:7). Let us, therefore, as we see Christ's return approaching, be "spiritually minded," submitting our wills to God's Word and will. To submit to God and His Word will bring "life and peace" in a world of increasing chaos (Rom. 8:6).

Deception Yields to Fleshly Demands

Our flesh constantly demands to be satisfied. That is why our principal battle is a veritable war between "the flesh and the spirit."

Unfortunately, deception plays upon fleshly demands. In fact, deception is a yielding to fleshly demands and, if left unchecked, will persist progressively to yield to ever-deeper demands until I become ruled by or under the dominion of the flesh.

This is precisely why Paul warns of the "itching ears" syndrome of the last days (II Tim. 4:3-4). The demands of the flesh and the world will be, and currently are, so great that even professing followers of Christ lose their love of the truth, demanding pastor, prophet and parachurch leader to tell them what they want to hear. Burger King has accurately defined our predominate theological methodology… "Gotta give the people what they want." "Have it your way."

Yet fleshly demands manifest themselves in many other ways, all of which are rooted in deception and produce poisonous fruit.

DAVID and BATHSHEBA

"At the time when kings go forth to battle," "David tarried in Jerusalem." In the evening, "David arose from off his bed, and walked upon the roof… and he saw a woman washing herself… very beautiful to look upon." "And David sent and enquired after the woman.. .and he lay with her" (II Sam. 11:1-4).

David was a man given to fleshly passions as are all men, moved by their eyes. When he should have been waging war with his men, he was entertaining himself in idleness. And that is precisely how 60-70 percent of Christian men and 30 percent of their pastors have become ensnared in the spirit-defiling, marriage-destroying deception of pornography. Now, even 34 percent of Christian women admit to seeking out pornography. Pursuit of the flesh is destroying our faith, opening our families to a host of demonic deceptions, leading those we deemed precious to perdition.

How or when will it stop? It will stop when we again become engaged in the real battles for the souls of men and stop giving ourselves to idleness, and entertainment and the lust of the flesh. All sin is addictive and monstrously deceptive, compromising our eternal destiny. If we sow to the flesh, we shall of the flesh reap corruption, "but he that soweth to the Spirit shall of the Spirit reap life everlasting" (Gal. 6:8).

"Let us not be weary in well doing: for in due season we shall reap, IF we faint not" (Gal. 6:9).

Deception Delights in Company

Deception demands validation. For that reason, those walking in deception or dancing peripherally with deception will always have plenty of company. As human beings, we want to believe that others think like us. One of our greatest needs is the desire to belong, to be accepted. We want to be in the "in" group or at least not part of some bunch we perceive are not generally accepted.

Since deception is the norm rather than the exception, as clearly portrayed in the Scriptures, the company of the deceived is not hard to find. People dancing with deception always tend to gravitate together. It is true… misery really does love company… birds of a feather really do flock together.

Because deception demands validation and because we tend to gravitate to like-minded or like-spirited people, deception tends to congregate over issues that bind us. For instance, if I want to divorce my spouse and re-marry, even if the Scriptures clearly say otherwise, my tendency will be to search for a pastor and congregation that will validate my desired position. The same is true for those seeking to walk in homosexuality or abortion. Whole congregations, then, will tend to be at least drawn to, if not driven by, one or more areas of deception.

This problem is exacerbated in democratic societies, particularly western culture. Cultural reliance upon a democratic majority to determine the course of action for a group or nation unwittingly becomes a system of validation for wrong ideas as well as right ideas. The popular phrase, "But everybody is doing it!" is an expression of just how deception delights in company. The rationale is that if a large enough number of people believe a certain way, it must provide adequate validation for me believing that way, or at least provide a measure of security that I am certainly not alone. Such thinking may be convenient, but not correct. In fact, it may be, and likely is, downright dangerous.

The Scriptures tell us why we cannot rely upon majority rule in determining truth, especially in these end times. Consider these carefully.

"Many will say…"

"Broad is the way, that leadeth to destruction, and many there be which go in thereat," said Jesus, "But narrow is the way, which leadeth unto life, and few there be that find it" (Matt. 7:13-14).

"Many will say to me in that day, Lord, Lord… and then will I profess unto them, I never knew you: depart from me…" (Matt. 7:22-23). "Not everyone that saith unto me, Lord, Lord, shall enter into the kingdom of heaven; but he that doeth the will of my Father which is in heaven" (Matt. 7:21). Whew! That begins to put things into profound perspective, doesn't it?

"Many shall… deceive many"

"Take heed lest any man deceive you," warned Jesus. Why is it that so many will be prone to deception? In addition to a rebellious spiritual environment where "the love of many shall wax cold" (Matt. 24:12), massive deception will be pervasive among the general "Christian" populace. The sheer numbers of the increasingly deceived, as "birds of a feather flock together," will create a kind of spiritual "jet stream," sucking the unsuspecting into its powerful draw. In that context, Jesus noted, "Many shall come in my name… and shall deceive many" (Mark 13:5-6).

It is critical to note that many who will be deceived will be deceived precisely because it comes in the name of Christ. Furthermore, it is not a peripheral minority but many who will be so deceived. Jesus, with great loving concern, gives us advance warning so that we will not be so deceived. Yet many will. Most do not believe they can be deceived. It's always "them," the other guy, or those "unbelievers." Yet the scriptural warnings are always to professing believers.

"Many shall follow…"

Notice again! Peter, warning of false teachers who, "through covetousness," "with feigned words make merchandise of you," makes clear that it is believers who become deceived (II Pet. 2:1-3)). Neither is his concern for a comparatively insignificant minority but rather for "many." "Many shall follow their pernicious [deadly] ways," he warns.

It should be increasingly clear that professing Christian believers are, and will be, at profound risk and must be forewarned so as to be fore-armed. So great does deception desire company that the end-time picture will be nothing short of a massive "falling away" (II Tim. 2:3, I Tim. 4:1).

Here is hope! Christ desires "to present you holy and unblameable and unreproveable in his sight." This hope is yours "If ye continue in the faith grounded and settled, and be not moved away from the hope of the gospel…" (Col. 1:22-23).

Chapter Six

Daring Thoughts
for *Deceptive Times*

1. Why is it that deception works progressively?

2. Can you think of any deception that is not ultimately dangerous?

3. Deception is always connected to either confusing or ignoring all or a portion of what God has said. In reviewing your own life with as much honesty as you can muster, can you see where you have danced with deception by confusing, ignoring or rationalizing what God has said?

4. Why is it that deception gains dominance by drawing us to yield to fleshly demands?

5. Have you been seduced into deceptive thinking or actions by the power of "democratic" majority thinking? Take a moment and trace the progress of your thinking on a specific area that the Holy Spirit now brings to light.

The Truth about Deception
Part 3

*"Let no man deceive you with vain words:
for because of these things cometh the wrath
of God upon the children of disobedience" (Eph. 5:6).*

DECEPTION IS DESTRUCTIVE! Satan wants to destroy you. "The thief cometh not, but for to steal, and to kill, and to destroy," said Jesus, but "I am come that they might have life, and that they might have it more abundantly" (Jn. 10:10).

If Jesus comes to bring us life under the Father's authority, Satan's primary tool, calculated for our destruction, is to undermine God's authority in our lives. He is clever. He is cool. And he is calculating. His weapons are carnal. But "the weapons of our warfare are not carnal, but mighty through God to the pulling down of strongholds" (I Cor. 10:4).

Satan plays upon our weaknesses "in the flesh." He always seeks to use the flesh and carnal desires against God's creation so as to get back at God. Unfortunately, we too often are willing pawns in this cosmic struggle. The real issue in all deception is God's authority.

Deception Defies Divine Authority

Remember! Satan is a rebel. He was the greatest, most glorious of all created beings. The Scriptures declare he was "full of wisdom, and perfect in beauty." This arch deceiver was "the anointed cherub that covereth," set by God Himself. He was "upon the holy mountain of God, and "walked up and down in the midst of the stones of fire" in heaven. God declared, "Thou wast perfect in thy ways from the day that thou wast created, till iniquity was found in thee" (Ezek. 28:12-15).

Just imagine Lucifer's glory. It was next to the very Creator of the universe. The prophet Ezekiel writes of the "prince of Tyrus" as a type of Lucifer, whose name meant "day star" or "son of the morning" (Eph. 28:29; Isa. 14:12). Ezekiel notes, "By thy great wisdom... hast thou increased thy riches, and thine heart is lifted up...." "Because thou hast set thine heart as the heart of God... they shall defile thy brightness. They shall bring thee down to the pit..." (Ezek. 28:5-8).

What was the driving issue between Lucifer and his Creator? It was authority. Who is and will be authority in heaven? Isaiah gets right to the point. "For thou has said in thine heart, I will ascend into heaven, I will exalt my throne above the stars of God: I will sit also upon the mount of the congregation... I will ascend above the heights of the clouds; I will be like the most High" (Isa. 14:13-14).

It seems that the "I's" have it. Five times Lucifer exalts himself to be equal with God. And that is precisely what Satan's seduction lures you to do. Lucifer seduced a third of the angels of heaven into his heavenly insurrection (Rev. 12:4, Dan. 8:10), for which prideful rebellion God cast him out (Ezek. 28:16). Now Satan seeks to draw not only the angels but men, you and me, into the same insurrection against the government of God. And if God would cast out the "anointed cherub that covereth" who was "perfect in beauty," "full of wisdom," he will likewise cast out His human creation who seek to make themselves equal with God by rebelling against His authority on earth.

How might Satan accomplish his nefarious goal? How might he seduce the maximum number of earth's men and women to join his rebellion?

There is growing arrogance in our world today to *defy* God and to *deify* man. It comes in many forms, some disguised and others blatant.

When scientists declare their goal in extending life is to develop "eternal life" as was stated in a national news magazine, there is a not-so-subtle intent to become "gods" in our own right and to eliminate the need for the Savior's offer of eternal life through His sacrifice for sin.

More shocking is the heart conviction declared by an international engineer for the Sony Corporation. As we chatted while waiting for our plane at the Los Angeles International Airport in 1995, he proudly reported on the recent amazing technological discoveries and those shortly to come, replacing much of the Creator's handiwork. Then, without missing a beat, and as if such a statement were natural and to be expected, he simply declared, "And the day is coming when we will be God."

Whew! It is shocking, isn't it? The sheer arrogance is truly breathtaking. This man showed no hint of any faith in anything beyond himself and the collective power and pride of man to save himself and become his own god. Yet what else should we ultimately expect as we approach the end of the age but just that mind set? Pagans will be pagans. Unbelievers who make no pretense of belief in anything other than man's inherent goodness and greatness will increasingly and necessarily continue in building a newly designed "tower of Babel" to secure man's destiny. Such are already clearly and convincingly in Satan's clutches. They need not be seduced. They are already deceived to eternal damnation unless they repent. These are not the object of Satan's seduction.

Satan's seduction is rather directed to those who profess to be believers... true believers. That is why they must be "seduced." The master deceiver knows he cannot win over professing followers of Christ by leading a direct, frontal, in-your-face rebellion against God. He must do it gradually, incrementally and deceptively, but no less deadly.

The deceiver's ploy is the same as that used in the Garden of Eden where Satan once deceived Eve to begin the earthly insurrection against God's authority. He must induce... yes, seduce us to differ with what God has said, either in implication or application. Remember, virtually all deception is either wrapped around a nugget of truth, or is untruth wrapped in a robe of seeming righteousness.

Remember also! The devil is in the details. The deception that comes to us is usually framed in the context that the "details" of what

God has said are insignificant. We accuse those who would teach or preach obedience to details as "legalists." The *label* then serves as a *libel* on both the message and the messenger, justifying us in our minds to marginalize, excuse, rationalize, ignore or debunk the details of what God has said to us in His loving kindness and mercy.

The net effect is to elevate our own reasonings and thoughts as equal to or even greater than what God has said. The ultimate result is that the individual professing Christian becomes the final authority on what is true. In this way, Christians have, like their pagan counterparts, become "moral relativists."

Most professing Christians are horror-struck over the moral-relativism of the day, claiming that "we must get back to the authority of God's Word." Yet it is equally true that most who claim Christ as Savior find little problem in entering into business partnerships with unbelievers despite the clear and contrary prohibition of Scripture.

"Be ye not unequally yoked together with unbelievers," warned Paul (II Cor. 6:14), yet scores of Christian businessmen do so daily. When the official publication of a well-known Christian business organization posed the question, "If you had opportunity to enter partnership with an unbeliever on what appeared to be a promising business deal, what would you do?". The vast majority of professing Christian businessmen responded by saying, "I'd do my due diligence, pray about it - then do it." The clear authority of what God had said was blithely swept away by pragmatic rationalization wrapped in prayer... as if somehow I, like Balaam, can pray myself out from under what God says (Num. 22-24).

The multiplied application of this dramatic willingness, even desire, to attempt to circumvent what God has said, wrapping rebellion in a multicolored robe of pragmatic rationalization, popular culture and prayerful obfuscation, reveals the ease with which we are currently seduced. At root, we don't much appreciate nor have the desire to yield to God's authority. If we can label such obedience to authority "legalism," we can freely indulge in the "license" to act as we please. This pattern explodes into full-scale rebellion. Satan is well aware of this propensity in your life, and he "plays his cards" accordingly. Are you soliciting his seduction? Deception defies divine authority.

Deception Denies and Distorts Truth

There are two effective ways to mask defiance of God's authority. I can *deny* the truth of what is written, or I can *distort* the truth of what is written. They are two sides of the same coin. It is currency that you can bank on in the Deceiver's system of deceptive seduction.

Outright denial of truth, even a seemingly isolated or single truth of Scripture, can, in the mind and heart of the denier, strike a death blow at the need to heed or obey anything God has said about or relating to that truth. To do so takes a level of unmitigated boldness and bald arrogancy that few professing Christians would embrace. The obvious and ultimate consequence of denying the truth of any single thing that God has said is, in effect, to render the remainder of Scripture equally without authority.

Evolution is such a denial of truth. It is an outright attack on the most fundamental statements God has made in the opening pages of the Bible. As the true Darwinian evolutionist well knows, if God is not Creator as claimed, one need not heed anything else "God" claims to be true in the pages that follow.

The more common ploy we use to mask our defiance of God's authority is to either equivocate with the meaning of the clear words of Scripture or to misapply those clear words so as to effectively modify or change the import of what was said to suit our feelings, pre-conceived notions or desired outcome. In other words, we put a "spin" on the truth.

This is what the Serpent did with Eve in the Garden of Eden. He did not urge Eve to deny the truth of what God said but to put a motivational "spin" on why God said it so as to encourage Eve to rationalize, thus elevating her own opinion, reasonings and thoughts as equal to or above what God had said. God considered it rebellion… defiance of His authority. He therefore banished Adam and Eve from the Garden, barring access to the Tree of Life (Gen. 3:1-24). Interestingly, the Bible concludes by saying, "Blessed are they that do his commandments, that they may have right to the tree of life…" (Rev. 22:14).

God yearns for us, as loving children, to submit our wills to His will, without denial, rationalization or manipulative "spin." When we do so, we are blessed. When we play the Deceiver's game, we are easily seduced, and jeopardize life in His Spirit.

King Saul was a prime example. We find his painful plight in I Samuel 15. God told him to "utterly destroy" the Amalekites and all that they had (vs. 3). Saul did not deny the truth of what God said, so "Saul smote the Amalekites" (vs. 7). His problem was that he put his own "spin" on what God had said, choosing rather to exalt his own view of what was required. Rather than "utterly destroying all that they have" (vs. 3), he chose to spare the best of the sheep and oxen (vs. 15).

When confronted by the Lord through the prophet Samuel, Saul then wrapped his rebellion (personal disagreement with a portion of what God had said) in a religious robe, saying, "the people spared the best... to sacrifice unto the Lord..." (vs. 15).

Saul's viewpoint determined his destiny. God, through Samuel, nailed Saul's defiance of authority with the now famous words, "Behold, to obey is better than sacrifice, and to hearken than the fat of rams." The ax was laid to the root. "For rebellion is as the sin of witchcraft, and stubbornness is as iniquity and idolatry" (vs. 22-23).

Saul's differing in part with what God had said cost him the kingdom. Will your partial obedience cost you the kingdom as well? Samuel, speaking for God, declared, "Because thou hast rejected the word of the Lord, he hath also rejected thee from being king" (vs. 26). One of the saddest verses in the entire Bible states, "But the Spirit of the Lord departed from Saul..." (I Sam. 16:14). Don't let it happen to you.

Partial obedience is no obedience. It is rebellion. It distorts God's truth. And wrapping it in a religious robe does not hide its defiance of God's authority. As A.W. Tozer reminded us, not even prayer is a substitute for obedience.

Deception Delights the Deceiver

Seduction brings a sense of fulfillment to the seducer. Seduction is not a passive enterprise. One who seduces another does so intentionally. And seduction, by its very nature, is selfish. Seduction is seductive precisely because the one seducing seeks to hide or camouflage the seductive motive. Perceived sincerity is the foil of the seducer. Seducers, therefore, are well equipped to quote scripture so as to lend authority or authenticity to the deception.

Satan is, and was, an expert at seduction. Even so are many who come in the name of Christ but who have cultivated the Deceiver's techniques to seduce their prey. Both Jesus and the apostles strongly warned of such individuals. Jesus spoke of wolves in sheep's clothing in describing false prophets (Matt. 7:15). He said we would ultimately "know them by their fruits" (Matt. 7:16). Beware the boastful or dramatic display of short-term fruit. It is long-term fruit that counts for the Kingdom.

Satan quotes scripture. He is a master at seduction. Just look at how he seduced Eve in the Garden. Notice his technique to entrap Jesus through the authority, but mis-application, of God's own Word in the wilderness (Matt. 4:1-11). Earthly deceivers often seduce their prey through mis-application or distortion of scriptural truth, playing upon our fleshly desires and tendencies. And their success rate is phenomenal.

The seducer's success is satisfying in a perverse sort of way. And as you well know, success breeds success. Successful seduction of a believer or group of believers metastasizes quickly. Since seduction usually preys and plays upon our fleshly nature, and since the war against the flesh has so many casualties who succumb to the flesh, they tend to spread the seductive spirit like wildfire. This results in the appearance of amazing success for the seducer, leading to even greater and more daring efforts to seduce. To the seducer, whether the Deceiver or a Doctor of Divinity, successful seduction can be intoxicating, driving the seducer and his prey to perdition.

Deception Defies Deliverance

One of the most deceptive aspects of deception is the rather blithe belief that, *Well, if I get off track I'll just get back on course*. But human nature, our sin nature, does not usually work that way. Once off course, we tend to remain off course unless acted upon by a profoundly powerful outside force.

We like to believe that reasoning and education will convince us to make course correction, but it seldom does. Consider, for instance, the matter of sex education in school. Has it reduced pre-marital sex? Has it reduced sexually transmitted diseases or AIDS? No! Out-of-wedlock births and abortions have soared since the advent of mandatory sex education. Cohabitation has increased 1000 percent since 1960. The flesh supercedes our faith and reason, driving us into the welcoming arms of deception.

God gives grave warning about this flippant idea that I can just turn things around at will. So grave are these warnings that few pastors or parachurch leaders will teach them or even read them to an audience. As we look at these, please remember these are not the words of this author, but rather God's words, inspired just like the rest of the Bible.

The first warning we will discuss is found in Hebrews 6. We are exhorted to "go on unto perfection" in Christ, not being content with "faith toward God" or "repentance" or "baptisms" or believing in the "resurrection" or even believing in "eternal judgment" (vs. 1-2). Why are we to press on unto perfection? It is because there is deceptive danger lurking if we do not.

> *For it is impossible for those who were once enlightened and*
> *have tasted of the heavenly gift, and were made partakers of*
> *the Holy Ghost, And have tasted the good word of God, and the*
> *powers of the world to come,*
> *If they shall fall away, to renew them again unto repentance;*
> *seeing they crucify to themselves the Son of God afresh, and put*
> *him to an open shame (vs. 4-6).*

Wow! It's breathtaking, isn't it? Yet we dare not ignore it. Certainly if we sin and confess our sin, turning from it in repentance, God "is faithful and just to forgive us our sins, and to cleanse us from all unrighteousness" (I Jn. 1:9). But how far "off track" must I get or where is the line drawn where it becomes "impossible" to be renewed again unto repentance" (vs. 4-6)? Do I really want to take that risk? Do you?

That leads us to the second warning found in Hebrews 10. Again, most pastors and parachurch leaders will neither read nor discuss this passage publically.

> *If we sin willfully after that we have received the knowledge of*
> *the truth, there remaineth no more sacrifice for sins, But a cer-*
> *tain fearful looking for judgment....*

*He that despised Moses' law died without mercy under two or
three witnesses: Of how much sorer punishment, suppose ye,
shall he be thought worthy, who hath trodden under foot the
Son of God, and hath counted the blood of the covenant… an
unholy thing, and hath done despite unto the Spirit of grace?
The Lord shall judge his people. It is a fearful thing to fall into
the hands of the living God (Heb. 10:26-31).*

The severity and sober nature of this passage is inescapable. Paul
conveyed a similar message to the church at Rome.

*Be not high minded, but fear: For if God spared not the natural
branches [Israel], take heed lest he also spare not thee.
Behold therefore the goodness and severity of God… toward
thee, goodness, if thou continue in his goodness: otherwise thou
also shalt be cut off (Rom. 11:20-22).*

Deception dulls the spiritual senses. It renders us progressively
insensitive to the serious nature of our salvation, seducing us to
become increasingly cavalier about our lives. Our attitudes and behaviors inevitably conform more and more to the ways of the world until
we regularly "sin willfully," with barely a twinge of conscience, quickly
justifying lives that have become abhorrent to God. The deceptive
drift becomes almost a drive to defy God's standards for living until
we reach a point where, from God's viewpoint, we have "done despite
unto the Spirit of grace" and have "trodden under foot the Son of
God" (Heb. 10:29).

At such a point, deception truly defies deliverance. God warns us
not to presume upon His grace. Remember, God's Spirit will never lead
you where His grace cannot keep you if you "seek first the kingdom of
God and his righteousness" (Matt. 6:33).

Deception Determines Destiny

It should be increasingly clear that deception leads us down the prim-
erose path to destruction. It is truly dangerous to dance with deception.

95

God yearns for us to follow Him with a whole heart. He craves fellowship with sons and daughters who obey His voice. He is, with great anticipation, preparing a bride to present to His only begotten Son. But that bride must be blameless, without spot or wrinkle or any such thing. That bride must be holy and without blemish (Eph. 5:27), for without holiness, no man shall see the Lord (Heb. 12:14).

Comparatively few will qualify (Matt. 7:14). This is unfortunately true despite the fact that God's heart desire is that none should perish, "but that all should come to repentance" (II Pet. 3:9). That should be profound warning to all who profess to follow Christ of the serious threat that seduction presents to the saints.

Deception will unfortunately determine the eternal destiny of vast numbers of professing believers who do not continue faithfully in living the truth. The picture of chosen Israel being taken by God's mighty arm of deliverance from the "house of bondage" in Egypt, yet, after 40 years of life testing, being prevented from entering the Promised Land, is a warning picture to each of us "upon whom the ends of the world are come" (I Cor. 10:1-12). Deception determined their destiny. Only Joshua and Caleb were given entrance to the land of promise because they had "another spirit" (Numb. 14:24). Today, God is calling you to that "other spirit," if you will hear His voice (Heb. 3:7-19).

There are many tests we face in life. God wants to prove us to confirm that we truly do love Him, that we trust Him. The "rich young ruler" failed the test because he did not truly trust. Instead, he trusted his riches. By the world's standards, he was a good man… even godly (he kept the commandments, so he thought). But Jesus said he did not make the cut into His kingdom. And Jesus watched him walk away (Mark 10:17-24). He was deceived. Deception cost him his destiny.

We will all face such tests, and many more. As we see the end of the age rapidly approaching, the testing will grow stronger. The testing will also be less forgiving.

There is coming a time, and it could be sooner than you want to believe, that you and I will have to make a choice whether or not to receive the "mark of the beast." All living upon the earth at that time will face the same test. It will be an ultimate test of your trust. Those who receive the mark, an act of worship of the Antichrist, will suffer eternal damnation for their deception. But those who will not be seduced will enjoy the eternal presence of God and His Son, Jesus Christ (Rev. 13:11-18, Rev. 14:9-12). This test is so important to your destiny that an entire chapter is reserved to prepare your heart.

Be not deceived. "Here is the patience of the saints: here are they that keep the commandments of God, and the faith of Jesus" (Rev. 14:12). Be one of them!

Chapter Seven

Daring Thoughts
for *Deceptive Times*

1. In what ways does deception defy divine authority?

2. Can you see how, in our post-modern world, the trend is to *defy* God but to *deify* man? Do examples come to mind?

3. Do you ever find yourself elevating your own reasonings and thoughts over what God has clearly said, thereby either denying or distorting the truth? Does any example come to mind that causes you to war within, not wanting to admit but rather to justify?

4. Why does deception actually delight the deceiver, thereby even increasing his or her deceptive methods or message?

5. Why is it that deception actually defies deliverance?

6. Do you believe deception can determine destiny? If not, why not, in light of the multiplied and grave biblical warnings?

Protecting Godly Paths

*"… ask for the old paths, where is the good way,
and walk therein, and ye shall find rest for your souls"
(Jer. 6:16).*

"**THE PATH OF THE JUST** is as the shining light, that shineth more and more unto the perfect day," said the wise writer of Proverbs (Prov. 4:18). I want that to describe my life and ways until the day Christ returns. Is that your desire as well? If so, we must explore what the "path of the just" looks like and how it is we are so prone to wander off of the path of life into deceptive pathways that lead to destruction.

Only Two Pathways

There are only two pathways in life. These paths follow the ways of two fathers, God and Satan. The Psalmist declared, "Thou wilt show me the path of life…" (Ps. 16:11). Yet, just four verses later, David proclaims, "… by the word of thy lips I have kept me from the paths of the destroyer" (Ps. 17:4).

God's pathway is called "the path of life" or "the path of the just." Since "the just shall live by faith" (Hab. 2:4, Rom. 4:3), the "path of life" must be walked by faith in simple trust and obedience. It is from the relative simplicity of following God's pathway that the gospel song, "Trust and Obey" was written. It is so simple that we must walk this path as a little child in absolute trust. For this reason Jesus rebuked his disciples, saying, "Whosoever shall not receive the Kingdom of God as a little child shall in no wise enter therein" (Luke 18:17). Jesus' disciples wanted to keep the kids away, thinking that the "path of the just" was too difficult and too complex for young children, but Jesus responded, "Suffer (allow) the little children to come unto me, and forbid them not, for of such is the kingdom of heaven" (Luke 18:16).

Satan's paths are always complex. They do not require simple trust and obedience but rather the interjection of mans' reasonings, thoughts, rationalizations, second-guessing and self will. David referred to them as "the paths of the destroyer" (Ps. 17:4). Satan's paths often offer purported shortcuts to salvation or blessing, but they inevitably lead to destruction. "There is a way [path] which seemeth right unto a man," says the Bible, "but the end thereof are the ways of death" (Prov. 14:12, 16:25). Mankind has been seduced to follow the Deceiver's pernicious paths, like children following the Pied Piper, since the Garden of Eden.

Why Are We Easily Seduced?

The record is unabashedly clear for at least 6,000 years. We humans, while made in the image of God (Gen. 1:26-27), do not much like walking in God's ways. God says, "This is the way, walk ye in it" (Isa. 30:21). He warns us not to turn off the path to the right or left, but we want to go our own way, don't we? We are easily seduced. What is it that renders us so easily seduced off of "the path of life?" It is our fleshly or carnal nature.

God has not made us robots of His divine will. Rather, in His sovereignty, our Creator has given us free will. He has given us free will because He desires our love from a willing mind and heart so that we might enjoy sweet fellowship. The only thing that He asks is that we trust Him... that we walk "the path of life" with Him, revealed in simple obedience as would a little child.

But in our pride, exercising our will under dominion of our carnal nature rather than yielding to God's Spirit, we succumb to the Tempter's lure onto alternative paths that promise shortcuts to peace and prosperity and the ultimate hope of a promised land. Our flesh does not want to simply walk by faith, knowing that faith will be tested and tried. We do not want to humbly obey as Christ did (Phil. 2:8), because we want to avoid suffering (I Pet. 2:21, Phil. 1:29).

The seducer of our souls convinces our carnal minds that his alternative paths will get us where we want to go without learning obedience, as Jesus did, through the things that we might suffer on God's pathway (Heb. 5:8). And so the majority of those who profess faith in Christ do not follow Christ on "the path of life." Rather, they claim the name of Christ while walking Satan's pathways leading to destruction. For this reason, Jesus gave clear warning:

> *"Strait is the gate, and narrow the way, which leadeth unto life, and few there be that find it" (Matt. 7:14).*

Jesus then exhorts you and me with fervent passion not to join the majority on the broad and seemingly easy paths that lead to perdition.

> *"Enter ye in at the strait gate: for wide is the gate, and broad is the way, that leadeth to destruction, and many there be which go in threat" (Matt. 7:13).*

How To Keep on The Path of Life

Given that we are so easily seduced off of the godly path that leads to life, how can we keep our feet on the right path?

The Psalmist David, though far from perfect, was called by God " a man after mine own heart" (Acts 13:22). That same David tells us directly how he avoided "the path of the destroyer." He notes: "… by the word of thy lips I have kept me from the paths of the destroyer" (Ps. 17:4). "The word of thy lips" is the written Word of God. The Psalmist declared, "Thy word is a lamp unto my feet, and a light unto my path" (Ps. 119:105). He asks God: "Order my steps in thy word" (Ps. 119:133).

"Through thy precepts I get understanding: therefore I hate every false way [path]" (Ps. 119:104, 128).

Listen to the Psalmist's cry, "With my whole heart have I sought thee: O let me not wander from thy commandments" (Ps. 119:10). "Thy word have I hid in my heart, that I might not sin against thee" (Ps. 119:11).

Do you love God's Word like that? Do you want to? Do you really want to keep your feet and those of your family or congregation from the paths of the destroyer? You can. But you must develop a pure love of God's Word as the most fundamental expression of God's heart. His Word describes and discloses the direction and destination of His pathway.

Unfortunately, the majority of those who profess to follow Christ do not truly love His Word. Their greatest desire is not to do the will of the Father as Christ did, but rather to have the Father do their will. If God's will as revealed in His Word does not clearly line up with the desires, proclivities and fickle feelings of the average "saint" today, he or she either ignores God's described pathway altogether when it comes to a point of disagreement or puts a "spin" on what God has said so as to redefine the path according to personal desires, i.e., the flesh. The end of such living is, as God warns, "the ways of death."

> *"There is a way which seemeth right unto a man, but the end thereof are the ways of death" (Prov. 14:12).*

How To Return To The Path of Life

What can I do if I have strayed off of "the path of life?" Is there hope? How can I find my way back? Does God care?

REMEMBER GOD CARES

Indeed God cares. He desires that none should perish but that all should come to repentance. And He has been patient, longsuffering toward you and all of us (II Pet. 3:9). Yet God's Spirit will not always strive with man (Gen. 6:3). "Now is the accepted time" to return to the ancient path (II Cor. 6:2). "Today if ye will hear his voice, harden not your heart…" (Heb. 3:7-8). God, in His great goodness is calling you right now to turn back to Him with all your heart (Rom. 2:4).

CHOOSE TO RETURN

It is not God who must turn but you and I. Years ago, my wife and I stayed at Monmouth, America's premier "bed and breakfast" plantation in Mississippi. Our attention was captured by a small but beautifully-framed plaque with a message we have never forgotten:

*IF YOU DO NOT FEEL CLOSE TO GOD,
GUESS WHO MOVED.*

God does not change, but we do. We drift away, wandering off of the divine path that leads to life. Sometimes we wander so far that we see no hope for return. The way back just seems too hard. We have lost our way. There just seems "too much water that has passed under the bridge." Yet it is precisely in such a place of lostness that God looks for us to choose.

"Choose you this day," says the Lord (Josh. 24:15). You make the choice… God will help you make the change… the necessary course of correction. Choose! His grace or enabling power is sufficient for you. His strength will be made perfect in your weakness (II Cor. 12:9).

RESTORE THE ANCIENT LANDMARKS

Landmarks have always been critical to navigation before the advent of (GPS) Global Positioning Systems. Pioneers made slashes on trees. Sailors were guided by the stars. Rock outcroppings, unusual trees, particular buildings and even stop signs or lights have been used to guide and give directions.

When identification of location was important not just for direction but for definition and ultimate destiny, it was and is necessary to insure that landmarks have permanence and can be depended on. Hence a surveyor's posts hammered deep into the ground mark the metes and bounds of land parcels so that we can rely upon land ownership records.

Can you imagine the chaos that would result in your city, your country… even in the world if we began to just uproot and discard the landmarks, of whatever type, that had guided and protected us? Every man would suddenly begin doing that which was right in his own eyes. Crime would explode. Violence would become the norm for resolving disputes. "Might makes right" would become the only rule of law.

And that is precisely what has happened in our modern and post-modern lives. We have removed, abandoned and even destroyed the ancient landmarks. Truths that were formerly accepted as absolute have been abandoned. Verities that gave us common voice have been vacated in our moral imagination. Behavioral taboos once defined by biblical truths have been banished from the Church House to the White House.

The sheer boldness and even arrogance of our times in removing the ancient landmarks was perhaps best expressed by the 42nd President of the United States. While carrying a large Bible regularly for photo ops, he journeyed in 1997 to California to be the first sitting American president to knowingly and purposely address an audience of homosexuals and homosexual activists, declaring...

> We are, in practical ways, redefining the immutable ideals
> that have guided us from the beginning.

Notice, this worldly president, professing to be a follower of Christ, did not hesitate to express the sheer spiritual defiance of his... and the nation's... position. He first acknowledged that the "ideals" or landmarks were "immutable," which is a term most commonly used to refer to God as *unchangeable*. He then admitted that these "ideals" or landmarks have "guided us from the beginning." Finally, he made clear that, as a people, we are "redefining" or changing truths and behavioral standards, which have, throughout history, been deemed unchangeable.

No sitting American president has ever made a more breathtakingly sweeping statement to pull the moral and spiritual anchors from the nation's soul than that man. Yet, while many recoil in horror, we must painfully admit that we, as a people, have indeed removed the ancient landmarks from our lives, in practical ways, redefining the unchangeable truths that have guided us from the beginning. Whether through embracing homosexual practice, abortion, divorce and re-marriage, Sabbath desecration, or a whole host of other manifestations of abandonment of moral and spiritual verities that have guided us, we are in a wholesale defiance of the clear truths of Scripture. We have removed the ancient landmarks.

"Remove not the ancient landmarks, which thy fathers have set," says the Lord (Prov. 22:28). Yet in our pride, we have done just that. The ancient moral and spiritual landmarks have been removed not only among the "unbelievers" but even more egregiously among those who profess Christ's name, whether of liberal or conservative, mainline or evangelical persuasion. We are lost! While professing to know *the* way, we have lost *our* way. We must individually, then, as families, and as congregations begin to restore the ancient landmarks of truth and righteousness. To fail to do so will leave us wandering in the wilderness of sin, deceived.

It is time to restore the ancient landmarks. That, alone, guided by the Holy Spirit, will help to keep us on the straight path that leads to life. The fear of legalism, that, for a generation, has served as a spiritual smokescreen to hide from God's heart-cry for obedience, must be replaced by the liberty in Christ to freely, and with humility, obey His will.

Where have you, your family, your congregation strayed from the ancient landmarks? Are you willing to restore those landmarks in your life that help to keep us on the straight path? Are you willing to begin today? The seduction of deception lies on the other side of "today."

SET STRAIGHT PATHS

"Make straight paths for your feet," says the Lord, "that you might be a partaker of his holiness" (Heb. 12:10-14). God is a father. He chastens and corrects those He loves. And in His chastening, He always directs us back to "straight paths."

Why does God repeatedly, both in the Old and New Testaments, call you and me to make straight our paths? Obviously, from His viewpoint, our paths have become crooked, threatening our eternal destiny. It is said, "The shortest distance between two points is a straight line." Whenever we introduce side paths, variations, interest points, diversions or even detours into our life path, at best life becomes more complicated, always running the risk of permanent diversion.

Given our sin nature, our flesh or carnal nature constantly beckons us to alternative paths. They appear more interesting. We even wrap them in a robe of righteousness, claiming them to be more "relevant," more apt to attract the "unbelieving" masses. Yet, in reality, these alluring alternative ways inevitably compel us to conform to the ways of the world, leading to our own deception or eventual destruction.

When God's people are seduced, they are lead astray from the straight and ancient paths through deception. And God's call is always the same: "Make straight paths for your feet." God provides the path, but we must choose to walk in it. Today, most call the straight path "legalism." The label of "legalism" actually libels the liberty God seeks to give us through His love. Satan has so seduced and deceived as to bring vitriol by professing Christians upon the very victory God offers us through the straight path. Let's face it! In the flesh, we just don't much like straight paths. They seem boring, restrictive. The reason is that we have taken our eyes off of the objective of our journey… to "Seek first the Kingdom of God and His righteousness" (Matt. 6:33). The shortest distance between where we are and God's goal is still a "straight path." Will you take it?

AVOID THE CROOKED AND BROAD WAY

The *straight* way is always perceived as the "narrow" way. Few seem to travel that way. The democratic majority follow the meandering, labyrinthine path that seems to offer more interest and cultural relevance. Jesus referred to that way as the "broad" way with a "wide" gate (Matt. 7:13). Jesus warned not to follow the majority who take that path.

The ancient prophets also warned Israel about that path. When Isaiah foretold of the coming Messiah and of the prophet who would prepare the way, he called that prophet a "voice crying in the wilderness" because most did not want to hear his message nor conform their ways to it. They were on "the broad path" that seemed popular. Yet Isaiah made clear that forerunner's central message and it remains the central message today on the near edge of the Messiah's Second Coming.

"Prepare ye the way of the Lord, make straight in the desert a highway for our God.

...the crooked shall be made straight, and the rough places plain" (Isa. 40:3-4).

When John the Baptist began his six-month ministry to prepare the way for Christ's first coming, his message was simple, concise and direct so that no willing heart could miss it. It is recorded with nearly identical words in all four gospels.

MAKE STRAIGHT THE WAY OF THE LORD, as said the prophet Isaiah (John 1:23).

Prepare ye the way of the Lord, MAKE HIS PATHS STRAIGHT (Matt. 3:3, Luke 3:4, Mark 1:3).

The crooked shall be made straight," cried Isaiah (Isa. 40:4). "I will lead them in paths that they have not known: I will make darkness light before them, and crooked things straight" (Isa. 42:16). If we are to be victorious in Christ and be prepared for His coming, we must choose to avoid the crooked , alternative paths and the broad way that seems popular and is persuasive to our carnal nature.

CHOOSE THE NARROW WAY

"Strait is the gate, and narrow is the way, which leadeth to life," said our Lord, "and few there be that find it" (Matt. 7:14).

How many will find, walk on, and complete the journey on the narrow path that leads to the joy of eternal fellowship with the Father, God? "Few," said Jesus. Put another way throughout the Scriptures, it will be only a small "remnant." That remnant will be deemed of little value to the majority. In fact, that remnant of true believers who choose to walk the straight and narrow path will be perceived as a "thorn in the flesh" to those who follow the broad and winding paths that Jesus said "leadeth to destruction" (Matt. 7:13).

Neither Jesus nor His apostles came to preach a "big tent" gospel but rather the Father's call to "the narrow way" that leads to life (Matt. 7:14). Yet the growing theme of pastor and people today is to embrace an ever-broader way, welcoming ever-greater numbers to an ever-easier and attractive winding path.

Which path will you choose? The seduction of the broad and meandering way is great. Will majority rule? Will you be a people-pleaser, or a God-pleaser? It is time to choose, for "the day of Christ is at hand" (II Thess. 2:2).

"Let no man deceive you by any means: for that day shall not come, except there come a falling away first…" (II Thess. 2:3). Make straight paths for your feet. Restore the ancient landmarks in your life. Avoid the wide gate and broad way that allures the flesh. And choose the narrow way that leads to life. "Today, if you will hear his voice, harden not your heart" (Heb. 3:7, 15).

Chapter Eight

Daring Thoughts
for *Deceptive Times*

1. There are only two life pathways. What are they?

2. Compare the Deceiver's pathway with God's pathway.

3. Why are we so easily seduced onto Satan's pathway?

4. What is essential to stay on God's pathway? How does that become a reality in your life?

5. Based upon your life ways, how important is it to you to walk God's "path of life?"

6. If you have gotten lost or wandered from God's pathway, how can you return? Do you want to?

7. In reality, which path are you choosing?

The Road to Hell

"Hell and destruction are never full" (Prov. 27:20).

"THE ROAD TO HELL is paved with good intentions," we are told. We believe this as a truism, but in actual truth, we act as if it is but an idle phrase, having little relevance. Though usually spoken in a jesting flair, the truth of this common aphorism should be taken to heart as an oft-repeated warning.

Good Intentions

Few intentionally embark with gusto on the road to hell. Why, therefore, do so many find themselves on that road, accelerating to full speed on the autobahn to eternal destruction? The answer lies with *good intentions*. Good intentions, alone, without an absolute anchor to unmoveable and unshakeable truth that does not drift, will inevitably lead down the on-ramp to the multi-lane expressway propelling all travelers thereon unsuspectingly to the abyss. Compromise becomes the engine that propels good intentions toward eternal deception.

Compromise Corner

In reality, the road to hell begins at compromise corner. Compromise corner is at the intersection of all the major roads of our lives. The decisions we make, the turns we negotiate at compromise corner, inevitably lead toward that multi-lane expressway to destruction, even while still believing we are headed in God's general direction.

All compromise as it relates to God's truth is "compromise," and all compromise on issues of truth is deceptive and profoundly seductive. The great danger is that few travelers realize the seriousness of the seduction, because they measure themselves and the correctness of their decisions by the overwhelming majority who seem headed with clarity and certainty toward the multi-laned expressway to hell. They reason, *if popular pastors, para-church leaders and the seeming majority seem comfortable with this direction, it must be okay,* even though deep in their heart they have this haunting suspicion that something is wrong. "It cannot be wrong if it feels so right," they muse. But in the end, compromise bites like a cobra, and is deadly.

Compromise corner is found at many intersections of our lives. In fact, it is at virtually every intersection where we are called upon to make decisions, whether great or small. Small compromises are more deceptive than great ones, yet we are able to so easily justify them. We reason, *Well, it's only a little compromise,* not realizing that the small compromise is on a series of secondary roads leading to ever larger compromises, all similarly justified. It is not *demons* but *decisions* that are our worst enemies.

Consider the following general ways in which we find ourselves at compromise corner:

- The CULTURAL CORNER - Image vs. Integrity
- The MORAL CORNER - Pragmatism vs. Principle
- The SPIRITUAL CORNER - Flesh vs. Faith

In the spiritual arena, we find ourselves "at the moment of truth, in the valley of decision" at many spiritual intersections where our decisions, whether small or great, persistently direct our destiny.

1. Our desires vs. God's desires (Eph. 2:1-3, Ps. 37:4, Matt. 6:33).
2. Our appetites vs. God's ordinance (I Pet. 2:11, Rom. 13:14, Mark 4:19).
3. Our fears vs. Godly faith (Matt. 10:28, Heb. 13:6, II Tim. 1:7).
4. Our happiness vs. God's holiness (I Pet. 1:13-16, I Thess. 4:7, Prov. 28:13-14, Prov. 29:18, I Pet. 3:14).
5. Our pleasure vs. God's purity (Heb. 11:25, Ps. 16:11, II Tim. 3:4, I Tim. 5:6,I Jn. 3:3).
6. Our comfort vs. God's call (II Tim. 2:3, II Cor. 11:22-27, 12:10).
7. Our purposes vs. God's purposes (Gen. 45:5-8, 50:19-20).
8. Our ways vs. God's ways (Prov. 14:12, Jam. 1:8).
9. Trusting man vs. Trusting God (Jer. 17:5-10, Isa. 30:1-3).

Collective compromises on these various tests of whether we will be governed by the flesh or by the Spirit lead almost inevitably to further compromise until compromise becomes a way of life. It takes radical confrontation through provocative preaching of the Word, with painful application, to reverse the ingrained pattern, usually coupled with divine discipline, which is never comfortable, and which is frequently dismissed as "an attack from Satan" (Heb. 12:5-11).

Since compromise has such a corrosive effect both on our character and on our lives as Christians, perhaps we should look further at patterns of compromise and how compromise corrupts, leading deeper into deception.

Patterns of Compromise

There are four distinct characteristics of compromise that collectively reveal its pattern in our lives.

COMPROMISE ALWAYS EXALTS PRAGMATISM OVER PRINCIPLE.

Pragmatism is a philosophy and method of decision making that defines value in life, families, activities, organizations, churches and governments on the basis of what seems practical, what produces a desired result. The foremost concern to the pragmatist is not whether something is true, right, just, moral, ethical or spiritually pure but whether it seems to work. Does the proposed idea, activity or action accomplish the desired objective?

The pragmatist finds it very difficult to value absolute truth as other than a theory. Truth gets in the way of what he values as practical. The pragmatic Christian may embrace a written creed or biblical principle as true, in the abstract, but his life seldom conforms to those claimed truths. What he says he believes is often very different from what he does. There is therefore a serious disconnect between what he sees as his "Christian" life and the way others (or God) see his real life. Obviously, such thinking leads to HYP-OCRISY. Such "pragmatic" faith can appear as little more than religious hype. It lacks integrity. And that lack of integrity dramatically affects decisions related to applied truth.

The great weakness of the pragmatist is that he finds it very difficult to trust God. While claiming to believe God's truth, he really does not trust God to honor that truth to produce the desired practical results. Therefore, the pragmatist relies principally on human reasoning, gospel gimmicks, and programs to accomplish his objectives, often leading to ever-increasing compromise.

Being practical and achieving objectives is not inherently wrong. But when principled living falls before the driving obsession of pragmatism, compromise and every evil way lurks for the slightest opportunity to strike. And strike, it has done, viciously.

A virile form of pragmatism rules now as a virtual dictator over American life. Rare is the pastor, parachurch leader, president or publisher whose life and decisions are not dictated by pragmatism. Principled thinking has received a post-mortem. Plaques declare our "principles," but our lives are written in the ink of pragmatism.

The compromising connection of the abandonment of living truth and anchoring principles can be found throughout the life of the church in this last generation. The entire church-growth movement has been driven by "what works" rather than what is true. Now it has been admitted that what was thought to "work" in the seeker-sensitive obsession for the last generation has failed. It produced *numbers* but failed to produce *disciples* as our Lord commanded (Matt. 28:19-20), resulting in the visionary of the entire seeker-sensitive movement to admit, "We made a mistake."[1] Such "mistakes" are multiplied thousands of times over with every decision we make, choosing pragmatism over principle. Just imagine the eternally devastating consequences for untold millions of such deception. And it was all driven by polls. "Christian" publishing, broadcasting and virtually every expression of the church and its ministry have been driven, not by what is true but by the market, what seems to work, what sells. It is a veritable addiction.

The MASTER of our souls now bows to the MARKET, the surrogate lord that now governs life and thought from pulpit to pew. Pragmatism has become a systemic infection, defying even the Word of Truth to purge it from our immoral imagination. In just forty years, the MARKET has become our MASTER. Just try to imagine where the spirit of compromise that has captured our moral imagination will take you in the trying days ahead as we approach the Second Coming.

COMPROMISE ALWAYS EXALTS FLESH OVER FAITH

While we claim to profess faith, we are often possessed by our flesh. The battle of the flesh against the spirit is undoubtedly the greatest and most recurring battle faced by followers of Christ. It is nothing short of all-out war. Sometimes it seems we face a vast array of enemy fleshly forces, but the more subtle and continuous assault we face is guerilla warfare, as individual and seemingly isolated skirmishes with our flesh. It is these that usually spell defeat. Losing one such skirmish of the flesh vs. the spirit after another defines the road to perpetual compromise.

Solomon was the wisest man who ever lived, at least in biblical times. Being the son of David, his was a godly and goodly heritage. "God gave Solomon wisdom and understanding exceeding much, and largeness of heart... he was wiser than all men" (I Kings 4:29, 31). And so God allowed Solomon to build Israel's first Temple. Its magnificence and the grandeur of Solomon's kingdom was so great that when the queen of Sheba saw it, "there was no more spirit in her" (I Kings 10:5). "Thy wisdom and prosperity exceedeth the fame which I heard," "... the half was not told me," she said (I Kings 10:7).

God's blessing was blatantly obvious. Because Solomon sought not for riches and honor but "for an understanding heart to judge thy people," God said, "I have given thee a wise and understanding heart; so that there was none like thee before thee, neither after thee shall any

115

arise like unto thee. I have also given thee that which thou hast not asked, both riches and honor…" (I Kings 3:9-13). God promised "I will establish the throne of thy kingdom upon Israel forever… but if ye or your children will not keep my commandments… then I will cut off Israel out of the land… and Israel shall be a proverb and a byword among all people" (I Kings 9:3-7).

"But king Solomon loved many strange women," say the Scriptures. "Of the nations concerning which the Lord said unto the children of Israel, Ye shall not go in unto them… for surely they will turn away your heart… Solomon clave unto these in love." "And his wives turned away his heart." "… and his heart was not perfect with the Lord his God, as was the heart of David his father" (I Kings 11:1-4). "And the Lord was angry with Solomon… Wherefore the Lord said I will surely rend the kingdom from you" (I Kings 11:9-11).

What an incredibly sad story… from riches to rags, spiritually. How did it happen? Solomon lost the battle through hundreds of guerilla skirmishes between his faith and his flesh. Yielding to fleshly demands over and over so compromised his faith that what remained was a grotesque caricature of a faith that once brought an outpouring of God's favor. Solomon still had his riches, but he lost his relationship with the God who had prospered him. He not only lost power with God, but ultimately the kingdom as well.

How many millions of professing Christians, pastors and people alike, have followed Solomon's example, especially over the years since the "Sexual Revolution," compromising their faith by submitting to the demands of their flesh? Statistics scream at us, showing the utter defilement of a once-vibrant faith to satisfy the flesh. No facts more painfully nor truthfully reveal the devastating reality of the massive victory of the flesh over our faith than these well-known facts:

- The divorce rate in the church has equaled or exceeded that of America as a whole for the last decade.
- The divorce rate in the "Bible Belt" of America has been 50 percent higher than the nation as a whole for the last decade.
- The divorce rate among America's pastors equals that of their parishioners and is the second highest of all professions.

- The out-of-wedlock birthrate continues to climb and currently stands at 50%. In the cities across America, the rate stands at 70%.
- Eighty percent of professing evangelical Christian young people admit they have engaged in pre-marital sex.

Like Solomon, we are expecting God to honor that which He says He hates and will consign our souls to hell unless we repent (I Cor. 6:9-10, Rev. 21:8, 27). We are losing our power with men because we have lost our purity before God. We fear man increasingly because the fear of the Lord has waned progressively from our moral imagination. Our faith is rapidly becoming little more than an orgy of the flesh wrapped in religious robes. Pastor and people have become complicit in this wholesale capitulation to the enemy of our souls.

COMPROMISE ALWAYS EXALTS SELF-CONSCIOUSNESS OVER GOD-CONSCIOUSNESS

It began in the Garden. Eden was the perfect environment, both physically and spiritually. God divinely designed every facet to perfectly provide for Adam and Eve whom God had created in His own image.

Perfect freedom was wedded to appropriate responsibility for the first man and his wife. All was theirs for the taking as they tended the garden. Life was simple. Simply take God, the Creator, at His word, and enjoy daily fellowship with God and spouse.

Then came the serpent. "Now the serpent [Satan] was more subtil.... And he said to the woman, Yea hath God said, Ye shall not eat of every tree of the garden?" To which Eve responded regarding the "tree of the knowledge of good and evil" in the midst of the garden, "God hath said, Ye shall not eat of it... lest ye die." Satan, in classic seductive deception, opening the way to the competing lordship of SELF that would seduce mankind throughout history, declared, "Ye shall not truly die." In fact, "... your eyes shall be opened, and ye shall be as gods, knowing good and evil" (Gen. 3:1-5).

The rest is history. "When the woman saw that the tree was good for food, and that it was pleasant to the eyes, and a tree to be desire to make one wise, she took of the fruit thereof, and did eat, and gave also unto her husband with her, and he did eat." The results were immediate.

1. "The eyes of them both were opened...;"
2. "They knew that they were naked...;"
3. "They sewed fig leaves together" to hide from each other; and
4. They "hid themselves from the presence of the Lord God..." (Gen. 3:6-8).

Satan's seduction was simple. Through a spiritual sleight-of-hand, shift the emphasis from God to SELF. Make what is *seen* to be the final arbiter of what God has *said*. Make it seem as if obedience to God is against SELF-interest. Cause temporal feelings to gain ascendancy over faith in the eternal wisdom of God. Express your SELF. Assert your SELF. "Ye shall be as gods..." (Gen. 3:5).

This was precisely the sin of Satan. It was the heart of his rebellion as the "anointed cherub that covereth," the most beautiful and powerful of all God's creation (Isa. 14:12-14, Ezek. 28:2-19). He exalted his SELF against the word and wisdom of God and was cast out of heaven. And ungodly exaltation of SELF will cast you out as well.

SELF consciousness rather than God consciousness is at the root or heart of most, if not all, compromise and sin. Jesus said, "Seek first the kingdom of God..." (Matt. 6:33). Man's wisdom says, "Seek first what's in it for me." Jesus said, "If any man will come after me, let him deny himself, and take up his cross, and follow me" (Matt. 16:24). The culture cries, "Have it your way." "I'll do it my way!" God says, "Obey my voice, and I will be your God, and ye shall be my people..." (Jer. 7:23, John 14:15, 21, 23, 24). We call the simplicity of our Creator's guidelines for our lives "legalism," alleging that any call to true obedience frustrates SELF-expression, SELF-will, SELF-desire, and SELF-fulfillment. As a culture and as a church, we have capitulated carte-blanche to the serpent's most elementary deception. SELF-help has replaced our need for God's help. We allege Jesus as savior, but SELF has become King. Faith is our lackey, but FEELINGS have become Lord.

COMPROMISE ALWAYS EXALTS TEMPORAL OVER ETERNAL

Remember Esau! He was the firstborn son of Isaac, grandson of Abraham. Esau was heir to the great promises of God through his grandfather with whom God had made an eternal covenant because of his faith revealed in his obedience (Gen. 12-15, Jam. 2:20-26). Yet Esau, entitled to a double portion of his father's blessing, squandered it for a mess of pottage. You know the story, don't you? It is found in Genesis 25:19-34.

The boys were twins. Jacob and Esau shared their mother Rebekah's womb. They had the same father and grandfather, born to the "son of promise" (Gen. 17:15-21) and heir to the divinely-declared heritage of the "Father of faith," Abraham. Such an heritage would be unparalleled in history, except only for the Messiah. Jacob, Esau's brother, despite his deceptive ways, wrestled with an angel for God's blessing, revealing the value he attached to the eternal. His name was changed to "Israel," for God said, "as a prince hast thou power with God and men, and has prevailed" (Gen. 32:34-28).

But Esau "despised his birthright" (Gen.25:34). In what way did Esau "despise" his birthright? He was a man of the field, a cunning hunter. He was his father's favorite son (Gen. 25:28), the firstborn, entitled to the incredible benefits delegated to the first son to carry his father's name. Yet, Jacob received the blessing. Why? And why is it important for you and your eternal destiny?

We dare not take this matter lightly. Esau came in exhausted from a hunting expedition and was faint. Jacob had been cooking up some red pottage. Esau, smelling the aroma, asked Jacob to feed him. Jacob bartered with his brother, "Sell me this day thy birthright." To which Esau responded, "I am at the point to die: and what profit shall this birthright be to me?" Jacob said, "Swear to me this day, and he sware unto him: and he sold his birthright to Jacob. Then Jacob gave Esau bread and pottage... he did eat and drink... and went his way" (Gen. 25:28-34).

Esau traded away a blessing of inestimable value for something grossly temporal and mundane. He "despised" his birthright. And the majority of Americans today who, like Esau, claim a heritage by faith through Abraham, nevertheless, are trading God's eternal promises for a mess of temporal pottage.

Untold millions of professing Christians, seduced by the promise of temporal gain, earthly prosperity, perks and position, are forfeiting eternal promise of inestimable value for a mess of earthly pottage. The pattern is well set. This deception is nearly complete. Jesus said, "Seek first the kingdom of God" (Matt. 6:33), but millions say, "No!" That will deprive me of opportunity. Valuing the temporal more than the eternal, they are committing themselves to seek "YOUR BEST LIFE NOW."

Do you have the spirit of Esau? Are you willing to allow the Holy Spirit to answer that question in the deepest recess of your heart? Which do you value more, the temporal or the eternal? What would a jury of your peers say? Your spouse? Your children? Your neighbors? God?

The road to hell begins at compromise corner. Compromise inevitably involves choosing the temporal over the eternal. Repeated choices set the life pattern. What is your life pattern? This is the area in which true "family values" are determined... God's family values.

God warns, "Jacob have I loved, but Esau have I hated" (Rom. 9:13, Mal. 1:2-3). This is a serious matter. It is so serious, that from God's viewpoint, he decreed the destruction of the Edomites, the descendants of Esau. Esau's viewpoint determined his destiny. Viewpoint always determines destiny, including yours and mine. So, where do you stand in valuing the temporal vs. the eternal? Destiny awaits your decision.

The "Conspiracy" of Compromise

Secret! Sinister! That is what both attracts and repels us from the concept of conspiracy. And there is good reason. *Conspiracy* is derived from the word *conspire*.

To *conspire* means to plan or plot together secretly. It requires the joining or acting together. It is the joining or acting together without the conscious awareness of the unwitting object of the conspiracy that renders it sinister and dangerous. The word *conspire* actually derives from two Latin words "com" - joined together as in "community," and "*spirare*" - to "breathe." Taken together, they literally mean "breathing together" for a secret, deceptive, undisclosed purpose designed to accomplish either a legal purpose by illegal or illegitimate means or an illegal purpose through seemingly legal or legitimate means.

That is precisely how compromise works. It involves several participants, but we are not usually aware that they work together in a sinister fashion to deceive and lead us to destruction. Compromise works through the interaction of people and ideas. When we are not moored safely in the harbor of God's absolute truth, we become vulnerable to the conspiratorial influences that threaten our souls at "The Cultural Corner," "The Moral Corner" and "The Spiritual Corner" where the "conspiracy" of compromise is hatched. At these corners we encounter the patterns of thought presenting life-defining choices that lead either to a deeper walk of faithfulness to our Lord or to an ever-deeper drift away toward "consorting with the enemy" of our souls.

The process of deceptive seduction ultimately leads to spiritual treason where we pretend to be followers of Christ and His kingdom outwardly, but in reality we have, like a spiritual "Mata-hari," gone to bed with and are fornicating with the enemy, all for some form of believed personal gain, i.e., acceptance, getting along, power, perks, position, favor, money, etc. The process inevitably begins at compromise corner where we are faced with choices of…

Pragmatism	vs.	Principle
Flesh	vs.	Faith
Self-focus	vs.	God-focus
Temporal	vs.	Eternal

These choices do not present themselves in isolation, one at a time, but actually work in sinister synergy to bring us to destruction. The Apostle Paul well understood this. He understood that our pre-eminent spiritual warfare, the battle for your soul and mine, takes place "between our ears," in the mind and heart, which Jeremiah warned is "deceitful above all things and desperately wicked" (Jer. 17:9). Let us consider Paul's exhortational warning.

Though we walk in the flesh, we do not war after the flesh:
For the weapons of our warfare are not carnal [fleshly], but mighty through God to the pulling down of strongholds [conspiratorial and sinister ideas contrary to God's will, Word, and kingdom].
Casting down imaginations [reasonings, thoughts and arguments], and every high thing that exalts itself against the knowledge of God, and bringing into captivity every thought to the obedience of Christ (II Cor. 10:3-5).

Jeremiah reminds, "I the Lord search the heart... to give every man according to his ways, and according to the fruit of his doings" (Jer. 17:10). As the Lord searches your heart, even now, what will He find concerning your own reasonings, thoughts and arguments? Have you been caught in the sinister "conspiratorial" web of fleshly and worldly choices at compromise corner? How long have you fraternized with the enemy of your soul through persistent and progressive compromise?

When Christ knocks at the door of your heart upon His return, will He find the enemy co-habitating in the "temple of the Holy Spirit," your mind and body? Are you entertaining strange spiritual bedfellows? Have you given place to compromise? Do you agree with God and His Word only in theory, or in actual daily practice? "Can two walk together unless they be agreed? (Amos 3:3)?

Isn't it time to kick out the co-habiters that conspire to seduce your soul? Isn't it time to "bring every thought into captivity to the obedience of Christ?"

"Behold, I come quickly," says the Lord (Rev. 22:7, 20). What thou doest, thou must do quickly. You make the choice and God, by His Spirit, will help you make the change.

Chapter Nine

Daring Thoughts
for Deceptive Times

1. Why is it said that "the road to hell is paved with good intentions?"

2. What decisions do you recall having made recently, or in the past, at "compromise corner?" How did you make the decision?

3. Have you found that compromise in your life ways and decisions is basically rotated around one or more of the four distinct characteristics of compromise described under "Patterns of Compromise?"

4. Where do you find your greatest temptation to compromise?

5. Judging from your life choices and pattern, would you describe yourself as a *Jacob* ... or an *Esau*?

PART IV

Gateways to Deception

"Wide is the gate… that leadeth to destruction"
(Matt. 7:13).

Gates have shown themselves to be of critical importance throughout history. The phrase, "storm the gates" reflects the importance of gates in keeping out enemies. The smaller or narrower the gate to the city, the more secure the city was to enemy invasion. For this reason, Jesus made clear that the access to His eternal city would be through a "strait" gate and a "narrow" way. The way would be so narrow and the gated access so limited that "few there be that find it" (Matt. 7:14).

Gates not only exclude but provide access. A shut gate declares warning that access to what lays beyond is prohibited. An open gate beckons one to enter. In all of our lives we encounter gates, both actual and figurative. They either provide us access or prohibit access to what lies beyond. A gateway becomes an entry point for ideas, practices, beliefs and yes, even deception to enter our lives.

The Psalmist prayed, "Open to me the gates of righteousness…." He called it the "gate of the Lord" into which the righteous shall enter

(Ps. 118:19-20). If there are "gates of righteousness," there are also Satan's counterfeit gates. Satan always seeks to open gates God closes and to close the gate God opens. The Deceiver's enticement is always to broad and popular gates.

In these chapters, we explore some of the broad and enticing gateways that draw millions unsuspectingly into the waiting arms of deception.

Cultural Seduction

"Be not conformed to this world:
but be ye transformed" (Rom. 12:2).

CULTURE IS A POWERFUL AND PERVASIVE LIFE INFLUENCE. With the exception of the "Laws of Nature" such as the Law of Gravity, the culture in which we live undoubtedly exerts the greatest influence in our lives during our earthly sojourn. The power and force of culture is so great that it can literally "lord it over" our lives. When culture becomes "lord," Christ is no longer our Master, but our mascot.

Cultural Imperatives

Every culture has its own imperatives. These are actions and attitudes, beliefs and behaviors that are considered a "given" for the culture. We might say, "Well, this is just what we do," or "We just think that way." These cultural mandates, by themselves, are neither good nor bad, righteous nor unrighteous, except to the extent that they require thinking or behavior that puts us in conflict with what God has revealed as His standards for attitude and action.

Many become confused in sorting out that which their prevailing culture requires versus that which Christ requires. The cultural influence is so strong that it often prevails in the life of professing Christians. Given a choice, we frequently opt for cultural acceptance and convenience over the ways God has clearly defined for His kingdom.

Jesus was uniquely confronted by this very issue concerning earthly power. Pontius Pilate, a crusty Roman governor in a proud Roman culture, valued and sought to protect Roman power. He was concerned whether Jesus presented a threat to earthly cultural and governmental authority, asking, "Art thou the King of the Jews?" Jesus, realizing the cultural tension, yet knowing he was the spiritual Messiah-King over Israel, did not directly confront Pilate's earthly power, but responded, "My kingdom is not of this world" (John 18:33-37).

In reality, from God's viewpoint, if you are a true follower of His only begotten son, Jesus, your "kingdom" is not of this world either. This world is not your home. You are a "stranger and pilgrim" (I Pet. 2:11), largely alien to the earthly culture in which you find yourself. Rather, you are a "fellow citizen" with the saints, and of the household of God (Eph. 2:19). You are an "ambassador" of the kingdom of Christ (II Cor. 5:20), with exclusive loyalty to the culture of His family. For this reason, we are said to be "in the world but not of it." For as Jesus is and was, "so are we in this world" (I John 4:17).

These are the spiritual ties that we all know and recognize. Our problem is not so much in what we *know* but in what we *do*. In reality, cultural imperatives increasingly have greater sway in our lives than biblical imperatives. We do not really much want to be strangers and pilgrims here, do we? We, like ancient Lot, have "pitched our tents toward Sodom" (Gen. 13:8-12), and like Lot's wife, look longingly over our shoulders at the happening scene surging around us. Perhaps that is why Jesus gave his end-time warning, "Remember Lot's wife" (Luke 17:32).

When Paul exhorted, "Be not conformed to this world...," he well knew the cultural imperative. He was well experienced in the powerful pull of prevailing culture to lure the weak and unsuspecting Christian into its seductive grasp. So, where do you stand? Have you been seduced?

Has the culture become your lord, leaving Christ as your mascot? The church, as a whole, has succumbed.

The Cultural Gateway to Deception

Prevailing culture is likely the widest gate onto the broad road to deception and destruction. Not only is it a dangerous gateway because it is wide, but also because it is so attractive, alluring and overwhelmingly trafficked. The sheer pressure of the multitudes passing through creates an almost irresistible impulse to "go with the flow." We have all heard the cultural demand to "go in threat." Lamentably, most are heeding the call.

We want to be loved and accepted. We want to feel that we are part of the "in crowd." We do not want to be ostracized or marginalized. And so we conform. We first follow reluctantly. But with each compromising step, the cultural lure grows stronger until we are embraced fully by its seductive arms. And that is where we find ourselves, especially as western Christians, on the near edge of the Second Coming.

The Church In Bed With The Culture

The church, both individual and corporate, has, like ancient Israel, committed adultery with the surrounding culture. Jeremiah's lament to God's chosen 2500 years ago echoes through the centuries. Like an arrow deftly released from God's unerring bow of truth, it strikes the bull's eye of our hearts, lives and ministries. It pierces to the depths of our souls. It finds its mark in the darkened corners of our lives where professing Christians and their pastors cuddle with the culture, finding seductive solace for souls parched for lack of intimacy with their Lord.

Hear the Lord's passionate plea through Jeremiah's pen.

Mine heart within me is broken because of the prophets... For the land is full of adulterers; Both prophet and priest are profane; yea, in my house I have found their wickedness, saith the Lord.
I have seen, also in the prophets of Jerusalem an horrible thing: they commit adultery and walk in lies... none doth return

from his wickedness: they are all to me as Sodom, and the inhabitants thereof as Gomorrah (Jeremiah 23:9-14).

Wow! The God who betrothed Israel to himself is a jilted lover. He is a jealous God (Ex. 20:5, 34:14). His own bride has fornicated with the worldly culture and committed adultery, both physical and spiritual. "Oh that my head were waters, and mine eyes a fountain of tears, that I might weep day and night... that I might leave my people, and go from them! For they be all adulterers, an assembly of treacherous men." "They are not valiant for the truth," declared Jeremiah (Jer. 9:1-4).

They will deceive every one his neighbor, and will not speak the truth: they have taught their tongues to speak lies.... Through deceit they refuse to know me, saith the Lord. Their tongue is an arrow shot out, it speaketh deceit.
Said the Lord: shall not my soul be avenged on such a nation as this (Jeremiah 9:5-9)?

The devil is always in the details. So is the truth. The common problem we have in reading and processing the words of the prophets, however potent they may be, is that they are generally interpreted to apply to someone other than me or to some group other than my group, my church, my culture or my situation. This enables us to mentally and spiritually dodge the arrow that would pierce our own hearts with our Lord's specific and passionate wooing and warning, fully applicable to our own lives. Unfortunately, if we persist in this dance away from truth and in this dodge from God's warning arrows... the proverbial "shot across the bow..." God will eventually abandon us, as He did with Israel and Judah, to our false lovers and our adulterous affairs with the surrounding culture. Adulterous deception may then direct and ultimately determine our destiny.

Adultery, Pure and Simple

The word *adultery* and its various derivatives occurs 69 times in the Scriptures, with 35 of those being in the New Testament. The word fornication and its various derivatives occurs 35 times in the Bible. Thirty of those are found in the New Testament.

Interestingly, God has chosen marriage specifically, and the sexual relationship, in general, to graphically depict His relationship both with Israel and with His church. God performed the first marriage to His created son, Adam, in the Garden of Eden. He betrothed Israel to Himself at Mt. Sinai to which the people responded, "I do" (Ex. 24:1-7). It was a blood covenant (Ex. 24:8). And God betrothed the church to His only begotten son, Jesus, the "last Adam" also through a covenant of His own blood.

The Father will ultimately present to His Son for consummation at the Great Marriage Supper of the Lamb a remnant of both Israel and the professing Gentile church who embrace Yeshua, Jesus, as Messiah and who have made themselves ready, "unspotted from the world" (Jam. 1:27), "not having spot, wrinkle, or any such thing" (Eph. 5:27). That bride, the true bride of Christ, must "be holy and without blemish" (Eph. 5:27), for without holiness, "no man shall see the Lord" (Heb. 12:14). "Wherefore, beloved,… be diligent," warned the apostle Peter, "that you may be found of him in peace, without spot, and blameless" (II Pet. 3:14).

Why the repeated references to purity and holiness? Why do the apostles so consistently and specifically declare that we live unspotted by the world and culture? Why are we repeatedly enjoined to be "Holy and blameless" and to be prepared as "a chaste virgin" to Christ (II Cor. 11:2)? The answer is simple. God is not going to present a whorish, adulterous or fornicating bride to His sinless Son.

The continuous message through both testaments is that God, wedding mercy and truth, is wooing His people back from their spiritual whoredoms to embrace a husband who is and will be true. He chastises "an adulterous and sinful generation" (Mark 8:38). He is jealous over those who claim to be betrothed but who, "upon every high hill and under every green tree they wander, playing the harlot" (Jer. 2:20). In holy frustration and with passionate plea he cries, "How canst thou say, I am not polluted" (Jer. 2:23)?

Surely as a wife treacherously departeth from her husband, so
have ye dealt treacherously with me… saith the Lord (Jer. 3:20).

The problem of spiritual adultery is yet even more deceptive and dangerous. This whorish embrace of the ways of the world and the seductive lure of the methods and messages of the decaying culture are not seen or recognized by us for what they really are in God's sight. We are so entrapped by the fun and fascination of the fickle world around us that we come to think this is normal - that it is acceptable to the Lord to whom we claim to be betrothed. We frolic in faith with Christ in an hour of worship and proceed to fornicate with the world during the week. "My people have forgotten me days without number," says the Lord (Jer. 2:32).

Even worse, we claim, in rebellion, to be innocent.

Yet thou sayest, Because I am innocent, surely his anger shall turn from me. Behold, I will plead with thee, because thou sayest, I have not sinned (Jer. 2:35).

"Thou has polluted the land with thy whoredoms and with wickedness. Therefore the showers have been withholden, and there hath been no latter rain, and thou hadst a whore's forehead, thou refusedst to be ashamed" (Jer. 3:2-3).

You may be thinking: *Get specific. What are you talking about? How does this "spiritual adultery" apply to me and my sphere of living?* It would be impossible to catalogue the hundreds, if not thousands, of ways we are prone to and have embraced the lure of worldly culture. The sphere of entertainment alone demonstrates an overwhelming whorish departure from the Lord of the household of faith whose ways are holy. Like Lot's wife, we lust for the world's ways, and the world seduces us through its lust, violence and debauchery. Pastors, convinced the Word of their professed Husband, Christ, is irrelevant, now substitute the "authority" of the seducing culture through its entertainment purportedly to introduce the world to marry Christ, expecting Christ to embrace our whorish ways because, as we argue to ourselves, "the end justifies the means." We then claim Scriptural authority as covering for our naked adultery, declaring "I must become all things to all men that I might win some."

Spiritual adultery now characterizes, in large part, how we live, how we spend our money and time, the choices we make, the values we espouse, our attitudes toward others, toward God and toward His kingdom. Adulterous thinking has become so pervasive in the church that it is indeed difficult to separate thoughts for the Lord to whom we allege betrothal from our thoughts of cultural and worldly suitors. This is true both in our individual lives and in our ministries.

Ministry, both its methods and message, are now dictated, not by the Master but by the Market. What the Master declares relevant to our souls, we deem irrelevant because it does not produce sales in a church driven by the carnal culture rather than by the Christ of the cross. The message of the cross itself has become a casualty to the siren call of culture. Preaching toward "felt needs" as perceived by culturally-driven seekers, we have increasingly failed to meet their true spiritual needs as defined by our Creator. *TIME* diagnosed the cultural seduction well, declaring that as Americans flooded back to church, church would never again be the same. Consider well the prophetic insight from one of America's leading news magazines.

AMERICANS ARE LOOKING FOR A CUSTOM-MADE GOD – ONE MADE IN THEIR OWN IMAGE.

The entire seeker-sensitive movement of the last generation, fueling the church-growth movement, has been culturally driven rather than Christ-driven. We have, in effect, sold America a false gospel based on a culturally re-defined Christ with a new "relevant" and marketable message from a God made in our own image whose modern message is not the pursuit of holiness but the pursuit of happiness.

There is a reason why "YOUR BEST LIFE NOW" has become the leading mantra of our time in both church and culture. It is born of spiritual fornication, producing progeny seeking first the temporal blessings of the culture rather than eternal hope in Christ. It is a re-defined faith that markets perfectly to the "ME" generation, and it has propelled its leading exponents to vast power, prominence and popularity while seducing both saints and sinners through a deceptively false message to embrace a false hope rooted not in repentance from sin but in restoration of self esteem. Feelings now trump faith.

Rather than coming out from among them, separating ourselves from the increasingly Christ-less culture, we, like ancient Israel, crave to be just like the Canaanitish culture. We have exchanged acceptance by God for acceptance by the world. Our increasingly whorish souls have made intercourse in the tents of wickedness. We love the praises of man more than the praises of God. Thus saith the Lord…

> *My people have committed two evils; they have forsaken me the*
> *fountain of living waters, and hewed them out cisterns, broken*
> *cisterns, that can hold no water.*
> *Know therefore and see that it is an evil thing and bitter, that*
> *thou hast forsaken the Lord thy God, and that my fear is not in*
> *thee….*
> *Thou saidst, I will not transgress; when upon every high hill*
> *and under every green tree thou wanderest, playing the harlot.*
> *The Lord hath rejected thy confidences, and thou shalt not*
> *prosper in them (Jer. 2:13, 19, 20, 37).*

Interestingly, and as a matter of hope for the church facing such "titanic" deception on a collision course with an unpleasant destiny, a profound confession was made even, as this chapter was nearly completed, by the progenitor and chief "prophet" of the seeker-sensitive movement. They had commissioned a study of the fruit issuing from the root of this massive spiritual experiment that has seduced thousands of pastors and millions of their followers worldwide. The results were compiled in a book titled *REVEAL*… resulting in the following heartbreaking, yet hope-filled confession by the leader… "We made a mistake."

Adultery in Heart… Adultery in Home

The consequences of the church dancing with the culture will inevitably lead first to explorative trysts followed by soul-sacrificing adultery. Consider this heart-rending portrait of the sexual life of the church.

As with the spiritual, so it is with the natural or physical aspects of our lives. The devastating pattern of spiritual adultery is reflected in massive physical or marital adultery and a lifestyle of fornication. The statistics are clear… and unadulterated.

Over the past 40 years since the late 1960's, the breakup of marriages in the church in America paralleled the breakup of marriages in the culture at large. In fact, the pattern of marital breakup in the culture at large became increasingly authoritative as a kind of measure of what was appropriate within the "Christian" realm of the broader culture. The philosophical shift and moral earthquake that occurred culturally was embraced increasingly by Christians of both liberal and conservative, mainline and evangelical stripe, including pastors and para church leaders. While protesting the breakdown of the family, as a matter of principle and concern, we progressively and pragmatically embraced not only the practices but also the underlying thinking of the broader culture that was abandoning wholesale the absolute truths of God's Word that had bound us in social contract from the beginning. Ignoring the warnings, the church boarded ship with the culture and pulled up her anchor of truth. Pitching her tent toward Sodom, she headed with reckless abandon toward the icebergs ahead. The casualties from the ultimate collision are still being numbered, and there is no end in sight. There were, and are, insufficient lifeboats to go around. The individual pain and collective agony has been incalculable… and the cost in fractured lives and undermined faith continues unabated.

Our "jealous" Lord winces in holy agony as His church has gone to bed with the worldly culture. His grief is without solace as those who claim to carry His surname run daily into the arms of lovers who are escorting them to a bed of temporal love, leading to eternal perdition. In no area of life is this adulterous apostasy more evident than in our marital and sexual behavior.

Spiritually Salacious

The statistical facts are piercing, persistent and even prophetic. So grave and spiritually salacious are these realities of church life in America that her leaders find every way possible to hide from them or rationalize them, secreting them from their parishioners and constituencies so as not to trouble their adulterous souls, thus affecting the flow of ministry resources. Consider this representative statistical sample, figures which, to an honest heart, are so well established as to be virtually incontrovertible.

PORTRAIT OF "CHRISTIAN" SEX

- 2/3 of "Christian" singles admit they are not virgins.
- 61% of students who signed abstinence cards that "True Love Waits" admit breaking their pledge – but – of the remaining 39% who say they kept their pledge, 55% had oral sex and did not consider it to be "sex."
- Evangelical college students do not consider anal intercourse to be "sex," and indulge in it accordingly.
- 34% of "Christian" women and 60-70% of "Christian" men admit seeking out pornography.
- 37% of pastors admit struggling with Internet pornography.
- 20% of pastors admit to an affair while in ministry.
- Cohabitation increased 72% from 1990-2000. The greatest increase was within the "Bible Belt."

PORTRAIT OF "CHRISTIAN" MARRIAGE

- By 1996, divorce in the church was 4% higher than the national average.
- By 1997, divorce in the "Bible Belt" was 50% higher than the national average, and still is.
- By 2000, divorce among pastors equaled their parishioners, the 2nd highest of all professions.
- By 2005, both the Church of England and Assemblies of God overturned historic doctrinal convictions to conform to Jezebel's cultural mandate, permitting pastors and parishioners to divorce and remarry even if their spouse is living.

HAS THE AMERICAN CHURCH BECOME A BROTHEL?

Said *Christianity Today*, "Sex beyond the bounds of true biblical marriage is embodied apostasy." Jeremiah aptly lamented, "... they were not at all ashamed, neither could they blush: (Jer. 8:12).

NOTE: For further, more in-depth understanding of our adulterous and fornicating culture, please refer to the following FACT SHEETS on our ministry website www.saveus.org.

- The Sexual Seduction of the Union
- The State of Ministry Marriage and Morals
- The Marital State of the Union
- The Spiritual State of the Union
- A Portrait of the Black Family

How Did It Happen?

The dangerous drift to destruction began in the 1960's with a massive truth quake. The spirit of the French Revolution, born of satanic "Enlightenment," resurfaced with massive philosophical and spiritual tectonic activity, overturning the truths of eternity that stabilized the social order. As the 42nd President of the United States declared with unabashed arrogance:

> We are redefining, in practical terms, the immutable ideals
> that have guided us from the beginning.[1]

Just as Robespierre, the chief engineer and voice of the French Revolution, dethroned the God of Creation, enthroning "REASON" as their reigning goddess, so did the West and Western Christians beginning in the 1960's. Following the siren call of the broader culture, the church and her leaders progressively embraced the spirit of human reason over the Spirit of the eternal God, who was given to lead and keep us in His Truth. Truth was no longer what the God of eternity declared it to be, but what modern and post-modern man desired it to be, wrapped in the pseudo-scientific robes of psych-ology for authority. The church crawled into bed with the culture, cavorting carnally, following BASIC INSTINCT rather than the basic inspiration of God's eternal WORD of TRUTH. Her bastard children now fill our churches, purporting to "resist the devil" but refusing to "submit to God" (Jam. 4:7). The apostasy of adultery is nearly complete. As with the natural, so with the spiritual.

The devil's dance steps to seduction were actually quite simple. We failed to resist because we, like a teenage damsel, yearned for cultural acceptance. It was not that pastor and people intended to go to bed with the world. We just yielded to its titillating advances, finding ourselves enraptured by the temporal thrill of eating the forbidden fruit. As it is written, there are "pleasures of sin for a season" (Heb. 11:25).

Just as in the French Revolution, it all began with rebellion against authority, discarding the verities of divine truth that directed both faith and family. The will of the people in democratic majority replaced the will of God in divine authority. Personal feelings replaced faith rooted in propositional truth. The "Encounter" movement of the culture in the 1970's was matched by the "God is Love" movement in the church. "How do you feel?" replaced "What is true... What hath God said?"

Divorce, virtually non-existent in both the broader culture and the church, became fashionable. Feelings had replaced an anchoring faith. Pastors fell in line with the cultural mandate, not willing to resist the people. It became "like people, like priest" (Hos. 4:9), so that the divorce rate among our pastors now equals that of their parishioners and is the second highest of all professions in America.

Since a secular divorce authorized re-marriage, the church reasoned, contrary to all of church history and biblical warning, that her increasingly divorced members should also be entitled to remarry. The cultural "pursuit of happiness" replaced Christ's call to holiness. *After all*, we reasoned, *God wants me happy. He wouldn't want me to remain faithful to the spouse to whom I had vowed loyalty "Till death do us part" if it would mean possible lack of SELF-fulfillment.* And so pastors, "willing to content the people" like Pilate (Mark 15:15), crucified Christ afresh by assisting the people in cavorting with the culture, authorizing their serial divorces and remarriages which Jesus had called "adultery" (Matt. 19:3-9), re-labeling their flagrant adulteries as "blessings," "answers to prayer," "manifestations of mercy," and "divine second chances."

The "gilded age" of the prosperous 1980's turned our hearts increasingly to worship the god of happiness rather than the God of holiness. Serial divorce and remarriage became the norm. That which God said He hated was wholeheartedly embraced in the headlong pursuit of happiness. That which God called "treachery" was now trumpeted from pulpit to pew as a triumph of God's grace (Mal. 2:13-16). The trumpeted "grace awakening" of the 1990's solidified this salacious baptism of the flesh, wrapping it in a robe of purported righteousness. Having "dissed" God's true grace given to enable us to obey His will, we re-defined "grace" to mean God's overlooking or winking at our willful disobedience.

Our affair with the worldly culture had inevitably led to a virtual divorce from the Lord whose name we yet bore. We now co-habitated with the world. The deception was complete. Our nakedness was revealed to the sexually craven culture. And the church, purporting to be betrothed to Christ, had betrayed the lover of her soul. Having abandoned marital faithfulness, she now took the lead in breaking up the family, leading the culture in unspeakable carnage. Grace had become dis-grace. And her Lord stands at her door and knocks (Rev. 3:19-20).

What Must We Do?

Jezebel rules jealously! "… thou sufferest that woman Jezebel, which calleth herself a prophetess, to teach and to seduce my servants to commit fornication…," saith the Lord (Rev. 2:20).

This is a warning both to the all-time church, but more specifically to the end-time church. The spirit of Jezebel is a jealous spirit, competing with a Jealous God for your affections. Only you have the ability to resist her tantalizing ways and the seductive allure of her temporal titillation. She flattereth with her words and causes you to forget the covenant with your God (Prov. 2:16-19). "Her feet go down to death: her steps take hold of hell" (Prov. 5:5).

In the face of this seductive spirit calling you into bed with the culture and its Jezebelish, Canaanitish ways, God says, "My grace [enabling power] is sufficient for thee, for my strength is made perfect in [your] weakness" (II Cor. 12:9).

To the married, "Drink waters out of thine own cistern…. Rejoice with the wife of thy youth. Let her breasts satisfy thee at all times: and be ravished always with her love. For the ways of a man are before the eyes of the Lord, and he pondereth all his goings" (Prov. 5:15-21). "Whoso committeth adultery… lacketh understanding: he that doeth it destroyeth his own soul" (Prov. 6:32). Pornography, many romance novels, sexually oriented magazines and movies lead you to virtual adultery (Matt. 5:27-28).

"Flee fornication" and all sexual immorality as God, not the culture, defines it (I Cor. 6:18). "Know ye not that your bodies are the members of

Christ... the temple of the Holy Ghost... and ye are not your own (I Cor. 6:15, 19)? Flee means to run from sexual temptation, not to dance with it. "There hath no temptation taken you but such as is common to man: but God is faithful, who... will with the temptation also make a way to escape, that ye may be able to bear it" (I Cor. 10:13).

Sexual sin is deadly, both physically and spiritually. Like a virulent cancer, it metasticizes rapidly throughout your body and the Body of Christ. It must be removed individually and corporately. To fail to deal with it as deadly is to dance with eternal destruction, jeopardizing the many, both now and future, by a false compassion for the few at present. Compassion for the individual must not trump the survival and spiritual vitality of the corporate body. Jezebel is very deceptive! We are mandated to "put away" unrepented wickedness from among us (I Cor. 5:1-13).

Failure to deal decisively with cultural fornication, spiritual adultery and marital infidelity will bring the wrath of God on the children of dis-obedience (Eph. 5:5-6). The beloved apostle Paul warned a sexually promiscuous, adulterous church:

> *Be not deceived: neither fornicators, nor idolators, nor adulterers, nor effeminate, not abusers of themselves with mankind [practicing homosexuals]... shall inherit the kingdom of God (I Cor. 6:9-10).*

We must repent! Adultery and fornication will keep you from the eternal presence of God. Jesus decried our serial divorces and remarriages as "adultery" (Matt. 5:32). We have exchanged, in Jezebelish fashion, the authority of Christ for the authority of a carnal culture. Our feelings have become our lord, and the Lord must now bow to our feelings. Feelings have trumped faith.

Jesus, addressing the Jezebelitish spirit that had invaded the church at Thyatira, declared:

> *I gave her space to repent of her fornication; and she repented not. Behold, I will cast her into a bed, and them that commit adultery with her into great tribulation, except they repent of their deeds. And I will kill her children with death; and all the*

churches shall know that I am he which searcheth the reins [inmost mind] and the hearts: and I will give every one of you according to your works (Rev. 2:21-23).

On any given day of corporate worship among professed Christians in America and the West, between 40 and 50 percent of those in the pews and pulpits are divorced, adulterers and fornicators by Christ's own definition. The remainder have, either tacitly or transitively, become enablers, "who knowing the judgment of God, that they which do such things are worthy of death, not only do the same, but have pleasure in [approve] them that do them" (Rom. 1:32). A democratic majority of rebellious Christians will not insulate us from the judgment of a holy God. We must repent!

A Triumphant Testimony

As this chapter was being written, a beautiful thing happened. I received an urgent call from a businessman in the Northeast. He said he had been listening to our national radio program, VIEWPOINT, for about a year, and had come under great conviction by the Holy Spirit. A number of our programs had dealt in various ways with the divorce and remarriage debacle. He had gone to our website **saveus.org**, reviewing the FACT SHEETS and a heart-rending, spirit-gripping outline of "What the Bible Really Teaches About Marriage, Divorce and Remarriage."

He had searched the Scriptures with an open mind, and the Holy Spirit, the Spirit of truth, had searched his heart. He said, "I am under conviction and I must deal with this now. I cannot wait. And that is why I called you from my office. Let me shut my door."

"Is there hope for my soul?" he cried out. "I am the adulterer and fornicator the Scriptures talk about. I am divorced and I remarried when my wife was still living. I've had affairs and have been unfaithful to my wife and the Lord. I have no peace. I go to church thinking it will go away. But I know I'm destined for hell, and now I'm on my way as a Reservist to Iraq. Please help! Is there hope for me?

It was a precious but pitiable plea. Fortunately, the Lord pities those who truly love him. Like as a father pitieth his children, so the

Lord pitieth them that fear him (Ps. 103:13). To those that fear Him, He will reveal His secret and show His covenant (Ps. 25:14). "What must I do?" pleaded the listener.

What a profound blessing! What a breath of fresh air in the midst of a self-justifying people who have abandoned the fear of the Lord, fearing man and pandering to a carnal culture for fulfillment.

"If you will simply and expressly confess your sin, in all of its heinous detail as the Holy Spirit has revealed it, not seeking to justify or hide from it, God is faithful and just to forgive and cleanse you from all unrighteousness," I responded, quoting I John 1:9. "But you must own up to it just as God has diagnosed it, and then turn from it in repentance," I continued.

The businessman broke forth in one of the most breathtakingly beautiful prayers of repentance I have witnessed in the last 40 years. His confession of particularized sin, including the selfish and unrighteous attitudes that drive him and how he had played loose, compromising with the culture in spiritual adultery, was characteristic of the great revivals of the past. And the peace that had eluded him came at once. Genuine joy replaced the gratuitous flatterings of the Jezebel spirit that had tyrannical governance over his life.

So dramatic was this divine encounter that I asked permission to share it with you. Is the Holy Spirit speaking to your heart? "Today, if you will hear his voice, harden not your heart" (Heb. 3:7). Weeping may endure for a night, but joy cometh in the morning" (Ps. 30:5). Jesus is coming soon. And He is not going to receive an adulterous bride.

A Message from Jesus' Brother

Blessed is the man that endureth temptation, for when he is tried, he shall receive the crown of life, which the Lord hath promised to them that love him (Jam. 1:12). "This is the love of God, that we keep his commandments..." (I Jn. 5:3, Rev. 14:12).

"But be ye doers of the word, and not hearers only, deceiving your own selves" (Jam. 1:22). "Pure religion and undefiled before God and the Father is this, To visit the fatherless and widows in their affliction [not to create virtual widows and fatherless children through divorce], and **to keep himself unspotted from the world** (Jam. 1:27).

"Ye adulterers and adulteresses, know ye not that the friendship of the world is enmity with God? Whosoever therefore will be a friend of the world is the enemy of God" (Jam. 4:4).

"Submit yourselves therefore to God. Resist the devil, and he will flee from you. Draw nigh [in true, unadulterated intimacy] to God, and he will draw nigh to you" (Jam. 4:7-8).

"A double-minded [two-souled] man is unstable in all his ways." "Receive with meekness the engrafted word, which is able to save your souls." "Humble yourselves in the sight of the Lord, and he shall lift you up" (Jam. 1:8, 21; 4:7).

"Ye have lived in pleasure on the earth, and been wanton; ye have nourished your hearts, as in a day of slaughter." "Behold, the judge standeth before the door" (Jam. 5:5, 9).

Surely, he comes quickly (Rev. 22:7, 12, 20)!

Chapter Ten

Daring Thoughts for *Deceptive Times*

1. Why does culture have such a powerful influence? How is it a gateway to deception?

2. Do you agree that the American church has "gone to bed with the culture?" What indications do you see?

3. Can you see why God described the waywardness of his people as "fornication" and as "adultery?" Are there ways that you see yourself having "fornicating with the world" or "adulterizing with the culture?"

4. What is your heart response to the statistics describing the sexual life of American "Christians?" Were you defensive, or grief-stricken?

5. Has the spirit of Jezebel vied in your life for dominion over the Spirit of God who is jealous for your soul?

6. How did you react to the broken-hearted testimony of the man who bitterly acknowledged his fornicating and adulterous lifestyle, crying out to God for forgiveness and in repentance? Did you cry out with him… or rise up in resistance?

7. Did Jesus' brother, James, say anything that stirred your own heart?

8. What is your current attitude toward deception, having read this far? Is this book relevant?

The Killer Virus

*"Let your communication be, Yea, yea; Nay, nay:
for whatsoever is more than these cometh of evil"
(Matt. 5:37).*

WARNING! There is a fatal virus that has been sweeping America and the world for a generation. It insidiously creeps in through our mail. It infects us without our knowledge as we read our newspapers and thumb through our magazines. Open wounds appear as we sit before our televisions and enter the theaters. Our minds become ulcerated as we speak to one another and our hearts are sometimes seared and cauterized even as we sit in our churches.

Who is Susceptible?

This virus is not partial to race, creed, or geographic region. The minds of the educated often appear more susceptible, but no heart is immune from damage. It is highly contagious! Every Christian is put on notice of the extreme danger of this virus.

Virus Can Be Fatal

In its advanced stages, the virus is fatal. Fortunately, the prognosis for recovery is good, if treated early. However, care should be taken to identify carriers of the virus to avoid contamination. It may be necessary, in some instances, to quarantine carriers - or at least take great caution in protecting your family from exposure and to de-contaminate promptly.

There is only one known cure if you or your family should become infected. The cure, however, can also prevent infection by the virus if taken regularly and in sufficient dosage. Special warning is issued to parents, teachers, pastors, youth leaders, political leaders, and any other persons who are in a position to expose others. If you should become infected, the potential damage to others is multiplied greatly. Due to the seriousness of this virus, any persons in the above categories who have knowingly become infected and continue to expose others will be subject to the social consequences now and to eternal accountability later.

This virus is known most commonly as "political correctness," a moral and spiritual disorder that infects the heart and mind, impairing and eventually neutralizing our ability to discern truth. It is systemic.

Truth and virtue were once part and parcel of what it meant to be American. Among the most popular lyrics of *The Battle Hymn of the Republic* are "His truth is marching on." Yet these days, it would be more accurate to add a word: "His truth is marching on *by*." As we watch it pass, the battle for some sense of moral rightness and biblically anchored direction becomes increasingly intense. This battle is becoming especially acute for professing followers of Christ.

Intentionalized Confusion

The concept of "political correctness" has become so common that it has even taken on its own acronym: "PC." One now stands to be thoroughly confused if he should use the initials "PC," having just learned from previous years that "PC" means "personal computer." But perhaps that's what political correctness is all about: confusion.

A functional definition of the term might be "speech that conforms to my perception of what is most generally acceptable among the most vocal people in politics, religion, business, society, and elsewhere so as to most likely avoid being made to feel I am not part of the *mainstream*. When we were teenagers, our parents called it "peer pressure." We used to cringe when it became obvious a man waited to see which way the wind was blowing before he spoke his mind. We thought such behavior spineless - a clear signal that he lacked moral fortitude. Today it has become a cultural mandate for all in the democratic West.

Symptoms of Political Correctness

So what are the practical, identifiable symptoms of this moral and spiritual virus. There are two predominant manifestations. The first is the inability to clearly distinguish truth and right from wrong. The second would involve unfortunate mutations of what used to be our common language.

Language has always evolved somewhat with general usage. Today it is modified with intent. An interesting case in point is a simple three-letter word: "*gay.*" In the large 1952 *Webster's Dictionary*, it is said to mean "excited and full of mirth." In a much smaller edition dated 1987, a second meaning was added: "homosexual."

When was the last time you used the word "gay" to describe a happy and mirthful person? Would you even dare? When was the last time you used the word to refer to homosexual behavior? Is it possible that you have contracted a case of political correctness?

Is this change a chance bit of linguistic evolution? Or is there an agenda at work? The word "homosexual" has always had negative con-notations within American society. Our moral and spiritual roots clearly establish sexual relations between a husband and wife of the opposite sex as the norm, the moral standard. Homosexuality is therefore immoral. The very word conveys that sense.

"If that's the case," some say, "let's change the word. Let's call it 'gay' and, in so doing, subtly reshape the public's perception of truth." Have you any doubt that this change in term is a strategic move? If it is not, why does the "gay" movement shun the word "homosexual" like the plague? Shakespeare was not totally correct when he said, "A rose by any other name would smell as sweet." That may be good for roses, but not for moral values and spiritual truth.

Words Count

Language and the words we use are critical to both preservation or extinction of moral values in society. The mere changing of *terms* of reference often changes also our moral *point* of reference. It dilutes or strips away the stark truth and muddies the waters of reason, perception, and reality. None can deny the effect in America and the world today. And it did not occur casually. It has been engineered.

Can you believe it? Those who teach their children that proper sexual relations are between a married man and woman are now referred to derogatorily as a "homophobe" and a "bigot." Since we don't want to be bigoted, we gradually conform to the incessant voices of the perceived cultural trend, silencing the voice of morality and truth. Society slips another foot down the slope of moral decay and spiritual seduction.

Let us begin to once again speak the truth. "Sexual preference" is sexual perversion. An "alternative lifestyle" is still homosexuality. "Cohabitation" is still adultery or fornication. One who "terminates a pregnancy" has had an abortion. The "products of conception" are a living human being residing in the womb. "Indiscretion" is still sin.

In the Bible, the American Founding Fathers found the source of real, dependable truth worthy of serving as the foundation of a nation. They were convinced that if they would continue believing in the Bible as God's Word, they would know **the** truth, and that truth would make them free (John 8:31-32). Should we do any less?

Truth is the only cure for political correctness. Apply it liberally. The future of America, and your children, depends on it. And the Church has no other foundation than Jesus Christ, who declared himself to be "the way, the truth and the life" (John 14:6).

"PC" in the Church

The paralyzing poison of political correctness is by no means isolated in the worldly culture. It has been purposely insinuated into the life of the church worldwide and has spread like wildfire.

The invasion of political correctness into the life of professing believers in Christ can be traced to two primary sources: (1) The church increasingly wanting to conform to the ways of the world for acceptance; and (2) Pastors and para-church leaders desiring to promote secondary agendas for personal and alleged "ministry" purposes.

Just as in the broader culture, political correctness in the church has become a major engine of warfare to destroy all opposition in pursuing and enforcing what philosophers and social engineers call "the will to power." It not only serves to destroy any common allegiance to truth but marginalizes any person or group that would dare to disagree. Its purpose is governance and dominance by intimidation or subterfuge. The pursued end, according to this new post-modern mind, always justifies the means... even if it means doing violence to the meaning of words.

The applications and implications for you, your family, your congregation... yes, even the truth of the gospel itself are vast and beyond the scope of this chapter. But a few illustrations of the insidious means of this "religious" correctness may help to strip off the seductive covers that camouflage the deception.

"Religious correctness" defiles both our message and our methods. It is always employed and justified in the name of accomplishing some spiritual purpose - hence the deception. *Grace,* for example, is no longer God's favor and enabling power to do what we ought, but has been redefined in the alleged "grace awakening" as God's willingness to overlook our sin, justifying our doing what we want. The new *Grace* has actually dissed true grace and has become *dis-grace.*

This has fueled the heresy of antinomianism. Lawlessness now abounds with a vengeance in God's own house, just as Christ and His apostles foretold. Why have we done this? It appears more loving, more inclusive and we believe it will help us grow our churches and "reach the lost." Now the "saints" live in sin equal to the "lost" we purport to reach. But we accomplished an objective - a short cut to church growth, through a re-interpretation or re-definition of *grace.*

Jesus said, "Make disciples." "Teach them to observe [obey] everything I have commanded" (Matt. 28:19-20) and "I'll build my church." (Matt. 16:18). We decided to build churches, have failed to teach obedience, and law-less-ness prevails - the premier behavioral characteristic of the end times. Anti-christ is called the "Lawless one" (NKJV).

Those who succumb to the anti-christ spirit are also lawless, deceived by unrighteousness, having pleasure in unrighteousness (II Thess. 2:8-12).

Consider the spiritual and moral consequences of "religious correctness" in merely re-defining and re-applying the simple word *grace*.

- The word *obey* has become the most hated word in the church, regardless of liberal or evangelical stripe. The very word our Lord and His apostles used to describe God's standard for loving and pleasing Him is now despised and denigrated by those who claim to be His followers (John 14:15-24, I Jn. 5:3, Rev. 14:12, Rom. 2:8-9).
- Those who attempt to teach or preach *obedience* to biblical standards or righteousness are intimidated to silence with the allegation "There's no *grace* in your message."
- The enabling power and favor of the God who declared, "My grace is sufficient for thee: for my strength is made perfect in your weakness" (II Cor. 12:9) is no longer deemed adequate to do His will. Instead, the new "PC"… politically/religiously correct *grace* approves or winks at our sin rather than strengthening us to overcome the enemy of our souls.
- The spirit of lawlessness has progressively replaced the law of the Spirit (Rom. 8:2-3).
- The carnal or fleshly mind has replaced Christ-mindedness (Rom. 8:5-7).
- Spiritual strength and moral stability have disintegrated.
- We now permit, justify… even approve… that which God prohibits.

Indeed, "political correctness" and its corollary expression of "religious correctness," neither of which is "correct," are the deceptive tools of an increasingly post-modern world, seducing the masses of both pagans and professing believers to change the immutable principles that have guided us from the beginning. And where there are changed principles, there are changed practices.

Consider soberly this shocking sequence. Sodomy was outlawed in America nationwide until the baby-boomer generation when the secular sexual revolution of the 1960's married the church's God-is-love movement of the 1970's, producing a bastard daughter who exchanged the "faith once delivered to the saints" for feelings, redefining grace to obey Christ as liberty to follow the culture. Divorce was virtually non-existent forty years ago. Scripture was accepted by most, believer and unbeliever alike, as the authoritative "Word of God" in the 1950's. Faith ruled, however imperfectly.

Today, mainline churches bless sodomy, evangelical churches bless divorce and feelings rule, almost exclusively. Since evangelicals, according to *Christianity Today*, have been "rethinking divorce,"[1] blessing what God says He hates (Mal. 2:16), when will evangelicals "rethink" sodomy? Surprise! It is already happening![2] Apparently God is so good that He has authorized His creatures (by grace of course) to become God. So much for the "emerging," or should we say, "evolving" church. Or is it God who is evolving? Just imagine! Is the eternal God, who declared "I change not" (Mal. 3:6), changing His unchangeable Word just for us who didn't much like what He originally said?

Believe it or not, this new "religiously correct" viewpoint is being enforced upon the entire church by pastor and people alike, both mainline and evangelical, in precisely the same manner as sodomy has been enforced through "political correctness" upon the nation and the world. "Political correctness," including all of its corollary expressions, is pernicious.

Just as the word "gay" has been redefined to put sodomy and homosexuality in a favorable light before men, so "grace" has been re-defined to substitute feelings for biblical faith and authenticate the power of culture over the power of Christ. Obedience - the evidence of our genuine trust in God - has been the casualty. They who live by their fleshly feelings cannot please God (Rom. 8:5-8). It is a dangerous thing to be at enmity with God (Rom. 8:7).

Indeed, "political correctness" is insidious. It is a potentially fatal virus to your soul. At first it produces spiritual blindness. Then, as it is allowed to proceed systemically, it corrupts the "hard drive" of your mind, preventing you from thinking biblically. Without repentance, you will progressively arrogate your will over God's will, until you are of a reprobate mind.

Though you claim to "know" God, you do not glorify or treat Him *as* God. You will become progressively vain in your imaginations, in your reasonings and thoughts. Your foolish heart will become darkened. Professing yourself to be wise, you will become a spiritual fool, finally changing the truth of God into a lie. Others who are infected will follow the same pattern. Though they know the judgment of God, they find solace in majority rule, shifting trust from the dependable God to the deceit of the masses. Finally, those gripped by this deadly virus will not only rebel against God by personally disobeying His written will, but will take pleasure in and approve others also in their rebellion (Rom. 1:21-32). At this point, the condition may well be spiritually terminal.

This is powerful deception! It's seductive ability is vast and lies in the desire to agree with those things that we think will either make us feel good or make others feel good. It is driven by false compassion, the fear of rejection, and willingness to follow the perceived crowd rather than to walk the narrow way in true obedience to Christ. You become vulnerable when your spiritual immune system is depleted by lack of sincere personal study of the Word. You are challenged with the choice of agreeing with Christ or the culture on life's important moral and spiritual issues. An ounce of prevention is worth a hundred pounds of cure in dealing with this deadly virus.

"Trust in the Lord with all your heart; and lean not unto your own [or other's understanding]. In all your ways acknowledge him, and he shall direct your paths. Be not wise in your own eyes: fear the Lord, and depart from evil. It shall be health to your navel, and marrow to your bones" (Prov. 3:5-8).

Chapter Eleven

Daring Thoughts
for *Deceptive Times*

1. We talk of "political correctness," but what is it? How does it work? Why is it effective?

2. How would you describe the symptoms of "political correctness?"

3. Does it make any difference what words we use to describe things? Do words count?

4. If our words do not count, how can we be sure God's Word means what it says and says what it means?

5. In what ways have you seen "political correctness" invade the church or your congregation? What about the religious version… "religious correctness?"

6. Have you noticed that the very use of the term "politically correct" does not mean correct at all, but actually means, "We're going to pretend that something is correct, though we know it isn't, in order to enforce our desired agenda on others?"

7. Have you succumbed, in any way, to the deceptive and pervasive power of "political correctness?" How?

The *Korah* Spirit

*"I will not be afraid of ten thousands
that have set themselves against me round about"
(Ps. 3:6).*

IN THE GUT-WRENCHING THROES of America's Civil War, Abraham Lincoln declared, "Now we are engaged in a great Civil War, testing whether this nation or any nation so conceived and so dedicated can long endure." Today, over 140 years later, America is engaged in a great spiritual war, testing whether this nation or any nation so conceived and so dedicated can long endure.

America was founded as "A nation of laws and not of men." Our politicians, in all democratic societies, have repeatedly reminded us of "the rule of law." This "Nation of laws" was predicated upon the nearly universal submission of its populace to the laws of God. For that reason, in 1830, the French secular observer, Alexis de Tocqueville, noted in his book, *Democracy in America*, after five years of careful observation of American society, "Everything in the moral field is certain and fixed" because "Christianity reigns without obstacles, by universal consent."

While recognizing that religion "never intervenes directly in the government of American society," de Tocqueville nevertheless considered it "the first of her political institutions." The Christian faith had the role of placing limits on individualism, hedging in self interest with proper concern for others. It introduced living guard rails to guide citizens in their mutual relationships, protecting society at large and individuals in particular from the ravages of man's unfettered sin nature. In other words, the law of God reigned supreme in the land.

The law of man, in a free society such as ours, has continuing validity and effect only to the extent that the law of God reigns in the hearts of men. For this reason, our second president, John Adams, declared, "Our government was made for a moral and religious people; it is wholly inadequate to the government of any other." Robert Winthrop, another American statesman, declared, "We will either be governed by a power within or by a power without, either by the Bible or by the bayonet." With these preliminary observations, let us explore the root problem, not only in America's most recent *Battles for the White House* but in our struggles in the Church House across America reflected also in our own houses throughout the Western world, as we watch violence explode, shattering all reasonable expectations of peace while proclaiming "Peace, peace." We will call it the "Korah Spirit."

The Korah Connection

One of the most frightening accounts in the entire Scripture is set forth in Numbers 16. Korah, a religious leader, great grandson of Levi for whom the tribe of the Levites was named, "gathered together 250 princes of the assembly, famous in the congregation, men of renown." "They gathered themselves together against Moses and against Aaron and said unto them, 'You take too much upon you, seeing all the congregation are holy, and everyone of them, and the Lord is among them: wherefore then lift ye up yourselves above the congregation of the Lord?'"

When Moses heard these words, the Scripture records that he fell upon his face. He was greatly distressed because he realized that these words, and the attitude or spirit behind them, put at risk the entire enterprise of God's having delivered His chosen people from the bondage of Egypt to lead them to the Promised Land. God's authority was at stake, and so was the rule of law. These religious and political leaders of Israel were unwilling to be satisfied with the roles and positions that they lawfully had in and among the people. They thought the entire congregation should be a democracy. Everyone should have equal place, equal title, equal authority, and the majority should rule and govern. God responded to this attempted hostile takeover by upstanding and religious folk, commanding Moses to separate the rest of the congregation from these men and their families. God then caused these men and their families to be destroyed. "The earth opened her mouth, and swallowed them up, and their houses, and all the men that appertained unto Korah and all their goods."

"They, and all that appertained unto them, went down alive into the pit and the earth closed upon them, and they perished from among the congregation." In addition to the earth swallowing up Korah and his two friends, Dathan and Abiram, "there came out a fire from the Lord and consumed the 250 men that offered incense." In other words, God brought summary judgment on those who believed that His Kingdom was to be ruled by pure democracy.

One would think that such a profound exhibition would have brought the balance of the congregation of Israel to their knees in repentance. It did not. Neither does it today. The very next day, "all the congregation of the children of Israel murmured against Moses and against Aaron saying, 'Ye have killed the people of the Lord.'" God's response was immediate. He will not tolerate lawlessness. A plague rose up among the people due to the wrath of God. Moses responded immediately, sending Aaron with the censor from off the altar, but 14,700 died in the plague due to their lawless spirit.

Democracy and the Korah Spirit

America and the entire West is dying morally and spiritually under plague from a lawless spirit that, with increasing vigor, prevails in the land. This lawless spirit masquerades politically under the rubric of democracy. Yet our founding fathers despised democracy. Democracy was a tyrannical form of government that was totally undependable. For that reason, they chose a Republic. When Benjamin Franklin, upon exiting the Constitutional Convention, was asked by a woman what form of government they had chosen, he responded, "A Republic, ma'am, if you can keep it."

The *Korah* spirit has manifested itself increasingly in American and Western society from the Church House to the White House and houses of Parliament. In the White House, we have seen Presidents of both political parties defying the laws that would limit the scope of presidential powers as Chief of the Executive Branch of government, defying the role of Congress as the lawmaking branch, establishing unprecedented Executive Orders to circumvent the Constitution and undermine the rule of law. Because the people themselves have become lawless, recent presidents were able to ride the crest of the common lawlessness to circumvent even removal from office for lawless behavior, including perjury, causing many to wonder how such a thing could happen. Perhaps this unfettered lawlessness is best expressed by a statement William Jefferson Clinton made at a gathering of supporters in Southern California in 1997. Listen to these words and take them to heart. **These may well be the most arrogant words ever uttered by an American President in office.**

We are, in practical ways, changing the immutable ideals that have guided us from the beginning.

Please note. The word *immutable* is a word most commonly used to describe the character of God, meaning "unchangeable." Our President declared, in effect, we are not only declaring, but we are acting in practical ways to change that which otherwise have been perceived to be unchangeable laws and ideals that have guided us from the beginning. One must ask, *On what authority does the President assume to change what he admits to be unchangeable ideals and laws that have guided us from the beginning?* The answer is simple. A lawless spirit requires no authority but his own, together with the perception of support by the coordinated, collective power of a lawless people behind him.

The AD 2000 battle for the White House revealed a media-enhanced expression of the spirit of lawlessness… the *Korah* spirit. The legislature of Florida established laws as the representative of the people under a Republican form of government. The democratically expressed will of the people through a popular vote was to be measured, tabulated, and certified, not by popular whim or by the vagaries of men's fleeting emotions, but according to very specific rules and guidelines set down, in advance, by the legislature, which had sole representative authority to establish Florida law.

The current sitting Vice President of the United States, having been well trained by the lawless example of our then sitting President, under whose authority he had governed for eight years, chose to ignore the rule of law to pursue personal and collective purposes of power. After the vote count, re-count, and further re-count, accomplished by numerous changes and exceptions to existing law, he was still unwilling to accede to the rule of law as set by the state legislature of Florida, nor to concede the election based upon the rule of law. He continued to echo the emotionally packed words, "Our Democracy" as the foundation for his lawless acts and attitude.

Mr. Gore then attempted to support his lawless acts by calling them "lawful" on the basis that he was pursuing remedies in the courts. In fact, what he did was seek to use the courts as a further expression of his lawlessness, co-opting them into overarching pursuit of pure Democracy, in absolute defiance of the existing form of government in Florida and in the United States of America. At the same time, he continued to advise America, "We want the will of the people." This was a mere cover-up for an otherwise lawless spirit, seeking to co-opt a major element of the American populace to override the rule of existing law in the pursuit of personal and collective power. It is precisely for this reason that our founders decried Democracy. Pure democracy, the unfettered rule of an ungodly people, inevitably produces chaos while rejecting the rule of Christ as well as legitimate earthly government in His name.

Edmund Randolf of Virginia, a founding father, said he wanted "to restrain the fury of Democracy." Elbridge Gerry of Massachusetts asserted that "the evils we experience flow from the excess of Democracy." George Washington, chairing the Constitutional Convention, urged the avoidance of "leveling principles" that flow from pure Democracy. John Adams, second President of the United States, reflected on this issue writing: "Democracy never lasts long. It soon wastes, exhausts and murders itself. There never was a Democracy that did not commit suicide." For that reason, Adams warned, "Our government is made for a moral and religious [Christian] people, and is wholly inadequate to the government of any other."

Although the seeds of lawlessness are endemic to the human heart because of the carnal or fleshly nature of man, those seeds, having been deeply sown in the "Age of Enlightenment" through the French Revolution, found their way into fertile soil in the American heart. By 1913, the election of Senators by State Legislatures as mandated by the Constitution was overturned by the 17th Amendment, allowing direct election of Senators. Constitutional "check and balance" was thus eradicated. The same year, the Federal Income Tax was introduced as well as the Federal Reserve System, all of which undermined the Republic.

The seeds of lawlessness have prospered to the point where sitting Presidents and Vice Presidents of both parties flaunt lawlessness in the name of Democracy, threatening the very existence of the Republic. Their collective conviction is clear: It is not too dear a price to pay to sacrifice the Republic that protected against raw abuse of power in order to secure and preserve their own power or a new global power. They now wage a campaign to abolish the Electoral College, because it is a built-in barrier to unfettered democracy and the lawless spirit that underlies it, when not submitted to God's absolute authority. **Pure democracy is the governmental incarnation of the *Korah* spirit.** This spirit has invaded not only our civil governments but also our churches and is raising its collective fist against God, daring the Creator to govern our lives and Christ's church. It is of critical importance, therefore, that we gain further insight into this highly destructive, deceptive and seductive spirit.

Diagnosing the Korah Spirit

The Korah spirit manifests itself in seven other spirits that, collectively, become so powerful as to sweep away all legitimate authority in favor of the tyranny of the majority. Here is a brief outline of those spirits.

1. A Religious Spirit

The *Korah* spirit usually reveals itself in religious cloak. That lends an aura of authenticity that it would not otherwise have. It is interesting that political observers note that our recent presidential elections were characterized by more religious God-talk than any other in American history. On the surface, this is not entirely bad. But when religion is used as a cloak, camouflaging other contrary intentions and spirits, it becomes exceedingly dangerous and deceptive.

2. An Egalitarian Spirit

Egalitarianism is the conviction that men are not only *created* equal, but that all should *function* equally, without authority, in the society. It was best expressed by the motto of the French Revolution, "Liberty, Equality, and Fraternity." Pursuit of this kind of "liberty," driven by what our Founding Fathers called "the Leveling Effect," ultimately undergirds anarchy which is political lawlessness. For this reason, the guillotine took the heads of all who were perceived as having any role of authority over their fellows at the time of the French Revolution. While America's Revolution was "Liberty Under God," the French Revolution was "Liberty From God." Therefore, since faith and family both represented authority, pure egalitarianism had to destroy both faith and family to achieve democratically-driven liberty. It is the egalitarian spirit that has driven the extreme feminist movement in America. Egalitarianism has fueled the fires of racial strife and is driving the blatant assault of the homosexual agenda, violently stripping the laws of God from the moral memory of the entire West and from the lawbooks of formerly God-fearing nations. It results in the unfettered pursuit of *rights* without godly *responsibility.*

3. A Lawless Spirit

A lawless spirit resists authority. That spirit is incarnated in a bumper sticker that has been sported from coast to coast stating, "Resist authority." Egalitarianism feeds a lawless spirit. For that reason, pure and unfettered democracy is the ultimate expression of lawlessness when invested in a people who are not under total submission to God's ultimate authority through the Scriptures.

4. A Usurping Spirit

A usurping spirit is a close cousin to the lawless spirit. A usurper is unwilling to accept authority based upon the common order for the society or the laws thereof. Rather, the usurper grasps for authority and will circumvent the rule of law and custom in order to gain position and power. The usurping spirit also is fed by the egalitarian and lawless spirits which empower it. For this reason, the apostle Paul warned women not "to usurp authority over the man" (I Tim. 2:12).

5. A Bitter Spirit

Bitterness is an underlying and motivating spirit. It is not a principle spirit but rather one which gives place to and empowers other ungodly spirits, twisting the truth so as to rebel against authority. It is for this reason that the writer of Hebrews warned to avoid allowing "A root of bitterness" to spring up in our hearts. Bitterness perverts an otherwise pure heart. It will defile many (Heb. 12:15).

6. A Rebellious Spirit

Stubbornness and rebellion are as the sin of witchcraft, according to the Scriptures (I Sam. 15:23). Rebellion, in America, masquerades as independence and hyper-individualism. Alexis de Tocqueville warned back in 1830 of a virulent form of individualism that would consume the nation if we did not come to grips with it. The rule of the people, unrestrained by submission to and governance by God's authority, evolves into the anarchy of pure democracy. Democracy then becomes the governmental manifestation of the collective rebellion of the people.

7. An Infectious Spirit

The *Korah* spirit is profoundly infectious. It does not *affect*, but rather *infects* groups both small and large, including entire nations and congregations. The *Korah* spirit, allowed to go unchecked, is perhaps the single most destructive element to face mankind. Its unleashing will produce the final worldwide government of rebellion against God.

The Korah Spirit and the End-time

The Scriptures make clear that one of the principle characteristics of the end-times will be lawlessness (Rom. 1:18-32, II Tim. 3:1-8). Lawlessness will abound. Men will despise authority. The anti-christ or counterfeit Christ, for this reason, is called the Lawless One (II Thess.2:8 NKJV). He will be the incarnation of the *Korah* spirit, leading the majority of humankind in a collective democratic rebellion against God Himself.

Democracy will be the anti-christ's governmental weapon. It is actually anti-government. That is the reason democracy is spreading so rapidly around the earth. Remember, our Founders despised democracy. Our leaders, today, embrace and promote it. The egalitarian spirit that levels all of creation into one collective power base ruled by their senses and the lust for power will fulfill Satan's false promise to Adam and Eve in the garden when he declared, "You shall be as God."

The reason the anti-christ or counterfeit-christ will have a false prophet is because he needs the religious component of the *Korah* spirit in order to effectuate and give a religious facade to man's ultimate rebellion. It is for that reason there are very few, even very few who profess the name of Christ, who will not be caught up in this end-time rebellion. Lawlessness will be the driving force behind the end-time apostasy.

Korah's Affect on the Church

The Church is God's ultimate plan for the fulfillment of His Kingdom. The True Church stands in stark contrast to the anti-christ's democratically motivated kingdom. Many professing Christians, in the name of Christ, will embrace the *Korah* spirit, and will ultimately persecute the True Church that refuses to embrace the lawless egalitarianism of the counterfeit church. For this reason, Jesus warned His disciples in

163

John 16:2, "The day is coming when he that killeth you will think that he doeth God a service."

How can we identify the *Korah* spirit working in our congregations? It causes men and women to become isolated from the Body. They come to believe that the Church, as a covenant community, is no longer necessary. They no longer believe that they must gather regularly for exhortation, ministering to one another, and refrain from gathering together "as the manner of some is." Secondly, they control their resources. Rather than seeing the tithe as a trust, returning it to God in thanksgiving, they want to control the resources. Third, there is a disrespect of the Body, a failure to discern the Body, a grasping for power, a growing bitterness leading to rebellion and anarchy even within the Church. Fourth, there is a collective uprising against what God has said in His Word on how we should live. The pursuit of happiness has replaced the pursuit of holiness. Professing Christians are elevating their own reason to godhood, just as the "Goddess of Reason" replaced the God of the Bible in the French Revolution. God's authority is cast down, replaced by the egalitarian heart and collective will of an increasing majority of "believers" embracing the ways of the world and repudiating, in practice, the will and Word of God. This is not the Church Christ is building. This is not the Church against which "the gates of hell shall not prevail." That is true only of the Church Christ is building. The church of *Korah* is the church that the anti-christ is building, the "synagogue of Satan" (Rev. 2:9).

Lawlessness has always been anathema to the heart of God. It will be the most identifiable characteristic of the end-times. It will reveal itself even in professing Christians and pastors, elevating their own will, thoughts, desires, and doctrines over the expressed and clear will of God, all for purportedly good reasons. The nearly wholesale embracing of divorce and remarriage among pastor and people is perhaps the most poignant expression of this doctrinaire democracy, with the majority shaking their collective fists in the face of God, declaring to God by a divorce rate higher among professing Christians than in their "unbelieving" counterparts, *We don't care that you hate divorce and call remarriage "adultery" while the former spouse yet lives* (Mal. 2:13-17, Mark 10:4-12, I Cor. 7:39). For this reason, Jesus, in His final address to His disciples on the Mt. of Olives, before His crucifixion said, "Beware of deception."

We are left with that warning as well. The culmination of history is at the door. The birth pangs are upon us.

Where do you stand? Are you already, perhaps unwittingly, an accomplice in the gathering end-time rebellion? The Korah spirit of this worldwide rebellion is gaining strength, gathering the masses in democratic demonstration of their collective will to defy God and His authority. To resist victoriously, you must valiantly put on the whole armor of God and do seven specific things that will protect you and those you hold dear (Eph. 6:10-18).

7 Requirements For Valiant Victory

1. STAND FIRM	girding yourself with God's truth (daily study and meditation on God's Word).
2. BE CLOTHED	with the breastplate of righteousness. Live with "clean hands and a pure heart" before God and man. Do not give place to the devil or his cohorts.
3. PUT ON	the true and complete gospel that will protect your feet in the rough and rugged spiritual terrain ahead.
4. LIFT UP	the shield of faith. Put your complete trust in God and His Word so that you will be able to deflect the fiery assault Satan will direct at you both by pagans and by many professing Christians. You must do this "above all."
5. PROTECT YOURSELF	with the helmet of salvation. Remember, it is God who works in and through you by His grace, but you must work out that salvation in fear and trembling (Phil. 2:12), realizing that Satan seeks to devour you (II Pet. 5:8).
6. TIGHTLY GRIP	the sword of the Spirit. The Word of God is both a shield and a sword that is sharp, alive and discerns even the

	thoughts and intents of your heart and those around you (Heb. 4:12).
7. WATCH and PRAY	Keep your mind and heart tuned to God's frequency so you are not overwhelmed by the enemy's deceptive and democratically rebellious chatter.

Finally, "be strong in the Lord and in the power of his might. Put on the whole armor of God, that you may be able to stand against the wiles [deception] of the devil (Eph.6:10-11). Remember, you are of God. "Greater is he that is in you than he that is in the world" (I John 4:4).

Chapter Twelve

Daring Thoughts
for *Deceptive Times*

1. Why was Korah, a recognized religious leader, viewed by both Moses and God as such a threat to God's purposes and God's people?

2. How did the majority of the Israelites respond to Korah and his two friends? Have you ever found yourself caught up in such a spirit?

3. Why is pure democracy dangerous? Why do you think our leaders almost never refer to the American *Republic* but rather to "our democracy?"

4. What one word best characterizes pure democracy exercised by people who refuse to submit to God's authority? Why do you think that word was also used by God to describe the attitudes and actions of men and women across the earth in the last days?

5. Have you seen evidence of the *Korah Spirit* in your life, attitudes or actions? How has it manifested itself?

6. Can you see the *Korah Spirit* rising up against God in the church? What do you think God's response will be?

Chapter Thirteen

Synthetic Authenticity

*"Through thy precepts I get understanding:
therefore I hate every false way" (Ps. 119:104).*

"THE AGE OF AUTHENTICITY" describes what *TIME* refers to as what "has led to a deep consumer yearning for the authentic." Yet, say two legendary business consultants, "America has 'toxic levels' of inauthenticity." Even the "authentic" is faked. As it is in the culture, so it is in the church.

It was *TIME's* cover story uncovering "10 ideas that are changing the world."[1] Number 7 of these world-changing ideas is titled, **Synthetic Authenticity**. It was not a joke. "Promoting products as 'authentic' is serious business these days." Yet the renowned authors of *Authenticity* (Harvard Business School Press) contend that to be truly authentic as a business or individual "puts a bull's-eye on your back" because of greater scrutiny by others requiring that behavior conform to alleged belief… that you are what you say, and say what you are. Therefore, James Gilmore and Joseph Pine II unabashedly declare, "The best strategy for many companies is to openly fake it….." Pretend to be authentic even by admitting your inauthenticity.

Get Real By Faking It

It truly is a fascinating concept: Get real by faking it. Pretend to embrace values of truth and relationship by intentionalized pretense. When the **false** is promulgated and even willingly embraced as **real** worldwide, there is little room left for that which is true. When faked authenticity is accepted, even desired, as normal or satisfying to the common man and his/her corporate, governmental, and organizational counterparts, there is no longer room for truth.

Pretense itself becomes *principle.* And even professing Christians, caught up in the tidal wave of culture, begin to celebrate faked faith as authentic.

Indeed, "promoting products as *authentic* is serious business." It is not only serious because false authenticity in the name of *authenticity* is being pursued in our businesses and ministries, but is more serious because of the inevitable consequences. When that which purports to be genuine is falsified, we gradually lose our taste for that which is true… the genuine article… and eventually lose even our will or ability to discern the true from the false. Finally, we begin gradually to despise the genuine article, being fully satisfied with the packaged pretense.

Justification comes easily to embrace the fake. We perceive it comes more cheaply. *And after all,* we reason, *its not the real thing that's important. Its that others think I have the real thing. Its not that I am in genuine relationship but that I "feel" like I have relationship that really matters.* Such thinking may be rationalized when it comes to products, but is devastating when it comes to principles or people or when our eternal relationship with the Potentate of our souls is at stake (I Tim. 6:14-15).

Marketing the Master

Authenticity has become the premier marketing tool of our time. According to *TIME*, "standard economic theory assumes that buyers are rational creatures who observe supply-and-demand laws." "Yet there is an ephemeral dimension of consumer behavior," observed business consultants Gilmore and Pink. They give a name to this "ephemeral dimension." "We are buying according to authenticity." "The crucial factor dividing success from failure… will be whether a business is perceived as real or fake, authentic or inauthentic."

Notice the profound shift. In a western culture in which we have all but abandoned "TRUTH" as anything other than a mere concept, marketing no longer emphasizes the actual merits of a product or service. Rather, post-modern marketing seeks to synthesize or fabricate a perception that will satisfy the ephemeral or fleeting feelings of a public that no longer has an appetite for truth or that which is truly real.

How can marketing get by with this deceptive sleight of hand - this bait and switch? It is because marketing experts accurately perceive that we want the *feeling* of authenticity rather than the genuine article. The real, the true, the genuine, the truly authentic is perceived as too costly. Yet, as has been said, "That which is obtained too cheaply is esteemed too lightly."[2] That is true of liberty as well as our relationships with others and our walk with the Lord.

Since the late 1960's, there has also been a profound shift in the ways we have presented or "marketed" the gospel of Christ. The substance of the faith once delivered to the saints has been gradually replaced by the lordship of feelings wrapped in the language of faith to appear authentic. It marketed well to a people who would no longer palate a crucified Christ who called His followers to "take up their cross." The cost of discipleship was deemed too great. "What hath God said?" was replaced with "How do you feel?" A new "cheap grace" became the product *du jour*.

Even as a new seeker-friendly faith was synthesized over a generation for the market, so too was God himself. The God of the Bible, as revealed by His own self-disclosure, was perceived unmarketable. We needed a new, a custom-made god, a god who would give us spiritual warm fuzzies without the demand of repentance and obedience. Churches and ministries obliged. Christian publishers and broadcasters advertised the new gospel "product" with a vengeance.

Gone were the messages of sin and salvation. In was the message of "healing" for the consequences of your sin. Gone was the cross and the call to holy living. In was becoming like the culture to better win the culture. The market had become the master, and the Master had become the mascot for "ministry" marketing.

Once again, *TIME* got it right, delivering a warning salvo to the church in its April 5, 1993, issue. It was the cover story. The cover proclaimed, "The Generation That Forgot God." The feature article, "The Church Search," noted that Americans were flooding back to church. It sounded good but lacked authenticity. The writer observed, "Church would never again be the same." Why would church in America never again be the same, you might wonder? *TIME's* answer was both prophetic and prognostic, pointing to the growing pretense of American Christianity being promulgated throughout the world. Church would never again be the same because...

Americans are looking for a custom-made god, one made in their own image.[3]

The Master had been remade. The church, pandering to the fickle (ephemeral) minds of a public seeking a spirituality of warm feelings, turned their taste against the truth that would make them free. Fake faith required a fabricated god. As *TIME* noted fifteen years later, as with commerce, so with Christ. "Jaded buyers love 'real' products - or at least ones that fake it well."

A Deceptive "Gospel"

Is the gospel of Jesus Christ deceptive? Absolutely NOT! Can the gospel be made deceptive or be presented deceptively? ABSOLUTELY! How the gospel is presented or marketed does, indeed, impact and even change the message.

The modern and post-modern mantra of the church marketing gurus is: "We're not changing the message, just the methods." The phrase may have a perceived ring of truth, but in principle, the message and its emphasis has been profoundly changed.

Just as commercial marketers seek to bring the fickle buying public to a pseudo-experience masquerading as the real thing, so do marketers of the faith. Even the very use of the word *faith* has been marketed to a non-committal people, pretending to offer the "authentic" while failing to present the requirements of the *authentic*, leading people to believe they are "people of faith" without ever truly meeting the Christ of Scripture who became obedient even to death.

The gospel presents not a product to be sold, but a Savior to be served. It is not a feeling, but a walk of obedient faith. It is not the freedom to do as I want, but the privilege to do as God wants. It is an exchange of the cultural mandate for Christ's mandate. It is being conformed to the image of God's dear Son, not being conformed to the culture of this world where, as one Christian magazine proclaimed on its cover, "IMAGE IS EVERYTHING." It seems that a principled life has been replaced by the pretense of false authenticity.

Millions now filling "Christian" churches as "people of faith" display little difference from the millions of others claiming to be "people of faith" in other religions… or even from those who claim no faith. Every significant poll for the last generation reveals no functional difference in behavior between professing Christians and their pagan or unbelieving counterparts. Why is that? They have been marketed a false gospel, claiming to believe IN God but refusing to BELIEVE Him. They are deceived. They have embraced a fake faith. "They don't want to cook," say the business consultants, "But they do want to package to say 'USDA ORGANIC.'"

People want the fruit without the root. They want to be clothed with *righteousness* without *repentance*. They want *healing* without *holiness*. They want *passion* without *purity*. They want *blessing* without *obedience*. They want *grace*, but live in *dis-grace*. They want a custom-made god, one made in their own image.

Faking the Faith

The reality is that untold millions are faking the faith. They and ministry leaders have been seduced by synthetic authenticity. And that is profoundly dangerous if we are on the near edge of Christ's Second Coming.

But instead of repenting of this adulterous affair with the world, dissimulating with the TRUTH, we look for even more seductive ways to market a "fake-real" gospel to fickle-minded folk. We entice them with half truths, with under or over-emphasized scriptures without biblical balance, hope without holiness, ritual to replace genuine relationship. We call Holy Spirit conviction, "condemnation," and a call to the obedience of faith, "legalism." The God of Creation cannot get a word in edgewise past the glib-mouthed marketers of synthetic authenticity.

Such profound fakery amid such prolific protestations of faith! Just as a vodka company ad campaign urges you to "Choose Authenticity," and a cigarette company proclaims, "Be Authentic," so the "authentic" buzzword of Christian publishing is this mantra of "fake-real." As Shakespeare once aptly said, "Methinks thou protesteth too much."

If we are truly authentic in our faith, it will become manifest in our attitude, behavior and even… eventually… in the polls. If we truly have authentic Christ-like marriages, the divorce rate will plummet precipitously, shocking the world with the amazing effects of a true gospel that is truly preached. Until then, we are left with little choice, and that is to fake it.

Business gurus Gilmore and Pine see little hope for the truly authentic despite the public's pretense of desire for it. "Therefore, the best strategy… is to openly fake it." "Does all this striving for authenticity make us more fake or more real," they ask? For a third option, they suggest: "fake-real." You don't have to be exactly what you say you are, they say. Just pretend.

TIME concludes its discourse on "Synthetic Authenticity" with these shocking words, "Today you are authentic when you acknowledge just how fake you really are." What do you think makes for genuine authenticity? What do you think God thinks? Have you, perhaps unwittingly, been creating a custom-made god, easier to serve, easier to believe, easier to market to a cynical and increasingly synthetic world? Are you a "fake-real" Christian? Remember, man looks on the outward appearance, but God looks on the heart (I Sam. 16:7). Are failings from fakery the predominant theme of your life testimony, or is genuine faith revealed in faithful obedience leading you to a transformed life of victory in Jesus.

A "Fake – Real" Christ

If you are a "fake-real" Christian masquerading in synthetic authenticity, you are already deceived but are also a prime candidate for the greatest seduction of all history.

Satan has no intention to go into eternal perdition without presenting you and the world with his custom-made, counterfeit Christ. The prophet Daniel says he will be crafty, shall work deceitfully, and shall gain dominion by flattery (Dan. 11:21-24, 8:23-25). Paul says this synthetic Christ will even "shew himself that he is God," yet this will not happen until many shall have first fallen away from genuine faith in Christ. Therefore warns Paul, "Let no man deceive you by any means" (I Thess. 2:2-4).

God himself is going to send strong delusion to those who walk in *synthetic authenticity,* "that they should believe a lie." The reason is that such people have already made clear their deceptive "fake-real" lives, not genuinely believing and obeying the truth but having "pleasure in unrighteousness" (II Thess. 2:11-12).

Those living a life of spiritual pretense, straddling the fence, wanting spirituality without humble submission to the Savior, will be deceived by Satan's final deception… the synthetic "fake-real" Christ. The apostle Paul warns, he will come "after the working of Satan, with all power and lying wonders, and with all deceivableness of unrighteousness… because they received not the love of the truth that they might be saved" (II Thess. 2:9-10).

Secure yourself against this final end-time deception. Remember, Paul's warning is to professing believers. How can you secure yourself?

1. PURIFY YOURSELF

The apostle John warned, "every man that hath this hope in him purifyeth himself even as [Christ] is pure (I Jn. 3:3). That means you must walk in repentance followed by obedient faith as a way of life.

2. LOVE GOD's TRUTH

The apostle Paul said that those who are deceived will not be "lovers of the truth" but will "believe a lie." Their alleged faith is fake (II Thess. 2:10-11). Be a lover of truth.

3. OBEY THE TRUTH

"Here is the patience of the [true] saints… "they that keep the commandments of God, and the faith of Jesus" (Rev. 14:12, I Jn. 5:3-4).

Obedience is the sole test of trust. If you love Jesus, you will obey God's commandments (I Jn. 5:2-3).

4. DO RIGHTEOUSNESS

The apostle Paul again makes clear that those who are deceived will have "pleasure in unrighteousness" (II Thess. 2:12). The apostle John confirms, saying, "let no man deceive you: he that doeth righteousness is righteous, even as he [Christ] is righteous (I Jn. 3:7). If you are truly righteous, you will do righteousness.

God Hates Synthetic Authenticity

It is true! God hates synthetic authenticity. He hates pretense. He despises the *false* masquerading as the *real*.

Jesus warned the end-time church at Laodecia, "I know your works, that ye are neither cold nor hot. So then because thou art lukewarm [a pretender], and neither cold nor hot, I will spew you out of my mouth" (Rev. 3:15-16).

Let's become red-hot for Jesus. Repent of "fake-real" faith. Love the truth. Obey the truth as an act of love. And do righteousness.

Be not deceived! A "fake-real" life will leave you open to Satan's end-time seduction.

Chapter Thirteen

Daring Thoughts
for *Deceptive Times*

1. Why do you think the hypocrisy of *synthetic authenticity* has become so popular?

2. What happens to our hearts when we fake our faith and when our supposed principles are mostly pretense?

3. Can you see how marketing has led over the past forty years to presenting the gospel deceptively, leading to a *false-real* faith?

4. In what ways have you found yourself faking the faith?

5. Have you found aspects of Christ's teachings too costly to commit to, leading you to embrace a watered-down version of true Christian living?

PART V

False Gospels for Synthetic Times

We are living in synthetic times. Our age, on the near edge of the Second Coming, is characterized by artificiality and pretense. It seems that the combined forces of government, law, business, philosophy and religion increasingly seek to market the false as genuine. The very spirit of our times is what business gurus have called the "fake-real."

As Christians, if we are to avoid deception and remain pure, we must identify the ways in which thoughts, ideas and philosophies begin to govern and change our thinking. As human beings, we are profoundly susceptible to being swayed, often unwittingly. We tend to drift with groups or the masses who are also being swayed, and therefore, we are unaware as to how far we have drifted from that which was genuine. We exchange *perceived* authenticity for that which is truly authentic. Isms often provide the vehicle for that exchange.

The world is filled with "isms." An ism is a doctrine, system or theory - a particular outlook, viewpoint or emphasis that purports to orient our thinking toward a particular way of processing the world, values, cultures, relationships and ideas that surround us.

In the following chapters, we will inspect five different categories of *isms*, which, either independently or collectively, contribute to corrupting the fulness or applicability of God's eternal, unvarnished truth in our lives. Some you will identify instantly as deception. Others may provoke you to re-think your own patterns of orientation. The broad classifications are:

SCIENCE   ISMS
SOCIAL   ISMS
POLITICAL   ISMS
RELIGIOUS   ISMS
GLOBAL   ISMS

Science Isms vs. the Gospel

"[they] changed the truth of God into a lie,
and worshipped and served the creature
more than the Creator…" (Rom. 1:25).

SCIENCE CAN BE DECEPTIVE. In fact, science can be and is seductively deceptive precisely because of how people popularly perceive it. Also, contrary to popular notions, science has profound spiritual implications and applications.

"Pure" Science is Not Pure

To use the term "pure science" is a virtual oxymoron. The reason is that every scientist, wittingly or unwittingly, brings to his or her "scientific" endeavor a host of isms and viewpoints that can either overtly or covertly affect the choice of projects promoted, the plan of inquiry, the perception for interpreting data, and even pre-conceived conclusions. The public is not usually privy to these hidden and undisclosed pre-conceptions and false-real conclusions. Hence, "pure science" is not truly *pure.*

The pretense of scientific purity is what prevails in the public mind. It is the *pretense* of purity that seduces the unsuspecting to sacrifice true principles, practices and profound beliefs on the altar of science.

Scient-ism May Not Be Sure

"Scientism" is the collection of attitudes and practices considered typical of scientists. It is based on the belief that the investigative methods of the physical sciences are applicable to all fields of inquiry, including the spiritual. The "scientific method" is the systematic procedure for scientific investigation involving observation of phenomena, experimentation to test the hypothesis, and a conclusion that validates, modifies, or rejects the hypothesis.

Scientists, using the scientific method, have brought and continue to bring amazing advances to modern life in nearly every field of genuine scientific exploration. Yet science has its limits. It can be used for good or for destruction. It can serve us or enslave us.

Science itself has become a modern ism. It has come to be seen in the modern and post-modern mind not just as a *means* of finding truth but rather as the *mediator* of truth. Rather than being our servant, it has become our master. The Spirit of the Creator which once governed and enervated the mind to legitimate and humble inquiry has been supplanted by the spirit of science which, in pride and illegitimate pursuit of power, seeks to silence the voice and remaining vestiges of the Creator.

A False Gospel

Science itself becomes a false gospel. It presents itself as a false gospel when it presents its theories as "gospel truth." When a theory is presented and marketed to the public as an idea or concept to be accepted without question and without proof, science has breached the wall of its own self-limitations, taking on the extra-scientific aura of philosophy and religious belief. Science has thus, since the middle of the nineteenth century, "evolved" into a new ism... a virtual "religious" belief system with its own dogma and high priests.

A Serious Dilemma

The ultimate issue subject to scientific exploration and hypothesis is the origin of all things, more particularly the origin of living things. The crown of this scientific conundrum is the origin of man. The potential answer to the question of origin of things material, life, and ultimately humankind poses a profound problem for the world of science, and indeed, for the entire world.

The explanation of origins presents a serious dilemma of monumental proportions, indeed eternal proportions, for it thrusts the theories of science into a no-holds-barred, battle-to-the-death confrontation with the biblical proclamation of truth as to the origin of all things, including man. You and I, indeed the inhabitants of the entire planet, are caught in the cross-fire of this war. Most have taken sides. Ultimately, it is a battle for the mind and heart of every man, woman and child. As with many (perhaps most) wars, its' true underlying motivations are camouflaged by the now-sacred robes of science.

Lurking within the question of origins are fundamental questions over which the battle lines are drawn.

- Was mankind created, or did he evolve naturally?
- Does mankind have a greater purpose than do animals?
- Is mankind accountable for his attitudes and actions? If so, to whom or what?
- Does mankind have any hope beyond the grave?

A Confluence of Isms

Historically, scientists, while pursuing answers and explanations in the natural world, did their investigative work with an over-arching consciousness that the secrets of this amazingly ordered world could only be truly uncovered because there was an originating intelligence that designed it. A distinct element of humility and increasing awe graced the scientist's exploration. But gradually, as the nineteenth century progressed, the "spirit" of science and scientific endeavor began to change. A search was on to explain the origin of things, in particular man, outside of the revelation of Biblical Scripture. That change was merging with emerging new isms in other fields of thought.

A new, virulent "humanism" exploded upon the world stage through the French Revolution; erecting the "Goddess of Reason" while purporting to topple the God of the Bible and all legitimate authority of faith and family.

Into this vacuum of authority came new political, social and religious isms. George Friedrich Hegel, abandoning traditional concepts of biblical spirituality, sought to explain the material world through "spiritual" principles, a dialectic or method of reasoning of: thesis, antithesis and synthesis. He envisioned a political utopia that could be synthesized by a kind of political evolution called Hegelianism. Karl Marx merged the method of Hegel with a message of "scientific socialism," luring one-third of the world's people into a man-centered, God-defying "communism."

It should not come as an historical surprise, then, that into this hot bed of radical new isms should come the modern and post-modern world's "synthesis" of origins, called "Darwinism."

Charles Darwin introduced his *Origin of Species* in 1859, in which he proposed his theory of natural selection. "He knew full well what he was up to," notes *NEWSWEEK*. "As early as 1844, he famously wrote to a friend that to publish his thoughts on evolution would be akin to 'confessing a murder'." "To a society accustomed to searching for truth in the pages of the Bible, Darwin introduced the notion of evolution… rather than as Genesis would have it."[1]

By1871, Darwin released his *Descent of Man*, claiming that man and ape could have evolved from the same ancestor. The shock waves swept the world, eventually reforming the viewpoint of pastors, presidents, popes and most people as to the origin of all things, including man. It was not by the hand… or voice… of God, but by natural selection. "To a world taught to see the hand of God in every part of Nature, he suggested a different creative force altogether, an undirected, morally-neutral process he called natural selection."[2]

If God did not create as stated in Genesis 1, does God exist? If Genesis 1-11 is not true, can any of the rest of the Bible be believed? Does Scripture carry any moral or spiritual authority? If Scripture has no ultimate authority and if God does not exist or did not create, who has authority in our lives and in our world?

Dr. Douglas Patina, author of an anti-creationist book, as quoted by Henry Morris, writes, "Creation and evolution between them exhaust the possible explanations for the origin of living things. Organisms either appeared on earth fully developed or they did not. If they did not, they must have developed from pre-existing species.... If they did appear in a fully developed state, they must indeed have been created by some omnipotent intelligence."[3] It is CREATION vs. NATURALISM. This is where science and biblical faith collide. Ultimately, it is not science at stake, but your soul. The real question remains... "Hath God said...?" Scientists well know the consequences. Do you?

NATURALISM vs. CREATION

Here is a clear-cut choice. The culture would seek to overlay the simplicity of this choice with a blanket of alleged complexity, spewing pseudo science to create a fog of obfuscation and confusion. In a world where the majority are convinced that "science does not lie" and that scientists have no ulterior motives for their projects and papers, naturalism wrapped in the concealing robe of "science" is both seductive and deceptive. The consequences of your choice are vast, beyond imagination. *VIEWPOINT DETERMINES DESTINY!*

Naturalism is a belief system. Just as it requires an element of faith to believe in CREATION, so it requires faith to believe in natural selection. In fact, it requires massive faith… irrational faith… to believe that nature, the physical world, has created itself from nothing.

Naturalism defies the most basic, accepted laws of science. The Second Law of Thermodynamics called the Law of Entropy, declares that all matter and energy, all of the physical world, is in the process of steady deterioration and that such deterioration is inevitable and cannot be avoided, just as the Bible declares. Sir Isaac Newton gave us the accepted and unrefuted "Laws of Motion." They include:

1. A body at rest tends to remain at rest until acted upon by some outside force.
2. A body in motion tends to remain in motion until acted upon by some outside force.

Using simple logic as a reasonable person, it should be obvious that if a body, or matter, including an atom, molecule, neutron or proton, will not advance, progress, or move in a developing direction unless acted upon by an outside force, that it would be even more difficult for something that does not exist at all to take on existence, either suddenly or gradually, unless and until acted upon by some outside force. That problem leads inevitably to a discussion of "First Cause." What caused the first thing, whatever it was?

For this question, science has no genuine answers. The scientific world is filled, however, with multiplied unproved "hypotheses" which change with every decade and generation, all of which amount to nothing more than speculation and hyper-ventilated imagination wrapped in the protective aura and mystique of "science." The Bible speaks simply to this conundrum: "The fool hath said in his heart, There is no God" (Ps. 14:1, 53:1). In other words, only a fool could come to the conclusion that there is no Creator God because of the manifold evidence to the contrary, obvious to any truly honest man. As the apostle Paul noted, the very existence and operation of the material world that can be observed and experienced is sufficient to conclude any man or woman without excuse as to the existence and eternal power of God (Rom. 1:20). James goes further, stating that even the devils believe in God and tremble (Jam. 2:19).

Why then is the nineteenth century conception of Darwinism and the militant march of naturalism presented not as theory but as dogma? Why did the British *The Independent* announce, "World scientists unite to attack creationism?" Why did "the national science academies of 67 countries warn parents and teachers to ensure that they did not undermine the teaching of evolution?[4] Why did they warn parents and teachers not to teach the concept of creation? What is driving this growing belligerence? Why are professors and researchers who even suggest the idea of "intelligent design" being fired and blacklisted worldwide?

The answer is quite simple. "It was apparent to many even in 1860 - when the Anglican Bishop Samuel Wilberforce debated Darwin's defender Thomas Huxley at Oxford - that Darwin wasn't merely contradicting the literal Biblical account of a six-day creation...." As *NEWSWEEK* noted, he "appeared to undercut the very basics of Christianity, if not indeed all theistic religion." Was this "undercut" the natural consequence of a legitimate scientific fact or the promulgation of a theory intentionally designed to avert the implications of an omnipotent Creator for modern man? If there is no intent to foreclose honest inquiry, why then did The Quebec Ministry of Education tell Christian evangelical schools that they "must teach Darwin's theory of evolution and sex education or close their doors…?"[5]

The true answer is that Naturalism is a non-theistic religion and belief system requiring immense faith, and is led by a passionate priesthood teaching and preaching the dogmas of Darwinism and humanism. It is an alternative faith to Biblical Christianity, with its own "authoritative" teaching on the origins of all things material, shifting ultimate allegiance from a Creator God to Man as his own god.

Eminent scientific philosopher and ardent Darwinist, Michael Ruse, even acknowledged that evolution is their religion!

> Evolution is promoted by its practitioners as more than mere science. Evolution is promulgated as an ideology, a secular religion – a full-fledged alternative to Christianity…. Evolution is a religion. This was true of evolution in the beginning and it is true of evolution still today.[6]

Revealing the massive deception perpetuated upon an often unsuspecting, yet willing public, Richard Levontin of Harvard, left no doubt.

> We take the side of science in spite of the patent absurdity of some of its constructs… in spite of the tolerance of the scientific community for unsubstantiated commitment to materialism…. We are forced by our *a priori* adherence to material causes to create an apparatus of investigation and set of concepts that produce material explanations, no matter how counterintuitive, no matter how mystifying to the uninitiated. Moreover, that materialism is absolute, for we cannot allow a Divine foot in the door.[7]

This pseudo-scientific deception has seduced most of the academic world as well as the common man who bows at its shrine. Speaking of the trust students naturally place in their highly educated college professors, physicist Mark Singham blatantly admitted the intentional abuse of that trust by professors.

> And I use that trust to effectively brainwash them… our teaching methods are primarily those of propaganda. We appeal – without demonstration – to evidence that supports our position. We only introduce arguments and evidence that supports the currently accepted theories and omit or gloss over any evidence to the contrary.[8]

Evolution is a religion… a religion without God. Julian Huxley, primary architect of neo-Darwinism, called evolution a "religion without revelation" and wrote a book by that title. In that book, he argued passionately that we must change "our pattern of religious thought from a God-centered to an evolution-centered pattern."[9] Huxley then boldly declared the underlying motivation behind the dogma of evolution or naturalism that demands its tenets be preached. Please try to absorb the sheer arrogance of this deception.

> "The God hypothesis… is becoming an intellectual and moral burden on thought." "We must construct something to take its place."[10]

The Heart of Deception

At the heart of deception lies a deceptive heart. The promulgators of evolution have chosen deception because they considered the alternative"religiously" intolerable. Robert Muller, a leader of the New Age movement and former assistant secretary general of the United Nations, said, "I believe the most fundamental thing we can do today is to believe in evolution… evolution is not merely a peripheral matter…, its basic in everything."[11]

Why is evolution considered "basic in everything" and "the most fundamental thing we can do"? The reason is quite simple. Evolution is not science but a philosophical and religious world view that precludes a Creator God who would have the authority to hold His creatures morally accountable to His own will. This is why Julian Huxley stated, "The God hypothesis is becoming an intellectual and moral burden." If the world is to create a global, godless system, defining its own "moral" standards rooted in sexual promiscuity and utopian unity that rejects the revealed truth of sin and salvation, the only alternative is naturalistic evolution to explain our existence.

In order for those intentionally self -deceived promoters of evolution to somehow live with themselves and promote their greater agendas, they need you to join them. If they can dupe the masses to democratically join them in the absurdity of their own deception, it somehow breathes legitimacy into a system that not only defies intellectual logic and mathematical probability but the most fundamental laws of science itself. Do we truly believe we can democratically overrule the laws of creation and the Creator by devising an artificial explanation for our existence, doubly deceiving ourselves by pretending it to be scientific? If you will believe this fundamental lie, what other lies are you prepared to believe built upon this lie?

Foundation of the Global Order

Evolution does not stand alone. It is, as the former assistant secretary general of the United Nations noted, "the most fundamental thing we can do"… "to believe in evolution" as "basic in everything." To what is evolution so "basic"? It is basic to a new vision of man. It is basic to a vision of a global utopia, man-centered rather than God-centered. It is a satanic "salvation" being prepared for the world as an "acceptable" alternative to the hope of salvation in Jesus Christ.

The Humanist Manifesto II gives us a preview of the thinking undergirding this New World Order now exploding boldly into the Brave New World. Take thoughtful heed.

> Traditional moral codes… fail to meet the pressing needs of today and tomorrow. False "theologies of hope" and messianic ideologies… cannot cope with existing world realities. They separate rather than unite peoples.

Humanity, to survive, requires bold and daring measures. We
need to extend the uses of the scientific method... in order
to build constructive social and moral values. Humanism can
provide the purpose and inspiration that so many seek; it can
give personal meaning and significance to human life.
We believe... that traditional dogmatic or authoritarian religions that place revelation, God, ritual, or creed above human
needs and experience do a disservice to the human species.
We can discover no divine purpose or providence for the
human species... humans are responsible for what we are or
will become. No deity will save us; we must save ourselves.[12]

Atheism in Disguise

Evolution is atheism in disguise. It is a religion in which man,
having denied a Creator God, declares himself "god." Evolution is foundational to all fields of thought undergirding the rapidly advancing
global evolutionary "church." The members of this "church" embrace
man as the center of the universe and natural selection as their "creation
story." Their priests are scientists and science teachers who have prostituted the legitimate purposes of science for an ulterior agenda. They
preach their doctrine dogmatically, and will brook no opposition from
within the ranks of science, labeling any who dare to suggest "Intelligent
Design" or a Creator as a scientific "heretic," excommunicating them,
burning their reputations at the stake.

Why the vengeance if this is science? It is because much more is at
stake. Evolution is atheism in disguise, and those who promote it are at
war with God. The atheistic nature of evolutionary thought is admitted,
even insisted upon by most of its leaders. Ernst Mayr, for example, says
that: "Darwinism rejects all supernatural phenomena and causations."[13]
A professor in the Department of Biology at Kansas State University
made clear:

Even if all the data points to an intelligent designer, such
a hypothesis is excluded from science because it is not
naturalistic.[14]

190

Evolution is, indeed, the false scientific basis of religious atheism. Will Provine at Cornell University frankly admits it. Consider the implications for your life, family and congregation.

> As the creationists claim, belief in modern evolution makes atheists of people. One can have a religious view that is compatible with evolution only if the religious view is indistinguishable from atheism.[15]

A Choice for Destiny

Evolution or naturalism is not simply a scientific viewpoint or theory that one can idly choose. The consequences of this choice are both temporal and eternal.

In the temporal realm of man's ongoing experience on this planet, evolutionary thinking has invaded and now pervades virtually every field of thought and endeavor, including the law. Nothing is deemed fixed or anchored in truth. Even the very concept of *truth* has largely vanished. "Truth" now is whatever I want it to be, morphing or "evolving" to suit the agenda *du jour*.

This abandonment of truth is leading inexorably to the embracing of a new evolving humanistic "truth," the revision of history, and the construction of a New Age utopian global order ostensibly to bring "salvation" to mankind and peace on earth through the New World Order announced over two hundred times by George Herbert Walker Bush during his presidency. At root is the religious belief of evolution. Julian Huxley, the first director general of UNESCO, could not have made it more plain.

> We must develop a world religion of evolutionary humanism.[16]

The choice of evolutionary humanism as the world's religious belief system will culminate in a counterfeit (fake-real) christ promising peace on earth. That temporary peace, enforced by compelling every man, woman and child to submit, will explode in the greatest devastation and reign of terror ever experienced or conceived by man, for without God, every man does that which is right in his own eyes. He has become "god."

The most devastating consequence remains. Eternity lies in the balance. One cannot embrace naturalistic evolution and the Word of God. They are mutually exclusive as clearly stated by evolution's strongest proponents. You must make a choice.

To choose evolution is to reject the God of Creation, the God of the Bible. The Bible declares that Jesus Christ created all things (Eph. 3:9, Col. 1:16). To embrace evolution is to reject Jesus Christ and to shift your worship to man. God's final warning to mankind before the outpouring of His wrath on the "children of disobedience" (those who refuse to humbly obey him) is a clear confrontation on the issue of creation. The Book of Revelation states that God will dispatch an angel to make one final plea to those on the earth, having "the everlasting gospel." Here is what the angel will say with a loud voice:

Fear God, and give glory to him; for the hour of his judgment is come: and **worship him that made heaven, and earth,** *and the sea, and the fountains of waters (Rev. 14:7).*

Whom you worship will determine your destiny. Those who believe in naturalistic evolution, by definition, cannot truly be worshipers of the God of Creation as revealed in the Scriptures. Will you worship man… or the Creator, God? Your viewpoint will determine your eternal destiny.

Postscript

Darwin's theory—that humankind was the product of a slow, evolutionary process from early forms of life—conflicts with the literal biblical account of creation. Notwithstanding, on October 23, 1996, Pope John Paul II declared that now knowledge confirms the theory of evolution to be "more than a hypothesis." The Vatican is evolving, again, from the authority of Scripture to the authority of the Pope. On February 9, 2009, the Vatican under Pope Benedict XVI, "admitted that Charles Darwin was on the right track when he claimed that man decended from apes," also declaring Intelligent Design to be but a "cultural phenomenon" rather than either a scientific or theological issue. *TIMESONLINE*, timesonline.co.uk 2/11/09.

Chapter Fourteen

Daring Thoughts
for Deceptive Times

1. Why is "pure" science not actually *pure*?

2. In what way does science itself become a false gospel?

3. Why was Darwinian naturalism developed and promoted as gospel truth and why do its adherents vehemently oppose presentation or discussion of either a Creator God or "intelligent design?"

4. Why is Darwinistic naturalism essential as a foundation for the global New World Order?

5. In what ways is evolution actually a religion rather than science?

6. How does evolution shift our worship from Creator to man and nature?

Chapter Fifteen

Social Isms vs. the Gospel

*"Professing themselves to be wise, they became fools...
who change the truth of God into a lie... (Rom. 1:22-25).*

IT IS THE NATURE OF ISMS to convert a nugget of truth into a full-fledged "gospel." By identifying and embracing that nugget of truth, the human mind and heart finds it very easy then to embrace and justify unending perversions and departures from the original truth. Sometimes those departures are subtle, but often they are dramatic, yet they are always seductive. The departures from truth are seductive precisely because there is within us a certain unspoken will to be deceived.

The Social Isms

In this chapter we confront the isms that compete and combine to form a social order and undergirding philosophy of life in conflict with the Christian faith as revealed in the Scriptures. It will be apparent that there is a sufficient nugget of truth in each to draw the unsuspecting into its welcoming arms. So great is the reach of these isms that they have infiltrated the entire earth, including the realms of evangelical Christianity and Jewish life as well.

These "social" isms are all rooted in our outlook on the world that places man at the center of the universe. Therefore, God is, at best, parenthetical to the driving force of these social isms, and is therefore either irrelevant or irreverently rejected. Yet they all purport to provide answers to the social needs of man, forming an environment for a variety of religions or spiritual viewpoints that reject, in whole or in part, the fulness of the gospel of Christ "once delivered to the saints." These social isms include communism, socialism, fascism, Freudianism, emotionalism rooted in psychology, feminism, hedonism and humanism. It is humanism, however, that undergirds each of the others.

Humanism - A God Substitute

Humanism is a way of thinking about man and his place in the earth. Humanists, whether religious or secular, emphasize this present life rather than the hereafter. Man is the center of the humanist's universe.

BECOMING GOD!

The fact that man is the center of the "religious" humanists' world view creates an immediate tension with the revealed Word of God. Jesus said the "Great" commandment - the commandment of overarching import - is to "love God with all your heart, soul, mind and strength" (Mark 29:30; Matt. 22:36-38). Issuing out of that great commandment and as an expression of it, Jesus said the second greatest commandment is to "love your neighbor as yourself" (Mark 29:31, Matt. 22:39). If I subtly drift, or more affirmatively, choose to elevate love of man over love of God, I will find myself not only at variance from God's truth but will become an unwitting participant in the tide of unintended consequences that flows from every deception.

Many humanists, however, are not "religiously" oriented in their humanism but rather embrace humanism as an alternate to a creator God. Julian Huxley, the first director of UNESCO, stated "We must develop a world religion of evolutionary humanism."[1] Interestingly, in the declared intention to avoid a creator carrying the corresponding religious obligation to obey Him, the "secular" humanist has developed a new faith rooted in a false gospel of "evolutionary humanism."

Evolution is the foundation of humanism. In denying a creator God, man is exalted above the Creator, beholden to no one but himself. Man, in effect, becomes "god." When people, acting under their humanistic belligerence toward the very concept of a Creator, collectivize that conviction through democracy, they feel empowered to enforce that conviction by whatever means necessary upon the shrinking remnant of the true Christian believers who do not share their views. That enforcement begins with "education" and will end with extermination, as the Scripture makes clear (Rev. 13-14).

A "NEW" GOSPEL for a NEW AGE

Interestingly, the American Humanist Association formed by John Dewey and others in 1933, the *Humanist Magazine*, and the *Humanist Manifesto* all appeared about the same time as the natural outflow of and supportive infrastructure for Darwinism.

Among the tenets of the first *Humanist Manifesto* were: "We believe that the universe was not created, it evolved." The second tenet declared: "We believe that man was not created; man evolved." That reduces mankind to nothing but an advanced animal with no obligation to restrain his passions or proclivities. It further replaces the gospel of "salvation from sin" with the new and alternative "gospel" of "survival of the fittest."

The hope of eternal salvation in Christ for those who, by grace through faith, repent and obey Him, is now, for the humanist, superceded by the hope of unfettered selfish pursuit to be a survivor among the masses in a dog-eat-dog world where only the most cunning and crafty are 'saved" until all hope is lost in death. It should come as no surprise that John Dewey, one of the leading founders of the American Humanist Society, should be known as the "father" of American public education. And it should further come as no surprise that the humanistic leaders of America's public school system have methodically and evangelistically sought to strip from the mind and memory of our students all vestiges of the Christian faith. Since "God has no grandchildren," we are now witnessing a generation of youth throughout the entire western world who are without hope, worshiping not at the altar of the faithful Savior but at the altar of a fleeting survival of the fittest. An entire generation has been seduced to a false "gospel" with a false "savior" and a false "hope." It has been called "a new gospel for a new age."

HUMANISM BREEDS UTOPIAN OFFSPRING

Humanism is, at root, a social ism that inevitably spawns utopian offspring that promise to bring "salvation" to the world by providing an alternative to the Second Great Commandment. Jesus said that the second "great commandment" was like the first... "Thou shalt love thy neighbor as thyself" (Mark 12:31).

Humanism, having rejected the Scripture's authority as to the attitudes and actions that enable followers of Christ to "love their neighbors," has invented fertile alternative utopian means to spin a thread from the true gospel of Christ into the fabric of new versions of "love." These include the economic and political systems of socialism, communism and fascism. Humanists further find it necessary to take a thread of truth from "love thy neighbor as thyself," spinning it into a counterfeit garment of "loving yourself" that does not biblically fit a true Christian believer. That is Freudianism in its multiplied manifestations of popular psychology.

Since socialism, communism, fascism and feminism not only seek to define and dictate social order but also operate co-extensively as major political and economic systems or viewpoints, we will reserve that discussion for our look at political isms. Here, however, we must look deeply into the unending well of Freudianism as it is manifested in the pervasive world of popular psychology.

Freudianism vs. Biblical Faith

The church historian, Martin Marty, characterized the three major thinkers of the nineteenth century, Charles Darwin, Karl Marx and Sigmund Freud, as "God-killers." Freud, known as the "Father of Psychoanalysis," wrote in a letter to Oskar Pfiser, October 9, 1918: "... why did none of the devout [religious] create psychoanalysis? Why did one have to wait for a completely Godless Jew?"[2] That is a question worth exploring.

SPIRITUAL VIEWPOINT DETERMINES
SCIENTIFIC VIEWPOINT

Psychology is known as the "science of human behavior." In truth, however, it is the study of the psyche... the study of the soul. But as we have discovered, science is not necessarily pure. A man's science is, contrary to popular belief, largely defined and directed by pre-conceived beliefs and viewpoints. These underlying beliefs and viewpoints establish theories, define methods of study and testing, often determine what is or is not researched, and become the environment in which conclusions are drawn and practices performed. The world of psychology and psychoanalysis, rooted in its seed bed of Freudianism, is no different.

While a medical student, Freud came under the influence of Dr. Ernst Brüche. Brüche was an evolutionary psychologist, committed to Darwin's view of man. Darwin had removed man from the Kingdom of God, ensconcing him in the animal kingdom. Brüche's philosophy of science left no room for the spiritual, for design or for ultimate purposes. All that could be either seen or experienced was merely matter in motion. Freud idolized Brüche. From Brüche, Freud adapted a God-less theology of human life and behavior. It was the natural progression of Darwinian naturalism. Man had no free will. All of his thoughts were determined. Therefore, human behavior had no moral quality.

AN ALTERNATIVE SALVATION

At root, then, Freudianism, in its common modern expressions of psychological study, counseling, therapy and the human potential movement, is an effort to explain man's behavior and correct his misbehavior by alternative means from those clearly expressed in God's revealed Word. Having fundamentally rejected God as Creator, the Bible carries no authoritative weight, being relegated to nothing more than antiquainted ideas expressed by unenlightened primitive man.

Psychology comes to man's rescue. Guilt from sin no longer required confession of sin and repentance but denial and massive injections of self-esteem. Rather than the probing search of the heart by God's Holy Spirit, convicting the soul through the divine surgery of the Word of God, leading to cleansing of eternal guilt by the sacrificial blood of Christ, psychology offers the couch, shifting salvation from forgiveness by God in

Christ to forgiveness by one's self. "SCREW GUILT" proclaim's psychology's bumper sticker theology. The pursuit of happiness has supplanted the pursuit of holiness. And this spiritual bait-and-switch has infiltrated and taken dominion over the Church throughout the West, from pulpit to pew, from the liberal to the evangelical. It is utterly breathtaking! How did it happen? Why at this unique moment in history?

DECEPTION for a DECISIVE HOUR

Sigmund Freud was born in 1856, just as Darwin's *Origin of Species* was being presented to the world for a godless explanation of man's existence, stripping away any divine authority over the lives of men. Wrapped in the robes of science, it took the aura of being scientifically authentic. At the same time, Karl Marx was presenting a godless utopianism of "scientific socialism" to the world, proclaiming its "salvation," securing the emancipation of all mankind without God. Thus, the Creator was replaced with naturalistic evolution, salvation was replaced with the survival of the fittest, and spiritual warfare against the enemy of our souls was replaced by class warfare rooted in revolution rather than Biblical revelation. The hope of eternal life under God's dominion through resurrection was supplanted by the earthly hope of violent protest to secure peace on earth under dictatorship. It was a time of converging deceptions for a decisive hour in history.

But a problem remained. Man's guilt would not go away. Guilt presents a formidable problem for Darwinian evolutionists. At what stage in the "evolutionary" process did man acquire the ability to feel guilt, and why? Even more troublesome was man's ability to feel guilt transmitted to future generations and to reflect on one's own actions as bearing some degree of responsibility.

A GOSPEL OF PLEASURE SEEKING

In response to this dilemma, Freud theorized his famous Oedipus complex. Freud proposed that a jealous male dominated primitive society, keeping women for his pleasure. When his sons were of age, sensing potential competition, he drove them away, but they conspired together, beating their father to death, causing them to feel guilt. In this way, Freud explained away the doctrine of "original sin" in Adam, arguing that human beings inherit a collective burden of guilt. All man needs to deal with this collective guilt is therapy. He must be put in touch with his past memories and current feelings.

During the first six decades of the twentieth century, psychological theories abounded. All were godless. Freud, in 1930, published his *Civilization and Its Discontents*, portraying man as hopelessly trapped in a struggle between his instincts and society's restrictions. Freud called religion an "illusion," viewing it as one of society's worst restrictions. Man's fundamental struggle, according to Freud, was not sinful rebellion against the will of a holy God but rather a struggle for expression between the id, ego and superego. The ego, said Freud, is the rational mind trapped between the id's unrestrained pleasure seeking and the superego's effort to impose a culturally-defined morality.

EXPERIENCE—THE HIGHEST AUTHORITY

In all their theoretical expressions, the psychologists and psychotherapists were humanists, always man-centered rather than God-centered. B.F. Skinner, in *Beyond Freedom and Dignity*, stated, "The idea of human freedom is a myth... the myth of the inner man who is somehow independent of the controlling influences of his environment. "Humanistic ethics," noted Eric Fromm, "is based on the principle that only man himself can determine the criterion for virtue and sin, and not an authority transcending him." Carl Rogers boldly declared, "Experience is, for me, the highest authority. Neither the Bible, nor prophets - neither Freud nor research - neither the revelations of God nor man - can take precedence over my direct experience."[3]

THE FRUIT REVEALS THE ROOT

Enter now the Sexual Revolution of the 1960's. Should we be surprised that just as psychotherapy and the world of psychology were gaining public acceptance that "free love" and unfettered sexual expression should explode onto the scene of American culture? Freudianism paved the way. The id now ruled. Feelings became lord as faith bowed to feelings. In discussing "Self-Actualization Psychology," Abraham Maslow had made clear, "We need a ... system of human values we can believe in... because they are true rather than because we are exhorted to 'believe and have faith.'"[4]

And believe we did! First the divorce rate soared. Cohabitation exploded! Abortion supported the free-love movement as the theology of psychology became America's normative believe system.

By the 1970's, the "theology" of psychology had invaded our churches from coast to coast. Jesus was still proclaimed as savior, but SELF had become king. Feelings increasingly trumped faith. The Encounter Movement in the world found willing adherents from pulpit to pew. Truth became relatively irrelevant. Therapists emerged as the new "high priests" of American culture. What therapists said about serving one's feelings superceded what God had said about living obediently in faith. Experience had become the ultimate arbiter of truth, mediated by fleeting and fickle feelings.

Pastors and parachurch leaders gradually but willingly redefined "the faith once delivered to the saints." The "God is Love" movement distorted the character of God's self-revelation; ignoring His truth, justice and judgment, while over-emphasizing His love and mercy. The Church of Christ was seduced by psychology's man-centered "theology," sacrificing moral purity before God to curry favor with man. Sin no longer separated from God or our fellow man. Self-esteem replaced self-denial. Preaching righteousness became a relic. We no longer needed to be saved from sin, but rather healed from the consequences of sin. Christ had become our mascot, the culture our master.

TRUTH and THERAPY INTERMARRY

By the late 1980's, the syncretism of faith and feelings was complete. The "Grace" movement of the 1990's wrapped it with a bow and presented it to the generation that may well see the long-awaited Second Coming. *Grace* was redefined from "God's favor enabling one to obey His will" to "God's winking at sin and overlooking our increasingly carnal ways." With feelings reigning supreme, the works of the flesh became flush. Hell froze over - at least as one could discern from the re-framed message of those charged to preach the truth. The promise of happiness replaced the preaching of holiness, and now we are neither happy nor holy. A marriage of convenience provided nothing but carnage wrapped in robes of false compassion.

The Church has prostituted her soul for the spiritually salacious offerings of a false salvation in order to savor Satan's tantalizing offer that "ye shall be as gods" (Gen 3:15).

As Paul Vitz, associate professor of psychology at New York University noted in *Psychology as Religion*:

> *Psychology has become a religion, a secular cult of the self. More specifically, contemporary psychology is a form of secular humanism based on the rejection of God and the* **worship of self**....[5]

WHEN FEELINGS BECOME LORD

Psychology is an opposing faith. It surreptitiously seeks to deliver a mortal blow to your own Christian faith. A psychiatrist admits, "The human relations we now call 'psychotherapy' are, in fact, matters of religion - and that we mislabel them as 'therapeutic' at great risk to our spiritual well-being..... It is not merely a religion that pretends to be a science; it is actually a fake religion that seeks to destroy true religion."[6]

The fruit reveals the root. Psychology is self-centered and man-centered. It exalts your feelings and emotions over your faith. It declares the lordship of the soul over the spirit. Consider where this orgy of feelings has led since the 1960's in America alone.

- The divorce rate for the last decade is at nearly 50 percent of new marriages.
- The divorce rate in the Church for the last decade has equaled or exceeded that of her secular counterparts.
- The divorce rate of our pastors became the second highest of all professions.
- The divorce rate in the Bible Belt has been 50 percent higher than the nation as a whole for the past decade.
- Cohabitation has increased over 1000 percent.
- Approximately 50 million American children have been aborted.
- Forty-eight percent of all black children are aborted.
- Of black children, 70 percent are born out of wedlock, 17 percent of white children.

- Eighty-five percent of black children do not live in a home with their father.
- The black family has degenerated more in the last 40 years than in the entire fourteen decades since slavery (*Ebony Magazine* – 75th Anniversary Issue).

CONSIDER THE CONTRASTS

The Bible and psychology are fundamentally incompatible. To attempt to mix them, one will be the loser. Consider these contrasts:

- Psychology is man centered; the Bible is God-centered.
- Psychology is self-centered; the Bible is God and other-centered.
- Psychology says man's basic need is to be happy; the Bible declares man's basic need is to be holy.
- Psychology says man's primary need is to be healed; the Bible says man's primary need is to be saved.
- Psychology says the root of man's problem is his environment; the Bible says the heart of man's problem is his heart.
- Psychology teaches man is basically good; the Bible teaches man is basically sinful.

LAST DAYS SELFISHNESS

Selfishness spreads like poison. A little of this leaven will leaven the whole lump of your life, your family, your congregation, your city and your nation - verily the whole world.

Think soberly about the Apostle Paul's warnings concerning the season ushering in Christ's Second Coming.

This know also, that in the last days perilous times shall come. For men shall be lovers of their own selves, covetous, boast- ers, proud, blasphemers, disobedient to parents, unthankful, unholy, without natural affection, truce breakers, false accus- ers, incontinent, fierce, despisers of those that are good, traitors, heady, high-minded, **lovers of pleasures more than lovers of God***; Having a form of godliness, but denying the power thereof: from such turn away (II Tim. 3:1-5).*

HEDONISM vs. HOLINESS

Hedonism is an ancient belief system and life philosophy. It lies at the heart of modern psychology. Hedonism is also embraced by humanism. Simply speaking, hedonism is the unfettered pursuit of happiness as man's highest goal - his life objective.

Three centuries before Christ, a Greek philosopher, Epicurus, defined philosophy as "the act of making life happy with pleasure as the highest and only good."[7] That virtually describes the message of modern psychology.

Epicurus preferred sense perception and experience to absolute truth. Feelings were his faith. "Eat, drink and be merry" was his motto. This is known as hedonism. In today's language we would say, "It's all about me." This last generation has been aptly called "the ME generation."

Hedonism is now the reigning philosophy of American life and of western civilization. God has been replaced by "ME." Is that not what Satan promised Adam and Eve? "You shall be as gods..." (Gen. 3:5). Psychology has been the engine to drive this profoundly seductive deception deep into our hearts and minds... even into our ministries.

Have you been seduced? For some, the deception remains subtle; for others it is substantive; but for all it is sinister, for it has defiled our purity, re-defined our purpose and distorted... or even destroyed... our eternal hope. The SELF cannot save. Therapy is not a substitute for obedience to God's Truth. Feelings do not replace faith. The soul is not the "alter-ego" of your spirit, for we are body, soul and spirit (I Thess. 5:23). And experience will never supersede the eternal Word of God that abides forever.

Chapter Fifteen

Daring Thoughts
for *Deceptive Times*

1. What is *humanism*? In what ways is it a God substitute?

2. What consequences might we expect to flow if we convince ourselves that man becomes god?

3. In what ways does Freudian psychology become an alternative faith?

4. Do you think there is any connection between the development of Darwinism, Marxism and Freudianism, all in the latter half of the 1800's?

5. In what ways did the emergence of psychology as a life authority lay the foundation for the Sexual Revolution in the 1960's and 1970's?

6. How has the normalization of psychology among the people changed the practical theology of the church?

7. Have you experienced the tension between *hedonism* and *holiness* in your life? Which is winning?

Chapter Sixteen

⤞⤝

Political Isms vs. the Gospel

"Ye shall cry out in that day because of your king
which ye shall have chosen you;
and the Lord will not hear you on that day" (I Sam. 8:18).

POLITICAL ISMS ARE DECEPTIVE, as with all other isms, precisely because they are wrapped around an element of truth. Political isms tend to extract authority from humanism and/or naturalism, making specific application in the realm of government and economics which affect untold millions or billions of people on our planet. We will now inspect some of the more prominent of these political isms, seeking to identify the spiritual sleight of hand which enables deception to be woven around a thread of truth.

The Seduction of Socialism

Socialism is powerfully persuasive and almost solemnly seductive to the natural mind. It carries with it somewhat of a spiritual aura of "doing good to all men" (Gal. 6:10). In fact, its proponents, while denying the authority of Scripture and the existence of a Creator, will often argue the authenticity of socialism by appealing to the Bible for authority.

GOOD REPLACES GOD

Social reformers love socialism. Socialism is a systemized substitute for the unselfish love and compassion God desires to flow from every human heart to his fellows made in God's image. The Apostle Paul exhorts, "… let us do good unto all men, especially to them who are of the household of faith" (Gal. 6:10). The unregenerate or biblically unbalanced human mind rationalizes in response, thinking… *If we should do good to all men, why not devise a society to* **compel** *all to "do good" so as to achieve a "just" society?*

COMPULSION REPLACES CONVICTION

Socialism, while seemingly driven by principles, is in reality driven by pragmatism. The purported "good" ends justify ignoring the heart-driven means which, from God's viewpoint, are as important as the ends. For the socialist, force supplants faith. Compulsion replaces heart conviction.

A SHIFT OF TRUST

It should be noted that the farther both America and the entire West have drifted from our biblical roots and Judeo-Christian convictions, the more we embrace socialism as a deceptive substitute to accomplish care in the social order. Inevitably, the source of trust for care of others is shifted from God to collective government. This issue of *trust* is truly significant. It will become the defining "truth" of end-time worship as the ultimate world care-giver, a counterfeit Christ, seeks to provide peace and safety to the world through a counterfeit salvation, compelling all inhabitants of earth to receive his mark to secure the final utopian provision. It will truly test your trust.

LOVE IS LOST

Yet many will argue, "Didn't the early church sell what they had, holding things in common, so that the needs of all were met (Acts 2:44-47)? Truly they did. However, their action was not driven by external compulsion but by internal conviction. Their genuine love of the Lord birthed a love for one another. The fruit revealed the root. "Behold how they love one another" became the living "marketing" motto in a pagan world to advance the message of salvation, turning man from a heart of sinful rebellion.

GOVERNMENT REPLACES GOD

Why should we be surprised at Satan's counterfeit in socialism? Why should we be shocked that the early seeds of socialistic utopianism revealed in Plato's *Republic* and Sir Thomas Moore's *Utopia* should be brought into focus by French revolutionary thinking in the rebellion of "Enlightenment" and be brought to full birth by Karl Marx and Friedrich Engels through the *Communist Manifesto* even as naturalistic Darwinism, a creation substitute, was also being born. Should we really be surprised that by the early 20th century, socialism had become the most potent political force in formerly "Christian" Europe?

A DRAMATIC DRIFT

As America drifts dramatically away from her godly roots and righteous ways, the conviction grows that a new society can be created that will improve mankind. God and His heart-driven gospel is being replaced by a man-centered "gospel." Longing for Heaven wanes in pursuit of heaven on earth. Capitalism must be destroyed, declare socialists, because it is fundamentally unjust. We must trust the saving and caring power of government to re-distribute wealth through taxes, nationalized health care, and cradle-to-grave social benefits.

As the Church reneges on its call to "love one another," embracing the self-serving cry of the godless culture, democratically-driven government increasingly fills the gap, leading inexorably toward a final shift of trust, paving the way for a global governmental "savior."

Have you been seduced? Where do you truly put your trust? Are you willing to be part of a re-birth of New Testament Christianity for the 21st Century where it can be truly said, "Behold how they love one another?"

Perhaps this is why the Apostle Peter warned, "But the end of all things is at hand... and above all things have fervent charity among yourselves... Use hospitality one to another without grudging" (I Pet. 4:7-9). Let the love of Christ constrain you.

Communism - A Synthetic Community

Even as socialism is a synthetic substitute for "loving your neighbor as yourself," so communism (commune-ism) presents a synthetic utopian government to enforce the perceived wonders of synthetic love through socialism on nations and the world. The driving motivation, at one level, almost seems biblical. After all, didn't the book of the Acts of the Apostles say that they "had all things in common," selling their possessions, parting them "as every man had need" (Acts 2:44-45)?

Where, then, is the deception? How does communism present a counterfeit? And why is and has that counterfeit been so persuasive, dominating nearly one-third of the planet's population?

SANCTIFIED CHURCH REPLACED BY SECULAR COMMUNITY

Broadly speaking, communism is a governmental belief system in which property used for production of goods and services is owned by a community or group instead of an individual. Such groups are frequently known as *communes* or cooperatives. The ancient Greet philosopher Plato in his *Republic* and Sir Thomas Moore in his *Utopia* (1516) advocated forms of communism. Communism effectively becomes a secular, surrogate church.

FORCE REPLACES FAITH

But communism, as more commonly discussed, finds its expression in what is called Marxism-Leninism. Karl Marx and V.I. Lenin contributed most to establishing Communist doctrine. During the latter part of the 19th century, as Darwinian naturalism had taken hold to present a godless explanation for men's existence, Karl Marx and Friedrich Engels advocated communism as a way of remedying the ills of society by replacing capitalism with a system where all the means of production were owned in common. The only way to achieve this grand utopian accomplishment, they concluded, was through violent revolution. Capitalism, they advocated, must be overthrown by force and must be replaced by a tightly controlled elite who would administer the system by totalitarian force. Communist doctrine was rooted in the *Communist Manifesto* (1848) just as evolution, an alternative "creator," was about to be presented to the world.

GOVERNMENT SUPPLANTS GOD

Interestingly, all Communist governments are officially atheistic. The Communist ideal is that all property is owned by the state and that everyone work for the common good at equal wages. The state becomes the ultimate and grand expression of "community" which is to be served as a veritable act of worship, not by free will but by threat of force.

UNIFIED BY COMMON GOOD RATHER THAN GOD

Communism ostensibly seeks the "common good" for the "community," but, having denied a Creator God, also fails to recognize man's sin nature, necessitating totalitarian government to compel men to do what God desires from the heart. Rather than elevating humankind as made in God's image, Communism oppresses man's spirit, and suppresses his desire and will to be productive, either for himself or anyone else. Incentive to be and become all that God makes available is stolen by the worshipful demands of the state. The government becomes a surrogate god, promising to meet all human need, with equality for all.

HOPE BECOMES HORROR

Social-ism thus merges with commune-ism to create one of mankind's greatest efforts to be governed without God. While giving the theoretical appearance of pursuing an equitable and just society, it denies the fundamentally sinful nature of man, necessitating replacement of mercy with merciless totalitarianism supported by secret police. False worship of the state coupled with lack of capitalistic incentive inevitably reveals the synthetic authenticity of socialistic communism. Hope is replaced with horror.

False Hope of Fascism

Fascism also replaces God's glory with the glory of the state. In a sense, Communism and Fascism are two sides of the same coin.

While Communism combines with Socialism, where property and production belong to the state, Fascism permits private enterprise, while maintaining dictatorial rule over the people. Fascism and Communism are similar, however, in that they are both undemocratic and totalitarian.

Intense nationalism and suppression of all opposition by force are typical of the Fascist state.

In the first half of the 20th century, Fascism threatened the entire world, first in Italy under Mussolini, where the Fascist creed was that people existed only for the glory of Italy. Italian Fascism appeared successful and metasticized to other countries. Under Adolf Hitler, the Nazis converted nationalism into a hate campaign against Jews. Hitler's dreams of glory led the world into a nightmare of war. Japan also embraced strong Fascist beliefs as did Spain under General Franco.

GLORY OF STATE REPLACES GLORY OF GOD

Fascism replaces the glory of God with the glory of the state. While seeking to avoid the economic dis-incentives of socialism by embracing capitalism, it lacks the conversion of heart needed to make men righteous before God, thus necessitating brutal force to perpetuate false faith in the state. Man's hope again turns to horror in idolatrous worship of a created being - the state. Without God, man becomes increasingly ungovernable. Force replaces faith. Mercy is crushed in merciless totalitarian oppression where the state is "lord" or in anarchy where "SELF" is king.

The Deception of Democracy or The Lie of Liberalism

This portion of our discussion on political isms is particularly difficult due to the danger that you, as the reader, will too soon react with some degree of horror rather than respond from the heart. The reason is that there is so much confusion, and even misunderstanding, related to the words *liberal* and *democracy*. Although this aspect of political isms could well demand an entire book to develop, risk is taken to reveal the essence of why *liberal-ism* and *democracy* are treated together, and why they link in leading to a final political deception that will govern the earth.

Democracy is high-risk government from the standpoint of millennia of mankind's sojourn on earth. With the limited exception of Israel's theocratic rule (rule by God under prophets and judges) from the Exodus out of Egypt until the coronation of Saul as her first king, the nations of the earth were governed by monarchs. Depending upon their subject, circumstances, personalities, customs and systems, their rule might be perceived as benevolent dictator or despot...or both. From this heritage came the concept of "the divine right of kings."

GOD'S DESIRE vs. MAN'S DESIRE

God desired to govern Israel, not through kings but through prophetic voices who would declare His will, guiding His chosen people in the ways of prosperity and peace, i.e. *shalom*, to fulfill His purposes in the Promised Land. It would serve as a type and shadow of the eternal rule of Messiah to come who would rule as "Prince of Peace" (Isa. 9:6-7). God was grieved when Israel demanded a king. They rejected Divine rule for the "divine right of kings." God warned them through Samuel's prophetic voice of the consequences of rule by man. But they would not listen in their rebellion. "We will have a king over us; that we also may be like all the nations" (I Sam 8:5-22), they insisted.

God relented. Israel exchanged the wisdom of God for the whim of man. The truth of a merciful and righteous God was bartered away for the tyranny of rebellious man. So the Lord said, "Make them a king."

DEMOCRACY BIRTHED IN PLURALISM

Kings ruled the earth for centuries... millennia. It was not until the pluralistic patrons of the Greek pantheon of gods began to conceive of the rule of man that the concept of democracy gained traction. Democratic rule was not god-less but celebrated in the names of deities too numerous to name, including "the UNKNOWN GOD" (Acts 17:22-23).

Rome, in its heyday, was a celebrated Republic with a bi-cameral legislature to provide checks and balances, wedding democratic governance by the people to elected senators and plebes who ruled under deified men called Caesars. Religious pluralism and multiculturalism were the Roman way, so long as one enjoyed Roman citizenship.

SEEKING GOD'S RULE

Twelve hundred years after the fall of Rome, Pilgrims and Puritans fled the farthest reaches of Roman rule. Fleeing the "divine rule of kings" in Britain, whose rule was more despotic than divine, they sought God's rule once again, convinced the king, by any name, could not be trusted with God's truth. Prison for some, the stake for others and stripes for many made clear that "his Grace" was no friend of those truly seeking God's grace, and desiring to live God's truth with a clear conscience. And so they left "Christian" Europe, choosing rather to suffer hardship in their "errand into the wilderness" of America rather than to enjoy the pleasure of sin for a season where tradition seemed always to triumph over God's truth.

SEEKING MAN'S RULE

Almost immediately, the dormant seeds of ancient Greek and Roman democracy began to emerge, first the blade, then the ear, then the full corn. Philosophers, economists and political theorists from John Locke to Montesque, from Voltaire to Rousseau, poured forth a new political liberal-ism. Reacting to the traditional rule of kings, political liberalism embraced the "social contract" under which citizens made the laws and agreed to abide by them. Political liberalism, thus through "rule of law" of, by and for the people, supported liberal democracy.

It was called the "AGE of ENLIGHTENMENT." Man could govern himself without a king. The goal was freedom. The only problem was defining the true meaning of freedom. And as has often been said, "The devil is in the details."

AMERICA EXPERIMENTS-PEOPLE RULE UNDER GOD

Liberalism begat democracy and democracy perpetuated liberal-ism. The people would now rule by consent. By 1776, the year America declared independence, economist Adam Smith had woven his liberal principles of free trade into *The Wealth of Nations*. A liberal economy would support a liberal democracy.

The American colonies preferred people's rule under God to the tyranny of King George. After a Tea Party and a Revolutionary War, America was the first nation to craft a constitution based on the concept of liberal government. The document began, "We the People…." John Adams declared, "Our government was made for a moral and religious people and is wholly inadequate to the government of any other." Robert Winthrop, in 1830, echoed the sentiments of John Winthrop, who had landed two boatloads of Puritans two centuries earlier:

We will be governed either by a power without or by a power within… either by the Bible or by the bayonet.

FRANCE EXPERIMENTS - PEOPLE RULE UNDER MAN

It was not so in France. The Age of Enlightenment brought the shadows of encroaching darkness. The Goddess of Reason replaced the God of the Bible. Heads rolled as "Madame Guillotine" liberally stripped life and liberty from thousands by the clamor of lawless tens of thousands. Truth was replaced with a Reign of Terror. Claiming "Liberty, Equality and Fraternity," faith and family were swallowed by moral famine.

The contrast between the liberalism which birthed the American Republic and that which detonated the French democratic Republic and the storming of the Bastille was profound. The secular French political observer, Alexis de Tocqueville, could not have painted the picture more clearly:

> Upon my arrival in the United States, the religious aspect of the country was the first thing that struck my attention. In France I had always seen the spirit of religion and the spirit of freedom marching in opposite directions. But in America I found they were intimately united and that they reigned in common over the same country.[1]

After five years studying life in the United States of America, de Tocqueville penned his observations in his famous *Democracy in America*.

> In the United States the sovereign authority is religious,… there is no country in the world where the Christian religion retains a greater influence over the souls of men than in America, and there can be no greater proof of its utility and of its conformity to human nature than that its influence is powerfully felt over the most enlightened and free nation on earth. In the United States the influence of religion [Christianity] is not confined to the masses, but it extends to the intelligence of the people….

Christianity, therefor, reigns without obstacle by universal consent. Christianity is the companion of liberty in all its conflicts - the cradle of its infancy, and the divine source of its claims.[2]

THE DESPOTISM of DEMOCRACY

By the late 18th century, liberalism became a major ideology in virtually all developed countries. On its face, what could be more full of hope and freedom than men governing themselves under the rule of law? What could be more just than a society that does not show favor to those of higher social rank?

But when men declare their freedom from God, under majority rule, unpleasant and dangerous results inevitably begin to manifest. When political liberalism, which most in the West embrace, interbreeds with cultural liberalism and libertarianism, traditions and truth held dear are vanquished in the name of individual liberty. Liberty degenerates into licentiousness. Promoters of biblical truth become "public enemy number one." Followers of the Prince of Peace are framed as the enemies of world peace.

HUMAN REASON REPLACES GODLY RIGHTEOUSNESS

The modern ideology of liberalism ensconced now in an increasingly Godless democracy can be traced back to humanism, which challenged the authority of the established church during the Renaissance. It found its historical moment of presentation to the world through the Enlightenment. Now, two centuries later, the God-less rule of the people is being exported as the political salvation of the world.

The spirit of the burgeoning democratic liberalism now surging through the veins of Americans and the entire West is perhaps best expressed by the 42nd President of the United States who, in 1997, declared to a Southern California gathering of the homosexual community these astounding words:

We are, in practical ways, changing the immutable ideals that have guided us from the beginning.

DECEPTION...DEMOCRATICALLY

Liberal democracy can serve us, or enslave us. If "We the People:" are truly "Under God," we will be under His governance. To the extent we spurn the government of God in our individual lives, we subject ourselves progressively to the godless tyranny of a godless majority.

Winston Churchill famously remarked, "... democracy is the worst form of government, except all the other forms...." True freedom is fragile. Democracy becomes demagoguery without the God of Creation. There is nothing about democracy alone that guarantees freedom from tyranny of the masses.

As the world, and even the church, hurtles inexorably toward the Second Coming of Christ in a spirit of blatant lawlessness, what form of government do you think will prevail to make possible the enthronement of a counterfeit Christ? Here is your first clue from the prophet Daniel: "... he shall come in peaceably to obtain the kingdom by flatteries" (Dan. 11:21).

The march of history reveals that, as Santayana once said, "The only thing we learn from history is that we don't learn from history." Soon, the deceptive devices of these political isms will be blended into a composite global governmental system that will seduce all but the most discerning into its fateful following. Will you discern the decisive differences, or will you be drawn in by the mass hysteria of global and Godless democracy?

UNIFYING THE WORLD AGAINST GOD

Consider well the days ahead. As with all the other categories of isms, including the religious isms yet to be discussed, a composite is and will be forming, blending the perceived best of all into an acceptable package to unify the world for peace, without the true Prince of Peace. A synthesized salvation will seduce the democratic majority. Will you be seduced?

POSTSCRIPT

Consider well! The cover of *Newsweek* February 16, 2009, bears the following headline: "WE ARE ALL SOCIALISTS NOW."

Chapter Sixteen

Daring Thoughts for *Deceptive Times*

1. What is socialism? Why is it seductive?

2. In what ways do socialism and communism serve to seduce us from trusting God?

3. How do communism and fascism result in false hope?

4. What is it about democracy that becomes deceptive?

5. What were the essential differences between the American Revolution and the French Revolution?

6. How will democracy become the governmental deception of the Anti-Christ?

Religious Plural-isms vs. the Gospel

"…there is none other name under heaven given among men, whereby we must be saved" (Acts 4:12).

"DON'T BELIEVE IN GOD?" a bright blue billboard asks. "You are not alone." The 20-by-60 foot sign along Interstate 95 was designed by a group of area atheists as an invitation to join the Greater Philadelphia Coalition of Reason. Steve Rade, who grew up as a Jew, is convinced neither God nor eternal life exists. "I'd like everyone to believe as I do," he said. "I think it would be a better world if they did."[1]

There are comparatively few atheists in the world and many more agnostics who thrive on intellectual doubt. Yet, only "the fool hath said in his heart, There is no God," observed the psalmist (Ps. 14:1, 53:1). The greater problem in our world today is belief in many gods and in a multitude of characterizations and representations of who God is, how to know Him, how to relate to Him and others, and how to be aligned with His will and purposes. For many it is not a Supreme Being but a *feeling* of spirituality that is sought.

Does it matter what religion you embrace… or none at all? Are all religions equal? Does it matter what your religious persuasions may be as long as you are sincere? Is spirituality all that matters? Do all roads lead to heaven? Has religious division become the greatest obstacle to world peace? Are there answers, and if so, what are the implications for you and me on the near edge of Christ's Second Coming?

In this chapter we will continue our exploration of the isms of our time as we wade into a world of religious pluralism. There is no subject more powerful nor pertinent to this unique moment in human history.

ISMS and PLURAL-ISM

As with the isms of science, the social order and politics, so too are the isms of religion. Any ism is generally framed around one or more nuggets or threads of truth. It is the element of truth, however small or large, that lends an aura of authenticity to the ism, elevating it above others in the pecking order of world isms. The greater the perceived authenticity, the greater the authority men are willing to attribute to the belief or religious system.

Culture also plays an enormous role in any discussion of religion. Over the past half century, as psychology and sociology have gained public respectability as "science," multicultural-ism has been wedded to religious plural-ism. The intended effect has been to diminish the authenticity of religion in favor of the authenticity of culture, thus rendering every religious belief or ism co-equal and every culture co-equal.

The post-modern repudiation of the very concept of absolute truth has completed the web of deception woven to wall out all but the bravest souls from challenging these presumptions. Many of these multicultural and religious pluralistic presumptions are increasingly codified into law or imposed by judicial activists on the bench in courts throughout the western world. The same sentiments have become part of the governing dogma of the United Nations.

Winds of Warning

Inclusivity is "IN." Exclusivity is "OUT." If an ism, faith, or belief system is to be currently considered "worthy" of the world's consideration, it must present itself as "inclusive," meaning that it makes no claim to being the only true faith or way to God. It wraps its arms warmly around all other beliefs as co-equal, equally valid.

Any religious belief that represents itself to be "THE" truth rather than one among many truths, is deemed to be "exclusive." Any religion that claims such exclusivity breaches the politically-correct presuppositions of the elite guardians of multiculturalism and religious pluralism and is deemed dangerous to the progress of the new global order and world peace.

World leaders are imminently cognizant of the squeeze of all religious beliefs into the "inclusive" mold. Beyond awareness, they actively promote the blending of religious beliefs. This blending of beliefs or isms is called syncretism.

The Seduction of Syncretism

"CAN'T WE ALL GET ALONG?" was the famous headline cry issuing out of the L.A. riots of 1991, related to persistent racial tensions. Yet that cry is now being superimposed upon the religions and isms of the world. Fear is fanning the flames. The world is a powder keg of highly explosive beliefs. "Peace on earth" is the global goal. And the pressure to set aside and/or disavow truths or principles heretofore deemed precious is powerful in the pursuit of peace.

But should people embrace peace at any price? Can, or should, the world's religions and isms compromise convictions to achieve a world order where all seem to "get along?" Will global peace trump godly peace? Or, is godly peace defined by mankind's best effort at global peace?

Many religions and isms are deemed non-exclusive and are therefore perceived as warm and welcoming. Others teach truths that are deemed compatible with other faiths, even though claiming exclusivity. Might they be convinced to set aside those things that divide in order to achieve peaceful co-existence? This process of gradually intermingling distinct beliefs, coupling to conceive more peaceful religious offspring, is called *syncretism*. It is and has been proceeding, for some passively, for others aggressively. All have reasons unique to their perceived role in the emerging global order.

Syncretism is profoundly seductive. After all, who, at heart, truly does not want to "get along with" or at least be perceived by others as "getting along with" other humans, even of differing persuasions. Tolerance, once practically defined as "putting up with the differences of others without violent reaction jeopardizing life, limb or property," has now come to mean "agreeing to disagree, considering another's viewpoint, even on matters of *truth* or *faith*, as co-equal to one's own beliefs and convictions."

The surging tide of syncretism seduces also by the unrelenting waves of media and marketing through church and culture that sweep over us, presenting polls in place of principles, tolerance instead of truth, feelings over faith, good works supplanting God's Word and the pursuit of happiness over holiness. Syncretism is converting priests and pastors into politicians and politicians into the high priests of a new religious order. Minority voices are given mega voices through activist courts while majority voices are muffled by a confluence of social and cultural stigma, godless media moguls and ministry mantras, preferring popular culture over Christ.

Sidebars of Seduction

A "sidebar" is used by writers and journalists to distill pertinent applications or illustrations supporting the thrust of the broader article published. Such "sidebar" notes and illustrations revealing the profound religious syncretism in our world, the fornication of faith and isms, could be so vast as to fill volumes. For our purposes here, by way only of eclectic illustration, "sidebar" stories are provided which emerged within only a single month period.

POLITICIAN BECOMES HIGH PRIEST

On May 30, 2008, the former Prime Minister of Britain, Tony Blair, unveiled The Tony Blair Faith Foundation, dedicated to "proving that collaboration among different religious faiths can help address some of the world's most pressing problems." Blair says, "faith and the values it brings with it are an essential part of making globalization work." "Blair and those working with him think religion is the key to the global agenda." Says Blair, "this is how I want to spend the rest of my life."[2]

POPE BECOMES POLITICIAN

On June 3, 2008, the *Ecumenical News Highlights* made this note. "After a visit to Russia, the Vatican's top official for Christian unity has said a meeting between Pope Benedict XVI and Patriarch Alexei II of the Russian Orthodox Church is 'possible.' Such an encounter would be **the first ever meeting between the Roman Pontiff and a Russian Orthodox patriarch.**" (Such is in planning with Alexei's sucessor).

MUSLIMS TALK TURKEY

TIME, on June 9, 2008, reported an astounding development in Turkey. "In the current turmoil over Turkey's identity that pits political Islam against staunch secularism in the courts and on the streets, the Alexes, a Turkish offshoot of Shi'ite Islam, offer a third way: a faith-based humanism big enough to incorporate both piety and modernity." "Their doctrine is unflinchingly progressive, favoring gay rights, access to abortion, equal opportunity for women and pacifism. They don't believe in heaven or hell." This group now is seen as a syncretic hope for uniting Turkey, comprising 15%-30% of the population.[3]

MILQUETOAST MANIFESTO

At the Washington Press Club, on May 7, 2008, a group of evangelicals presented a 20-page declaration entitled "An Evangelical Manifesto," trying to change widespread perceptions of evangelical Christians in the culture. As one Christian publication declared on its cover "IMAGE IS EVERYTHING."

One passage of the manifesto affirms evangelical's commitment to religious freedom: "A right for a Christian is a right for a Jew, and a right for a secularist, and a right for a Mormon and a right for a Muslim, and a right for a Scientologist, and a right for all believers in all the faiths across the land." Here was a Milquetoast effort to claim an "evangelical" position while pandering to a culture that accepts any religion or ism other than genuine Christian faith, a faith that declares the exclusivity that Jesus Christ is "the way, the truth, and the life: no man cometh unto the Father, but by me" (John 14:6).

Interestingly, one of the principle signers of the manifesto was then president of the Council for America's First Freedom (Freedom of Religion). That organization celebrates the freedom of expression of every religious faith and ism other than the exclusive claims of salvation through Christ alone ostensibly taught and believed by true evangelicals. *Belief Watch*, for *Newsweek*, on June 2, 2008, aptly called the image effort, "The Milquetoast Manifesto." "As Wheaton College professor Alan Jacobs rightly observed, the problem with the 'Evangelical Manifesto' is that it's not a manifesto at all. It's polite and embracing… porridge. America's evangelicals, especially those struggling with consciences… deserve better."[4]

When we seek and love the approval of men and their culture more than the favor and approval of God, we actually will to be deceived and will participate in the syncretistic seduction. Perhaps this is an appropriate moment to measure your own spiritual temperature. Are you a God pleaser? Or have you become a people pleaser? Is the message of your life mighty through God, or Milquetoast?

POPE REACHES TO OTHER FAITHS

The Vatican announced May 30, 2008, that "Pope Benedict XVI will meet representatives from other Christian faiths as well as other religions" during his visit to Australia.[5]

PASTORS ADMIT SKEWING MESSAGE

Over half (55%) of pastors admit "one or more topics they would not preach or only preach sparingly because the sermon could negatively affect their hearers' willingness to attend church in the future."[6]

PASTORS THREATENED FOR PREACHING

Two American-born pastors handing out gospel leaflets in a predominantly Muslim area of Birmingham, England, were threatened with arrest. Officers contended spreading the Christian message was a "hate crime." The incident fuels concerns that in Britain, "the Christian message is increasingly unwelcome."[7]

QUOTING SCRIPTURE BANNED IN LIBRARY

"Quoting from the Bible has been banned in a community room at the public library in Clermont County, Ohio." A couple requested use of the community room for a financial planning seminar. A library employee asked if there would be any quotes from the *Bible* in the presentation. When the employee was told of the intent to include biblical quotes, use of the premises was twice denied, claiming Library Policy prohibited use of the Bible or biblical quotes in the public meeting room, which was open to private groups upon application.[8]

SCHOOL REMOVES PLEDGE OF ALLEGIANCE

A Portland, Oregon elementary school principal unilaterally decided to discontinue using the Pledge of Allegiance. She explained the pledge was removed "out of respect for the diversity of faiths."[9]

RENOUNCE YOUR FAITH

"A Canadian human rights tribunal ordered a Christian pastor to renounce his faith and never again express moral opposition to homosexuality...." In a decision dated May 30, 2008, the Alberta Human Rights Tribunal banned pastor Stephen Bossion from expressing his biblical perspective on homosexuality and he was ordered to pay $5,000 for "damages for pain and suffering" as well as to apologize to the activist who reported him and complained.

"As for the future," the lawyer, acting as judge, wrote; "Mr. Boisson and The Concerned Christian Coalition Inc. shall cease publishing in newspapers, by email, on the radio, in public speeches, or on the Internet disparaging remarks about gays or homosexuals... and is further directed to remove from current Web sites and publications all disparaging remarks versus homosexuals."

An attorney similarly attacked noted: "In essence, the Alberta Human Rights Tribunal is ordering the minister to renounce his faith, since his opposition to homosexuality is based upon the Judeo-Christian Bible."[10]

SCHOOL ART POLICY BANNED BIBLE

"An art policy at a Wisconsin high school that allowed images of Buddha, the Grim Reaper, demons and Medusa, banned a Bible reference to John 3:16." "The student was told by his teacher that the cross and biblical reference on his drawing needed to be covered...."[11]

225

WARNING - QUOTING BIBLE ALIENATES PEOPLE

A respected Christian evangelical writer warned evangelical writers not to quote the Bible on issues affecting non-believers in the culture because it might alienate them. "Let's not call marriage 'biblical,' as we like to, but 'healthy,'" posed Tim McLaughlin. He urged Christian writers to write from a non-believer's viewpoint rather than from God's viewpoint as expressed in the Scriptures, so that people would not be offended.[12]

KABBALAH for KIDS

"Hollywood's A-list stars are bringing the cult of Kabbalah to inner-city schools in London," according to the *TIMES ONLINE* from London. "It's all about finding your light and sharing it," says actress Demi Moore. She, together with designer Donna Karan and actor-husband Ashton Kucher, teamed with Madonna for a high-powered fundraiser, focusing on "Spirituality for Kids." What connects them is Kabbalah. And they are seeking to fund SFK, a global youth program already working within six British schools, as part of the curriculum, with more on the waiting list. SFK claims to "encourage children to see their own goodness, to see the light and have more spiritual powers."[13]

BIBLE CRIMINALIZED IN COLORADO

A new Colorado law prohibits Christians from teaching or talking about biblical prohibitions against homosexuality, except behind the closed doors of their sanctuaries. The intent was to silence public expression of biblical truth by Christians as it applies to politically-correct cultural issues, in particular those related to sex and gender, and to, in effect, make it unlawful to oppose homosexuality and same-sex marriage, even in the courts.[14]

RELIGION - THE NEW POLITICS

Tony Blair, former British Prime Minister, formally launched the Tony Blair Faith Foundation in New York. A British online paper observed, "For Mr. Blair, rhetorically and professionally, religion is the new politics." Blair said, "Religious faith will be of the same significance to the 21st century as political ideology was to the 20th century."

Blair further noted, "In an era of globalization, there is nothing more important than getting people of different faiths and culture to understand each other better and live in peace and mutual respect... to give faith its proper place in the future."[15]

The Spirituality of Seduction

It should be increasingly apparent that the world is not becoming more atheistic, in the classic sense, but more "spiritual," in an individual sense. Every man's, every group's or every culture's religious ideas and persuasions are no longer seen as competing for absolute religious authority. Since all are deemed co-equal, the walls separating religious beliefs are crumbling. Political Correctness has bred its offspring, Religious Correctness, which increasingly defines the rising global spirituality. What matters now is not what faith you embrace but merely whether you embrace a faith, however you may define it or whatever it may be, however vague. Hence the common phrase... "People of faith."

The term "people of faith" is very slippery. It allows common discussion of religious and cultural, even global, issues without a moment's concern about the tenets of that faith or the convictions, if any, connected to it. It is warm, fuzzy, cuddly, and culturally embracing. It is a term perfectly tailored to a developing global spirituality ushering in a false peace-maker, the counterfeit Christ.

Note carefully! Consider the characteristics of the various "sidebar" illustrations of religious development both in the United States and worldwide.

1. They either oppose from the outside or seek to diminish from the inside the exclusivity of true, Bible-believing Christian faith.
2. They embrace other faiths or generic spirituality as desirable.
3. They seek to silence the Bible as authority.
4. They seek to exalt culture rather than Christ.
5. They envision a global peace by uniting religious sentiment rather than a Godly peace uniting mankind in righteous truth.

The warm womb of end-time spiritual deception has been long in preparation, receiving implantation of the seed of many religious suitors for centuries, ready to conceive the final and false faith in the fulness of time bearing the DNA of Satan himself. It will be a composite faith giving a sense of warm togetherness, something the various religious streams of the world can and will embrace, including a cosmic "Christ."

The religious isms of the world will be, and are being, drawn together, weaving the emerging tapestry of this "inclusive" global faith. Many within the broader Christian community have been and are becoming unwitting accomplices.

The pattern is clearly discernable since the founding of America. The earliest settlers sought to establish a genuine, full-blooded expression of fundamental Christian faith in view of Europe's growing apostasy, establishing Harvard and Yale to train well-educated pastors and leaders to continue their work. Universal Unitarianism soon took the reigns. Despite two great awakenings and other revival movements, by the late 1800's and early 1900's, liberal theology invaded North America from the European continent, particularly from Germany, the seed-bed of the Reformation.

Alarm bells went off to protect "the faith once delivered to the saints." "We must restore the fundamentals of the Christian faith," was the cry, and *The FUNDAMENTALS* was penned to preserve them. But a rising and popular "social gospel" movement threatened to swamp the fundamental boat. The battles raged with much bad blood. To avoid controversy and seek a more culturally acceptable expression of the Christian faith while preserving the essentials, the new "evangelical" movement was given birth by Billy Graham and Carl F. H. Henry and others.

Despite lip service to the contrary, compromise with the culture persisted, increasing momentum from the 1960's forward. The "Church Growth Movement" began to slip away from clear confidence in the gospel into even more imaginative gospel gimmicks to lure even more fickle customers into church. Pastoral seminars to grow big churches replaced sermons to grow deep disciples. The "Seeker Sensitive" movement polled people to determine what sinners wanted to hear rather than petitioning God for what they needed to hear.

Pandering to the culture increasingly became the premise for church growth. Truth became a casualty. Hypocrisy reeked. And a growing disillusionment developed among the younger generation craving authenticity, however synthetically it may be presented to achieve the feeling. The new "Emerging Church" movement, pursuing relevance over revelation, developed as the "seeker sensitive" movement realized it was failing to make genuine disciples. Now only nine percent of professing younger Christians claim to believe in absolute truth.

We believe IN God, but we just don't BELIEVE Him or His Word anymore with any genuine level of certainty. Pursuit of *relevance* has replaced biblical *revelation*. When some of the most prominent evangelical leaders in the world today refuse on national television to admit that Jesus Christ is the "only way, the only truth, and the only life" and that "no man cometh to the Father, but by me" (Jn. 14:6), the womb is ripe to give birth to a hybrid faith of the world's isms that will please the masses who will march to the drumbeat of the final world order before Christ's return. The spirit of seduction is palpable. The birth pangs are upon us. The bastard child of religious fornication is about to be born.

Interfaith-Ism

The year was 1893. Religious leaders from around the world gathered in Chicago for an unprecedented ecumenical event - the Parliament of the World's Religions. It was the largest interfaith conference in the history of the world up to that time.

In 1948, the same year Israel became a nation, the modern ecumenical movement was born with the founding of the World Council of Churches. The purpose was clear: to help create the religious atmosphere for a new global order. The World Council of Churches declared:

> After the Second World War, the establishment of the World Council of Churches in 1948 signaled the resolve of the ecumenical community both to work for the fuller unity of the church and to participate in the struggle for a new just world order.[16]

Ecumenism has been seen as an effort to unify Christian churches. Ecumenism has evolved into Inter faith-ism. Interfaith-ism is calculated to unify the religions of the world. It can be seen in operation in every community and is virtually enforced by the cultural embrace of religious pluralism and multiculturalism. Those who resist the wave of interfaith-ism sweeping the earth become culturally marginalized and politically ostracized, perceived as resisting peace and brotherhood.

Vatican II, which the *Catholic Encyclopedia* declared, "The greatest religious event of the twentieth century...," merged the ecumenical movement with the interfaith movement. The Council, which opened October 11, 1962, urged, "all Christians... to act positively to preserve and even promote all that is good in other religions: Hinduism, Buddhism, and other world religions." This was to be carried out by the Secretariat for World Religions.

Pope John Paul II was embraced lovingly by the world largely because he embraced the world's religions in an unprecedented way. He traveled to 130 countries currying favor. He then, in carrying out Vatican II, held an actual interfaith summit in Assisi, Italy, and an interfaith prayer meeting with world leaders of approximately one hundred of the world's pagan religions. What was the purpose for the "VICAR of CHRIST" to be unequally yoking himself with unbelievers in direct violation of the Scriptures (II Cor. 6:14)? Its purpose was the merging of world religions under the "motherhood" of the Roman Catholic Church. Pope Benedict XVI continues wooing world religions for the interfaith agenda.

ISMS

If we are truly honest, all isms, including religious isms, gain their following and authority because of some level of truth, emphasis or practice that binds the adherents. Deception lies in those aspects that are untrue, wrongly applied, or unduly emphasized or de-emphasized. This is true both for pagan-isms and those isms purporting to be Christian. Such isms are vast and beyond the scope of this discussion. But by way of illustration, a few prominent isms bear our focus.

HINDUISM

Hinduism is arguably the oldest of the great religions and the only religion without a founder. It is actually a collection of many native Indian religions, having about 200 sects, and is embraced by about one billion adherents, most of whom live in India. Nearly all sects respect the Vedas ("revealed knowledge"), the ancient collection of religious writings.

The fundamental doctrine is that of the identity of the individual soul with the universal soul (Brahman), or God. This merging of the individual soul in identity with God is a significant component of much New Age religious belief. Hinduism is very mystical and stresses non-violence. Historically, Hinduism has not tried to win converts by force and has generally, until recently, tolerated other religions, absorbing ideas from them.

Those characteristics make Hinduism, or aspects of its teachings, highly desirable and easily assimilated in a world that has embraced religious pluralism and multi-culturalism as foundational for a global social order.

BUDDHISM

About one fifth of the world's population is Buddhist. Buddhism was founded by Siddhartha Gautama ("Buddha" meaning "The Enlightened One") in India around 500 BC. It is the primary religion of the Far East.

Buddhism was originally a reform movement that rejected certain beliefs and practices of Hinduism and therefore shares many of the same beliefs, including reincarnation, the law of karma, and liberation. *Liberation* is achieved through understanding and practicing the Four Noble Truths which include "The Eightfold Path." The Buddhist must at all times observe the high moral principles of the Eightfold Path which emphasizes non-violence and the brotherhood of all.

The fact that Buddhists comprise a commanding segment of the earth's population makes it essential for world leaders to assimilate principles and concepts from it into a religious composite that the emerging pluralistic and multi-culturalistic world can embrace. The emphasis on enlightenment in pursuit of Nirvana, where peace and harmony are attained, is now embraced and promoted throughout the West. The Buddhist concept of world brotherhood is promoted unwittingly even by Christians, whereas the Bible teaches only a brotherhood in Christ.

Both Buddhism and Hinduism are therefore perceived as non-exclusionary and therefore globally acceptable within a pluralistic system pursuing world peace. Yoga has become a not-so-innocent tool in advancing the normalcy of eastern religions throughout the West, yes, even in our churches.

PANTHEISM

Pantheism is the belief that God, or supreme being, and the universe are a unity. Everything that exists is merely an aspect of God. Pantheism undergirds or is woven through most New Age thinking and spiritualism. All persons and things merge into a vague "oneness" where all, in effect, become gods.

It does not take much imagination to understand why pantheistic thinking increasingly prevails in the emerging global society. We are "one" with the world and all are merging into spiritual oneness, it is believed. Therefore a global religion binding us into a global society with global government is seen as the most natural and desirable destiny, however dangerous it may be.

ENVIRONMENTALISM

Pantheism undergirds much of the environmental movement. Since humans and nature are really "one" in a supreme being (unity), environmentalism itself becomes "religious." It is promoted religiously by preaching from its most prominent priests... our politicians.

It is important, as Christians, to demonstrate good stewardship of our environment. It is quite another thing to turn the environment into an object of worship, or to establish man and nature as co-equals in "God." The world was made for man, not man for the world. Yet environmentalism, as a quasi-religious belief system, has been co-opted by those intent on a utopian global order to draw the nations into a false unity, shedding freedoms under false pretenses for a false hope of peace, where man becomes his own savior.

GNOSTICISM

Gnosticism is a religious movement that emerged in the early Christian period. It became so widespread that by the beginning of the third century AD, most of the intellectual Christian congregations were infected by it to some degree. In the second century AD, the movement "spread with the swiftness of an epidemic over the church from Syria to Gaul."

As the spirit of a resurrecting Rome now spreads throughout the earth, Gnosticism is once again spreading like an epidemic to undermine the truth of the gospel of Jesus Christ, destroying faith and replacing it with intellectualisms masquerading as genuine spiritual faith. This new

Gnosticism is being driven by popular novels and tomes in the popular culture such as the explosive *DaVinci Code* and *The Secret* together with pseudo-intellectual "higher criticism" by the Jesus Seminar, all of which eat like spiritual termites at the heart and soul, replacing genuine faith in Biblical truth with intellectual doubt and informational pride.

The apostle Paul warned of the early vestiges of gnosticism, against "what is falsely called knowledge [gnosis]" (I Tim. 6:20). Such persons, said Paul, are "proud, knowing nothing, but doting about questions and strifes of words..." (I Tim. 6:4).

Gnosticism comes from the Greek *gnosis* meaning "knowledge." It fused elements of Oriental mysticism, Greek philosophy, and Judaism with Christian ideas. It endeavored to introduce into Christianity a so-called "higher knowledge" of which the ordinary believer was incapable and of which genuine salvation consisted. The resulting intellectual pride of the Gnostics changed the gospel into nothing more than philosophical romanticism. For the Gnostics, God became the ultimate, nameless, unknowable being.

Ancient Gnosticism disappeared largely by the 5th century, but its spirit has now reappeared. Once condemned as heresy, it now thrives, undergirding the new popular spirituality, infatuated with sources of evil but denying sin and biblical salvation.

Aspects of Gnostic teaching are reproduced in modern pantheistic philosophies and in forms of religious teaching that deny biblical atonement. This renders neo-Gnosticism a welcome influence in the developing global "gospel" of religious syncretism. This teaching strikes at the heart of the Christian faith and morality. The personality of God, free will of mankind, the existence of moral evil, the deity and incarnation of Christ, His redemption for the world, His resurrection – all is denied. A new, redefined and "cosmic" Christ is resurrected for global consumption. This new "Christ" loves everyone, is in everyone, makes no moral demands, calls for no repentance from sin and is non-exclusive, thus wedding the world in a new spiritual "unity."

Uniting the Nations

In 1993, the Parliament of World Religions again met in Chicago. Its purpose was both to commemorate the 100th anniversary of the first Parliament (1893) and to plan for the world's "spiritual future." Approximately 5500 religious leaders from a vast array of denominations and religions attended, including voodoo and druid priests, Freemasons, wiccans, snake charmers, Zoroastrian sun worshipers, occultists and Luciferians. Diversity was the defining spirit. During the nine-day gathering attended by 857 persons issued press passes, over 500 seminars and workshops were held, pursuing Interfaith Understanding and various dimensions of global spirituality.

Robert Muller delivered the Parliament's keynote address, forcefully calling for creation of a "permanent institution" dedicated to pursuing religious unity. As the United Nation's "Prophet of Hope," Muller believes world unity can only be achieved with a one-world government and a one-world religion. Although raised a Catholic, it was a Buddhist who left the deepest impression on his life. In his *New Genesis: Shaping a Global Spirituality*, Muller discloses the profound impact of the former U.N. Secretary General U Thant.

Perhaps the most significant event of the 1993 Parliament of World Religions was the convening of an inner circle of interfaith religious "authorities," consisting of Robert Muller and his closest allies. The group endorsed an interfaith document *Towards a Global Ethic* calling for "a common set of core values… found in the teachings of the religions." Catholic theologian Hans Küng makes clear that participation in the new "ethic" (religion) will not be optional. "The undivided world increasingly needs an undivided ethic," wrote Küng. "What we need is an ecumenical world order."

Robert Muller contends that religions claiming to "have the total truth" miss the real point of Jesus and other religious "emissaries." He contends that each religion (ism) provides part of the truth, and that collectively, the core of the world's religions contain the complete truth. This position is rapidly becoming the culturally accepted norm in America, the entire West and, indeed, worldwide. Indeed, U.S Presidents Barak Obama and George W. Bush have declared, despite their professed "Christianity" that all religions worship the same God. The emerging global religious syncretism is nearly complete.

The Pew Religious Landscape report released in mid 2008 found that 70% of Americans say "many religions can lead to eternal life." But most amazing is that 57% of evangelicals say many religions can lead to eternal life. Given that the most fundamental fact of the Christian faith is that salvation comes through Christ alone (John 14:6), the Editor-in-Chief of *BELIEFNET* observed, "this finding ought to rattle Christian leaders."[17]

Where Do You Stand?

The stage has been set. A one-world ecumenical blended religion (ethic) is not only contemplated but nearing consummation. All who refuse to embrace this false unity movement are now being culturally and politically marginalized and will soon be deemed the chiefest of enemies of the new "Roman" and "Babylonian" order. They are, even now as we have seen, persecuted through proliferating hate-crimes legislation and the rising choir of voices of world peace seeking to drown out the lone voice of the Prince of Peace and His faithful followers.

So… where do you stand? Have you already been seduced? Have you been sorely tempted? Has the promise of "unity" caused you to forget that, for the true follower of Christ, our unity is in Him and in Him alone? What are you saying to your children and grandchildren? Pastor, can your voice be clearly heard and discerned among the flock, calling them to "come out from among them and be separate" so that "I will receive you, and ye shall be my sons and daughters, saith the Lord"?

This is the growing hour of temptation. Deception is knocking at your door. If you, in weakness, open that door, the risk to your eternal destiny is incalculable. The river of seduction is swift and the currents capture most who venture close.

Remember the Master's words, "But he that shall endure to the end, the same shall be saved" (Matt. 24:13). By God's grace, His enabling power, you can remain pure and resist the tide in loving faith. Perfect love will cast out fear (I Jn. 4:18). Fear not!

Chapter Seventeen

Daring Thoughts
for *Deceptive Times*

1. Why do you think that the exclusive claim that Jesus is "the only way, the only truth and the only life" is falling on increasingly hard times? Have you noticed the growing rejection?

2. What is religious *syncretism*? Have you seen how it is creeping even into the church under the guise of *unity*?

3. Why is the term "people of faith" deceptive? Have you noticed how professing Christians and their leaders have increasingly adopted this phrase? Can you see how this term of "political correctness" is being used to normalize syncretism and prepare the way for a global religion?

4. How has *ecumenism* now evolved into *interfaith-ism*? What do you see as the deceptive consequence?

5. What was your reaction to Catholic theologian Hans Küng's bold statement, "What we need is an ecumenical world order?"

6. What can you do, as pastor or parishioner, to help protect those you love and serve from being seduced by the rising pluralistic, ecumenical, inter-faith, syncretistic global faith?

Chapter Eighteen

Global-ism – the Anti-Gospel

*"The kings of the earth set themselves, and the rulers
take counsel together, against the Lord,
and, against His anointed…" (Ps. 2:2).*

"**WE SHALL HAVE WORLD GOVERNMENT**, whether or not we like it," declared James Paul Warburg on February 17, 1950, speaking before the United States Senate. "The only question is whether World Government will be achieved by conquest or consent."

Men's Dream of Dominion

World government has been the dream and dominion of men throughout the ages to this present age. From the Tower of Babel in Genesis 11 to the trumpeting of the New World Order in our generation, mankind and its various kingdoms and rulers have sought to govern the then-known world in power and glory. Inevitably, man's lust for power and glory seeks to eclipse, escape, or even defy the power and glory of the Creator.

The problem with pursuit of global government is not in the nature of government itself, for God has ordained government as "the minister of God to thee for good," to protect against evil and praise that which is good (Rom. 13:1-4). Civil government among mankind is to be conducted under the overarching fear of the God of the Bible and His governance. When humans forsake the fear of the Lord, God's ways of government and covenantal oversight and revelation are no longer available (Ps. 25:14). Man thus devises his own ways, seeking inevitably to create a utopian world order promising peace on earth.

The promise and hope of a global order ushering in world peace is profoundly alluring to the natural mind. After all, who in their right mind would not yearn for peace to avert a nuclear holocaust? Those under thirty years of age today have haunting fears that their lives or the lives of their children will be cut short in a worldwide conflagration. The aura of fear with empty promises of peace recalls the oft -repeated phrase, "Peace, peace; when there is no peace" (Jer. 6:14, 8:11).

In this chapter we will briefly explore the advanced stage of preparation in every major sphere of man's endeavor for a One World government and a new global order. We will unveil the massive deceptions paving the way, why these are of potential eternal consequence to you and the world's inhabitants, and how you can live pure, avoiding the *Seduction of the Saints.*

Daniel's Dominion Dream

While the prophet Daniel was captive in Babylon, God gave him a prophetic dream (Dan. 7). In that dream, he saw four great beasts representing the existing and future great powers of the earth that would rule until the "latter days" and the great "time of trouble." These kingdoms have been commonly interpreted as:

FIRST:	A Lion - Babylon
SECOND:	A Bear- Medo-Persia
THIRD:	A Leopard- Greece
FOURTH:	An "Exceedingly Dreadful Beast"- Rome

The fourth beast, "dreadful and terrible," "exceedingly strong," was different from all the others. It had ten horns representing governing powers. The book of Revelation describes this same beast as having "seven heads and ten horns" with "ten crowns" (Rev. 13:1). These ten horns are further described as to "receive power one hour with the beast. These have one mind, and shall give their power and strength to the beast." These ten kings or powers "shall make war with the Lamb..." (Rev. 17:12-14).

This great and fearsome fourth beast that "shall devour the whole earth, and shall tread it down, and break it in pieces" (Dan. 7:23) is undoubtedly a resurrected or revived Roman Empire. Ancient Rome, a democratic republic, was diverse in government from the monarchies that preceded it. Rome governed the then-known world with an iron fist through its legendary legions, amassing great wealth, ushering in the *Pax Romana* or "Roman Peace" even as Christ, the Prince of Peace was being born.

Rome declared the government of the world to be upon its shoulder, even as the King of kings was sent by God to re-introduce God's governance in the world.

Isaiah had prophesied:

For unto us a child is born, unto us a son is given: and **the government shall be upon his shoulder:**
Of the increase of his government and peace there shall be no end, *upon the throne of David [not Rome], and upon his kingdom, to order it, and to establish it with judgment and with justice from henceforth even forever (Isa. 9:6-7).*

The battle lines for dominion were drawn. God had promised His "Prince of Peace" (Isa. 9:6), and Satan, the dragon, would empower His counterfeit "prince" with a global government promising peace on earth. That final world government would be a composite of the previous world powers, blending the best man had to offer to blasphemously compete with the Christ of God.

And the beast which I saw was like unto a leopard, and his feet were as the feet of a bear, and his mouth the mouth of a lion:

and the dragon gave him his power, and his seat, and great authority."
And they worshiped the beast, saying, Who is able to make war with him?
And he opened his mouth in blasphemy against God…
(Rev. 13:2-6).

The Battle for Dominion

The battle for dominion rages. The great dragon (Satan) is determined to dominate the planet to satisfy his personal vendetta against God. He is marshalling every tool at his disposal, and he knows destiny is in the balance. His determination is to "deceive the whole world" (Rev. 12:9). He is convinced his spiritual cunning and clever seduction will draw the vast majority into his final global conspiracy against the Christ of God through a counterfeit christ. That is why Jesus warned us in his final words before his crucifixion, "Take heed that no man deceive you" (Matt. 24:4).

How will such diabolical deception take place? Why will the vast majority be deceived? What is the Deceiver's scheme or *modus operandi*? What is wrong with globalization? Will you be able to discern the difference between truth and deception?

The Moment To Be Seized

The date was September 11, 1990. U.S. President George Herbert Walker Bush stood before a joint session of Congress, a fresh wind of patriotism blowing across the country. Consider closely the words of the 41st president.

> The crisis in the Persian Gulf, as grave as it is, also offers a rare opportunity to move toward an historic period of cooperation. Out of these troubled times… **a new world order can emerge**: a new era – freer from the threat of terror, stronger in the pursuit of justice, and more secure in the quest for peace.[1]

That "new world," declared President George H.W. Bush, "is struggling to be born." The "opportunity" that he so eagerly desired to seize, was the building of a "new-world order." Over 200 times, the senior President Bush declared this "new world order" during his administration. It was historic. It was as if the world had become pregnant and the president of its reigning superpower was deputized to announce the conception long-thought to be but the rantings of conspiracy theorists. But the gestation period was not given. The birth would come in the "fulness of time"… heaven's prophetic time and Satan's false-gospel hour to seduce the world.

It would be man's glorious gospel of self-salvation, of utopian peace and of global safety without the God of Creation and of biblical revelation. A substitute god would be prepared, designed democratically, without dogma or doctrine offensive to a multicultural, religiously pluralistic world intent on global unity. The Scriptures had warned, "when they shall say, Peace and safety; then sudden destruction cometh upon them, as travail upon a woman with child; and they shall not escape" (I Thess. 5:3). But such warnings, however dire, are deemed unworthy in the face of such lofty ambitions as a global order of unprecedented peace and prosperity.

Eleven years later, the Prime Minister of Britain could not contain his enthusiasm. Two weeks after the infamous Islamic attack on the World Trade Center Towers and the United States Pentagon, Tony Blair delivered "the most powerful speech of his career," causing one member of Parliament to remark, "He spoke as if he were President of the World." Note well his words.

> This is the moment to seize. The kaleidoscope has been shaken… let us reorder this world around us. Today, humankind has the technology to destroy itself or to provide prosperity to all. Yet science can't make that choice for us. Only the moral power of a world acting as a community, can."[2]

The very concept of a grand global order almost defies the imagination. For thousands of years, the world, its people and nations, being inherently sinful and selfish, have sought self-gain by grinding others into submission. Europe is a classic study. It's various nations and peoples have been in almost perpetual warfare from the purported fall of Rome to the end of World War II. So, what is so unusual about this moment of history? Will the world now become "one"? Since the failure of Charlemagne's "Holy Roman Empire," what "gospel" will now gather and what glue will now bond the world into a bold new order of the ages?

Unity Fever

The pressure for and toward world unity, at every level, is unprecedented. This pressure has reached a fever pitch. The flames of global fever are fanned by fear of global conflagration and by a utopian vision for a global peace and prosperity that has heretofore escaped mans' grasp.

The great and growing river of unity gradually becoming a global sea is fed by the confluence of many streams and tributaries, both religious and secular. Neither time nor space here permit detailed delineation of the vast and pervasive scope of this movement. We must therefore limit our latitude of observation to that which enables us to bring into focus the emerging sculpture of a global order being forged as mans' ultimate achievement and salvation.

This emerging global-ism is being forged out of the multitude of prevalent isms in our world, the most significant of which we have broadly distilled as the "science isms," "social-isms," "political-isms" and "religious-isms," with the ultimate goal of unprecedented material-ism. While seemingly separate in their respective disciplines, upon closer inspection one cannot escape the merging and synergetic interaction of these various broad categories of isms, each reinforcing the other and developing a kind of "magnetic" attraction, chasing each other ever closer into an uncanny bond now universally defined as *global-ism*. While jointly and severally becoming mutually interdependent, it is the religious isms that globalists increasingly, although often reluctantly, acknowledge as the ultimate catalyst to bind the world in the final thrust for global unity.

It is fascinating to watch the threads of the emerging global tapestry being woven into a discernable pattern through the unprecedented pursuit of unity. One can easily be trapped in its seductive web of deception, especially because of the sheer weight of the supposed "authorities" and their massing majorities embracing global-ism as a veritable new "gospel."

Emerging "Oneness"

The year was 1630 AD, John Winthrop, a godly English attorney, was preparing to settle four boatloads of Puritans seeking "Promised Land" in the "New Canaan" called America. Before landing, he penned *A Model of Christian Charity*, setting forth the vision of biblical unity that would bind this "New Israel" in their "errand into the wilderness" to establish that "City upon a hill" Jesus had spoken about that "could not be hid" (Matt. 5:14). Winthrop wrote:

> ...we are a company professing ourselves fellow members of Christ.... We ought to account ourselves knitted together by this bond of love, and live in the exercise of it, if we would have the comfort of being in Christ.
> We must delight in each other, make others conditions our own, rejoice together, mourn together, labor and suffer together, always having before our eyes, our community, as members of the same body.[3]

BIBLICAL ONENESS

Note the oneness of purpose and practice in Winthrop's early declaration. This oneness was rooted in righteous relationships which were rooted and grounded in Jesus Christ and His truth. There was no desire, direction or decision to achieve earthly unity apart from the Scriptures which bound them into the commonality of Christ who declared himself to be "the way, the truth and the life (John 14:6).

So great was that unifying holy purpose and practice that 200 years later, the secular French philosopher and observer, Alexis de Tocqueville, noted with amazement in his *Democracy in America*:

> In the United States the sovereign authority is religious, ...there is no country in the world where the Christian

religion retains greater influence over the souls of men than in America, and there can be no greater proof of its utility... than that its influence is powerfully felt over the most enlightened and free nation of the earth.[4]

EVOLUTIONARY ONENESS

Just 29 years after de Tocqueville penned *Democracy in America*, Charles Darwin released *The Origin of Species* in 1859, sowing the spiritual seeds of an alternative unity, defying the Creator and denying that man was made in God's image. Scientists embraced this alternative unity in Naturalism, lending to it an aura of authenticity to persuade the unsuspecting masses. Evolution thus became the unifying "creation doctrine" of the developing global alternative gospel.

"The survival of the fittest was quickly interpreted as an ethical precept that sanctioned cutthroat, economic competition, embraced by the most ruthless capitalist giants to justify their practices. Andrew Carnegie said in his autobiography that evolution came in like a light, because it not only eliminated the need for God, but it justified him in his business practices."[5] A century later, the same "survival of the fittest" philosophy had grown into massive multi-national corporations functioning as quasi world and regional governments, globalizing a new business bond, unifying the world in material "oneness."

Evolution became the unseen bond, facilitating the emerging world unity in virtually every sphere, whether political, scientific, social or religious... even material.

SOCIAL ONENESS

Into the growing spiritual vacuum of the soul, sweeping like a plague throughout the western world, as evolution sucked the god-image from man, came a new unifying alternative to the Creator's gospel of the soul. Freud's war against God meshed well with man having been cut loose from his Creator through evolution.

Humankind needed a new bond to unify socially. A new "acceptable" version of love was needed - SELF love. Through Freudian psychology, feelings replaced biblical faith and human experience replaced biblical truth. *Eros* and ***phileo*** love supplanted the selfless ***agape*** love of

Scripture. Oneness of feelings now progressively replaces oneness in biblical faith as experience trumps truth even in our churches. Psychology had become the unifying ethos of an emerging global social order where increasingly god-less men could embrace *feelings* as lord and *SELF* as king.

The church divorced the God of mercy from the God of truth, abandoning the fear of the Lord for the fear of man, thus baptizing the new psychologized "gospel" with the aura of a man-centered faith. Few can resist the universal secularization of feelings. The faith "once delivered to the saints " is being offered as a socially "spiritual" sacrifice on the altar of world peace to usher in the enticing era of global oneness. Unity born of feelings has been deemed vastly preferable in the emerging global culture to the "divisive" unity that sets people apart as followers of an exclusive truth in Christ that alone will make and keep men free (Jn. 8:31-32, Jn. 17:17-19).

POLITICAL ONENESS

Just as Israel, the "apple of God's eye" (Zech 2:8), was entering the prophetic birth canal to be re-born as a nation, the Deceiver sought to pre-empt the divine drama with an equally dramatic birth.

Pursuit of Peace and Prosperity

World War II had shaken the world. Germany had decimated the Jews. The nations were in despair and Europe was destroyed. And so the United Nations was founded to provide "world peace and security." Interestingly, the Hebrew word "Shalom" might be best translated "peace and security" or "security and prosperity." The divine plan was to send forth His anointed One, the Prince of Peace, to unify the "Israel of God," genuine believing Jews and Gentiles, into "one new man" in Christ," "so making peace" (Rom. 2:28-29, Rom. 9:4-8, Rom. 11:25-26, Eph. 2:12-22).

Satan's Counterfeit

But Satan seduced the nations with his own alternative peace plan. Unite the nations, contrary to God's express command, and let them build a global "tower" system that will reach heaven, or at least create man's best heaven on earth, thus "saving" the earth from the inevitable consequence of sinful rebellion. Unwittingly, history would repeat itself. The God-dispersed tower of Babel of Genesis 11 would now become global. The world would become **one**, under the Deceiver's direction, until its final destruction.

The United Nations was thus founded in 1945. One of its earliest official acts was to partition the land of Palestine, which God had eternally deeded to Israel, into two nations, one for the Jews and one for Arabs. The partition was to transpire in 1948. The Deceiver was deft in his direction: Divide Israel, which God decreed to be united as one, and unite the nations which God had commanded to separate. The divine penalty would be severe... ultimate divine judgment (Joel 3:1-2, Zech. 12:8-9). Israel was re-born May 14, 1948, and the world has been haunted for its division to this day, and will repeat that debacle.

Just as God would breathe life into the house of Israel (Ezek. 37:1-4), so Satan would breathe life into the unifying of the Gentile nations. Satan's counterfeit is nearing completion. Let us further trace Satan's historical tracks in our time and his deceptive plan for global dominion.

A Global Phenomena

From the ruins of World War II, a global phenomena began. Just as Israel began its phenomenal resurrection from historical obscurity in fulfillment of biblical prophecy on May 14, 1948, so Europe began a breathtaking rise to world prominence in 1951 with the establishment of the European Coal and Steel Community or "Common Market." Established by the Treaties of Rome in 1957 and 1958, the declared aim was to give Western Europe greater influence in world trade and economic affairs. By 1999, a single European currency, the Euro, was created, and now competes with the dollar for global acceptance.

The Maastrict Treaty of 1993 established the political entity known as the European Union. The renowned Roman Empire of antiquity faded into diverse peoples and countries from the Mediterranean to the Baltic and North Seas for 2000 years. As the curtain is drawn on the "church age," the countries now clamour to be included in the spectacular "resurrection" of "Rome." Twenty-seven nations, historically at enmity, now embrace as political "friends," all in pursuit of *security* and *prosperity* (shalom).

Never before in history has a nation, obliterated from its roots and dispersed to the four winds for two thousand years, been resurrected in its own land, as has Israel, against all social, political and economic odds. By contrast, never before in history have so many countries and peoples, now nearing 500 million, voluntarily come together in time of peace, as has the European Union. Said Jacques Delos, former head of the resurrecting "Rome," "We must hurry, History is waiting."

Prophecy is not waiting, but rather surging inexorably toward the Second Coming of Christ, God's promised "Prince of Shalom" (Isa. 9:6). In less than a generation of seventy years, the world has witnessed the rebirth of Israel, the "apple of God's eye," and the rebirth of "Rome," the Deceiver's counterfeit, merging the spirit of Egypt, the spirit of Babylon and the spirit of Rome into one global enterprise destined to declare dominion over the souls of men. Babel of Babylon (Gen. 11) is being rebuilt in men's hearts as "Mystery Babylon" (Rev. 17:5), just as the Kingdom of God, through the "Israel of God" is being given life through the hearts of men as the "Mystery of God" (Rev. 10:7).

The Reviving Roman Empire

The two kingdoms are coming into mortal and eternal conflict. Satan, as the "god of this world" (II Cor. 4:4), is drawing the peoples of this planet into godless oneness. In drafting the historic Treaty of Lisbon as the constitution for the reviving Roman Empire, the European Union elite refused even to recognize God, having embraced the godless antipathy of the French Revolution. Rather, this expanding union chose to declare its rebellion against the Creator by adopting symbols to set itself blatantly against Christ's coming kingdom.

The twelve stars of the European Union flag set themselves against Christ's twelve disciples and the twelve tribes of Israel. The Tower of Babel, through a variety of European posters and other depictions, displays open contempt for oneness in Christ, boldly declaring man's intent to unify for his own salvation. The European Parliament in Strasburg is even architecturally designed to visually replicate, with a modern flair, the ancient Tower of Babel.

A "Radical New Dream"

But the political rebuilding of "Rome" is not yet complete. The nations, observing the seeming phenomenal success of the European Union in such historically short order, are seeking to create similar regional unions throughout the world, all for *security* and *prosperity*. The goal is "global consciousness." The first transnational political entity in history, the "United States of Europe," represents "the rise of a new ideal that could eclipse the United States as focus for the world's yearnings for well-being and prosperity [shalom], declared Jeremy Rifkin in a profound editorial analysis.[6] Rifkin noted, as an American, "Yet our country is largely unaware of and unprepared for the vast changes that are quickly transforming the Old World and giving birth to the new European Dream." His words should grip the heart and soul of every Christian believer worldwide.

> The European Dream, with its emphasis on inclusivity, diversity, sustainable development, and interconnectedness is **the world's first attempt at creating global consciousness.**

Interestingly, it is precisely Barack Obama's open embrace of this vision that connected him so powerfully with America's youth and ingratiated him as a veritable "rock star" throughout the European continent, earning him the moniker of "messiah" by *Der Spiegel*, a German magazine.[7] Oprah Winfrey announced the Obama election as "a change in global consciousness." His presidential campaigning counterpart, John McCain, also embraced the new global vision, calling for creation of a new "League of Democracies" which its boosters argue, "would have not only the moral legitimacy but also the will to right the world's wrongs effectively"...[8] a utopian vision.

Columnist Jeremy Rifkin reveals the cataclysmic "change" that is enervating the vision of global-ism modeled by the New "European Dream," replacing the American Dream whose life support has been nearly severed from its original Godly roots. Europe now represents *peace* and *prosperity* to the world.

- Europe has the largest internal market in the world.
- The Euro has vied for superiority with the dollar.
- Europeans are the world's bankers, claiming 14 of the world's 20 largest commercial banks.
- Sixty-one of the 140 biggest companies on the Global Fortune 500 are European, while only 50 are U.S. Companies.
- The American homicide rate is four times that of Europe.
- Europeans provide 47 percent of the world's humanitarian assistance, the United States contributes 36 percent.

"Utopian as it sounds," notes Rifkin, "remember that 200 years ago, America's Founders created a new dream for humanity that transformed the world. Today, a new generation of Europeans is creating a radical new dream." "Romano Prodi, the President of the European Commission, has admitted that the EU's goal is to establish 'a superpower on the European continent that stands equal to the United States." When Prodi was asked to explain what he meant, Rifkin notes, "he spoke of the European vision as one of a new type of power... a new kind of superpower based on waging peace."[9]

Imitation as Flattery

It is said that imitation is the ultimate flattery. If that be so, the European Union, the resurrecting bones of the Roman Empire, stands profoundly flattered, for the entire world is in hot pursuit of "waging peace" to achieve *security* and *prosperity* (Shalom) by forming regional unions.

Most prominent, perhaps, has been the "Security and Prosperity Partnership" or SPP signed in secrecy by U.S. President George W. Bush with Mexican President Vincente Fox and Canadian Prime Minister Paul Martin in Waco, Texas on March 25, 2005. Although long publically denied, the North American Union to merge the United States, Mexico and Canada is well under way to emulate the European pursuit of *security* and *prosperity*, all without act of Congress.

On April 30, 2008, President George W. Bush signed the "Transatlantic Economic Integration" agreement between the U.S. and the European Union, citing the same ostensible economic purpose to which the rise of the European Union was attributed. Co-signatories included German Chancellor Angela Merkel, current president of the European Council, and European Commission President José Manuel Barroso. The United States became committed to a Transatlantic Common Market between the U.S. and the European Union by 2015, a period of seven years, without ratification of a treaty or act of Congress.[10]

This plan, being implemented by the White House with the aid of six U.S. senators and 49 congressmen as advisors, appears to follow a plan written in 1939 by a world government advocate who sought to create a Transatlantic Union as an international governing body. An economist from the World Bank agreed in print that the foundation of this Transatlantic Common Market "is designed to follow the blueprint of Jean Monnet, a key intellectual architect of the European Union," who admitted the true purposes of the Common Market were intentionally not disclosed to Europeans, intending rather that it lead inevitably from economic integration to political integration and a European superstate.[11]

Where will this process now end, and what are its implications not only for the world but for those who profess ultimate allegiance to Jesus Christ?

On February 1, 1992, then President Herbert Walker Bush, having over 200 times announced the coming New World Order, declared:

> It is the sacred principles enshrined in the UN Charter to which we will henceforth pledge our allegiance."

In 1993, President William Jefferson Clinton pushed congressional approval of NAFTA, the North American Free Trade Agreement and in 1995, CAFTA, the Central American Free Trade Agreement. These laid the foundation for George W. Bush's North American Union and an ultimate merger with the European Union.

The echo of these events continues to circle the earth. Even as this chapter was being written, the Mediterranean Union was announced, established July 13, 2008, to "form a bridge between Europe, North Africa and the Middle East." It was the brainchild of French President Nicholos Sarkozy, composed of 43 member nations. The Union committed to "peace, stability and security" (Shalom), was formed "to ensure the region's people could love each other instead of making war," emulating the European Union. Announcement was timed to coincide with the French presidency of the European Union. As *The Guardian* in Britain noted, "Sarkozy's big idea is to **use imperial Rome's centre of the world as a unifying factor,** linking 44 countries that are home to 800 million people."[12]

Now established or in process are the following global unions, some with overlapping nations:

European Union	27 nations	Actual
Mediterranean Union	43 nations	Actual
North American Union	3 nations	Formative
Trans Atlantic Union	30 nations	Formative
South American Union	12 nations	Actual
Central American Union	8 nations	Actual
Pacific Union	13 nations	Formative
Russia and Belarus Union	2 nations	Actual
Indian Union	25 states	Actual
African Union	53 nations	Actual
Central Asian Union	5 nations	Formative
South Asian Union	44 nations	Formative

The Anti-Gospel

Global governance is not a conspiracy theory but a confrontive truth. The "gospel" of global government and the unification of the world is secularly described as ***global-ism***. Its spiritual roots draw life not from trusting God's wisdom, grace and power but rather from mans' desire to sever dependance on his Creator and to depend upon mankind's "good nature" to do the right thing for the "common good," and hence save himself. It is the "anti-gospel" precisely because it denies mans' fundamental sinful condition necessitating a savior other than himself, shifting ultimate trust to the "arm of flesh," which brings a curse. (Jer. 17:5).

Israel, continuing her search to be like all the other nations (I Sam. 8:5-7), and to be included among them despite God's declaration they "shall not be reckoned among the nations" (Numb. 23:9), now seeks inclusion in the European Union and has just been received into the Mediterranean Union. Having rejected her Messiah, she continues to proclaim, "We have no king but Caesar" (Jn. 19:15), trusting the proffered *shalom* (security and prosperity) of man's systems rather than her Savior's sacrifice. And so a European Commissioner wrote in one of Israel's key daily newspapers, "We will also work with Israel to promote and uphold the values we share and which we believe hold the key to prosperity in Europe and everywhere else in the world."[13]

America, as a Gentile "New Canaan," has followed the path of Israel. Having progressively abandoned the God of her fathers and the fear of the Lord, she now fears man. Having lost actual trust in the Creator, she desperately clings to a motto, *In God We Trust*, that has become little more than a faded symbol and an empty mantra. The God who "made and preserved her a nation" had set her apart from all other nations, yet now, in growing fear, she seeks to wed herself to their pagan global enterprise for *shalom* (security and prosperity).

The Unbelief of False Trust

Both Jew and Gentile, "God has concluded them all in unbelief..." (Rom. 11:32). The rabbis of the Supreme Judicial Court of the Jewish People, the Sanhedrin, reconstituted in 2004 after nearly 2000 years of dispersion, have presented their "peace initiative." In a letter drafted in 70 languages to "all government institutions of the world," the rabbis warn that "the world is nearing a catastrophe" and that the "only way to bring peace among nations, states and religions is by building a house for God." The rabbis, having little seeming trust in God as their "I AM," call on "non-Jews to help the people of Israel fulfill their destiny and build the Temple, in order to prevent bloodshed across the globe."[14]

Nature abhors a vacuum. When our genuine trust in God and His Word wanes, Satan is quick to interject an alternative, inevitably shifting our focus from authentic faith to a fleshly counterfeit. Israel, as with the West and the western Gentile church, suffers from acute spiritual anemia. We are wide open for Satan's final spiritual deception. It has been well designed to entrap both Jew and Gentile, and its final manifestation is soon to be revealed for those who have an eye to see.

For the Jew, the Temple may well be the perfect trap, diverting trust from God's "Anointed One" to Satan's appointed one, the "Son of Perdition" who makes ingratiating promises as "the little horn" emerging from the "ten horns" of the resurrecting Roman Empire (Dan. 7:7-8). He will "speak great words against the most High, and shall even wear out the saints...", both Jew and Gentile (Dan. 7:19-25), once he gains power. The mere flattering promise of security and prosperity will be sufficient bait to ensnare and co-opt the trust of most Gentiles, for by the pursuit of peace this imposter will destroy many (Dan. 8:23-25).

Yet, for this latter-time trader in trust to gain global dominion so as to invite men to sacrifice their eternal souls for the promise of temporal peace and prosperity, Satan's global governmental "gospel" must become nearly universally embraced. Shockingly, even now, "Anyone Who Resists the EU Is A Terrorist" according to Italian President Giorgio Napolitano at a news conference. The German President, Horst Kohler, also present at the Siena conference, nodded in agreement.[15] But those broadly labeled "terrorist" today will be deemed "traitor" tomorrow. Just as with ancient Rome, the resurrecting end-time "Rome" will brook no opposition once enthroned.

How will such universal acceptance be achieved? What will win the mind and heart of the world to passionately embrace global-ism as the ultimate "gospel" for "peace on earth, goodwill toward man" (Luke 2:14)?

Will you recognize Satan's duplicity in the hour of deception? Or will you dance with the Deceiver, seduced by his offer of counterfeit *shalom*, packaged alluringly in religious robes calculated to convince all but those who "keep the commandments of God, and the faith of Jesus" (Rev. 14:12)? Is it not time to "prepare the way of the Lord" in your life and in the life of those in your sphere of influence so that you "may be able to withstand in the evil day" (Eph. 6:14)?

RELIGIOUS ONENESS

Massive spiritual deception is mounting as the final bridge, bidding pastors, priests, parishioners and parachurch leaders to cross over a worldly "Jordan" into a counterfeit "Promised Land" of global *security* and *prosperity* (Shalom). The rivers and rivulets of the world's religious isms are now combining to propel even professing Christians in the powerful currents of global "oneness" into the counterfeit Christ's new global order. As Jesus well warned, "if it were possible, they shall deceive the very elect" (Matt. 24:24).

We will pull back the curtain from what may be the final acts of this deceptive drama in the next chapter. Please prepare your mind and heart in an attitude of profound humility and prayer, for of necessity we must hereafter increasingly delve into delicate issues of doctrine and tradition that potentially impact destiny. Remember, if we are truly "in Christ," He must always trump culture and His truth must always trump our traditions.

Chapter Eighteen

Daring Thoughts
for *Deceptive Times*

1. Why do you think mankind has repeatedly sought to form global government despite God's command to disperse throughout the earth and despite His obvious displeasure with those at the Tower of Babel?

2. What is God's goal for ultimate government bringing "peace on earth?"

3. What, according to Daniel's prophecy, will be the final world government before the Messiah returns?

4. What is it about this time in history that is so unique as to cause Tony Blair to declare, "This is the moment to be seized?" What did President H. W. Bush mean when he boldly stated, "The new world is struggling to be born?"

5. How has the press for unity, both locally and globally, unwittingly caused pastors and people to play into the ungodly spirit of the emerging counterfeit satanic government, economy and religion?

6. Are you able to discern the difference between genuine oneness in Christ and the emerging counterfeit "oneness" movement?

7. Can you see how the promise of the New "European Dream" actually vied dramatically, luring the American heart in the Presidential election campaign of 2008, seducing vast numbers of American citizens into the waiting arms of socialistic global-ism, deftly offered to satisfy a longing hope for governmental salvation?

8. Why is *global-ism* the anti-gospel?

Chapter Nineteen

Mystery of the Woman

*"The angel said… I will tell thee
the mystery of the woman, and of the beast
that carrieth her…" (Rev. 17:7).*

THE **"PROPHET of HOPE"** is the unusual title ascribed to Dr. Robert Muller, former Assistant Secretary General of the United Nations. Dr. Muller has made it clear that world unity cannot be achieved simply through political unions and alliances. Such unity, according to Muller, requires a one-world religion.[1]

A Counterfeit Body

In his book, *New Genesis: Shaping a Global Spirituality*, Robert Muller reflects: "I would never have thought that I would discover spirituality in the United Nations…! Perhaps spirituality is a such a fundamental human need that it always reappears in one form or another in life and throughout history and we are about to witness now its renaissance in a global, planetary context."[2] In 1993, Dr. Muller delivered the historic Parliament of World Religion's first keynote address, calling for a "permanent institution" dedicated to pursuing religious unity.[3]

Dr. Muller believed we were entering "a new period of spiritual evolution," a period of rising planetary consciousness and global living which is expected to result in the perfect unity of the human family. Central to his theology are views of "a divine United Nations" and a "cosmic Christ." "If Christ came back to earth, his first visit would be to the United Nations to see if his dream of human oneness and brotherhood had come true," wrote Muller. "I often visualize," said Dr. Muller, "of a United Nations which would be the body of Christ."[4]

In every chapter of *New Genesis*, writes Gary H. Kah in his *The New World Religion*, Robert Muller calls for a U.N.-based world government and a new world religion "as the only answers to mankind's problems." "Through it all," notes Kah, "Muller maintains his status as a Catholic Christian," ultimately linking the U.N.'s mission to Roman Catholicism. Note well his passionate pseudo prophecy.

> Pope John Paul II said that we were the stone cutters and artisans of a cathedral which we might never see in its finished beauty.
> All this is part of one of the most prodigious pages of evolution. It will require the detachment and objectivity of future historians to appraise… the real significance of the United Nations.[5]

The de Chardin Connection

Pierre Teilhard de Chardin was born in France in 1881. Evolution was the passion of his life. As a Jesuit priest of the Catholic Church, Teilhard pursued his first love - blending the physical and spiritual worlds under the banner of evolution.[6] The "Christ" of de Chardin was not the Christ of the Gospels. For him, Christ had to fit into the theory of evolution. According to Teilhard's concept of evolution, God had not previously evolved enough to express himself through human consciousness. Chardin's process of evolution concludes with man becoming conscious of who he is - "God."[7]

"Christ is above all the God of Evolution," wrote de Chardin. "He is the supreme summit of the evolutionary movement... evolving into a Super-Christ. Humanity is the highest phase so far of evolution... beginning to change into a Super-Humanity... the Omega Point."[8] He is the most widely-read author of the New Age movement, and his ideas "gained acceptance among many Catholic leaders, including Pope John Paul II."[9]

Father Teilhard de Chardin influenced most of the prominent United Nations leaders of his day. Norman Cousins, former president of the World Federalist Association, made the connection, writing in the Forward to Robert Muller's autobiography...

> Whatever the uncertainties of the future may be... oncoming generations will need living examples of the conspiracy of love that Teilhard de Chardin has said will be essential to man's salvation. Robert Muller is involved in such a conspiracy."[10]

Muller, in *New Era Magazine*, made the final connection, saying, "It is necessary that we have a World Government centered on the United Nations." ... we can credit the coming World Government to the 'influence of the writings of Tielhard de Chardin'."[11]

Bringing all the world's religions into cooperation with the United Nations was Robert Muller's top priority. "My great personal dream," he explained, "is to get a tremendous alliance between all the major religions and the U.N.". Muller, in 1997, exulted, "... during the 50th Anniversary of the United Nations... we launched again the idea of United Religions... and a meeting... to draft and give birth to a United Religions.... I will be the father of the United Religions."[12]

The March of Inter-Faith Ecumenism

Even as the vision for uniting the nations through a common religion advances through the United Nations, the systematic spirit of interfaithism and ecumenism is marching lock step to the spiritual drumbeat of a deceptive "unity" movement worldwide. The cry of "UNITY" in our churches, cities and throughout the various religious expressions globally, as well as through a variety of governmental and (NGO) Non-governmental yet quasi-governmental structures, is in itself becoming a common voice and unifying mantra.

It is profoundly seductive, for who, in the current market of polit-ically-correct ideas, desires or even dares to resist the tide. And where is the deceptive danger?

Exchanging trust in the truth of God's revealed Word for trust in man's experience and relationships is becoming the new model of "Christian" ecumenism. It is subtle and it is seductive. To break down walls of division, the new approach is to ignore divine proposition in favor of personal testimony. As Cecil "Mel" Robeck of Fuller Seminary, an Assemblies of God minister said, "We will not get embroiled in dis-putes involving scripture or homosexuality because it "would have the potential to derail our effort."[13]

Cecil Robeck is on a 12-member committee for Global Christian Forum. The *Christian Century* reported, "After keeping a low profile for several years, advocates of a fresh approach to ecumenism are going public...." "About 240 leaders from the Vatican, World Evangelical Alliance, Orthodox Churches, historic Anglican and Protestant communions, and Pentecostal and independent churches" gathered November 6-9, 2007, for the Global Christian Forum, to advance the new approach based on "per-sonal testimony." Just one month earlier, Cardinal Avery Dulles admitted the potential for harmonizing doctrines was exhausted, necessitating "an ecumenism of mutual enrichment by means of personal testimony."[14]

"How then can Christian unity be envisaged?" asked Cardinal Dulles. Testimony must trump truth so as to build trust in man. As Dulles declared, "Our words, they may find, carry the trademark of truth."[15] We would do well to remember the warning of the Psalmist.

It is better to trust in the Lord than to put confidence in man.
It is better to trust in the Lord than to put confidence in princes
[pastors, priests, popes and presidents] (Ps. 118:8-9).

Once again, this false unity movement requires that you spiritu-ally dance with the devil, the very Deceiver himself. Remember, there is a great eternal battle between Satan and God for the souls of men.

Satan seeks to seduce your soul from the faithful trust and allegiance to *HaShem*, the one true God, and His Son, *Yeshua*, Jesus Christ.

Jesus, the "Anointed One," the Meshiach, the Holy one of Israel, is the "express image" of God's person, "upholding all things by the word of his power." He declared, "I and my Father are one" (Jn. 10:30). He said, "He that hath seen me hath seen the Father" (Jn. 14:9). And Yeshua also said, "I am *the* way, *the* truth, and *the* life: no man cometh to the Father but by me" (Jn. 14:6). Jesus made clear that the only true unity pleasing to God was that which is the fruit of being *sanctified* or set apart through God's truth as found in the Scriptures. It was this unity "through the truth" that would cause the rest of the world to "believe that thou has sent me" and would display God's glory as true followers of Yeshua (Christ) became "one" even as Yeshua was one with the Father (Jn. 17:16-23). Never forget! It is our trust in the truth of God's Word that binds us in biblical oneness. Anything else is a counterfeit, however attractive it may appear and however broadly it may be embraced. We are *in* the world, but not *of* it.

Yet interfaith-ism and ecumenism march on to a louder and more incessant drumbeat. The Third Parliament of the World's Religions met in December, 1999, in South Africa, with 6000 delegates from more than 200 different religious groups. Catholic theologian, Hans Küng, said he maintains a "horizon of hope" that the 21st century might witness "unity among churches, peace among religions, and community among nations."[16]

The most ambitious organization in today's interfaith movement has been the United Religions Initiative (URI), founded by William Swing, the Episcopal bishop of California. Although this movement is little known to the public, "it now provides a spiritual face for globalization, the economic and political forces leading from nationalism to a one-world system," says Lee Penn, an investigative reporter. The interfaith movement "is no longer... a coterie of little-heeded religious idealists..." he says. "The URI's proponents range from billionaire George Soros to President George W. Bush, from the far-right Rev. Sun Myung Moon to liberal Catholic theologian Hans Küng, and from the Dalai Lama to the leaders of governmental-approved Protestant churches in China."[17] Penn warns in his *False Dawn* that the United Religions

Initiative and the interfaith movement are poised to become the spiritual foundation of the New World Order - the "new civilization" now proposed by Mikhail Gorbachev, the last leader of the Soviet Union.[18]

A Geo-Political Struggle

We dare not lose sight of the global context in which the accelerating move toward ecumenism and interfaith-ism is taking place. To do so runs the risk of being assimilated into a compromised faith system that is sucking an unsuspecting and naive world into a deception from which few will be delivered. What is truly at stake is a massive geo-political struggle for governance of the earth in which religious faith is but a pawn. Again, it is mankind's rebellious pursuit of a counterfeit peace or *shalom* outside of the true claims of Yeshua, Jesus the Christ.

Illustrative of this geo-political struggle is the historic battle between the Vatican and Russia, in which Russia symbolizes a *secular* vision and the Vatican a *spiritual* vision for a New World Order. Each, however, utilizes the counterpart, whether spiritual or secular, to achieve its long-term objective of global dominance.

Under Vladimir Putin, the Russian Orthodox Church was exalted to near unprecedented favor, with Putin having to kiss the ring of the reigning archbishop. Secular power embraced religious power in pursuit of global dominance. Moscow, thus empowered and supported by massive petrol dollars, signaled its "place in the new world order."[19]

Seeking global influence, Vladimir Putin declared Russia "Defender of the Islamic World," thus uniting the world's greatest concentration of oil and gas production and reserves in an embrace of Islam, the goal of which is world domination.[20]

The Vatican had earlier moved to neutralize the clearly growing wedding of Russian Orthodoxy to Russian nationalism being parlayed into global power. Pope John Paul II, seeing Russia as the greatest opposition to ultimate Vatican objectives, did everything he could to romance the Russian Orthodox Church back into the fold of Rome after a 1000 year schism. As of July, 2008, the Archbishop of Moscow said to Pope Benedict XVI, "the right conditions do not yet exist for Pope Benedict to visit Russia." "He needs an explicit invitation."[21]

Looking back to the time of the fall of the Iron Curtain and the dissolution of the Soviet Union by Mikhail Gorbachev, Vatican insider, Malachi Martin noted that "These two men [Gorbachev and John Paul II] are the only two among world leaders who not only head geopolitical institutions but have geopolitical aims. Geopolitics is their business." But, observed Martin, "for the vast majority of onlookers and for many in government… the gargantuan change being effected in the shifting ground escapes them." Malachi Martin called Gorbachev and Pope John Paul II "Forces of the 'New Order': The Two Models of a Geopolitical House."[22]

The Vatican - " A Geopolitical House"

"The newest game in the City of Man," declared Vatican insider Malachi Martin in *The Keys of This Blood*, "is the building of a geopolitical structure. Everyone who is anyone in terms of sociopolitical and economic power is engaging in it… and ultimately… all nations, great and small, will be involved. It is the millennium endgame." But where does the Vatican fit? Why would a Vatican insider be talking so seriously about geopolitics? Most people undoubtedly think of religion when they hear words like *Vatican* and *Pope*. What then is the geo-political connection?

According to Malachi Martin, since the start of his pontificate in October 1978, Pope John Paul II was a consummate geopolitician. "He heralds a new and as yet unrecognized force in the geopolitics of nations, a force that he actually claims, will be the ultimate and decisive factor determining the new world order." He further notes, "… there are no other feasible ways of rationalizing this Pope's performance on the world stage." "His Holiness has assiduously carved out for himself an international profile" which "no pope ever did on a like scale. Nor has any human being known in history attempted it."[23]

During his Pontificate, John Paul II visited 130 countries, establishing personal relationships with governmental leaders in most of them. He invited representatives of 100 of the world's largest religions to join him in Italy for the ultimate multicultural, religious-pluralistic prayer meeting, directing prayers to over 300 million gods. He was the most traveled Pope in history. He even re-established relations with Israel after 2000 years of rejection, resulting in the first official visit by an Israeli head of state to the Vatican seat of Roman Catholicism.

Vatican City is not just the locus of Roman Catholicism but is an independent state. The Vatican is "considered among the nations" whereas God declared Israel "shall not be reckoned among the nations" (Num. 23:9) and that true followers of Christ would be as "strangers and pilgrims" on the earth (I Pet. 2:11).

The Vatican lies within Rome, Italy, and is the world's smallest state, having no commerce of its own. As a sovereign state, it has its own flag, currency and postal system. It has diplomatic relations with most of the nations of the earth. The Pope, as "Bishop of Rome" known as the "VICAR of Christ," has absolute legislative, executive and judicial power, the ultimate merger of church and state. He resides in the largest and grandest palace in the world with 1400 rooms, while Christ himself had no place to lay his head (Matt. 8:20).

John Paul II was the only Pope in history to actually call for a New World Order. A CNN news release from VATICAN CITY January 1, 2004, is instructive.

> Pope John Paul II rang in the New Year with a renewed call for peace... and the **creation of a new world order** based on respect for the dignity of man and equality among nations.... He stressed that to bring about peace, there needs to be a new respect for international law and the **creation of a "new international order" based on the goals of the United Nations.**[24]

It should come as no surprise that upon the death of Pope John Paul II, 4 million pilgrims and 100 heads of state gathered in Rome to mourn, surrounding hundreds of scarlet-clad cardinals and bishops shown surrounding a golden, crucified Christ. He had ingratiated himself and the smallest of all states to the world for a generation, wooing all faiths and political powers to come under papal authority.

But why did Pope John Paul II wait for 25 years before announcing his clear embrace of a "New World Order?" Perhaps the only real answer why John Paul II took this opportune moment to declare the New World Order as his objective is that the world stands at the threshold of the appearance of the first "beast" of Revelation, a beast "having seven heads and ten horns… and upon his heads the name of blasphemy" (Rev. 13:1-8).

Rise of the Beast

The Scripture makes clear that a "beast," as used metaphorically in both Old and New Testaments, refers to a political kingdom or power. The prophet Daniel's great vision of the world's kingdoms portrayed them as "four great beasts." The fourth and last beast was "dreadful and terrible, and strong exceedingly… it was diverse (different) from all the beasts that were before it; and it had ten horns." Out of these ten horns or governing powers came a "little horn" that would rule through the others, using their consolidated global power. This "little horn" had "eyes like a man," "a mouth speaking great (pompous) things," and will ultimately speak blasphemous things about God and Yeshua, His Son, wearing out the true saints, and even changing divine times and laws (Dan 7). These "ten horns" envisioned by Daniel would appear to be the same "ten horns" described in Revelation 13:1-8 and Revelation 17. Scholars almost universally identify that fourth and final "beast" in Daniel's vision as the Roman Empire.

RESURRECTING THE *PAX ROMANA*

The Roman Empire never fully "died." Just as with Israel, in its prosperity it was greatly weakened and decayed internally, incapable of resisting its enemies. Its citizens were, in effect, dispersed (as it was with Israel) throughout the then-known world, having largely lost their Roman identity. But the emergence of "Rom-ance" languages and Roman-esque laws, and culture and architecture over the centuries that spread throughout the European continent revealed the Roman root.

Eventually that Roman root spread across the Atlantic and Pacific to the Americas, revealed largely in laws, government, language and culture… and even in religious practices. The *Pax Romana* or "Roman Peace" was, two millennia later, identified as the *Pax Americana*. English became the lingua franca (common language) of the western world, indeed of the entire earth. America, with her glorious eagle wings spread, had become the reigning "Roman" superpower with a Roman capital and a Roman government seeking to export a Roman democracy to an ever expanding Roman world to bring a Roman "peace on earth." Yet in her prosperity, she also progressively abandoned the Prince of Peace, the only true source of **shalom** (security and prosperity). And as with ancient Israel and Rome, she also began a precipitous internal decay. As her moral and spiritual foundations crumble, fear and fragmentation grow even as her citizens and "caesars" pump their chests in Roman pride. And so America's President, George W. Bush, in the waning days of his presidency, reached for security and prosperity from the new and rising Roman star, the European Union,[25] envisioned as the pulpit from which the new counterfeit gospel of Satan's false Roman peace will be preached as "man's last best hope of earth."

PLEA for PROPHETIC PERSPECTIVE

A bird's-eye view or heavenly top-view perspective on earthly history reveals valuable prophetic insights not otherwise apparent on this plane of casual life experience. By analogy, it may appear like a chess game being played in three dimensions at once. That may already have become apparent, but if not, it is necessary to point out that in the "end game" of geopolitics compounded by religious objectives, the actual significance or prophetic connection of historical events may not be superficially apparent or even recognizable for centuries. Deception for many arises in failure or refusal to "connect the dots" biblically.

As we complete this chapter, our difficulty, in very limited space, will be to translate, in distilled fashion, the vast historical and more recent information available in an attempt to convey the convergence of geopolitics in pursuit of a new Roman global government with the pursuit of a unified global religion that is preparing to usher in and undergird the New World Order that will set itself "against the Lord, and against his anointed" (Ps. 2:2).

Many without prophetic perspective will be seduced to swim in the surging stream of global-ism and of interfaith-ism, caught up in its politically-correct euphoria, unaware that deception is leading them to destruction. But those who are truly "looking for that blessed hope, and the glorious appearing of the great God and our Savior Jesus Christ" will "purify themselves even as he is pure" (Tit. 2:13; I Jn. 3:3).

E PLURIBUS UNUM

E Pluribus Unum is a Latin phrase out of ancient Rome meaning "Out of Many, One." It was proposed by Franklin, Jefferson and Adams in 1776 as a motto for the United States. It first appeared on the Great Seal of the U.S. in 1782 and has continually appeared on America's coins. However, the official motto of the United States is "In God We Trust."

The original settlers on American shores sought to display the kingdom of God as described in the Bible in living color. What Israel had failed to do, they intended to complete for God's glory until Christ's return. Many were joined together from the European continent for one holy purpose – to spread the gospel of Jesus Christ across the seven seas and seven continents, as described in their founding documents. That vision gave rise to a secular dream... the American Dream, magnetizing mankind everywhere. As prosperity multiplied, trust in God waned. Discipling people to obey the commands of the Master was exchanged for an increasingly godless democracy worshiping at the feet of the Market. For the last generation, America has exported to the world the salvation power of democracy bowing to the Market. Lamentably, that model has become our global legacy.

As with Israel, God called America to be separate for His glory, and blessed her with power and prosperity. But as with Israel's abandonment of obedience to God in her prosperity, so it is with America. She now joins the world system with vigor and vengeance and is preparing to pass the baton to the new rising star modeling unity for the emerging global order.

"The POST-AMERICAN WORLD" was *NEWSWEEK's* shocking cover story May 12, 2008. "Over the last 20 years, globalism has been gaining depth and breadth," writes Fareed Zakaria. "To bring others into the world, the United States needs to make its own commitment to the system clear." "For America to continue to lead the world, we will have to first join it," he notes. He closed the article with this painful observation: "… when historians write about these times, they might note that by the turn of the 21st century, the United States had succeeded in its great, historical vision – globalizing the world."[26] Having abandoned our unity "Under God," we have sown the seeds of a false trust. We have exchanged our divine call of globally preaching the "Great Commission" for a mess of globalizing material "pottage." The baton of leadership is being passed.

The European Union now models the new global mantra. "Unity in diversity" is the motto of the European Union. According to the EU website, the motto means that Europeans are "united in working together for peace and prosperity."

Notice the continual recurrence of the words "peace and prosperity" or "security and prosperity." These have become the marketing mantra for the coalescing of nations in pursuit of global government. God desires that we enjoy *peace and prosperity* in pursuit of Him. When we seek the fruit without the root of righteousness in Christ, it becomes idolatrous.

When men or nations collectivize themselves in idolatrous pursuit, rejecting God's governance, God rejects them and despises their efforts as open and notorious violation of the first three of the Ten Commandments. That is what brought God's judgment on the builders of Babel and what will bring His judgment on Europe's end-time effort to "union-ize" the world into a godless democracy.

Godless unionizing of the world is an act of collective rebellion against the rule of the Creator. And that is why the European Union, in establishing its constitution, refused to even give God a polite "goodbye" or "au revoir", refusing even to recognize His name in a historical sense or to acknowledge Him or the Christian faith in historically "Christian" Europe.

FROM CONSTANTINE TO CHARLEMAGNE

In order to understand the European Union's prophetic role today, it is necessary to recall Europe's papal past. This becomes a sensitive matter for those raised within or currently embracing the Roman Catholic Church and its Vatican governance through absolute papal authority and the "Holy See." Yet to remain pure and escape the seductive snare being laid for your soul, it cannot be avoided. Please read prayerfully rather than through the lens either of tradition or of political correctness. We are about to pull back the curtain, beginning the final ACT of an unfolding historical drama that will reveal the Deceiver's choreography of a masterful counterfeit to deceive the nations and consign the seduced masses to eternal perdition. It will lead us to solve the "Mystery of the Woman."

We begin this final dramatic ACT by looking back over the shoulder of history to the ancient Roman Empire. But before we begin this fascinating journey, we can gain perspective by re-visiting a most recent dramatic and historic event – the founding of the Mediterranean Union July 13, 2008.

Nicolas Sarkozy, the French president who conceived the concept for the Mediterranean Union in the womb of his Roman mind, declared its birth just as he began his presidency of the European Union, hosting an "unprecedented gathering of leaders from Europe and all sides of the Mediterranean."[27] The summit's participants committed themselves to "peace, stability and security" with "the same goal and the same method" as the European Union.[28] *The Guardian* from Britain noted: "Sarkozy's big idea is to **use imperial Rome's centre of the world as a unifying factor** linking 44 countries that are home to 800 million people."[29]

Let us now fasten the seat belts of our chariots and return to ancient Rome whose *Pax Romana* promised peace, stability and security (shalom) to the world just as God's "Prince of Peace was being born.

In 63BC, Julius Caesar, who had been elected *Pontifex Maximus*, became emperor of Rome and vested the governmental office of Roman emperor with ultimate priestly powers. From that time forward, the title *Pontifex Maximus*, which had been used solely among the pagan priesthood, was appropriated by the Roman Caesars. The Caesars not only merged the role of supreme governmental ruler with that of supreme religious leader (Pontiff), but also claimed to be deity or god in the flesh and were worshiped as such.

In 376 AD, Gratian became the first Roman Emperor to refuse the idolatrous title of *Pontifex Maximus* and presented that role to the Bishop of Rome. By this time, Roman bishops had gleaned substantial political power, and in 378 AD, Bishop Damasus was elected *Pontifex Maximus*, the first pope in history to bear the title. All the pomp and ceremony that had characterized Rome's pagan worship was imported into the Roman version of Christianity.

Historian Will Durant in *Caesar and Christ* succinctly describes the transfer of the power of Rome's decaying government to the increasingly politically powerful Roman version of the Christian Church.

> The Roman See increased its power.... Its wealth and ecumenical charities exalted its prestige.
> By the middle of the third century, the position and resources of the papacy were so strong that Decius vowed he would rather have a rival emperor at Rome than a pope. The capitol of the Empire became the capitol of the [Roman Catholic] Church.
> Rome absorbed a dozen rival faiths and entered into Christian synthesis. It was not merely that the Church took over some religious customs and forms common in pre-Christian Rome – the stole and other vestments of pagan priests, the use of incense and holy water, the burning of candles... the worship of the saints... the law of Rome as the basis of canon law, the title of *Pontifex Maximus* for the Supreme Pontiff, and... the Latin language as the enduring vehicle of Catholic ritual.[30]

Durant, in concluding his history of the growth of the Roman Catholic Church, makes secular observations that have had profound spiritual implications echoing down to this fulcrum moment of world history. He notes that "as secular failed," Roman government "became the structure of ecclesiastical rule." Consider well his concluding remark and its implications for our time.

> The Roman Church followed in the footsteps of the Roman state; it conquered the provinces, established discipline and unity from frontier to frontier. Rome died in giving birth to the [Roman Catholic] Church; the Church... inheriting and accepting the responsibilities of Rome.[31]

The prophetic pattern emerging from the merger of political and spiritual authority in the pope is best captured in the lives of two emperors, Constantine and Charlemagne.

Constantine is credited with declaring Christianity to be the official religion of the Roman realm. In the Edict of Milan, he granted toleration to all religions and increasingly showed favor to Christians, "But as the Roman empire became Christian, Christianity in turn became imperially Roman."[32]

Despite his ostensible "conversion" to Christianity, Constantine was a consummate politician deeply rooted in a pervasively pagan empire. "He treated the bishops as his political aides; he summoned them, presided over their councils, and agreed to enforce whatever opinion their majority should formulate," observed Will Durant. "A real believer would have been a Christian first and a statesman afterward; with Constantine it was the reverse. Christianity was to him a means, not an end. "Constantine's support of Christianity was worth a dozen legions to him...."[33]

"Constantine aspired to an absolute monarchy; such a government would profit from religious support," noted Durant in *Caesar and Christ*. "Perhaps that marvelous organization of bishops and priests could become an instrument of pacification, , unification and rule."[34] Perhaps, as we await the return of Christ, the visionaries of global government will again utilize the power of the Roman church to gain and authenticate power for a resurrected "Rome." Constantine, while claiming to be a "Christian," maintained the pagan title of *Pontifex Maximus*. His coins were inscribed: "SOL INVICTO COMITI" (Committed to the Invisible Sun). During his reign, Constantine blended pagan worship with worship of the Creator, ordering the Roman realm and the Roman Church to change the biblical Sabbath of the Fourth Commandment so that all would worship "on the venerable day of the Sun," Sunday.

In a powerful sense, surrounded by a profound aura of mystery, Rome never truly expired in 476 AD as often written in the obituaries of nations. Rather, Rome was revived in 800 AD when Pope Leo III, in desperation, fled to Charlemagne for protection. On Christmas Day, with Charlemagne at Rome, Pope Leo III crowned Charlemagne emperor of the Holy Roman Empire. He was the first in a line of emperors that continued for the next one thousand years.

And that vision was revived under Pope John Paul II, the "geo-political" pope, throughout his papacy from 1978 to his death in 2005 AD. The world's near universal obeisance and adulation at his Vatican state funeral by Protestant, Catholic, Hindu, Buddhist and a hundred other faiths revealed that the scarlet-robed bishops led by the *Pontifiex Maximus* ruled a global "Roman" world. As the *BBC News* noted, it was "history's largest funeral," attended by millions and broadcast world-wide to billions. The then leader of the free world, George W. Bush, eulogized the pope as "a hero of the ages."

Indeed, as Nigel Rodgers notes in *Roman Empire,* "The Catholic Church, with its hierarchy and universalist ambitions, is the most obvious inheritor of ancient Rome."[35]

All Roads Lead to Rome

A British newspaper headline read, "Pope declares EC (European Community) heaven sent." In 2004 AD, Pope John Paul II began the process of canonization for Konrad Adenauer, Alaide de Gasperi and Robert Schuman, founders of the European Union. Indeed it is "extraordinary" for a politician to be canonized, declared the Catholic newspaper, *The Tablet. The Daily Telegraph* quoted one attending the canonization synod as saying, "The European Union is a design not only of human beings but of God." He added that the canonization of the politicians would show that the European Union was "built on a rock,"[36] the very biblical words used to describe the pre-figured Christ of God.

Why the historical and accelerating role of the Roman Catholic Church in global political matters? Why did Pope John Paul II make history with his journeys to 130 nations and the building of connections with heads of state worldwide. What are the goals of the smallest nation-state, the Vatican, and its *Pontifex Maximus*, increasingly seeking to merge the religious role with political power? Indeed, it appears that all roads are leading inexorably to Rome, setting the stage for the great apocalyptic showdown between a prostituted religious power and the global political powers that pimp her for personal gain until she is cast away in disdain.

The Treaty of Rome in 1957 established the European Economic Community now known as the European Union. In 2004, the European

Parliament presented to the member states of the EU the text of a proposed constitution to be ratified. EU leaders agreed in Brussels that the constitution should be officially adopted in Rome in November 2004; if ratified by all member countries, an event not far off, it will replace the Treaty of Rome (1957).

Also in 2004, the Vatican received additional political power as a representative of the United Nations. Rome now has the right to be heard at the UN General Assembly.

The Vatican sees its role in the United Nations as essential to fulfill its geopolitical ambitions. The UN sees the pope as the world's greatest "moral leader" to persuade global citizens of the glories of the New World Order. Each needs the other. The matter of religion in the global scheme is taking "front row-center." In his final address before the U.N. General Assembly September 21, 2006, Secretary General Kofi Annan warned of a "new war of religion on a global scale" and declared only the United Nations can solve the world's problems.

Israel has become complicit. President Moshe Katsav visited Pope Benedict XVI at the Vatican on November 17, 2005. It was the first official visit by an Israeli head of state to the seat of Roman Catholicism after John Paul II had recognized Israel for the first time in history. Israel, as with the world's nations, fears catastrophe and seeks global religious union. On February 19, 2006, *Arutz Sheva*, Israeli National News, delivered this news brief:

> Israel's Ashkenazi chief rabbi, Yonah Metzger, meeting with the Dalai Lama, a Buddhist monk... suggested that representatives of the world's religions establish a United Nations in Jerusalem, representing religions instead of nations, like the UN currently based in New York.
> "Instead of planning for nuclear war... it will invest in peace," Metzger said.
> Also at the meeting was Chief Sephardic Rabbi Shlomo Amar, Rabbi David Rosen of the American Jewish Committee (who is on good terms with the Roman Catholic Church), Rabbi Menachem Froman of Tekoa, Ethiopian rabbis and various Islamic sheikhs.[37]

The Woman Rides the Beast

In the 1990's, unusual biblical symbolism began to appear throughout Europe. Britain issued a stamp to commemorate the European Parliamentary elections. The stamp depicted a woman riding a beast. Paintings and statues of the woman and the beast appeared in official Brussels' circles and on a poster. A mural of the woman and the beast even decorated the Brussels' airport lounge.

"The woman on the beast is now the official picture of the EU," according to Rev. Dr. Ian Paisley, a Northern Ireland minister who was also a member of both the Westminster and European parliaments. He said that when the multibillion dollar new parliament building in Brussels, Belgium, was completed, at the end of where the parliament meets is a dome. On the dome is a colossal painting, three times life size, of the woman riding the beast.

In Strasburg, France, the rival new headquarters of the parliament, designed like the Tower of Babel, is a painting of a naked woman riding the beast. When designs for the new Euro coin were unveiled, there was the woman riding the beast on the back of the Greek euro-coin. In 1992 a German ECU coin was issued showing Europa and the beast. In the new Brussels building of the Council of Europe is a bronze statue of the woman riding the beast.

A United Airlines' pocket-seat magazine contained this headline in German, "Good morning, Europe." The article began with these words.

> This May, a daring picture appeared on the cover of *Der Spiegel*, one of Europe's most prestigious news magazines: a pitch black bull, horns lowered, charging straight at the reader. On its back sat a young woman draped in dark blue cloth and waving the blue flag of a United Europe. The cover was a delight for European readers since the woman was the very popular French supermodel Laetitia Casto, who had also recently been selected as the "Marianne 2000" in France - the feminine personification of the French Revolution...[38]

According to tradition, Europa is the Great Goddess, mother of the European continent. According to mythology, Zeus, also known in Rome as Jupiter, fell in love with Europa, the beautiful daughter of a Phoenician king. He seduced her attention by assuming the form of a white bull. When she sat on his back, he whisked her away, returned to his normal form, and she bore him three sons. This supreme deity of mythology also bore other names including *Pater* (father) and *Soter* (Savior).

All this may be fascinating history, but why should we be concerned about mythological figures even if they have been adopted for the identity of the resurrecting Roman Empire? The reason is simple. The Bible gives specific description and warning concerning a woman sitting upon such a beast which figuratively depicts the merging of religious power and political power ushering in the grand finale of Satan's deceptive drama of the ages. Shockingly, the final ACT of this drama is now happening before our eyes, and most, whether rich or poor, and regardless of status, race, color or religion, are predisposed to embrace the coming counterfeit salvation offered by a false "Christ" bearing false promises of *security* and *prosperity*. What, then, has God said concerning this mystery woman? The answers are found in the book of Revelation, chapter 17.

MYSTERY OF THE WOMAN

Revelation 17 and 18 are perhaps the most explicit prophetic chapters of Scripture. They may also be the most dramatic. The sheer scope of their historical applications and prophetic implications is breathtaking as well as heart-rending.

God despises "whoredom." God actually "hated" Esau because he prostituted his birthright for a mess of temporal pottage (Mal. 1:1-6, Rom. 9:13, Gen. 28:7-9). He ultimately dispersed Israel, the "apple of his eye," throughout the nations because of her spiritual whoredoms (Jer. 3:1-3). Our Creator is pure and holy. He despises those who, for personal or institutional gain, will compromise their principles. He hates those who will exchange eternal favor and power with God for temporal favor and power with man. Consequently, when the Scripture speaks of a "great whore," we should universally take notice.

THE GREAT WHORE

According to Revelation 17:1-2, this *whore* is like no other in the spiritual monstrosity of her prostitution. She is a "great" whore! And she sits on "many waters." The sheer magnitude of her influence and those with whom she has prostituted herself are global. Both the kings and political power brokers of earth as well as the world's common inhabitants are dramatically affected by her spiritual fornication and have become, in one way or another, complicit in it.

A WOMAN of SCARLET and PURPLE

The great whore of Revelation 17 is "arrayed in purple and scarlet" and "decked with gold and precious stones…," "having a golden cup in her hand." The cup is "full of abominations and filthiness of her fornication" (vs. 4).

MOTHER of HARLOTS

This "great whore" is not content with her own prostituted life and ways but seeks to birth others who will likewise prostitute themselves as she, so that she can bring them in under her mothering wings, claiming them as her own. She is "THE MOTHER OF HARLOTS." Her home is also the seedbed, supply center, and seductive cover of "ABOMINATIONS OF THE EARTH," all under the cover of "sainthood" (vs. 5).

PERSECUTOR of TRUE SAINTS

The "Mother of Harlots" fiercely protects her global prostitution ring and will brook no opposition. True saints cannot be tolerated, since the true gospel light of their lives shines into the dark corner, revealing the shocking spiritual debauchery characterizing the "Great Whore's" prostitution system. Persecution of true saints is inevitable for the Mother of Harlots to maintain the global spiritual brothel that decks her with "gold and precious stones" and vast wealth. Throughout history, she has become "drunken with the blood of the [true] saints, and with the blood of the martyrs of Jesus" (vs. 6).

She is a great mystery. The political leaders and peoples of the planet stand in amazement, "with great admiration" at her immense earthly power and glory (vs. 6). They seek her influence, long for her prosperity and lust for her power, The Whore needs them, but they need her. Can this brothel relationship persist indefinitely, or will one prevail?

The Woman and the Beast

The Great Whore sits upon "a scarlet colored beast, full of the names of blasphemy, having seven heads and ten horns" (vs. 3). These ten horns or powers would appear to be the same "ten horns" spoken of by the prophet Daniel in describing the "fourth beast" and final world empire, Rome (Daniel 7:7-25). Just as Rome seemed to rise triumphant, fall into obscurity, and now resurrect with astonishing vitality, so the world is wondering with amazement at the dramatic rise of the European Union now merged with the Mediterranean Union which the nations now regionally strive to emulate. It is "the beast that was, and is not, and yet is" (Rev. 17:8).

Here is "the mystery of the woman, and of the beast that carrieth her" (Rev. 17:7). This "mystery" is made historically and prophetically manifest to those with an eye to see; an ear to hear; and with a mind, heart and will to understand. Please contemplate with conviction of heart and conscience the inherent warning of this prophetic passage:

> *...they that dwell on the earth shall wonder, whose names were not written in the book of life from the foundation of the world, when they behold the beast that was, and is not, and yet is (Rev. 17:8).*

The Beast

The beast that carries the woman is something to behold. It will captivate the entire world, the overwhelming majority of the earth's population. It is a global political or governmental system "which hath seven heads and ten horns" (verse 7). The "ten horns" are component governmental powers that give global governing power to "the beast" which is the fourth and final world empire (Dan. 7:16-25). The ten horns are "ten kings" (governing authorities) which have not had ongoing historical existence but rise throughout the earth in the final season ushering in the end of the age, and they receive power one hour (a short time) with the beast." "These have one mind, and shall give their power and strength to the beast" (Rev. 17:12-13).

The spirit and purpose of this beast that carries the woman is not only secular but in serious rebellion against God, having declared evolution as the "creator" so as to vacate all vestiges of divine dominion. All who truly submit to the God of Creation, in obedience to His Word and commandments, and who walk faithfully in the spirit and truth of Jesus, Yeshua the Messiah, will be seriously persecuted, as they were in ancient Rome, in the beast's "war with the Lamb" (Rev. 17:14, 14:12, Dan. 7:21). But "he that shall endure unto the end, the same shall be saved" (Matt. 24:13).

The mushrooming power of "the beast" and of the "ten horns" from whence it receives power are inadequate, by themselves, to fully convince the world's citizens of the great glory and authenticity of their enterprise. Once again, as with ancient Rome, so it is with the final emerging global "Rome." The power of the secular is seen as insufficient. A religious power must be embraced. They will accomplish global dominion together. The woman "drunken with the blood of the saints" will ride the beast (Rev. 17:6-7), out of which partnership each hopes to gain preeminence.

The Whorish Woman

The "kings of the earth have committed fornication" with the "great whore" that rides the beast (Rev. 17:1-2). Each has, historically, and will, prophetically, use the other for illicit self gain. That is the nature of prostitution. Each seeks to gain through geopolitical intercourse the perceived power and favor of the other so as to gain ultimate power and favor with the people.

The beast is described as having "seven heads and ten horns" (Rev. 17:7). The "horns," we have seen, are political governing powers. The "seven heads," however, are "seven mountains on which the woman sitteth" (Rev. 17:9). This woman that rides the beast into global power "sitteth on many waters" (vs. 1). The "waters" are "peoples, and multitudes, and nations and tongues" (vs. 15). The whore's influence is vast, multicultural and perceived as the most globally influential religious power.

The "beast," despising the God of Creation; determines to use the "woman," and her feigned and prostituted faith to establish the beast's global authority, until she is no longer needed. The "ten horns," then, "shall hate the whore," and "shall make her desolate and naked," and "shall eat her flesh," and "shall burn her with fire" for "God hath put in their hearts to fulfill his will" (Rev. 17:16-17).

We must now establish the woman's identity. Her identity is established geographically and geopolitically. God makes her identity historically recognizable so that no one honest of heart, "keeping God's commandments" AND "having the faith of Jesus" (Rev. 14:12), could mistake His message. The identification is an implicit warning to beware and not participate overtly or covertly in the whore's deception.

The woman which thou sawest is that great city, which reigneth over the kings of the earth" (Rev. 17:18).

The seven heads are seven mountains [hills] on which the woman sits" (Rev. 17:9).

The "great whore" is also symbolically described as "Babylon the great" (Rev. 18:2). Many of the same descriptions given of the "woman" that rides the beast in Revelation 17 are given of "Babylon the great" in Revelation 18. "The kings of the earth, who have committed fornication and lived deliciously with her, shall bewail her, and lament for her, when they shall see the smoke of her burning… saying, Alas, alas, that great city Babylon, that mighty city, for in one hour is thy judgment come" (Rev. 18:9-10).

The global merchants that have participated with the beast in prostitution with the "great whore" shall weep and wail, saying, "Alas, alas, that great city, that was clothed in fine linen, purple and scarlet, and decked with gold and precious stones…! They "cried when they saw the smoke of her burning, saying, What city is like unto this great city" (Rev. 18:15-18).

The "Great City"

The rhetorical question of Revelation 18 echoes to our time… "What city is like unto this great city?" Is there any historical and continuing city on earth that matches the geopolitical and religious descriptions of Revelation 17 and 18?

There is only one city on earth that for more than 2000 years has been known and identified globally as the city on seven hills. That city is Rome. And the Bible unambiguously declares that the "great whore," the woman that rides the geopolitical "beast," is "that great city, which reigneth over the kings of the earth" (Rom. 17:18). She has prostituted eternal truth for temporal power and prosperity, [39] becoming the wealthiest institution on earth. Much of her wealth has been acquired through the sale of salvation. Under her proclaimed power to mediate heaven and hell, millions gave untold billions, thinking they could purchase heaven on the installment plan, not by the free grace of God but by the forceful merchandising of a false gospel by "His grace," the Pope.

There is only one city in history that could be characterized globally as fornicating with the kings of the earth, mixing the persuasive power of religion with the power of politics to gain dominion over the world's people. It is Vatican City. *The Catholic Encyclopedia* states: "It is within the city of Rome, called the city of seven hills, that the entire area of Vatican State proper is now confined." [40] The words *Vatican* and *Rome* are used interchangeably. When one speaks of *Rome*, the most common reference is to the hierarchy that rules the Roman Catholic Church.

The Pope, claiming to be the "Vicar of Christ" (in essence, "Christ in the flesh") has absolute monarchal rulership over Vatican State, the world's smallest political state, yet "reigning over the kings of the earth" (Rev. 17:18). Popes have claimed dominion over kings and kingdoms throughout history and claim their word and that of the Roman Catholic Church, which the Pope mediates, has authority over and supercedes the authority of the Scriptures. And now, at the end of the age, the Vatican seeks to bring the entire "Christian" and pagan world under its whorish motherhood.

The Scriptures describe her as "MYSTERY, BABYLON THE GREAT, THE MOTHER OF HARLOTS..." (Rev. 17:5). The Roman Catholic Church describes herself as "The Mother Church." But having prostituted herself for earthly wealth and power with political suitors, she became the "MOTHER OF HARLOTS." She presents herself as a great "MYSTERY" to the world, claiming global moral authority while committing global fornication; claiming to be a bearer of the truth while embracing treachery in her heart. Her prostituted power reigns supreme through threat of political blackmail. Hell hath no fury like the "great whore's" scorn mediated by the *Pontifex Maximus*.

The Pope has become the most powerful ruler on earth today. Ambassadors from every major country come to the Vatican to do obeisance to "His Holiness." As Pope Gregory IX thundered, the pope was lord and master of everyone and everything. As one historian noted, the papacy in Rome is "a single spiritual and temporal authority exercising powers which, in the end, exceed those that had ever lain within the grasp of the Roman Emperor."[41]

Usurpation of Authority

In the name of Christ, the Roman Catholic Church has, in effect, usurped God's authority in the earth. With blasphemy of the highest order, the Pope, claiming to be "The Holy Father," has declared his pontifications to be co-equal with or superceding the very Word of God. The Scriptures admonish: "Ye shall be holy: for I the Lord your God am holy" (Lev. 19:1). But the Pope claims the title, "YOUR HOLINESS." Jesus Christ is declared "King of kings and Lord of lords" (Rev. 19:16), yet the Pope is coronated, declaring him: "Father of princes and kings, Ruler of the world…."

The Deceiver's culminating act to defy God's authority in the earth is to exalt his counterfeit as "Father of princes and kings, Ruler of the world," bringing every tongue, tribe and nation under his dominion and authority in religious defiance of what God hath said. The Roman *Pontifex Maximus* is about to proclaim that authority and dominion as the woman rides the beast into global glory and power. It has begun in Europe.

Religion - The New Politics

A veteran European journalist wrote: "what is emerging in Europe is a Holy European Empire, an attempt to rebuild the old empire united under the pope. This is becoming blatant: The stained glass window of the Council of Europe at Strasbourg Cathedral features the Virgin Mary under a halo of twelve stars, the same stars you see on the EU flag. The Vatican is playing a major role in the creation of a new Holy European

Empire." "The pope repeatedly called for religious unity in Europe. This means a united Catholic Europe, which was consecrated to Mary by the Vatican in 1309 AD."[42]

Otto von Habsburg, head of the house of Habsburg, whose family dominated Europe for centuries as the continent's leading Catholic layman, wrote in *The Social Order of Tomorrow*:

> Now we do possess **a European symbol which belongs to all nations** equally. This is the crown of **the Holy Roman Empire**, which embodies the tradition of Charlemagne, the ruler of a united occident....[43]

How then does this "European symbol which belongs to all nations" extend the "Holy European Empire" to become a global "Holy Roman Empire?"

On May 29, 2008, the former British Prime Minister, Tony Blair, declared, "I'll dedicate the rest of my life to uniting the world's religions." "Faith is part of our future… an essential part of making globalization work." He said faith could be a "civilizing force in globalization."[44]

In December 2007, Tony Blair converted to Catholicism, after meeting numerous times in private with the pope. On May 30, 2008, Mr. Blair formally announced the Tony Blair Faith Foundation. He declared, "Into this new world, comes the force of religious faith." His goal is to bring the six leading faiths together: Christian, Muslim, Hindu, Buddhist, Sikh and Jewish. "Religion is the new politics," declared the new Catholic convertee. "Religious faith will be of the same significance to the 21st century as political ideology was to the 20th century."[45]

Blair, who serves also as Middle East peacemaker – the official emissary of the United States, the European Union, the United Nations and Russia – told *TIME* he "converted to Catholicism to fully share his family's faith. But he plainly enjoys being part of a worldwide community with shared value, traditions and rituals." "In a sense," observed *TIME*, *"The Catholic Church has long embodied the attributes of globalization that now engage Blair."*[46]

Several European papers now report that President George W. Bush "may follow in the footsteps" of Blair and his own brother, Jeb, converting to Catholicism after leaving office. He, like Tony Blair, has held an intimate meeting in Rome with Pope Benedict XVI as rumours mount. A close friend of George W. Bush, who converted in 1979, told the Catholic News Agency that "Bush is not unaware of how evangelicalism, by comparison with Catholicism, may seem more limited both theologically and historically."[47] [48]

The rising spirit of globalism is compelling and profoundly deceptive. It is drawing business and corporate leaders, political leaders and spiritual leaders, yes, even professed Christian leaders and Protestants of every stripe. It has become the "IN" thing, a mark of modern savvy and of market and ministry success, but the Master becomes little more than a mascot in pursuit of secondary agendas that wed the world in counterfeit unity or oneness.

A classic, but by no means exclusive, example of this global fever is the cover story of *TIME*, August 18, 2008. The cover title reveals the globalizing spirit: "THE PURPOSE DRIVEN PASTOR – RICK WARREN – America's most powerful religious leader takes on the world." But the title of the feature article goes straight to the heart of the matter: "The Global Ambition of Rick Warren."[49] In the seeming righteous pursuit of ridding the world of material poverty, an unrighteous wedding, "unequal yoking," of religious pluralism is embraced to accomplish the secondary agenda (II Cor. 6:14). The *purity* of the faith once delivered to the saints is inevitably compromised. The apparent "goodness" of the global agenda becomes a subtle substitute for the God who commands us to care for the poor. We may be "purpose driven" but not "purity and principle – driven." The *good* has seductively replaced *God* in the pursuit of a compromised and more universally acceptable *global gospel*… all in the name of Christ. It lures world leaders, not to the foot of the Cross, but to a counterfeit faith rooted in false unity.

As Tony Blair declared, "Religion is the new politics." The global spirit uniting religion and politics is also politically uniting Protestants under the *Pontifex Maximus*. The British *TIMESONLINE* reported "Churches back plan to unite under Pope."[50] These efforts are well under way as the report set forth.

> Radical proposals to reunite Anglicans with the Roman
> Catholic Church under the leadership of the pope were

published… and have been agreed by senior bishops of both churches. In a 42 page statement prepared by an international commission of both churches, Anglicans and Roman Catholics are urged to explore how they might reunite under the Pope. Rome has already shown itself willing to be flexible [on doctrinal issues]. In England and Wales, the Catholic Church is set to overtake Anglicanism as the predominant Christian denomination for the first time since the Reformation….

The document titled *Growing Together in Unity and Mission* significantly reported:

The Roman Catholic Church teaches that the ministry of the Bishop of Rome [the Pope] as a universal primate is in accordance with Christ's will for the Church and an essential element of maintaining unity and truth.
We urge Anglicans and Roman Catholics to explore together how the ministry of the Bishop of Rome might be offered and received in order to assist our Communions to grow towards full, ecclesial communion.[51]

Reports throughout the Protestant and Charismatic world show a similar pattern of pastor, priest and people drifting toward and embracing the catholicism of Rome, ultimately leading to papal primacy and submission to the *Pontifex Maximus* who embodies both the spirit and substance of the resurrecting Roman Empire, leading the Roman Church to ride the Roman political beast to world domination and ultimate destruction. The Deceiver's seductive system is clever but will prove cataclysmic.

"Come out of Her"

Jesus, King of kings and Lord of lords, will not countenance a counterfeit that seeks to usurp both His glory and His authority. He will not tolerate those who trifle with His truth. He cannot and will not bless those who blasphemously claim authority to change His eternal Word for political or pontifical gain or to arrogate themselves to change even

His Ten Commandments, proudly declaring the papal magesterium's authority to change the very "times and laws" God hath put in His own hand (Dan. 2:21, 7:25).

The "great whore" is seducing kings and kingdoms, both political and religious. Her bed is spread with "purple and scarlet, and decked with precious stones... having a golden cup in her hand full of abominations and filthiness of her fornication" (Rev. 17:4). As she lures many into her lair, she becomes "THE MOTHER OF HARLOTS" (Rev. 17:5). She has gathered to herself the very colors worn by Roman Caesars and with which Christ was mockingly clothed. *The Catholic Encyclopedia* declares her golden chalice "the most important of the sacred vessels... of gold or silver... and the inside surfaced with gold."[52]

For more than a thousand years, the Roman Catholic Church under the *Pontifex Maximus* exercised both religious and civil control over Rome. The Pope abolished the Roman Senate and placed all authority under his hand. The *Curia Romana* that once governed Rome was adopted by the Roman Catholic Church as the "Roman Curia" that is now "the whole ensemble of administrative and judicial offices through which the Pope directs the operations of the Catholic Church."[53] That usurped authority is once again being merged as the "woman" rides the "beast" of a resurrecting global Roman empire. Her symbolic name is "Babylon." "Catholic apologist Karl Keating admits that Rome has long been known as *Babylon*. Keating claims that Peter's statement 'The church here in Babylon... sends you her greeting' (from I Peter 5:13) proves that Peter was writing from Rome. He further explains, "Babylon is a code word for Rome."[54]

To all, whether Catholic or Protestant, or of whatever religious or political persuasion, the God of Creation warns from heaven...

> "COME OUT OF HER, MY PEOPLE, that ye be not partakers of her sins, and that ye receive not of her plagues. For her sins have reached unto heaven, and God hath remembered her iniquities" (Rev. 18:4-5).

He that hath an ear to hear, let him hear what the spirit saith to the church.

Chapter Nineteen

Daring Thoughts
for *Deceptive Times*

1. What do you think is the significance of the "United Religions" campaign under the United Nations?

2. How is the continual call to "unity" propelling the world into a "spiritual force for globalism?"

3. Did you know that Pope John Paul II called for "the creation of a new world order" based "on the goals of the United Nations?" How does that reflect upon a *geopolitical* role for the Vatican as opposed to a *spiritual* role?

4. Can you see how the political and spiritual history of Rome and of the Vatican connects the prophecies of Daniel and Revelation? Does this history reveal the nature of the final "beast" empire? In what ways?

5. Historian Nigel Rodgers noted, "The Catholic Church, with its hierarchy and universalist ambitions, is the most obvious inheritor of ancient Rome." How does this provide foundation for massive deception, particularly among Roman Catholics?

6. In what ways do you think Tony Blair was right in declaring: "Religion is the new politics?"

7. Does it appear to you that the promoters of global government and the Roman Catholic Church (The Vatican) are working in concert, each for their own purposes of global dominion?

8. What should be the attitude and response of true followers of Christ?

Chapter Twenty

∼⊱⊰∼

The Mark and Your Master

*"If any man worship the beast… and receive his mark
on his forehead or in his hand, the same shall drink
of the wine of the wrath of God" (Rev. 14:9-10).*

THE "MARK OF THE BEAST" is undoubtedly the most familiar and
feared of the multi-faceted aspects of Biblical prophecy. People will go
to great lengths to avoid a telephone number, address or social security
number containing the successive digits 6-6-6, requesting changes from
business and governmental agencies to remain distanced and dis-associated
from the infamous number of the "beast" of Revelation 13, 14, and 17 as
well as of Daniel 7:19-25. Yet to what degree, if at all, do people understand the spiritual significance of that mark of identification? If, indeed,
it is of such potent prophetic significance, why does the Bible seem to
imply that the *mark of the beast* will be nearly universally accepted? And
what are the implications for you, your family and your congregation?

Plan For The Mark

Plans are well underway for the implementation of the perfect
identification marker to solve national and international problems that

are proliferating with the rise of electronic technology and globalism. These plans take a variety of expressions throughout the nations. Israel's recent action provides a classic illustration, as revealed by an editorial in HAARETZ.com, an Israeli news publication.

> The Interior Ministry wants identity cards to contain fingerprints and a biometric photograph, in order to prevent forgeries and impersonation. The cabinet approved the proposal unanimously... but there has already been a public outcry.

In its editorial titled "Who's afraid of fingerprints?", follow now the rationale responding to the public reaction. It is illustrative of arguments presented around the globe, justifying the rapid implementation of privacy-invading technology.

> It is hard to understand why a fingerprint, though unique and thus enabling absolute identification, is arousing opposition in a society where most personal information is available via court order or illegally. It is impossible to prevent the existence of databases that are potentially injurious to privacy, but technical and legal means must be created to keep information from passing between bodies.
> The main objection is to the database, and not to the biometric ID cards. The fear of the data being misused is justified.... However the argument that only totalitarian states fingerprint their citizens is wrong. England is gradually shifting to biometric passports; and the United States fingerprints every government employee. Israel already has a fingerprint database of all Israeli Defense Force conscripts since 1973. The new database will be accessible only by judicial order.
> As with any legislation that infringes on a basic right to some extent, the potential damage must be weighed against the benefits.
> If there is a simple, available technical means that can prevent hostile elements... and can also replace worse, more

invasive means like wiretapping, interrogation under torture, arrest and surveillance, then it should be welcomed, and should be put to use sensibly and soon.[1]

Ehud Olmert, Israel's then Prime Minister, exulted over the government's decision to implement a central data base containing every citizen's fingerprints and photograph. He called it an "unprecedented revolution" in order to combat counterfeiting. The Prime Minister added: "What will be done is an integration of biometric elements to create the highest level of accuracy in personal identification known to today's science world.[2]

Prophecy of the Mark

The mark is coming. God, in His great love and mercy, foretold through the prophet Daniel and through the apostle John that a great "beast" government would arise as man's final and ultimate expression of government without God. That final resurrected "Roman Empire" will be "exceedingly dreadful" (Dan. 7:19).

The power of this empire promising peace will be such as to deprive the citizens of the world of privacy in order to solidify its all-encompassing control. In order to accomplish such control, this beast "causeth all, both small and great, rich and poor, free and bond, to receive a mark in their right hand or in their foreheads" (Rev. 13:16). The Greek word translated "mark" means "scratch or etch." This mark signifies "the number of a man" which is "the number of the beast." That number is "Six hundred three-score and six" or 666 (Rev. 13:18).

There has been much speculation and theorization over the centuries, attempting to identify "the beast" by means of interpretation of the significance of the number 666. It is not our purpose here to engage in that particular discussion. The Scripture advises: "Let him that hath understanding count the number of the beast" (Rev. 13:18). It should be noted, however, that the number "7" signifies God and His perfection. The number "6" signifies man, "a little lower than the angels" (Ps. 8), but not equal to God. Man was given six days to do all his labor and the seventh he was to rest, showing his trust in God rather than himself, even in Creation (Gen.2:3). The number "3" signifies God in His god-head, a word that occurs only three times in Scripture. It would appear then, at minimum, regardless of whatever else it may signify, that the number 666 is the number of man seeking godhood. Expressed in different terms, it is a man claiming to be as God heading up an earthly empire attempting, under Satan's authority, to replace God's authority in the earth in a final act of arrogant rebellion against a loving Creator.

Purpose of the Mark

The purpose of the "mark of the beast" is to confirm your identification with and your allegiance to mankind's ultimate expression of "SELF-government," without submission to man's Creator. Your willingness to carry that mark will reflect both the condition of your heart before God and your willingness to conform to the will and ways of a world system calculated to replace your trust in your Creator with trust in man.

The purpose of the mark, as you can well see, is of profound spiritual and eternal significance. It involves the necessity of making a choice. And that choice will be rendered more or less difficult by your true spiritual condition preceding the presentation of the mark. Jeremiah warned:

> *Cursed is the man that trusteth in man, and maketh flesh his*
> *arm, and whose heart departed the from the Lord.*
> *But…Blessed is the man that trusteth in the Lord, and whose*
> *hope the Lord is (Jer. 17:5-7).*

It is extremely important to note that the Scriptures give no indication that professing believers in Christ will not be faced with this profound choice. In fact, to the contrary, all of the warnings of Scripture are to believers. To conclude that believers are somehow exempt is to render the warnings of Christ, His apostles and the apostle Paul meaningless.

Consider that Daniel, one of the three most righteous men in the Bible (Ezek. 14), faced a similar choice resulting in his being cast into the lion's den (Dan. 6). The three godly Hebrew young men who refused to bow down to Babylon's golden anti-God authority were cast into the fiery furnace (Dan. 3). And thousands of faithful first, second and third-century Christians met frightening fates in the Coliseum, refusing to recant their faiths by bowing down to Rome's rule that demanded they make a choice, either for Caesar or for Christ.

Once again the choice will be… Caesar or Christ. Rome ruled at Christ's first coming and will rule at His Second Coming. At Yeshua's first coming, the evangelical Pharisees and mainline Sadducees declared "We have no king but Caesar" (John 19:15). What will you say by your life choices before Jesus' Second Coming? The presentation of the mark will profoundly test your trust.

Presentation of the Mark

The phenomenal advance of technology over the past half century is both historic and prophetic. Over the course of this writer's lifetime, the atomic bomb and neutron bomb, threatening global holocaust, now holds the world hostage. The unraveling of DNA is an unrivaled biological development, causing man to aspire now to compete with the Creator. The computer has rendered computation so quickly, and the accumulation and processing of information so vast as to make available the life histories of every man, woman and child on earth, including their pictures, medical histories, biometric identification and financial affairs. Satellite systems now enable the tracking and positioning, within six feet, of every person on the globe. In the precise words of an international engineer for the Sony Corporation in conversation with this author… "The day is coming when we will be god."

That is the emerging spirit of the resurrecting Roman Empire, empowered by technology so astounding and seemingly unending as to cause a "little horn" with "eyes like the eyes of man," speaking "great words against the Most High," standing up against Christ himself, the "Prince of princes" to arise, becoming the last "Caesar" to rule the earth (Dan 7:8, 25; 8:25).

Jesus warned us just before His crucifixion to "Render unto Caesar the things which be Caesar's, and unto God the things which be God's" (Luke 20:25). But what happens when Caesar claims Christ-hood and his romanized kingdom usurps the authority of the Kingdom of God? That is the picture portrayed in Scripture of one called the "son of perdition," the one in whom Satan invests final authority as the Deceiver, to draw all men to worship his counterfeit christ, thus making "Caesar" the savior of the world.

A MARKED MAN

A "marked man" is one who is identified in some way for a particular purpose, whether good or evil. Both your Creator and His arch enemy, Satan, wants to you to be a "marked man or woman."

When God would deliver Israel from their Egyptian "house of bondage" and from the iron furnace of Pharaoh, God, through Moses, instructed the children of Israel to mark their homes by painting the blood of the Passover lamb on their doorposts (Exod. 12). Pharaoh, a type of Satan and his anti-christ, bellowed "Who is the Lord, that I should obey his voice, to let Israel go" (Exod. 5:2)? Pharaoh had marked the people for slavery, but God marked those who would obey and trust Him for deliverance.

When Israel and then Judah refused to trust God as revealed by their rebellion and disobedience, God promised their destruction because He was "broken with their whorish heart," but as always, God said He would "yet leave a remnant" (Ezek. 5, 6:8-9). How would God identify the *remnant* to be spared? God instructed an angel with an inkhorn to "set a mark upon the foreheads of the men that sigh and that cry for all the abominations that be done...." To those not then bearing God's mark, other angels were instructed to go through the city, "and smite: let not your eye spare, neither have ye any pity." God instructed the angels to "begin at my sanctuary" (Ezek. 9:4-7).

It is critical to be "marked" by God! Men and women *marked* by God are those who, by faith, "paint" the "blood of the Lamb" on the "doorposts" of their life and heart, who come Out of Egypt and its spirit of bondage to Satan's ways, and who live in the humble holiness of obedience, being "a doer of the word, and not a hearer only, deceiving your own selves" (Jam. 1:22, Ezek 33:7-33, Matt. 7:21-29, Heb. 12:14). It is also critical to note that though all Israel were "heirs according to the promise" and were the "seed of Abraham," most were not *marked* by

God as the elect remnant because their life of purported faith did not reflect righteous living demanded by God of those who claimed to be His sons and daughters.

Satan also intends that you be a *marked* man or woman. He knows the unlikelihood that he can accomplish this directly, and so he relies upon seduction. He is adept at employing simple deception to lead the unsuspecting to destruction. Ultimately, however, most will succumb and receive his mark. Lamentably, all "whose names are not written in the book of life of the Lamb…" will receive Lucifer's mark of worship of the end-time "Caesar" who will rule in his stead (Rev. 13:8, 14:9-10).

A MARKETING METHOD

Mankind will not readily receive a mark that many or most find suspicious. Like all products and promises, it must be promoted. The people must be persuaded to forfeit principle for pragmatism, privacy for the promise of protection and provision marketed as *security* and *prosperity.* Even professing Christians must be targeted to compromise their trust.

The mark is being marketed by the gospel of gradualism. Technological advances are trumpeted as solutions for trying circumstances and troubling problems. Private convictions are gradually softened in favor of the purported public "common good." Headlines and commercials scream dire threats demanding technological salvation. Proliferating international drug trading, identity theft, economic meltdown and the terrifying prospect of terrorism conspire to induce compromise. Citizens demand solutions and politicians pander to provide security through governmental salvation. Trust is gradually, yet inexorably, shifted from God and the gospel to the government and global saviors. We have witnessed the willingness of American politicians, their president and the people they represent to abandon the very foundational principle of America's prosperity in order to purportedly "rescue" the world from financial collapse.

Dramatic technological developments in virtually every sphere of life, coupled with the explosion of the *Information Age,* have gradually normalized both the concept and practice of universal identification. Few give it much thought. Although frought with corrupting consequences, most choose to embrace greater and more intrusive identification for the government promised *security* and *prosperity.* Blood-bought freedom is cavalierly sacrificed on the altar of personal peace and prosperity.

The multitudinous rivulets of technological developments cours-ing down the mountains of commerce worldwide over the past fifty years have made their way to common expression in a global river sweep-ing everything in its path toward global government and global control ostensibly for global security and prosperity or *shalom*. Consider the following by way of illustration:

1. In 1935, the Social Security Act was passed in the U.S.A to pro-vide old-age insurance and unemployment compensation. A number was issued for all participants with guarantees it would never be used for general identification. Now, through a number of amendments, this supposedly innocuous program marketed for security and prosperity covers cradle to grave care and it is virtually impossible to accomplish financial transactions or obtain medical care without the universally-required social secu-rity number.

2. The RFID or radio frequency identification chip is becoming a universally required device on every commercial product to increase corporate prosperity and to track purchasers with items purchased.

3. GPS (global positioning systems) enable instant mapping from home or auto to desired destinations but also facilitate instant tracking of your whereabouts.

4. Governmental regulations now require every new vehicle sold in America to be embedded with a chip, allowing you and your vehi-cle to be tracked any time or any where, ostensibly for your safety.

5. As of 2009, the US federal governmental requires, through the National Animal Identification System, that every agricultural animal be equipped with an identification device enabling its movement to be traced from birth to slaughter, with penalty fines up to $1000 per day. This program is not limited to commercial producers, but includes animals at home. Both animal and prem-ises must be registered. The marketing purpose is to prevent ter-rorism. The effect is to place in the hands of government absolute control of animal food supply.[3]

6. London has a publicly-funded spy network of 10,000 crime-fight-ing closed circuit television cameras.[4]

7. Israel boasts a "revolutionary new processor" cell that will deliver ten times the performance of today's PC processors.[5]

8. The University of Maryland is perfecting a surveillance system whereby your facial image can be matched to your gait, your height, your weight and other elements so a computer can instantly identify you. It is but a small step from tracking a terrorist to tracking a toddler, teacher or trumpeter of God's Word.[6]

9. Leaders of a U.N. Internet panel plan to set up a global system where cyberspace would be under the control of the United Nations.[7]

10. The US National Security Agency (NSA) has filed for a top-secret patent for technology, enabling the government to track anyone surfing the web to their physical address. It will build a "network latency topology map" for all internet users.[8]

11. The FDA (Federal Drug Administration) has now approved an implantable medical chip to store all of your medical information.[9]

12. Mexico's attorney general publically announced that senior members of his staff and 160 employees received a subdermal "anti-kidnap" chip due to the kidnapping plague terrorizing Mexico. Russia, Switzerland, Venezuela and Columbia have also purchased such chips.[10]

13. Europe's fastest supercomputer - an IBM that can make 40 trillion calculations per second - recently booted up in Spain. Its memory is equivalent to the combined memories of nearly 20,000 personal computers and has a storage capacity equivalent to the information that could be found in 29 million books. IBM intends to make such accessible computers available to governments.[11]

14. The U.S. Department of Homeland Security is funding research of a new implantable chip called MMEA (Multiple Micro Electrode Array). This chip can be surgically implanted into a human nerve or into the brain, enabling an outside controller to read a person's thoughts, feelings or emotions and to control feelings, thoughts and actions, thus empowering an outside controller to direct people or entire populations.[12]

15. Big Brother Europe is alive and well. The European Commission, as an anti-crime measure, has decreed a computerized collection

of personal details drawn from every citizen of the 27-nation European Union, which was set to be operational by the end of 2008. The central database is to be maintained in Brussels.[13]

As should be readily apparent, technology is marching lockstep to the incessant drumbeat of commercial globalism and global government. All that remains to complete "marketing" to the masses is an event of global significance, causing those increasingly addicted to *security* and *prosperity* to readily forfeit freedom for a false faith in a God-defying global government to provide their needs. The stage for the ultimate transactional exchange of trust in God to trust in man will have been set. That moment is accelerating at breathtaking speed. Might the current global economic meltdown precipitate such prophetic fulfillment? Will you be ready? How about your family? And pastor, will your congregation stand the test?

Presentation of the Mark

The technological groundwork for implementation of a global mark is nearing completion. Popular applications of supporting technologies are now readily received and resistence is diminishing. Demand for solutions to pervasive problems such as identity theft, counterfeiting, terrorism and drug trafficking is growing exponentially. And globalists wait patiently for the propitious moment and method to present their mark so that people will clamor for its promised benefits, willingly and with gratitude releasing precious freedoms for pernicious false promises of peace and prosperity.

The presentation of the mark will require a religious component to complete the deception. A miracle-working false prophet, called "another beast" will come up "out of the earth," exercising all the power of the first beast which the great whore rides (Rev. 13:11-13). This "beast" prophet will cause all who dwell on the earth, "both small and great, rich and poor, free and bond, to receive a mark in their right hand or in their foreheads" (Rev. 13:16). The purpose is to enforce and facilitate the power and control of the final beast government, the revived Holy Roman Empire, "that no man might buy or sell" without the mark, the name of the beast, or the number of his name" (Rev. 13:17).

Spiritual deception will be accomplished "by means of those miracles" which the false prophet has "power to do in the sight of the beast." This "beast" prophet will be vastly persuasive, capturing the minds and hearts of the vast majority into the seductive false trust of a counterfeit savior. The apostle Paul reveals why people will be deceived (II Thess. 2:10-12):

1. "They love not the truth"
2. "They have pleasure in unrighteousness."

Protect yourself and those in your charge. Be a lover of God's truth. "Seek first the kingdom of God and His righteousness" (Matt. 6:33). "Trust in the Lord with all your heart; and lean not on your own understanding. In all your ways acknowledge Him, and He shall direct your paths" (Prov. 3:5-6).

The Power of the Mark

Possession of the *mark of the beast* on your person is a public declaration of your allegiance and submission to the power of the final "beast" empire... the resurrected Roman Empire. It is a testimony to your true trust.

The *mark of the beast* represents the promise and power of man to protect you and to provide for your needs. Since this final global empire is man's best and ultimate effort to govern without God and since the mark is the indicia of "a man" (Rev. 13:18) in whom Satan, the master deceiver, will "incarnate" himself as a false christ, a person's choice to receive that mark, regardless of whatever rationalization he may conjur up, will have the power to separate or "sanctify" that person unto Satan.

The mark becomes powerful leverage to compel every man, woman and child to bow to the beast. The only powers over which the beast and its mark have no ultimate dominion are the power of God and your power to choose. Satan, through his anti-christ, will be very persuasive, however. His persuasive power, as the "son of perdition," is the power of life or death. Your choice will be perceived as a choice of life or death on earth. If you do not receive the mark, you will be unable to buy or sell within the global economic system, jeopardizing survival. You may also risk execution as a traitor to the Empire, just as it was for the early Christians.

On the other hand, if you receive the mark in fear rather than reject it by faith, you will have failed the ultimate and final test of your trust. Those who take the mark will do so, from God's perspective, as an act of worship of deified man and of the Deceiver, Satan. Therefore, taking of the mark also has the power to deprive you of eternal life with our Lord Jesus Christ, the God of Creation.

Choosing to receive the mark promises temporal peace, provision and security. Choosing to reject the *mark of the beast* may result in loss of earthly life but in the gaining of eternal peace and salvation. "If any man worship the beast and his image, and receive his mark in his forehead, or in his hand, the same shall drink of the wine of the wrath of God… and he shall be tormented with fire and brimstone in the presence of the holy angels, and in the presence of the Lamb" (Rev. 14:9-10).

Permanency of the Mark

The historic battle between God and Satan is a battle for your soul. The *mark of the beast* is not just some clever marketing device but will determine your eternal destiny.

To receive the *mark of the beast* is to reveal your true heart. It reveals what you truly value – the temporal or the eternal. Isaac had two sons, Jacob and Esau. Esau foolishly sold his precious birthright, as the first-born, for a mess of pottage (Gen. 28:7-9). God despised Esau for treating trivially that which had true value. Therefore said the Lord, "Jacob have I loved, but Esau have I hated" (Rom. 9:13, Mal. 1:3).

Where do you place true value? What would those around you say? Where do you invest your time, your talent, your treasure? Do you seek first the kingdom of God and His righteousness? If that does not define your life now, how will it suddenly become foremost when your very life is on the line?

No one can definitively and precisely say how or when the *mark of the beast* will ultimately be presented or what form it will have. There are many theories. Some say it will be a computer chip. Others say it will be some mark of the first-day Sabbath as ordered by the *Pontifex Maximus* of ancient Rome and re-confirmed by the Papacy contrary to the fourth commandment. Yet others have said it will be the six-pointed star or the mere number 666. The Scriptures merely call it a mark or "etching." The important thing is to recognize and understand what that mark represents, that from God's viewpoint it is a declaration of where you choose to put your trust, and that once made, the choice is permanent.

A national news article titled, "The Dangerous Art of the Tattoo," observed that "Tattoos are fast becoming a mark of the 21st century." At least 25% of people under 30 now sport at least one tattoo. Marks and piercings of the body have become normalized on the near edge of Christ's Second Coming as never before in history. Dr. Bernadine Healy notes, "… most people get tattooed without a clue about the implications." The risks, she warns, are significant, "the most obvious one being a major case of remorse." Unfortunately, notes Dr. Healy, "tattooing is designed to last forever."[14]

The *mark of the beast*, whatever it may actually prove to be and whatever form it may take, will be permanent. It will reflect a permanent and unchangeable choice. The mark demonstrates a choice of faith, trust and worship, regardless of whatever rationalizing "spin" one might employ to justify receiving it. God's warnings are direct, they are dire, and they determine eternal destiny.

Anyone who chooses to receive the mark of identification indicating trust in the counterfeit christ, his false miracle-working prophet, and his Creator-defying and denying system of salvation, will not have their names "written in the book of life of the Lamb slain from the foundation of the world" (Rev. 13:8). Consider well!

> *All that dwell upon the earth shall worship him [the counterfeit christ representing the final beast empire] whose names are not written in the book of life of the Lamb…" (Rev. 13:8).*

By far, the majority, both Jew and Gentile, will display their trust in a false christ representing Satan's kingdom. Yeshua specifically warned his Jewish brethren, "I am come in my Father's name, and ye receive me not: if another shall come in his own name [the counterfeit christ or self-anointed one], him ye will receive" (John 5:43).

"If any man worship the beast and his image, and receive his mark in his forehead, or in his hand, the same shall drink of the wine of the wrath of God...." "And they have no rest day or night, who worship the beast and his image, and whoever receiveth the mark of his name" (Rev. 14:9-11). "... there fell a noisome and grievous sore upon the men which had the mark of the beast, and upon them which worshiped his image"(Rev. 16:1-2).

People "Not Appointed To Wrath"

Many have devised theological systems to purportedly prevent professing believers in Yeshua from being faced with and having to make the profound choice discussed in this chapter. Such systems may themselves be dangerously deceptive, for if we do not believe we may face such a challenge to our faith and trust, it induces weakness, spiritual indolence, and great susceptibility to the seduction that will lure most to receive the mark. Remember, all of the end-time warnings of Scripture are to professing believers. Therefore, the wise believer will prepare for the worst and hope for the best, always cementing our confidence in Christ.

"Yourselves know perfectly that the day of the Lord so cometh as a thief in the night." "But ye, brethren, are not in darkness, that that day should overtake you as a thief." "Therefore, let us not sleep, as do others; but let us watch and be sober [serious minded]." "Let us, who are of the day, be sober, putting on the breastplate of faith and love; and for an helmet, the hope of salvation. For God hath not appointed us to wrath..." (I Thess. 5:2-9).

The Bible references three main sources of wrath: the wrath of Satan, the wrath of man and the wrath of God. The "wrath of God" is reserved for the unbeliever (John 3:36) and will also be poured out on "the children of disobedience." The apostle Paul warns believers, "Let no man deceive you with vain words: for because of these things [unrighteous living] cometh the wrath of God upon the children of disobedience" (Eph. 5:1-11).

The wrath of God is reserved for those who reject Yeshua as His Anointed One, who refuse to trust Jesus Christ as Savior, who reveal their lack of love and trust by rebellion and disobedience and who shift their ultimate trust and allegiance in time of testing to Satan's counterfeit kingdom and false christ. "Here is the patience of the saints," however. Saints that are not seduced "are they that keep the commandments of God, and the faith of Jesus" (Rev. 14:12).

Praise God that He has not appointed those who truly love and trust Jesus Christ, as evidenced by their faithful lives, to the outpouring of His wrath. God has and will prepare a way of escape from the final and unprecedented outpouring of His wrath. God's fury of righteous indignation brought as judgment on the earth is not to be trifled with. The remnant who are truly faithful will be "raptured" or "caught up" to meet the Lord (I Thess. 4:16-17), just as His wrath is ready to be out-poured, beginning at the Sixth Seal, "for the great day of [God's] wrath is come; and who shall be able to stand" (Rev. 6:17)? Little wonder that Paul enjoined, "… comfort one another with these words" (I Thess. 4:18).

While true believers are protected from the wrath of God, the Scripture provides no assurance that believers will be protected from the end-time wrath of man. On the contrary, Jesus and the apostles repeat-edly warned of the last days assault against Christ and his true followers. "Then shall they deliver you up to be afflicted, and shall kill you: and ye shall be hated of all nations for my name's sake." Notice, it is not the name of **God** that will be deemed offensive but the name of **Jesus**. "Then shall many be offended, and shall betray one another…." This betrayal will most likely be by those who fail the trust test by receiving the mark, betraying true believers to deliver them over to the Roman system that persecuted believers in the early church and will multiply that persecution against the end-time church, in great fury. For this reason, Jesus warned, "But he that shall endure to the end, the same shall be saved" (Matt. 24:9-13).

Preparing Your Life

The pictures portrayed by the end-time prophecies of both Covenants are, to the natural man, terrifying. Jesus warned of "Men's hearts failing them for fear, and for looking after those things which are coming upon the earth…" (Luke 21:26). Daniel warned that the "little horn" anti-christ power "made war with the saints, and prevailed against them" (Dan. 7:21). The counterfeit christ, given over totally to Satan, will blatantly blaspheme against God, "and it was given over unto him to make war with the saints, and to overcome them…" (Rev. 13:7).

How then should we live? How will you stand in the evil day? Will you walk in fear… or in faith? Will you live in trust… or in terror? Today is the day to decide, before the final deception makes it a hundred times more difficult.

"Finally, my brethren, be strong in the Lord, and in the power of his might. Put on the whole armor of God, that ye may be able to stand against the wiles of the devil." "Stand therefore, having your loins girt about with truth, and having on the breastplate of righteousness." "Above all, taking the shield of faith, wherewith ye shall be able to quench all the fiery darts of the wicked. And take the helmet of salvation, and the sword of the Spirit, which is the word of God." "Praying always… and watching… with all perseverance" (Eph. 6:10-18).

"The great dragon was cast out, that old serpent, called the Devil and Satan, which deceiveth the whole world: he was cast into the earth, and his angels were cast out with him" (Rev. 12:9). They accused the brethren continuously. And how do we overcome him? Here are the three most important things to remember for spiritual victory. Process these prayerfully. "And they overcame him (1) by the blood of the Lamb, and (2) by the word of their testimony [their life matches their profession of faith]: and (3) they loved not their lives unto death" (Rev. 12:11). Be warned, "for the devil is come down unto you with great wrath, because he knoweth that he hath but a short time" (Rev. 12:12).

Protected by God's Mark

Satan has his mark, but God also has His mark. One is a mark of eternal destruction, the other a mark of eternal deliverance. "The foundation of God standeth sure, having this seal, The Lord knoweth them that are his. And let everyone that nameth the name of Christ depart from iniquity" (II Tim. 2:19). If we name the name of Christ, the only name by which we can be saved, God expects us to depart from the sinful ways that define those who will ultimately take the Deceiver's mark.

Immediately before God pours out His wrath, he instructs an angel "having the seal of the living God" to seal "the servants of our God in their forehead." Which seal will you receive… the seal of God… or the mark of the beast? Will your trust be in man… or the MASTER?

Chapter Twenty

Daring Thoughts
for *Deceptive Times*

1. What is the real purpose of *the mark of the beast*?

2. In what ways does receiving that mark reveal where a person truly puts his or her trust?

3. How do you think the *mark* of the beast empire will be marketed so that the vast majority, even professing believers, will accept it?

4. What are the two clear spiritual reasons the Apostle Paul gave as to why professing believers will be deceived?

5. What part will *fear of man* vs. *fear of God* play in choosing the mark of the beast?

6. Caesar… or Christ? Which will you choose in which to place your trust? Are you prepared for this test?

7. What steps can you take to prepare your life and the lives of those in your spheres of influence to pass this ultimate test of trust?

PART VI

Seducing Spirits and *Doctrines*

"IN THE LATER TIMES, some shall depart from the faith, giving heed to seducing spirits and doctrines…" (I Tim. 4:1). The warning of the apostle Paul is clear and should be convincing to any sober-minded saint.

Please note! It is those who profess to be *saints* who are warned, for a person cannot *depart* from a place or position in which he or she has never been. Again Paul warns the saints, "That ye be not soon shaken in mind, or be troubled in spirit… as that day of Christ is at hand." **"Let no man deceive you by any means: for that day shall not come, except there come a falling away first…"** (II Thess. 2:2-3).

In the chapters following, we focus on some of the more common aspects of doctrinal deception and spiritual seduction, ranging from classic cults to challenges within our churches. Depending upon your historical background and your current exposure within the broader Christian community, some aspects of this discussion may prove challenging to pre-conceived notions or to theological positions you may deem sacrosanct. Please consider these chapters carefully and prayerfully, striving to avoid a knee-jerk defensiveness that may frustrate the very purpose of the point being made, potentially leading to deception by elevating tradition over truth and heritage over holiness, thus opening the door to unsuspected seduction.

We now begin a three-chapter exploration of falsity that threatens our faith. Remember, the Deceiver is a master counterfeiter. He is adept at seducing saints to receive and believe falsity as if it were the truth. It is precisely because believers believe the false to be the truth that they are seduced by unsound doctrine and the purveyors thereof. We will discover that doctrinal deception can be broadly identified by…

FALSE PROPHETS
FALSE TEACHING
FALSE HOPE

Let's walk this path together prayerfully.

Chapter Twenty-One

False Prophets

"Beloved, believe not every spirit, but try the spirits whether they are of God: because many false prophets are gone out into the world" (I John 4:1).

THE WARNING WAS CLEAR! Just before His crucifixion, Jesus poured out His heart to those dearest to Him… His disciples. As they sat on the Mount of Olives overlooking the eastern gate of Jerusalem, those who had followed the Lord for over three years were concerned about what lay ahead. And so they asked… "what shall be the sign of thy coming, and of the end of the world. And Jesus answered… Take heed that no man deceive you" (Matt. 24:3). If the disciples were incapable of being deceived, Jesus warning was worthless, wasn't it?

Many Will Be Deceived

Jesus minced no words. Many false prophets shall arise, and shall deceive many," he declared (Matt. 24:11). It may not be what we want to believe, whether we be pastor or parishioner, but the Master said the church would be plagued by many false prophets and that many will be deceived.

The environment will be and now is ripe for deception. It is as if every avenue and form of historical deception has been repackaged for maximum allure to a fence-straddling, culture-driven, all-about-ME generation that has virtually abandoned the very concept of absolute truth in favor of the false authority of feelings and experiences. The apostle Paul gravely warned that "in the last days perilous times shall come" in which "evil men and seducers shall wax worse and worse, deceiving and being deceived" (II Tim. 3:1, 13). Interestingly, if the false prophets were perceived to be *evil*, they would be incapable of deceiving. The *many* will be prone to deception precisely because their minds and hearts are prepared to receive falsehood and to either reject or fail to properly identify truth.

The counterfeit will be convincing. Christ will have largely become a mascot rather than the Master. "Because iniquity shall abound, the love of many shall wax cold" (Matt. 24:12). Men shall be "ever learning, and never able to come to the knowledge of the truth" (II Tim. 3:7). They will rush to and fro from convention to convention, meeting to meeting, prophet to prophet to have their "itching ears" scratched (II Tim. 4:3), looking for purveyors of falsehood to speak smooth words in the name of Christ, seducing them into compromising complacency and deceptive dependancy. "Through covetousness shall they with feigned words make merchandise of you…" (II Pet. 2:3).

With warnings this dire of deception lurking in the growing doctrinal darkness as we sit poised on the near edge of our Lord's Second Coming, it behooves us to explore what God reveals in His Word concerning the discerning of false prophets. And if we are to discern the counterfeit, we must also discern the authentic. We must also discern the difference between a *prophet* and a *pastor* or *priest*.

What Is A Prophet?

The Church Christ is building is "built upon the foundation of the apostles and prophets…." "Jesus Christ himself is the chief corner stone," the chief of the prophets (Eph. 2:20). Jesus, God the Son, incarnated the three distinct spiritual offices on earth for God the Father: (1) Prophet, (2) Priest, and (3) King.

The so-called "divine right of kings" in the sphere of civil government drew its authority from Christ as "King of kings and Lord of lords (Rev. 19:16). All earthly rulers are then kings under the ultimate dominion and authority of the King of kings, and are said to derive their authority from Him to rule with judgment and justice. Similarly, the earthly prophets and priests among men derive both their calling or office and authority from Christ as Prophet of prophets and Priest of priests. All authentic prophets or priests must therefore model their respective roles or offices as exemplified by Christ. Failure to do so renders one a "false prophet" or a "false priest." A *false prophet* is one who either counterfeits his calling as an imposter or perverts his calling to please men.

The office of the prophet in the Church or in the Kingdom of God is profound. The entire Church is, as Paul stated, "built upon the foundation of the apostles and prophets" (Eph. 2:20). It is important to note that the Church is not built on the foundation of pastors or priests, whether past or present. This popularly held notion displayed in the practices of the church has led to much doctrinal deception and moral decay within the body of Christ. The true prophet is no more desired in the church today than were the prophets sent to ancient Israel and Judah, or even Christ himself among the priests and religious potentates of His day. We must clearly distinguish, then, between the offices of prophet and of priest or pastor. Confusion can lead to counterfeiting and false prophecy.

Paul reminds us that God gave to the church five specific ministry callings or offices. Note the order… apostles, prophets, evangelists, pastors and teachers (Eph. 4:11). These offices are current and active in the New Testament church. These are sometimes referred to as "the five-fold ministry gifts." Many pastors seek to co-opt these all for themselves, claiming to incarnate "the five-fold ministry gifts." But these are separate and distinct offices, each with a unique and necessary function, "for the perfecting of the saints, for the work of the ministry, for the edifying of the body of Christ…"

- Till we all come in the unity of the faith…
- That we henceforth be no more children, tossed to and fro, and carried about with every wind of doctrine, by the sleight of men, and cunning craftiness, whereby they lie in wait to deceive (Eph. 4:12-14).

Let's define the terms together by definition and by function. A pastor rules over the pasture. He feeds and guides the sheep as a constant companion. He is a shepherd, charged not only with feeding the sheep but with guarding them on an ongoing friendship basis. His greatest weakness is that he grows so much to identify with the sheep and their voice that it begins to muffle or render him increasingly tone-deaf to the still small voice of God. For this reason, as the people increasingly conform to the ways of the ungodly culture, drifting away from the truth, the pastor, over time, tends to drift with the people to retain their favor. He comes to "love the praises of men more than the praise of God" (John 12:43). Finally, over time, perhaps a generation, the picture becomes clear to an unattached observer. It has become, "like people, like priest" (Hos. 4:9). Apostasy has set in and becomes increasingly normative.

The *priest* officiates in spiritual things for God to and among the people. In all but "high church" settings today, the role of priest and pastor are practically merged. The pastor or priest, therefore, is a daily shepherd over a local flock of believers, officiating as God's hand extended, representing the people to God. The true prophet, on the other hand, operating in the office of prophet, represents God to the people. The nature and level of the prophet's inspiration to speak on God's behalf is qualitatively different than that of pastor or priest, hence the difference in designation.

While many or even most prophets are *foretellers*, the prevailing role of all prophets is to be a *forth-teller*. The nature of a true prophet's forth-telling is dramatically different in spirit, force, message and solemnity from the preaching and teaching of most pastors and priests, unless a pastor actually is a true prophet, of which there are precious few. The pastor/priest is primarily concerned with nurture and feeding. Both are needed, but the prophet bears the burden of rejection for a message neither pastor nor people really want to hear or deliver. For this reason Jesus mourned over Jerusalem, representing all Israel: "O Jerusalem, Jerusalem, thou that killest the prophets, and stonest them which are sent unto thee…" (Matt. 23:37). The Savior said they refused to receive God's correction, and so it is today.

The true prophet is the ultimate patriot. He speaks pointedly for God to the people, bringing precise warning and powerful wooing with the objective of turning their hearts back to holy purpose and practice. The true prophetic voice becomes most identifiable when the people have drifted away from pure doctrine and godly living, calling both pastor/priest and people to repent. The prophet lifts up his voice like a trumpet to show God's people their transgressions and sins (Isa. 58:1). He cries aloud to turn hearts from religious pretense to righteous purpose so that the people and their land might again rejoice in God's perfect plan to give them a hope and a future (Jer. 29:11). God raises up the provocative voice of the prophet when He can no longer trust the pastor/priest to preach righteousness, for they have become "like people - like priest."

When the Scripture warns of "false prophets," however, such warnings include a broader range of religious persons who purport to lift up their voices to the people on God's behalf as if they speak "prophetically." These might include:

- Prophets having a genuine prophetic office but who are unfaithful to the call.
- Pastors or priests who purport to speak for God but who distort or pervert the purity of God's message, thus leading the trusting flock astray.
- People having no genuine prophetic office nor being a pastor or priest but being a prophetic imposter, gaining purported "prophetic authority" through the force of personality or the sensationalism of their prognostications.
- People purporting to exercise the "gift of prophecy" (I Cor. 12:10) but who conjur their own prophetic message, it being not truly of or from God.

Having attempted to define the office and role of the true prophet, it is time to trace the identifiable characteristics of a false prophet.

Identifying The False Prophet

The false prophet is *false*, either in calling or in consistency of message with either the whole of the Scripture or God's greater purposes. A true prophet, Jeremiah, lamented loudly, "Mine heart within me is broken because of the prophets" (Jer. 23:9). This broken-hearted prophet thundered his warnings about false prophets because he saw their devastating moral and spiritual effect upon the people. Although they may have been well-intentioned, they undermined God's prophetic purposes by seducing the people to *comfort* rather than *conviction*; embracing ritual over righteousness. They resisted the true call to repentance and obedience by popular pandering to the people's perceived self interest.

Jeremiah paints a dramatic contrast between the true and the false prophet. His picture presents the false prophet as "profane" or prostituted in purpose, practice and message (Jer. 23:11), causing God's people to err. His portraiture of the prophetic counterfeit coincides shockingly with the patterns of so-called prophetic "ministry" today. Do we dare get specific? Let's take a look at Jeremiah's list of the Terrible Ten.

THEIR LIFE and MESSAGE ARE INCONSISTENT

"I have seen in the prophets... an horrible thing: they commit adultery, and walk in lies" (Jer. 23:14).

The divorce and remarriage rate among pastors and those claiming prophetic voices today is equal to that of their parishioners and is the second highest among all American professions. Jesus, a true prophet, said, "Whosoever shall put away his wife, and marry another, committeth adultery against her" (Mark 10:11). At least thirty percent of our pastors play with pornography, by their own admissions, and are therefore adulterers by Jesus' definition (Matt. 5:27-28).

THEY STRENGTHEN EVILDOERS

"I have seen in the prophets an horrible thing... they strengthen the hands of the evildoers" (Jer. 23:14).

The prevailing preponderance of so-called "prophetic voices," at least in western culture, have increasingly over the past generation set aside biblical standards of righteousness in favor of disintegrating cultural standards, thus seducing those who follow them to believe their false message to be truth. By false precept and folly in life practice, they have modeled and massaged, coddled and encultured evil, falsely authenticating the growing sinful practices of their parishioners. By exalting feelings over faith, they have, among other things, justified the divorces that God says he hates, calling them "answers to prayer," "God's second chances," or "a new beginning."

THEY DO NOT REPENT

Said Jeremiah, "… none doth return from his wickedness… they have become unto me as Sodom and as Gomorrah" (Jer. 23:14).

Despite a generation of prayers for revival and restoration, there has been almost no cry among voices generally deemed "prophetic" calling for professing believers and their pastors/priests to truly repent. It is as if sin has become sacrosanct. As *U.S. News and World Report* declared on its cover, "Pre-marital Sex is the Sin America's Wink At." The magazine writers were unable to get any prominent "Christian" leader to comment, because the problem was so vast within the evangelical church that they risked losing popular support and finances for their projects and thus remained silent.

THEIR VISION IS NOT FROM GOD

"Hearken not unto the words of the prophets," warned Jeremiah. "They make you vain: they speak a vision of their own heart, and not out of the mouth of the Lord" (Jer. 23:16).

While purporting to speak for God, they speak their own thoughts, schemes and ideas. Their own lives are not in order, and they are unwilling to clearly see God's order. Their "visions" lead to progressive vacuity rather than lasting victory.

THEY PROMISE PEACE

"They say… The Lord hath said, Ye shall have peace… No evil shall come upon you" (Jer. 23:17).

False prophets pander to the people, telling them favorable things to gain their favor. They refuse to risk their own reputation to restore God's reputation, choosing to preach renewal without repentance and revival without a return to righteousness. Rather than declare God's portending judgment, they promise peace and prosperity, thus undermining the eternal purposes of God to advance their temporal agendas.

THEY DO NOT TURN THE PEOPLE FROM EVIL

"If They had stood in my counsel… then they should have turned them from their evil way… (Jer. 23:22).

The true prophet is usually called to come forth openly when the people and their leaders are wandering from the straight path. Pastors should so speak. But when the cultural drift has metasticized dramatically among both pastor and people, pastors become the guardians of the status quo while claiming to guard the flock. They become unwilling to address moral decadence and unrighteous living, not wanting to offend so as to risk favor or the flow of finances. They thus, in effect, become false prophets, for their ministry becomes a pretense.

THEY MISAPPROPRIATE GOD'S NAME

"I have heard what the prophets said," says the Lord, "that prophecy lies in my name, saying, I have dreamed, I have dreamed. "… they are prophets of the deceit of their own heart" (Jer. 23:25-26).

It is a serious thing to appropriate the name of the Lord, to say "Thus saith the Lord" or "The Lord told me…." As our faith becomes ever more fickle through the exaltation of feelings as the arbiter of truth, the misappropriation of the name of the Lord by pastor, prophet and people to baptize fleeting feelings as truth will increase. The pattern is prominent now and becoming pervasive. Before using the phrase "God told me…," we might well be advised to re-consider the seriousness of cavalierly assaulting the third commandment, "Thou shalt not take the name of the Lord they God in vain," by deifying our feelings or using God's name to manipulate the fickle masses.

THEY PREACH and PROPHESY UNFAITHFULLY

"The prophet… that hath my word, let him speak my word faithfully" (Jer. 26:28).

Obviously, it is possible from God's perspective to preach His word unfaithfully and to prophesy in an unfaithful manner. Interestingly, the common comeback to any expression of concern regarding the faithful-ness of a pastor's or prophet's message is the almost inevitable defense, "My pastor preaches the Word." So how do we discern and disavow falsehood? Can it be done without being perceived as mean-spirited or divisive?

In general, under the current hyper-ventilated exaltation of feel-ings over genuine faith, the mere mention that a word of prophecy or preaching may be in error in some way is almost automatically labeled divisive. Therefore, any criticism of doctrine or of prophetic declaration requires first a solemn evaluation of one's heart motivation and humble discernment of a range of personal or group traditions that we may be prone to superimpose on the Word of God. We must not yield to the temptation, however, to allow such sensitivities to cause us to dance with deception while claiming self-righteously to disavow it. Unfortunately, this the has become the all-too-common pattern.

God's viewpoint on His Word differs from that most common in today's churches, whether mainline, evangelical or pentecostal. Generally speaking, pastors and their people as well as self-proclaimed prophets see God's Word as comforting, encouraging, loving and motivating, as these terms are understood in modern and post-modern western cul-ture. While there is truth in these concepts, it is by no means the whole truth. Deception lies in the chasm between how we choose to embrace God's Word and how God sees it.

God's viewpoint is virtually anathema to our feelings that continually fight to replace our faith, rendering us very susceptible to the seduction of false prophecy. God's Word, through His eyes, is not only *comforting* but *convicting*, it is not only loving but lashes out at sin and unrighteousness. The Scriptures introduce us to peace with God, but also pierce over hearts with the "Sword of the Spirit which is the Word of God" (Eph. 6:17). God rebukes false prophets and pastors who speak only the soft side of Scripture, thundering, "Is not my word like as a fire? And like a hammer that breaketh the rock in pieces" (Jer. 23:29)? So… what do you say?

THEY COPY-CAT THEIR PROPHECIES

"… behold, I am against the prophets, saith the Lord, that steal my words every one from his neighbor… that use their tongues and say, He saith (Jer. 23:30-31).

It has become commonplace for pastors and prophets to mimic one another. Like politicians, they like to take their cues, not from God but from others perceived as more successful. They travel from seminar to seminar, conference to conference, to get their marching orders, then placing God's name upon their own thoughts to authenticate them before others. Again, like politicians, they do "spiritual" polling to determine the "wind of the Spirit."

It is deception, leading their disciples into false confidence in their communication with God. Man becomes the master while the Master becomes little more than a spiritual mascot, giving a false illusion that God has spoken. When a pastor purports to speak "prophetically" through a message he has plagiarized from the Internet because he does not actually hear from God himself, you know the people are in trouble.

THEIR MESSAGE IS "GOSPEL-LITE"

"Behold, I am against them that prophesy … and cause my people to err by their lies, and by their lightness; therefore they shall not profit this people at all, saith the Lord" (Jer. 23:32).

Here are the two principle ways those purporting to speak prophetically deceive. They lie, and they turn God's weighty Word into little more than a motivational mantra of self-help slogans and systems. They pander to the people in the name of Christ, thus bordering on blaspheming God's ultimate Prophet (Yeshua) who died to tell and live the whole truth as the Truth made flesh (Jn. 1:14).

Lying is not only defined by what is said but also by what is not said. If we preach only of God's promises and blessings but skirt away from His warnings, correction and judgment, have we indeed "preached the Word?" If we speak of His love, mercy, favor and forgiveness but refuse to speak equally of His Truth, His justice and judgment and the necessity of our obedience and repentance, have we not presented an unbalanced and therefore false gospel. Will "gospel-lite" save a people weighted down with sin and unrighteousness just because we bring them inside the doors of churches filled with parishioners who refuse to repent because our pastors and prophets are more concerned with personal reputation than a true prophet's reward?

Counterfeit Christ Needs Counterfeit Prophet

As we have seen, the marketing of messages today, whether secular or spiritual, is deeply rooted in creating perceptions that are fabricated or are a pretense, purporting to be "the real thing" but are designed primarily to promote an image. This has been called "synthetic authenticity." It has become the prevailing way to promote products and persons in a world where "image is everything." When the realm, role and ministry of the prophet is fabricated, we are destined for deep and dramatic deception.

The prophet is intended by God to be a messenger of profound purpose, a "voice crying in the wilderness." He is God's ultimate voice to His people and the world when pastor, priest and people have become dull of hearing, and when the ways of the people have become morally degenerate. When the prophet or prophetic voice becomes a pretense, God is provoked and the people are led astray, as by a spiritual "pied piper," to deception and destruction. Such synthetic "prophetic" voices have proliferated over the past generation, priming the church to be seduced by the "false-real." These false-real "prophets" are, in a sense, a premonition of the ultimate false prophet described in the Book of Revelation.

A counterfeit "christ" needs a counterfeit prophet to declare his message so as to convince the people of his authenticity. As the Anti-Christ begins to be exalted as a political savior "anointed" by the final "beast" empire prophesied by Daniel (Dan. 7:12-21), gaining phenomenal favor with the global citizens through crafty politics, promises of peace and flattery (Dan. 8:23-25, 11:21), another "beast" will arise. This second beast is identified commonly as "the false prophet."

The false prophet "exerciseth all the power of the first beast… and causeth the earth and them which dwell therein to worship the first beast, whose deadly wound was healed." He, like the counterfeit christ he represents, will undoubtedly employ "flattery" to gain favor with the people. Like so many false prophets today and in the past, he will tell the people what he thinks they want to hear. He may even quote Scripture to seduce the saints who have failed to study the Word diligently, so as to rightly divide the Word of truth (II Tim. 2:15).

Interestingly, this false prophet will be a miracle worker. He will even counterfeit the prophet Elijah so as to deceive both Jew and Gentile, making "fire come down from heaven on the earth in the sight of men."

317

"He deceiveth… by means of those miracles," using them to confirm his authority so as to compel those deceived to make an image to the beast. "He causeth all, both small and great, rich or poor, free and bond" to receive the identifying "mark of the beast" and causes "as many as would not worship the image of the beast should be killed" (Rev. 13:11-15).

What, then, are the pertinent principles we should glean from these descriptions so as to avoid this massive end-time deception that leads the masses to eternal destruction?

1. We must be personally anchored in the truth of God's Word so that we can rightly divide the Word of truth and not be seduced by having it turned against us.
2. We must realize that miracles are no substitute for the ministry of the truth through the Word of God.
3. We must be committed to the whole Word of God, both Old and New Testament, and live out God's truth in spirit and in truth through obedient, holy lives.
4. We must not be seduced by our feelings and choreographed emotionalism in the name either of God or government.
5. We must build a tower of trust in the God of truth through a continuous cycle of loving obedience and repentance, restoring and maintaining true spiritual sensitivity to God's still small voice.
6. We must seek first the kingdom of God and His righteousness.
7. We must be prepared to stand alone and not be seduced by the massive majorities who value temporal life and peace over eternal life and peace, thus rejecting the true Prince of Peace in favor of Satan's imposter.

The Door to Deception

There are two principal doorways into the chambers of false prophets and by which their voices gain access to the chambers of your heart and mind. These are:

1. When we do not truly love the truth.
2. When we take pleasure in unrighteousness.

Paul makes it abundantly clear. When the "son of perdition," the "man of sin," or the counterfeit christ is presented and that "Wicked" is revealed, he will have first gained his deceptive dominion "with all deceivableness of unrighteousness in them that perish, because they received not the love of the truth that they might be saved." That deceivability of unrighteousness will be camouflaged by the false prophet's religious appearance, purportedly confirmed by "the working of Satan with all power and signs and lying wonders" (II Thess. 2:2-11).

Therefore, brethren, "be strong in the Lord, and in the power of His might. Put on the whole armour of God, that ye may be able to stand against the wiles of the devil." "Stand, therefore, having your loins girt about with truth…" "That ye may be able to stand in the evil day, and having done all to stand" (Eph. 6:10). Pray always, watching with all perseverance (Eph. 6:18).

Chapter Twenty-One

Daring Thoughts
for *Deceptive Times*

1. What is a *false prophet*?

2. How many will be deceived by false prophets? Could that possibly include you? Your loved ones? Your congregation?

3. What is a true prophet?

4. As you read Jeremiah's "Terrible Ten" characteristics of false prophets, did any specific persons come to mind? Why?

5. Have you found yourself taken in by the glib promises and prophecies of someone claiming to speak prophetically? Why did you respond favorably?

6. Why does the counterfeit christ need a false or counterfeit prophet? Are you presently equipped to discern the counterfeit nature of the miracle-working false prophet?

7. There are two primary doors to deception. Are either of these doors open in your life?

Chapter Twenty-Two

≈≋≈

False Teachers

"…there shall be false teachers among you…
Many shall follow their pernicious ways" (II Pet. 2:1-2).

FALSE TEACHERS AND FALSE PROPHETS are cut largely from the same cloth. There is something about their message, and perhaps methods and attitudes, that is deceptive and dangerous.

Forewarning

In this chapter we will explore the nature of false teaching, ways that the truth can be falsified, and tests for truth. We will bridge from cults to Christian denominationalism and from small groups to the mega-church phenomena. We will probe the deceptive side of doctrines often held dear. This chapter, by its very nature, will likely be challenging to many. The religious and spiritual land mines that are laid throughout the world… even throughout the world of professing Christians… are so voluminous and carefully placed so as to dare anyone with good will to deign to approach the subject of doctrinal deception without risking violent reaction and explosive retribution. For that reason, you are urged to make every effort to read with a heart toward righteous response rather than reactionary, knee-jerk reaction.

The issues presented here are identified as the result of sixty-three years of exposure to, in and with the broader body of Christ, from coast to coast and in a variety of mainline, evangelical and pentecostal/charismatic persuasions and denominations. The author is the son of a man who ministered for seventy years in a variety of denominations, and this author has also engaged in ongoing pastoral and media ministry for twenty-five years.

Over the past generations of personal ministry and broad church exposure, it has become glaringly apparent that dramatic changes have taken place in the lives and beliefs of professing Christians, causing any honest, knowledgeable and careful observer to shake his or her head in disbelief at such dangerous drift. The church is in grave danger of being dashed to pieces on the shoals of deception! And this is precisely as both Jesus and the apostles warned. "Take heed that no man deceive you," declared our Lord" (Matt. 24:4). If followers of Christ could not be deceived, Jesus the Christ was certainly unaware of it. Neither was Peter, the apostle.

> ...*there shall be false teachers among you, who privily shall bring in damnable heresies, even denying the Lord that bought them, and bring on themselves swift destruction.*
> *And many shall follow their pernicious ways; by reason of whom the way of truth shall be evil spoken of. And through covetousness shall they with feigned words make merchandise of you (II Pet. 1-3).*

Why People Believe Falsehood

If, as the Bible indicates, the vast majority of people on the planet will "believe a lie" (II Thess. 2:11) and "few there be" that will walk the narrow way and find the strait gate that leadeth to eternal life (Matt. 7:13-14), we need to understand why that will be true. Understanding *why* is our first defense against false teaching.

We must return to the simple warning words of the apostle Paul. People will be seduced by false teaching and false prophecy for either or both of the following basic reasons:

1. They love not the truth; and
2. They have pleasure in unrighteousness (II Thess. 2:9-12).

The underlying heart condition of those who will be deceived is that there is either a latent desire or active will to be deceived. If that were not true, they would be lovers of the truth and take pleasure in righteousness. So… at this juncture, where do you honestly fit as the Holy Spirit searches your heart? Do you honestly consider yourself a *lover of the truth*? Do you embrace the truth… the whole truth… even if it hurts? Do you *take pleasure in righteousness*… God's standard, that is… or do you dance with the deteriorating and continually re-defined cultural standards rooted in compromise?

"Strong delusion" characterizes those seduced into deception (II Thess. 2:11). *Delusion* is a false belief or opinion, strongly held in spite of invalidating evidence. Why are such false beliefs strongly held in spite of biblical evidence to the contrary? Consider these ten biblical reasons carefully.

1. They love not the truth (II Thess. 2:10).
2. They prefer unrighteousness (II Thess. 2:12).
3. They prefer "wonders" over the Word (II Thess. 2:9).
4. They actually love unrighteousness (II Tim. 3:1-4).
5. They have only a form of godliness (II Tim. 3:5).
6. They are easily led due to fleshly desires (II Tim. 3:6).
7. They seek information, but reject the transforming truth (II Tim. 3:7).
8. They actually resist the truth when it is perceived as undesirable to the flesh, because their minds have become corrupt and reprobate (II Tim. 3:8).
9. They will not endure sound doctrine but seek teachers who will tell them what they want to hear (II Tim. 4:3).

10. They turn their ears from truth, preferring falsity and even fables presented by seducers who "wax worse and worse, deceiving and being deceived," just like their hearers (II Tim. 4:4, 3:13).

Identifying Features of Falsehood

Now that we have discovered, from God's viewpoint, why people become deceived, we must attempt to discover the most decisive characteristics of falsehood as it relates to biblical truth. As we do this, it is important to again be reminded that Scriptural warnings about deception are directed to disciples... people who claim to be followers of Christ and who sincerely believe they are what they claim to be. God is concerned about the *Seduction of the Saints*, particularly as we enter the "last days" (II Tim. 3).

There are at least seven clear characteristics of falsehood and its carriers worthy of our consideration. Space permits but a brief review.

1. FALSE CHARACTER of TEACHER

The Scriptures enjoin us to truly "know them which labor among you" (I Thess. 5:12). This calls for a level of confidence born of relational intimacy and observably consistent Christian character. Concerning character, the standard has little to do with *charisma* but everything to do with consistent *Christ-likeness*. Christians are easily seduced by celebrity charisma. We like to be WOWed rather than to be won by hard truth.

Paul provides necessary attitudinal and behavioral standards for all persons considered as leadership in Christ's body. These are precisely stated in I Tim. 3:2-13 and in Titus 1:6-14. We do well to review these regularly and apply them faithfully, first to ourselves and then to others. As a point of illustration, a pastor, prophet or teacher who is not "given to hospitality" will be given to SELF-ishness. His or her self focus will affect what they say, what they do not say, and how they say it.

One who teaches, preaches or prophesies as well as one appointed publically to serve must hold "the mystery of the faith in a pure conscience" (I Tim. 3:9). A corrupt conscience will translate into a corrupted and deceptive message. The condition of one's life determines how and what he declares as truth.

2. FALSE CALLING

It has been frequently said that many a pastor or priest has been "called by his mother" rather than "called by God." Many men enter ministry with corrupt minds, bearing a carnal message that connects with carnal hearers who sing their carnal, celebrity praises. Most men, however, begin with a clear conscience, but many become corrupted within an increasingly corrupting church system, seeking to please an increasingly carnal constituency. A teacher, pastor or prophet who panders to the people, refusing to teach or preach the hard and heart-convicting truths of the Bible, has become a hireling and has shifted his calling from Christ to the culture. Deception of the disciples is inevitable.

3. FALSE CHARACTER OF GOD

When the very character of God is falsified, the call of God in our lives is distorted, resulting in deception that can well lead to an undesired destiny. This may well be one of the most serious problems seducing saints today. The deceptive nature of such teaching is usually not that it is totally untrue but rather that it is a half-truth leading to a false understanding and false faith in a false God. It stems from an inherent desire to give God a make-over so that He might be more palatable to our fickle feelings and fast-food tastes.

"God is love" says the Bible (I Jn. 4:8), yet the prophet Malachi excoriates those who claimed to be God's chosen, saying that they have forgotten "the God of judgment" (Mal. 2:17). God is compassionate and merciful, and for that we are eternally grateful, but He is also the God of truth and righteousness (Deut. 32:4, Ps. 45:7, Heb. 1:9), and expects those who claim His name to live righteously (I Jn. 2:29). God desires that we be blessed and happy (Matt. 5:1-12, Prov. 16:20), yet He commands that we be holy (Lev. 20:7, I Pet. 1:14-16), and without holiness "no man shall see the Lord" (Heb. 12:14).

In this last generation, as we approach Christ's Second Coming, we have perversely and pragmatically re-defined the faith so as to promote power, perks and position by maligning the character of a holy God, recasting Him as a cosmic Santa Clause. *TIME* perfectly captured the popular deception on April 5, 1993, in its cover story. As Americans were flooding back to church for a brief season following Gulf War I, the news magazine noted that church would never again be the same. The reason was not cause for rejoicing. This liberal publication labeled the problem with the discernment of a prophet, declaring, "Americans are looking for a custom-made God, one made in their own image."

What kind of God do you seek, or serve? Have you, perhaps unwittingly, become complicit in the customizing of God... a false God for deceptive times? Do you truly and joyously embrace His whole truth, or have you subtly re-defined His character to suit yours? And what of Christ?

4. FALSE CHRIST

As with God the Father, so with God the Son. Mis-characterization of the Father leads inevitably to a re-defining of the Son. Jesus said, "He that hath seen me hath seen the Father" (Jn. 14:9). Therefore, mis-characterization of Jesus also leads necessarily to re-creating God the Father in a false image. It was precisely Jesus' specific identification in oneness with the Father that caused the religious leaders to label Jesus a "deceiver" and a blasphemer worthy of death (Jn. 5:18, 7:12, 10:30-31).

Consider that in all honesty neither pagans nor professing believers, including their pastors, care much for the God of the Old Testament. He is seen as mean-spirited, judgmental and oppressive. Jesus, on the other hand, is generally perceived as loving, tolerant, compassionate and generally light on sin, yet as Jesus said, "He that hath seen me hath seen the Father" (Jn. 14:9).

From God's viewpoint, it is clear that we have grossly misinterpreted not only the Father but His "Anointed One," the Son. How can we truly say we love God, God the Father, or Jesus the Christ when we so casually and cooly ignore their self-disclosed and self-described character? The reality is that we have not only created a custom-made God but also a re-designed Jesus. This alone reveals our latent will to be deceived and even to self-deceive.

What we defectively choose to believe about God, about the character and ministry of Jesus, and about the entirety of the biblical message has distorted the gospel truth into a patchwork of half truths opening the floodgate to fallacious faith and false security, for even the New Covenant declares, "Our God is a consuming fire" (Heb. 12:29). As it is written, "Jesus Christ the same yesterday, today and forever" (Heb. 13:8).

A "false" Christ, therefore is not just the imposter who presents himself saying "I am Christ," but is also a falsified Christ, re-designed, re-defined and re-imagined, who is re-constructed to meet our carnal, cultural re-defining of the Christian faith. Jesus the Great Physician is "IN" but Jesus the Prophet and ruling King is "OUT." We crucify Him afresh when we cavalierly reject His divine character, self-disclosed not only as "full of grace" but also as "full of truth" (Jn. 1:14).

When we yield to the temptation as pastors, parachurch leaders and people to feel compelled to "market" Jesus to an unbelieving and resistant culture, we inevitably manipulate His character to "sell" Him. We-recast Jesus in ways we think will make Him more palatable to a culture with ungodly tastes, thus seducing unbelievers to embrace a false Christ who gives them false hope with *synthetic authenticity*. The saints gradually sell themselves on a *false-real* Jesus, becoming self-seduced. Such "saints" are the prime candidates to be further seduced by the many false Christs and false prophets coming in the name of the Lord.

Take heed! These false Christs and false prophets come *in the name of the Lord*. "Many will come in my name, saying I am Christ; and shall deceive many," warned Jesus (Matt. 24:5). They may or may not claim to be Christ but will, in any event, present a false Christ claiming Scriptural authority. Some will supposedly confirm their words with miracles, as will the Anti-Christ's false prophet. Said Jesus, these "shall show great signs and wonders; insomuch that, if it were possible, they shall deceive the very elect" (Matt. 24:24). Little wonder, then, that our Lord cried… "Take heed that no man deceive you" (Matt. 24:4).

Have you subtly redefined or re-cast Jesus to suit the fancy of your feelings? Have you attempted to "market" Jesus to others so as to "win" them to Christ, misrepresenting the totality of His character so as to present our Lord in what you believe to be a light most favorable so as to pander to a compromising culture? Have you set yourself up, as well as those you love and serve, to easily embrace false Christs and the person and message of false prophets?

5. FALSE CONTROVERSY

Who is on the Lord's side, and how do we know? God has a controversy over this question. In fact, God has basically two controversies, one with pagans and the other with those who profess His name. One controversy we easily understand; the other we easily reject, for we often live on the edge of presumption.

"The Lord hath a controversy with the nations," warned Jeremiah. He will plead with all flesh; He will give them that are wicked to the sword...." "And the slain of the Lord will be at that day from one end of the earth even unto the other...." (Jer. 25:31-33). Those who do not call themselves by the name of the Lord and believe are "condemned already," said Jesus, because "men loved darkness rather than light... their deeds were evil" (Jn. 3:18-19).

Yet God also says He has a controversy with those who claim His name. It is a controversy which few truly acknowledge, leading to serious deception and destruction, compromising destiny.

The prophet Micah lifted up his voice like a trumpet to Israel and Judah, those who called themselves by the name of the Lord and who claimed the promises of Abraham. "Hear... the Lord's controversy... for the Lord hath a controversy with his people, and he will plead with Israel" (Micah 6:2). What is the root cause of God's controversy? The prophets and pastors keep telling the people, "Is not the Lord among us? no evil shall come upon us" (Micah 3:11).

This feel-good, flattering message carries much favor among professing saints, yet it seduces them to a false trust when they have, in actuality, lost their love for truth. It portrays the precise condition of the church today, claiming to love Jesus but largely rejecting God's truth by walking in unrighteousness. In such an environment, God cannot get a word in edgewise to bring correction and conviction because the increasing majority of pastors and prophets, loving the praises of men more than the praises of God, continue proclaiming, "The Lord is among us; no evil shall befall us."

Hosea reinforced God's warning concerning this dangerous deception. God's real controversy is not with the pagans but with those who profess His name. If we can re-frame the focus of God's controversy, pretending it is not with "US" but with "THEM," we think we escape the finger of God's corrective hand. *After all, we reason, WE wear the "white hats" and THEY wear the black hats.* This thinking has driven thirty years of "Culture Wars," resulting in almost no visible or lasting moral or spiritual change. Christians have insulated themselves from the Holy Spirit's conviction, hence, no real revival.

And so Hosea pierces this "Christianized" paganism among God's people with a serious warning.

> *Hear the word of the Lord… for the Lord hath a controversy*
> *with the inhabitants of the land, because there is no truth,*
> *mercy, nor [true] knowledge of God in the land.*
> *By swearing, and lying, and killing, and stealing, and com-*
> *mitting adultery, they break out…. Therefore shalt thou fall in*
> *the day, and the prophet also shall fall with thee… and I will*
> *destroy thy mother.*
> *My people are destroyed for lack of knowledge; because though*
> *hast rejected knowledge, I also will reject thee…: seeing thou hast*
> *forgotten the law of thy God, I will also forget thy children…*
> *because they have left off to take heed to the Lord (Hosea 4:1-6).*

> *They will not frame their doings to turn unto their God: for the*
> *spirit of whoredoms is in the midst of them, and they have not*
> *known the Lord. They shall… seek the Lord; but they shall not*
> *find him; he hath withdrawn himself from them (Hosea 5:1-6).*

A falsely-focused controversy seduces the heart of the professing saints into a false sense of security, vehemently claiming "God is among us," when in fact, "he hath withdrawn himself from them" (Hosea 5:6). It is professing believers that "backslide," and when they persist in or are "bent to backsliding," God will give sway to their self-deceived wills (Hosea 11:7). In His mercy He woos and warns, " return unto the Lord thy God; for thou hast fallen by thine iniquity" (Hosea 14:11).

The question remains. Have we, have you, has your congregation presumed that God's warnings were for "THEM" rather than for you or "US?" If so, deception lies at the door and has most likely taken up residence in your house.

6. FALSE COMMITMENT.

To whom is God committed? To whom are you committed? To whom is your congregation or group committed? These questions open the door to discussion of areas in which both pastor and people unwittingly find themselves in deception, and which provide the axis around which some forms of deception turn. We will look at just a few examples.

A. People versus God

God loves people and we are inspired to love them as well. Yet frequently our professed love of God conflicts with our admonition to love people. Some engage in isolation from people as a practice, claiming it is because they are so in love with God. Others spend their time with people, virtually ignoring a personal and intimate relationship with God. Most pastors and parachurch leaders can relate to this problem. If allowed to persist as a practice, it becomes a practice of self-deception justified as "serving God." It reveals an unbalanced life.

Similarly, since we are called to love and serve people in the name of Christ, our invariable human tendency is to shift our focus to people while losing our focus on the Lord, again justified as "serving God." When this pattern persists, without correction, it inevitably results in us becoming "people pleasers" rather than "God pleasers." This is one of the most serious deceptions in the church today. It has led to unbalanced and therefore unbiblical teaching and unbalanced lives? As we seek increasingly to please (and not offend) people in our ministries and lives, we decreasingly seek to please God.

Pleasing God requires teaching and preaching the whole truth of His Word, not just those parts we think will please and patronize the fickle feelings of saints and sinners. It means not only telling folks they are forgiven but also that they must forgive or forfeit God's favor (Matt. 6:15). It means not only teaching friends that God is love but that He hates evil and sin and will not countenance rebellion in His presence (Ps. 97:10, Prov. 8:13, Heb. 12:14). It includes not only proclaiming the precious mercies of God but that His mercy extends only to those who fear Him and will obey Him (Ps. 103:13, 17-18). It requires not only offering Christ's salvation from sin but warning that upon Christ's return, "he cometh to judge the earth: He shall judge the world with righteousness, and the people with His truth" (Ps. 96:13), and that "mercy and truth" are two sides of the coin of God's character.

Woe to the professing Christian, and especially pastors and prophets, who prepare, on the day of judgment, to rely on the defense, "I did it to please the people" or "I just didn't want to offend them by telling them the whole truth." It cost king Saul the kingdom (I Sam. 15). What will it cost you?

B. Government versus God

The choice between God and government has been an age-old issue, used by saint and sinner as both sword and shield. It has been used to establish and protect both political and religious power. And it will become a quintessential tool of deception in the mouth of a false christ and his false prophet.

Government is ordained by God, we are told, and indeed it is. "For government is the minister of God to thee for good. But if you do that which is evil, be afraid; for he beareth not the sword in vain: for he is the minister of God, a revenger to execute wrath upon him that doeth evil. Wherefore, ye must needs be subject, not only for wrath, but for conscience sake" (Rom. 13:4-5). In all realms, the God-given authority of government is simply to maintain order in a fallen world. It is to protect sinner and saint from external and internal attack perpetuated by sinful men.

The apostle Paul calls believers to submit to such government as a "minister of God for good." We are not only to submit and obey its laws because of the threat of force but also because of our faith. "Let every soul be subject unto the higher powers. For there is no power but of God: the powers that be are ordained of God. Whosoever therefore resisteth the power, resisteth the ordinance of God: and they that resist shall receive to themselves damnation. For rulers are not a terror to good works, but to evil (Rom. 13:1-3).

What then are we to do if government becomes a terror to the "doers of good works?" What are we to do if a government becomes so corrupt and perverted as to become the enemy of the righteous rather than of the evil doer? The last words of Israel's king David were, "He that ruleth over men must be just, ruling in the fear of God" (II Sam. 23:3). But what do we do when rulers fear men more than God and when God-ordained government becomes an engine of corruption and unrighteousness?

Daniel and three Hebrew young men taken captive to Babylon found themselves in that predicament. Daniel, through conspiratorial decree, was ordered not to pray to anyone but the king for thirty days, which order he respectfully declined to follow and suffered the decreed consequences of the lion's den. Shadrach, Meshach and Abednego were commanded to bow down and worship Nebuchadnezzar's golden image, which demand they respectfully declined to follow, suffering the consequences of a ravaging fiery furnace. Peter and John were ordered not to speak or teach in the name of Jesus, which they respectfully refused to obey, stating, "We ought to obey God rather than men (Acts 4:18-21, 5:16-42). They were beaten and imprisoned, "rejoicing that they were worthy to suffer shame for his name" (Acts 5:41).

Increasingly, government is bringing a heavy hand upon Christians worldwide in the name of Jesus. Through laws, incitement of marauding bands, threat of force and refusal to enforce laws, otherwise law-abiding believers are suffering and dying so as to declare their faith and decide their eternal destiny, respectfully refusing to bow to tyrants who wage war against God through unbiblical laws. The times are tightening and the faith of true believers will be tried, even as by fire.

It is never wrong to do right; and it is never right to do wrong. We serve a higher Master than government. We must always respect the role of government and our leaders, but we must not bow down to their ungodly, unbiblical edicts that defy God and His Word. Government is to be our protector against evil doers, not a perpetrator of evil. Government is to be our servant, not our master. Furthermore, government is ordained by God to be our *protector*, not our *provider* (Rom. 13:4). When government overreaches its ordained purpose, purporting to be our provider, it will shift your trust from God to government. That is precisely the purpose of the *mark of the beast*.

Yield not to the temptation or teacher that would seek to justify your receiving the mark of the counterfeit christ, arguing that "the powers that be are of God," therefore you must "be subject unto the higher powers." A true Christian believer will respectfully decline, having prepared by faith to trust God come what may. Are you prepared to make such a decision… or will you be seduced into deception, depriving you of an eternal destiny with a loving God who now, in His mercy, warns you?

7. FALSE CONTENT

False teaching, by its very nature, contains false content. False content presents itself as either *unbiblical* or as *unbalanced*.

Unbiblical teaching is easier to identify than unbalanced teaching. By "unbiblical" we mean any teaching that is clearly contrary to or inconsistent with the foundations of the Christian faith as defined by both the Old and New Testaments. By "unbalanced" we mean teaching that may find support by certain passages but which is presented in such a way as to ignore other equally important and counterbalancing passages, thus leading to deceptive theology that seduces the saints into what, in actuality, are unbiblical beliefs and false trusts.

A. Unbiblical Teaching

Obvious unbiblical teaching normally conjures mental concepts of pagan religions and cults. Today, however, even these historically *unbiblical* teachings are being syncretized into a religious stew with the historically "Christian" faith to suit the politically-correct environment of post-modern thinking where there is no toleration for absolute truth. For those under forty years of age, discerning and discipling in "the faith once delivered to the saints" is becoming exceedingly difficult. All of the global cultural forces now virtually demand inclusion, embracing all beliefs as co-equal in value; what in effect is universal salvation. As the reasoning goes, *If God is love, none will be lost and all will be saved*, based upon the sincerity of one's belief, however false it may be.

Such obvious unbiblical teaching would include, but not be limited to, New Age, Buddhism, Hinduism, Pantheism, and Mohammedanism (ISLAM). Of particular danger here are cultural celebrities and media icons who increasingly embrace these teachings, purporting to normalize them as the "IN" thing for modern man who truly loves his neighbor.

In January 2008, Oprah Winfrey, having declared, "The Bible deceived me," embarked upon a massive media program through "Oprah and Friends" to disciple untold millions to forsake the truth of Scripture, embracing the "gospel" of Eckhart Tolle's *A New Earth* and Marianne Williamson's *A Course in Miracles*. Winfrey now boldly proclaims you have no need of a savior - "You are your own savior." Millions of adoring fans, including a vast "Christian" audience, have been progressively seduced by her false gospel embellished by an emotionally-driven cult of celebrity.

Traditionally recognized cults such as Jehovah's Witness, Christian Science, Scientology and Mormonism, which present books claimed as co-equal with or superceding the Biblical revelation, rely upon extra-biblical writings to re-cast the Scriptures with emphases and doctrines that are not consistent with the Bible. They attempt to combine the Scriptures with other writings which, in effect, create a new hybrid faith or religion.

Judaism presents a similar problem, claiming the Tanach or the Old Testament's 39 books to be true and God-inspired, yet combining with it vast rabbinical writings and interpretations taken as functionally co-equal in authority. Thus, Rabbinic Judaism often re-constructs, re-defines and sometimes actually de-constructs the well-understood faith of the prophets. Yeshua himself, as a rabbi, rebuked the Sadducees and Pharisees for their unbiblical traditions. Jesus excoriated their twisting of truth by rabbinical "spin," declaring, "ye have made the commandment of God of none effect by your tradition." "In vain they do worship me, teaching for doctrine the commandments of men," lamented our Lord (Matt. 15:1-9).

Roman Catholicism, purporting to be "Christian" by embracing Christ as savior, exalts the magesterium of the Roman church to a place co-equal to and with authority superceding Christ himself. The pope, purporting to speak *FOR* God, is deemed to speak *AS* God. His words and papal edicts are declared to supercede and overrule the written Scriptures, including the omission of the Second Commandment and the arbitrary re-defining of the Fourth Commandment. So extensive are these papal positions contrary to the writings of the apostles, prophets and Christ himself that many are set forth in the table at the conclusion of this chapter.

The examples of groups and religious persuasions presenting unbiblical teaching are too numerous to enumerate. Even as this chapter was being written, the author received a call from a leading member of the Unification Church led by Rev. Sun Yung Moon. This gentleman has listened regularly to the author's daily radio broadcast, *VIEWPOINT*, being greatly encouraged by our continued focus on strong marriages and families. For twenty minutes he gracefully sought to wed our biblical focus on marriage and family to Rev. Moon's doctrine that he and he wife are the True Parents sent by God and that Rev. Moon is, indeed, the awaited Messiah, which claim was boldly announced recently to the United States Congress.

What simple tests might we employ in order to discern the deception presented by what should be clearly distinguished as "unbiblical" teaching? Such tests for evaluating unbiblical teaching might include:

1. Does it seek to rely upon writings outside of the Bible itself?
2. Does it elevate the authority or opinion of any man, woman or group over that of Christ and both the Old and New Testaments?
3. Does it point exclusively to Yeshua (Jesus Christ) as the Messiah and as the only savior and only mediator between God and man?

While there is a multitude of clearly unbiblical teaching relatively easily discerned by a true and sincere disciple of Christ, there are equally as many teachings that, while purporting to be biblical, are actually unbiblical because of their lack of proper biblical balance. These are often more difficult for unsuspecting saints to see and therefore lead seductively to unexpected distortions of truth and damaging- even dangerous - unintended consequences.

B. Unbalanced Teaching

Unbalanced teaching usually bases its authority on some portion of Scripture, hence its profound capability of deceiving by leading unsuspecting or unknowledgeable believers astray. Pastors and parachurch leaders are particularly prone to be snared in the trap of unbalanced teaching because they have congregations and constituencies they feel compelled to please. Since *BIG* is almost always deemed to be *BETTER*, compromise in choosing what will be taught, what will not be taught and the relative weight that will be given to particular aspects of the biblical message is inevitable and has unfortunately become normative.

The problems of unbalanced teaching are seriously exacerbated by a host of Christian ISMS including such commonly accepted isms as liberalism, conservatism, Calvanism, Armenianism, Protestantism, and

Catholicism. Add to these various other doctrinal systems and the risk of unbalanced teaching increases dramatically. Then introduce the 2000 denominations in America and the 20,000 such denominations world-wide and biblical truth becomes fragmented into thousands of camps, each choosing to emphasize an aspect of Scripture to the diminution or even exclusion of other profoundly important biblical principles.

The land mines of these various theological positions are strewn dangerously across the broader Christian community, threatening rejection and destruction to anyone daring to question their biblical balance. These explosive "land mines" serve to insulate whole groups from question or correction, thus perpetuating a hybrid form of deception under the aegis of "protecting truth." We must humbly admit that even our denominations and doctrinal associations were nearly all formed out of division, testifying to the fact that deception was lurking about. And they cannot all be right.

Unbalanced teaching often, if not usually, presents itself by forcing an unbiblical choice or emphasis, pitting one truth against another, mandating an either/or decision. Some of the more common of these false choices are:

The love of God	vs.	The truth of God
The mercy of God	vs.	The judgment of God
The grace of God	vs.	The holiness of God
The wooing of God	vs.	The wrath of God
The forgiveness of God	vs.	The righteousness of God

Each one of these characteristics of God are set in opposition, creating a divine tension that is woven like a thread throughout the Bible. As human beings, our fleshly minds resist these holy tensions, demanding resolve for our comfort. Yet to resolve in favor of one or the other seemingly opposite characteristics is to eviscerate God himself, reconstructing His character as our human mind desires. Such arrogance borders on blasphemy. We must accept and teach God as He reveals himself... not as we want to relate to Him. In each instance, God is not "either/or" but rather a hard-core "both/and."

If we shift the balance either way to overemphasize a characteristic of God we prefer over one we tacitly reject, we have, in effect, created God in our own image. The Church, professing Christians and their pastors, having purposely chosen for an entire generation to emphasize the love, mercy, grace, wooing and forgiveness of God, while rejecting in very real ways, the judgment, truth, holiness, wrath and righteousness of God, have led pastor and people alike into a moral cesspool where the fear of the Lord is mocked and "obey" is deemed a four-letter word to be avoided at all costs. The wheel of the church is so out-of-balance as to be thumping dangerously down the broad path to destruction.

The so-called "Emerging Church" is but the latest in a generational series of re-defining and re-emphasizing the Word of God to pander to a culture that increasingly hates Christ. The emphasis is not to become more Christ-like but to become more culture-like so that presenting Christ can be more comfortable and without real risk. For the "Emerging Church" and its leaders, the very thought of teaching doctrinal truth is tantamount to heresy. Why? The "Emerging Church" is choosing an even more dramatic shift in favor of the love, mercy, grace, wooing and forgiveness of God to the virtual, if not open and vitriolic, exclusion of the judgment, truth, holiness, wrath and righteousness of God.

If we are truly on the near edge of our Lord's Second Coming, these unbalanced choices and teachings that virtually defy the fulness and truth of God's self-revealed character put vast numbers of professing believers who place their trust in such teaching at great spiritual risk of deception. And those who are purportedly converted under such false teaching are led to trust a false gospel and a false God.

Is it not time to take seriously the command to teach the whole counsel of God? Parishioners will exclaim, "But my pastor teaches the Word." But what they fail to realize is that he may be teaching primarily those aspects of the Word he chooses to teach so as to preserve favor with the people. Judgment will begin first at the house of God (I Pet. 4:17). And as James reminds us, pastors and teachers "shall receive the greater condemnation" (Jam. 3:1).

The vast deception that defines these last days requires special discernment by the saints. "Take heed that no man deceive you" (Matt. 24:4).

Chapter Twenty-Two

Daring Thoughts
for *Deceptive Times*

⁓◦⁓

1. How would you identify a *false teacher*?

2. Why are people prone to believe false teaching?

3. Is it possible to teach from the Bible and still be a false teacher? How?

4. As you read through the seven characteristics of false teaching and false teachers, did any persons or teachings come to mind? Why?

5. What is the difference between a clearly *unbiblical* teaching and an *unbalanced* teaching? Can you see how, in reality, they are both actually unbiblical?

6. How do both clearly unbiblical and unbalanced teaching lead professing believers into false trust and, in effect, to a false gospel?

7. Why will pastors and teachers receive "greater condemnation?" Does their greater condemnation leave you off the hook for failing to discern deception?

8. Have you truly "studied to show yourself approved unto God a workman that needeth not to be ashamed, rightly dividing the word of truth?" What do you intend to do about your deficiency? When will you start? Will you faithfully persist?

Is the Roman Church Christ's Church?
A Biblical Comparison

ISSUE	ROMAN CATHOLIC	vs. GOD'S WORD
Holy Father	Pope & Priests	"Call no man Father"
Intermediary	Pope - priest - Christ through Mary	"The man Christ Jesus"
Blessing	To those who obey the Church	To those who obey Christ
Mary	"Mother of God"	Mother of Jesus
Priesthood	Appointed by Vatican System	All who are reborn in Christ
Final Authority	Pope and Church tradition	Word of God
Sabbath	1st Day	7th Day
Marriage	Pope and priests forbidden to marry	Forbidding marriage a "Doctrine of devils"
Access to Word	Pope and Priests	All Believers
Governance	Vatican System	Holy Spirit
Salvation	Faith + Works, mediated by Church	Faith alone thru Christ alone
Eternal City	Rome	Jerusalem
Temple Mount	Vatican	Mt. Zion
His Holiness	Pope	God Alone
Prayer	Ask Christ in Mary's name	"Ask the Father in my name"
Truth	Defined and determined by Pope & tradition	Defined and determined by Word and Spirit
Judgment	Once to die, then purgatory	"Once to die, then judgment"
Saints	Those beatified & sanctified by Vatican	All believers sanctified by Christ
Wisdom's Source	Fear of the Church	Fear of the Lord
Forgiveness	By Pope and Priests	By God - as acknowledged by saints
Interpretation of Word	By Pope and Church Tradition	No private interpretation
Supreme Head of Church	The Roman Pontiff	Jesus Christ
"Immutability"/Unchangeable	The Roman Church and its Traditions	God and His Word
The Church	All who submit to Rome as representative of Christ	All who submit to Christ

"'The Pope': A Scandal and A Mystery"

"This man who is called the Pope is a mystery…a sign of contradication. He is even considered a challenge or a 'scandal' to logic or good sense…"

"Confronted with the Pope, one must make a choice. The leader of the Catholic Church is defined by the faith as the Vicar of Jesus Christ. The Pope is considered the man on earth who represents the Son of God, who 'takes the place' of the Second Person of the omnipotent God of the Trinity."

"Have no fear when people call me the 'Vicar of Christ,' when they say to me 'Holy Father,' or 'Your Holiness,' or use titles similar to these, which seem even inimical [contrary or opposed] to the Gospel. Christ himself declared: 'Call no one on earth your father; you had but one master, the Messiah' (Mt. 23: 9-10).

These expressions, nevertheless, have evolved out of a long tradition, becoming part of common usage. One must not be afraid of these words either."

Quoted from *Crossing the Threshhold of Hope*
by "His Holiness" John Paul II © 1994
Chapter 1, "The Pope": A Scandal and a Mystery", pg. 3, 6.

THE CHOICE: To take the Creator God at His Word, or, to take the Pope and Roman Catholic Traditions as the final authority for life, faith and practice.

False Hope

*"Every man that hath this hope in him purifieth himself,
even as he [Christ] is pure" (I Jn. 3:3).*

TRUE HOPE "MAKETH NOT ASHAMED" (Rom. 5:5), but a false hope leads only to deception and destruction. Hope lies at the heart of the gospel. It is the firm and trusting expectation of being restored to righteous relationship with a holy God who will welcome holy people into His heavenly home in the fulness of time. Such a hope becomes truly "GOOD NEWS" in light of the horror of eternal anguish and separation from God that awaits those who do not truly place their trust in the "God of hope" (Rom. 15:13). Rest assured: Hell is not a place of hope.

The Seduction of Syncretism

Just as the Arch-deceiver, Satan, seeks to seduce saints in other areas of life and belief, so he never ceases to seduce us to a false hope. He is the Deceiver and works through deception to destroy the saints through false hope. Truly, "the devil is in the details."

False teaching often becomes *false* because it represents or is susceptible to implying a false hope. In the case of false and pagan religions, the risk of false hope to the saints is slim. To the extent the Bible becomes intermingled with other belief systems, the risk of embracing a false hope increases for professing followers of Christ. This is the great danger of *syncretism*, the blending of religious beliefs, to both saint and sinner. It is syncretism that is preparing the way for a unifying global religious faith that will lure the masses to a counterfeit master. But there remains a more subtle assault on the hope of the saints that is the principle focus of this chapter.

A Plea for Purity of Heart

Please bathe your heart in prayer as we seek to surgically dissect significant areas of false hope or susceptibility to false hope in those who profess to be the "body of Christ." Many are the land mines that are laid to render this surgical exploitation delicate.

For many, this chapter will be a challenge. Rather than yield to the fleshly temptation to respond in "knee-jerk" fashion to protect a position you or your group holds, please seek to listen with your heart as the Holy Spirit may reveal concerns you have not considered. Remember, our goal is oneness in Christ. Our hope is in Christ. And our purpose is to "seek first the kingdom of God and his righteousness" (Matt. 6:33) that all the blessings we seek "shall be added unto us."

One Faith, One Hope

Consider these words. There is only "one hope of your calling." "There is only one body, and one Spirit… one Lord, one faith, one baptism, one God and Father of all [believers] (Eph. 4:4-6). For this reason, we are called to "walk worthy of the vocation [or invitation] wherewith ye are called… endeavoring to keep the unity of the Spirit in the bond of peace" (Eph. 4:1-3).

If we are truly seeking to "keep the unity of the Spirit in the bond of peace" and if we truly believe there is "only one Lord, one faith, one baptism, one God, one Father" for all professing saints, how then do we explain the substantial differences that have driven the American church into over 2000 denominations and the global church into over 20,000 denominations? Is Christ divided? Does the Holy Spirit, who is "the Spirit of truth" (Jn. 14:17), lead those who claim to follow Christ's Spirit to embrace diverse and often diametrically opposed positions concerning both the written Word of God and Yeshua, the "Word made flesh?"

To claim such confusion and chaos is of Christ is again to border on blasphemy. If we are truly honest, this condition exists and persists because of two problems: (1) our fleshly lack of understanding of the fulness of God's Word (both Old and New Covenants) and His intent; (2) Our fleshly unwillingness to embrace the fulness of biblical truth and of the character of God as revealed in Christ and its implications for us as His followers. The painful truth is that we choose to believe what we want to believe.

To resolve this chaotic confusion within the ostensible "body of Christ," many call for compromise so as to achieve what, at best, may be artificial "oneness…" *synthetic authenticity*. For others, compromise is a polite word for *heresy*, and they remain hunkered in theological bunkers of belief systems, often refusing even to fellowship with those outside their denomination or theological persuasion. The reality is that Christ calls us neither to compromise nor to isolated communities but to humble conviction that if we were truly "in Christ," we would be at one with one another. The universal life goal, then, of all Christians believers must be to humbly press into Christ as "**the** way, **the** truth and **the** life" (Jn. 14:16) rather than pressing into our quasi-political theological conventions that bind us together, clinging to our crystallized theological positions rather than to the cross. The Christian life is not a theology to be formed but a life to be lived.

James pierced to the heart of a *theology* of faith disconnected from the *life* of faith, declaring, "Faith, if it hath not works, is dead, being alone" (Jam. 2:17). The brother of our Lord truly expressed the Hebraic heart in which the gospel was birthed, attacking the Greco-Roman cerebral faith composed primarily of cognitive assent to religious facts. He called such a believer a "vain man," repeating that "faith without works is dead" (Jam. 2:20). Life ways must line up with professed beliefs or the professed beliefs, however sincerely made, are bogus. "For as the body without the spirit is dead, so [professed] faith without works [consistent Christ-like life] is dead also (Jam. 2:26).

Convictions Have Consequences

Beliefs or convictions all have consequences. Theological constructs also have consequences. For as a man thinketh in his heart, so is he" (Prov. 23:7).

What we say we believe about God, about men, about eternity, about salvation and about the Christian life all affect a man's behavior. God has designed life so that consequences will flow dependant not only upon what we say we believe but also upon the alignment of our ways and will with God's will and ways. For this reason, God exhorts:

Let the wicked forsake his ways, and the unrighteous man
his thoughts: and let him return unto the Lord, and he will
have mercy upon him; and to our God, for he will abundantly
pardon (Isa. 55:7).

Repentance that lies at the heart of restoration of relationship with God, in both New and Old Testaments, demands not only a change of mind, belief or will, but also a corresponding change of heart, behavior or ways reflecting God's own ways. When this does not occur, belief, however true, becomes hypocrisy and is branded by God as "unbelief." It is precisely this kind of "unbelief" that kept all but two of Abraham's heirs, who God delivered from Egypt, from entering the Promised Land. And it is the same "unbelief" that will keep many from the eternal "Promised Land." God warned, these "believers"… "they do alway err in their heart; and they have not known my ways. So I sware in my wrath, They shall not enter into my rest" (Heb. 3:10-11).

The apostle Paul affirms this very understanding, reciting the history of God's chosen coming out of Egypt, whose true ways did not line up with their profession of God's favor as the seed of Abraham. "With many of them God was not well pleased." Paul says they were our examples that we, also professing to be the seed of Abraham by faith, should not fall as they did through the "unbelief" of failing to live in accordance with their claimed faith (I Cor. 10:1-10).

> *Now all these things happened unto them for ensamples: and are written for our admonition; upon whom the ends of the world are come.*
> *Wherefore, let him that thinketh he standeth take heed lest he fall (I Cor. 10:11-12).*

We see, then, that beliefs or convictions have consequences. The majority of the seed of Abraham, taken out of Egypt by God's mighty and merciful hand, were denied access by the same merciful God to the Promised Land. Although they were "heirs according to the promise to Abraham," they did not receive the promise. What kept them from receiving the promise? Their ways did not conform to God's ways. The disconnect between their professed belief and their life ways disqualified them from their desired destiny. God's response was not passive, for they provoked Him to wrath. "And the Lord's anger was kindled... and he sware, saying, Surely none of the men... shall see the land which I sware unto Abraham... because they have not wholly followed me... save Caleb... and Joshua... for they have wholly followed the Lord" (Num. 32:10-12).

Important questions naturally flow. Have you wholly followed the Lord? Do your ways reflect His ways? Do your thoughts reveal His thoughts? Does your will line up with His will? These are serious questions and cannot be taken lightly by brushing them off cavalierly, simply because you have embraced teaching that has led you to believe that how you live is relatively irrelevant to God and has no affect on your eternal destiny. Five hundred ninety-nine thousand, nine hundred ninety-eight Israelite men who believed in the God of Abraham and considered themselves heirs according to God's promise would now strongly beg to differ with your theology. They believed "IN" God, but they did not *BELIEVE* Him.

With this foundational background, we now explore the deceptive dangers lurking in the shadows of a number of popular doctrines that could work destiny-determining deception.

The Horror of False Hope

False hope, preached from pulpits and taught from pews, can be devastating to unsuspecting saints. It is not that either pastor or people intend to deceive by the unbalanced presentation of certain doctrines. On the contrary, they have become absolutely convinced as to their truth. Many would rather die on the hill guarding their theological camp than they would for Christ.

Most, if not all, such doctrines are built around substantial truth. That is where they gain their persuasive authority. Unfortunately, and often unwittingly, these doctrines are presented with great passion while precluding and excluding major balancing principles of Scripture, convincing the unwary of the absolute truth of these doctrines, luring the unsuspecting to a false hope.

Neither time nor space permit an extensive exploration of these teachings, so each will be given only such attention as is necessary to reveal the deception lurking in the doctrine. Because most of these are passionately promoted, to merely propose a concern is to provoke reaction. However, if we are truly on the near edge of Christ's return, it behooves us to humbly reassess beliefs that may have profoundly deceptive consequences for those who trust us as purveyors of truth.

Remember - Jesus warned, "Take heed that no man deceive you" (Matt. 24:4). This writer does not want to be an unwitting agent of deception. Certainly **you** would likewise want to avoid deception at all costs, even cost to your pride, power, perks or position. Finally, before we probe where "angels fear to tread," let us remember also that "A man, convinced against his will, will be of the same opinion still." Let us prayerfully proceed.

How is A Person Saved?

How is a person *saved*? From what is a person *saved*? And to what or for what purpose is a person *saved*?

Although what is about to be said is no longer considered "kosher" in certain "Emerging Church" circles, the Scriptures make clear that a person must be *saved* because he or she is *lost*. Jesus declared, "For the Son of man is come to seek and to save that which is lost" (Luke 19:10).

God's kingdom is the ultimate Lost and Found Department. But the good news of the gospel is hidden from the lost (II Cor. 4:3), because "the god of this world hath blinded the minds" (II Cor. 4:4) and their natural minds are incapable of perceiving their spiritual condition and spiritual truth (I Cor. 2:14).

God's law must be presented to a lost man so that he can see his true state, recognizing his need for a savior, "for all have sinned and come short of the glory of God" (Rom. 3:23), for the "wages of sin is death…" (Rom. 6:23). "The law was our schoolmaster to bring us to Christ" (Rom. 3:24). Once we, through the "schoolmaster" of the Law, see the utter hopelessness of our lost condition, and we humble ourselves to "repent and be baptized every one of you in the name of Jesus Christ for the remission of sins ye/we shall receive the gift of the Holy Ghost" (Acts 2:38). As it is written, "Believe on the Lord Jesus Christ and thou shalt be saved…" (Acts 16:31).

Our salvation is by God's grace [His enabling power], through faith [our trusting Christ's substitutionary sacrifice taking upon himself the death penalty for our sin], and it is not by our own good works, so that no man can boast, claiming he saved himself (Eph. 2:8-9). For "if thou shalt confess with thy mouth the Lord Jesus, and shalt believe in thine heart that God hath raised him from the dead, thou shalt be saved" (Rom. 10:9).

So… what does it take to be "saved?" One passage says "believe," another says "repent and be baptized," yet another says "confess and believe" and yet another says "baptism doth now save us" (I Pet. 3:21). What is the formula for saving faith? Is God decreeing a formula, or is He, through His earthly mouthpieces, describing in simple terms a profound life change that re-sets our minds and re-calibrates our hearts by His Spirit to serve the Lord our God with all our heart, soul, mind and strength revealed in loving our neighbor as ourselves. Is God seeking a *CONFESSION* or a *CONVERSION*?

Herein lies the latent deception of our westernized Greco-Roman delight in formularized faith. The formula of "believe and be baptized" confirmed only by "confession" actually confuses, shifting the weight of God's concern from *conversion* to *confession*, from a changed life to a blythe confession of faith. Many a man, under the evangelistic passion to get people "saved," makes his purported "confession of faith," yet is never truly convinced of his sinful lostness. Not fully comprehending the fulness of the good news of the gospel, he is neither converted, nor does his life reveal the inward change suggested by the outward confession. Yet he is assured he is saved because he followed the formula.

Is this what God desires? Did Yeshua sacrifice His life that we might feverishly follow a formula to get people a "get out of hell free" card? Are such people making such freewheeling, formula-driven confessions without truly repenting of their sinful ways actually "saved?" And then we notch our belts in evangelistic pride, numbering those that we claim to be "saved" to justify our compromised marketing of the Master, massive budgets, and manipulated statistics on church growth so as to gain greater recognition among religious men for our success.

Are we not dancing with deception? Can you imagine the Devil's delight with such spiritual seduction? We induce *confessions* of faith where there is no genuine *conversion* of heart, assuring the unsuspecting soul of his salvation. Are we not unwittingly increasing the population of hell rather than the hope of heaven? Are we not aware that Christ commanded us not to make *converts* but to make *disciples*? Did not our Lord focus His Great Commission on teaching folks to obey everything He had commanded rather than to blythly follow a formularized faith (Matt. 28:19-20)? And what does it mean to truly "believe?" Is this an exercise in lip service, giving intellectual assent to religious facts, or does it mean a radical shift in one's life, producing the fruit of the Spirit (Gal. 5:19-25)? The "devil is in the details."

Question! Have we unwittingly become complicit in proclaiming a false hope through a formula that is not revealing genuine faith? This is worth serious consideration if we are truly sincere about winning the lost. The consequences are eternal.

Is Salvation Secure?

A man goes forward at a Billy Graham rally. A woman checks a card at a revival meeting. A teenager raises his hand in a youth conference. Each, probably through a counselor asking a few quick questions, makes a confession of faith, reciting assent to the appropriate religious facts. They are likely then assured that now that they are *saved*, they could never again be lost, because "no man is able to pluck them out of my hand" (Jn. 10:29). They are said to have "eternal sincerity," or as it is often said, "Once saved, always saved." Is this true? Does this common doctrine lead to devastating deception, and if so, how?

This subject has been debated passionately by well-meaning pastors and parishioners ever since John Calvin replaced Jesus Christ as the locus of biblical authority for many. When Calvin became the mediator of truth, Christ went to the back of the bus, being called forward only when convenient to support Calvin. The Apostle Paul had warned of the deceptive danger of idolatrously following men and their systems, yet we nevertheless persist in the practice, revealing our carnal immaturity (I Cor, 3:1-23). "Therefore," declared Paul, "let no man glory in men" (I Cor. 3:21).

This subject is one of the most explosive, volatile land-mines strewn throughout the church. It separates very brothers. It fractures relationships. But even more troubling, it has incalculable potential to seduce untold millions to a false hope and an unsuspecting destiny. Our purpose here is not to attack the doctrine as such, but rather to reveal the dangerous deception inherent in the doctrine. Therefore, please consider these thoughts prayerfully.

There are a variety of biblical passages upon which the doctrine or teaching of "eternal security" is based. No effort is made to try to re-define or re-construct the meaning of those scriptures, nor is it necessary even to recite them. If they did not appear to substantiate the concept of eternal security, the doctrine would never have been fashioned within Calvin's "TULIP" theological system. The problem is that there are vastly more scriptures that suggest or even appear drastically opposed to the concept of "once saved, always saved" than can be gleaned to support it.

Why then would we choose, virtually without question, to believe that if we once confessed Christ as savior, we are eternally secure and could never fall away, given such a vast array of scriptures to the contrary? There are two main reasons. First, men, especially Greco-Roman western thinkers, love and virtually demand systems in which to try to organize their thoughts. Once such systems are constructed, they demand that every verse or passage that seems not to follow the system either be systematically ignored or systematically forced through a kind of mental gymnastics to fit the system, attempting through a variety of intellectual devices to explain away the obvious inconsistencies. Second, the teaching of "once saved, always saved" is highly desirable to the natural-minded man. It is easy to believe, purporting to guarantee a "get out of hell free" card regardless of how one lives his or her life. Who would not want to believe such a teaching?

This discussion admittedly launches into the theological deep where entrenched proponents would rather drown than admit the decidedly troublesome biblical problems that threaten to swamp the spiritual boats of untold millions of believers. However, it is not necessary here to further discuss the theological merits or biblical support for or against "eternal security" as a doctrine. The sole purpose here is to probe the profound deception that lurks in the dark corners of the doctrine. The author begs of you to consider seriously how this pernicious doctrine, so widely preached, seduces the saints.

The primary deception of the doctrine of "once saved, always saved" can be expressed in one sentence. **To preach and teach the doctrine of eternal security renders meaningless every warning of Scripture to the saints**. Since all of the then-time and end-time warnings of Jesus and His apostles, including Peter, James, John and Paul are directed to the saints (the followers of Yeshua, and the professing believers, all of which constitute the church), to teach that all such are "saved" notwithstanding their rebellious refusal to live righteous lives is to make a mockery of both the Master's life and the Master's sacrifice.

Do we... do you... really want to risk leading vast numbers of professing saints unsuspectingly to eternal damnation because we persistently cling to a doctrine that renders the Word of God of none effect? Do we really want to take a mental razor blade and effectively excise all of the dire warnings our loving Lord, and those who gave their lives to follow Him, delivered to save future disciples from deception and deceptive lives that would alter their eternal destiny?

Consider the supreme foolishness of declaring a "faith" that fails to declare the Scriptural mandate that our lives reveal and reflect the transforming, converting power of the Holy Spirit, and then secure such a false faith with a false hope as defined by "eternal security." The true gospel is scandalized, seducing the saints in the name of salvation. Satan himself could not conjure a more effective deception.

Salvation without repentance revealed in righteous living is nothing but the dissing of God's grace. It is precisely this "cheap grace" that has led to the disgrace of America, far-reachingly evangelized yet radically undiscipled.

We are eternally secure if we are eternally faithful, being saved solely by faith in and through the enabling power of God, who is willing and able to work in us "both to will and to do of His good pleasure" (Phil. 2:13). Therefore, as Paul warned, "work out your own salvation with fear and trembling" (Phil. 2:12).

Are We Saved By Faith… or By Works?

Nothing could be clearer! We are not saved by our good works but by our faith and trust in Christ's accomplished work. "For by grace are we saved through faith; and that not of ourselves: it is the gift of God: Not of works lest any man should boast." But, "we are… created in Christ Jesus unto good works…" (Eph. 2:8-10).

Here is the deception, resulting not from an unbiblical view but rather from an unbalanced view born largely of formularized faith and fear. Faith is first rooted in the fear of the Lord, which calls for loving obedience to the law, written not in stone but on the fleshly tablets of our hearts (Heb. 8:8-10; Jer. 31:31-33). Obedience is the sole biblical test of our love and trust of our Lord, as He and His disciples made clear repeatedly (Jn. 14:15-24; I Jn. 2:3-4, 3:22-24, 5:2-3). In reality, it is our obedience that reveals our faith (I Jn. 5:2-4).

Yet commonly expressed formulas seem to fight against the very evidence of faith that pleases God. It is an oft-repeated evangelical mantra that "We are saved by grace alone, through faith alone, in Christ alone." That is gospel truth, but the devil again deceives in wrongly defined and ill-discerned details. Is *faith* a recitation of facts formed into a recitable creed, or is it the willingness to hang one's entire hope on what God has promised, conforming one's will to God's ways? Is *grace* God's willingness to wink at our willfulness and sin, or is it God's unmerited favor and enabling power making possible our ability to do His will and obey

His voice? Does "faith in Christ alone" mean that His followers need not obey the Father's will as Christ himself did?

Anyone reading evangelical magazines, books and other publications over the last generation has witnessed a profound antipathy toward the very concept of obedience. "Grace" is the most loved and repeated word on the lips of pastors and people today, while "obey" is the most despised four-letter word in the Christian vocabulary. How in God's name did a word and concept that, from God's viewpoint, most closely defines the reality and existence of our love for and faith in Him become the most despicable word in the church in these last days?

Listen to the passionate words of John, the "beloved" disciple.

By this we know that we are the children of God, when we love God, and keep His commandments.
For this is the love of God, that we keep His commandments: and His commandments are not grievous *(I Jn. 5:2-3).*

Our problem is that we have swung the pendulum of biblical truth to an unbalanced extreme. We have chosen to major on *grace* and minor on *obedience*. Such a shift not only results in *false teaching* but also in *false hope*. We have blatantly chosen to emphasize only that which made us and our evangelistic targets feel comfortable, lowering the bar for Christ's body so low as to disembowel its holy character, rendering it but a parade of unrighteousness to brazenly assault the Pearly Gates.

This profound unpopularity of the biblical call to obedience, from Genesis to Revelation, is predicated on two things: (1) Our fleshly or carnal desire for eternal assurance without temporal endurance; (2) Our paralyzing fear that somehow we will heretically violate the doctrinal motto "by grace alone, through faith alone, in Christ alone" if we preach obedience. The result has been nothing short of a cataclysmic disaster, producing perhaps the most rebellious, undiscipled, undisciplined and spiritually disobedient generation to have ever inhabited western shores since the First Great Awakening. The divorce rate in the American church that has equaled or exceeded that of the nation for nearly two decades is the embarrassing witness to this debacle.

Will All Be Saved?

Let's be clear. The Lord is "not willing that any should perish, but that all should come to repentance" (II Pet. 3:9). It is clearly implicit in this statement of Christ's heart by Peter that some... perhaps many... will "perish." Those who *perish* will not inherit their preferred eternal destiny. Those whose names are "not found in the book of life" will be "cast into the lake of fire" (Rev. 20:15). No one should therefore aspire to intentionally, or even inadvertently, seduce any unsuspecting soul to believe that all humans on the planet will ultimately be saved.

The teaching of universal salvation is, and will become, increasingly popular as we approach the Second Coming of Christ. It will lure many, through false hope, to perdition. Why is such blatantly unbiblical teaching becoming a growing phenomena when it is so dangerous to eternal destiny? How does such open deception take root?

False teaching promoting false hope inevitably results from either unbiblical or biblically unbalanced ideas. Here are some of the "reasonings and thoughts" leading to the false hope of universalism:

1. The Bible says that "God is love" (I Jn. 4:16). Since God is love, He could never allow or even contemplate the eternal torment or punishment of His human creation made in His image. It is argued that this would violate His essential nature. The obvious problem with this position is that it is biblically unbalanced. While it is true that "God is love," it is equally true that God is truth, righteousness and a God of judgment (Deut. 32:4; Ps.31:5; Ps. 97:2, Isa.30:18). We cannot give God an earthly makeover to conform the eternal God into a temporal caricature to suit our carnal whims.

2. *But how can I lead others to embrace such a brutal God?* Many reason. This argument, again, mis-characterizes God. Is a judge *brutal* because he pronounces sentence on one who knowingly violated the law? God is as just as He is loving and merciful. He hates sin and cannot countenance it in His holy presence (Ps. 119:104, 128; Heb. 12:14). We also are to hate evil if we love God (Ps. 97:10).

God, in His great mercy as a reflection of His love, has provided a means of escaping His wrath that will be poured out on the children of disobedience. We must receive the blood and sacrifice of Yeshua for the remission of our sins; we must repent or reverse our ways to conform to God's ways, and rejoice in the hope of the resurrection.

3. Would God consign seemingly good people, or people who sincerely follow other gods or faiths, or my beloved relatives to eternal damnation? Many, including an increasing number of pastors, have increasingly substituted their own reasonings and thoughts on these questions for what the Bible says. The spirit of this age is to elevate feelings over God's revelation of truth. When we do this, we make ourselves equal to or greater than God. That was the essence of Satan's rebellion. Satan then caused Adam and Eve to superimpose their reasonings over what God had said, and it cost them Paradise, for they were cast out of the Garden of Eden. What will it cost you?

Is Salvation for Now or Later?

For centuries in the western Christian church, salvation from sin has been preached as providing a ticket to eternal life… later sometime. This was a significant change from the long-prevailing Hebraic viewpoint that salvation was as transforming for the here and now as it was to be for the still-awaited Messianic future.

The Psalmist, David, gave testimony to this truth as a "man after God's own heart." In Psalm 103:1-5, David praises God for the overreaching breadth of His salvation.

Bless the Lord, O my soul: and all that is within me, bless His holy name. Bless the Lord, O my soul, and forget not all His benefits:
- *Who forgiveth all thine iniquities;*
- *Who healeth all thy diseases;*
- *Who redeemeth thy life from destruction;*
- *Who crowneth thee with loving kindness and tender mercies;*
- *Who satisfieth thy mouth with good things….*

Then came Jesus. He declared that "the kingdom of God is come unto you" (Matt. 12:28). Healing and deliverance were evidence that God's kingdom had come, that His will was being done on earth as it was in heaven. Yet the kingdom was not manifested in its fullness. It had broken into Satan's domain on earth but was yet to be fully experienced. True disciples of Christ were deputized to carry on the work of the kingdom (Jn. 20:21) until the Savior's return to judge the earth in righteousness (Ps. 96:13).

So where, in this context, do we find false hope. We find it in unbalanced representations of God's kingdom that distort the truth and can become dangerously deceptive, as we shall see. Before proceeding further, however, we must see God's kingdom from His viewpoint as disclosed in Scripture.

- God's kingdom is both present (Matt. 12:28) and future (II Pet. 1:11).
- Jesus is the reigning king over God's kingdom (Rev. 19:1-6).
- Jesus, as reigning king, expects His subject to submit to His authority and obey His words (Jn. 14:15-24; I Jn. 2:3-6, 5:2-3).
- To enter the kingdom of God as a recognized citizen, a person must be "born again" of the Holy Spirit (Jn. 3:3), which means he must "believe" on the Lord Jesus Christ (Acts 16:30-31) he must "confess with his mouth that Jesus is Lord" (Rom. 10:9-10), he must "repent" and "be baptized" (Acts 2:38), and he must "bring forth fruits worthy of [as evidence of] repentance" (Luke 3:8). We generally and historically call this process "conversion."
- One who is "born again" or converted by faith in Christ through God's grace [enabling favor and power], is ordained to do "good works," the works of Christ and His kingdom now (Eph. 2:10).
- The throne or seat of power in God's kingdom is rooted in and eternally established in "righteousness and judgment" (Ps. 97:1-2).
- Those who love the Lord as citizens of his kingdom "hate evil" just as He does (Ps. 97:10).

Herein can be found a host of deceptions based upon biblically incomplete or unbalanced views, teaching and emphases, leading to a dangerously compromised destiny. This is not a matter of complicated theology or word-parsing legalities. It is about the fullness of authentic relationship with the Creator of the universe. He welcomes no pretenders and has no patience with religiously synthetic authenticity. Yet He waits… longsuffering… "not willing that any should perish but that all should come to repentance" (II Pet. 3:9).

Consider these concerns in which lurk the seeds of false hope.

1. If I emphasize in my life and teaching that God's kingdom is now rather than future, the focus of hope inevitably turns to the temporal rather than the eternal, thus compromising future glory for present gain. This has become a gospel perversion for the western church that has permeated the world in this last generation, leading to profoundly unrighteous living from pulpit to pew. If, on the other hand, I emphasize only the future heavenly kingdom, my life and teaching will be so concerned with getting people "saved" and making "confessions of faith" that I will likely miss the "kingdom now" life of Christ to be displayed as the truth made flesh," demonstrated by the present power of God to "save" by healing and deliverance. Both Jesus and His disciples displayed the complementary balance, and Paul poignantly stated, "The kingdom of God is not in word, but in power" (I Cor. 5:20).

2. If we succumb to the global and cultural pressure to use the word *God* rather than *Jesus*, we reveal our shame of the only name by which men must be saved (Acts 4:10-12). If we refuse to publicly recognize our King, are we yet His subjects (Matt. 10:32)? And if we are not, in both spirit and in truth, His subjects, then whose subjects are we?

3. If we despise the word *obey* in fear that we violate "salvation by grace through faith," do we not communicate, either expressly or implicitly, that it is not God's will but rather our own that is to be done, leaving it to professing believers to pick and choose how they wish to live? Do we not defy Christ's kingdom while deifying our own? Can such rebels claim life in the eternal kingdom?

4. If we fail to declare and display the "works of the kingdom" in the present, is not our gospel of future salvation missing the ring of

authenticity? Didn't Jesus' own disciples confirm the word with signs following (Mark 16:20)?

5. Is there a biblical commodity called "faith in the abstract?" Is Jesus Lord if I refuse to obey Him? If I persistently refuse to obey the "King" in the present, will He welcome me into His eternal presence in the future? Is Christ looking for a *confession of faith* or a *conversion of life?* Given that Christ is returning soon, how much weight do we want to give to parsing theological confessional jargon rather than the living of a pure, holy and righteous life as the true evidence of faith? Destiny may lie in the decision, for without holiness, no man shall even see the Lord (Heb. 12:14).

6. Are we only saved *from* sin, or are we saved *to* something? If we fail to manifest what we are saved *to*, what credence or authenticity is there in what we profess to be saved *from*? If we do not display the "fruit of the Spirit," do we have the Spirit of Christ? If we do not preach righteousness and pretend God does not see the rebellious "works of the flesh" which we allow to persist in our churches, are we not providing false hope? The Apostle Paul wasted no time in correcting such distortion of the gospel truth, declaring of unrighteous and fleshly behavior, "they which do such things shall not inherit the kingdom of God" (Gal. 5:21, I Cor. 6:9-10).

If we purport to live in the Spirit, claiming a place in the eternal kingdom, let us also walk in the Spirit now, revealing that the Kingdom of God is among us (Gal. 5:25). Deception lurks dangerously if we don't.

When Will Christ Return?

Few questions garner more interest than when Christ will return. The return of Jesus Christ to claim His bride, the Church, was known throughout most of New Testament history as "the blessed hope of the Church." However, it was our Lord who declared, "But of that day and hour knoweth no man, no, not the angels of heaven, but my Father only (Matt. 24:36). While we may not know the *day* or the *hour* of His return, we are enjoined by the Apostle Paul to recognize the *season*, and therefore be prepared, "lest it overtake you as a thief" (I Thess. 5:4).

It is not our intention here to shed specific light on when Jesus will make His glorious appearance, but rather to reveal the latent deception in the most popular and currently prevalent teaching on the subject known as the "Pre-Tribulation Rapture." Since this teaching is so popular, to express concern is to "dare to walk where angels fear to tread." But we must. Please consider this brief discussion and with an open heart in light of the whole of Scripture. If there were not great danger lurking within this teaching, we would not dare to discuss it. Amazingly, there are many who would more easily abandon the cross than the concept of the Pre-tribulation rapture. Why does this teaching have such a hold on our hearts? Why do we insist on embracing it despite the overwhelming biblical evidence to the contrary?

Before we proceed further, the reader should recognize that this writer believed and embraced the Pre-trib Rapture doctrine for nearly fifty years. It was the prevailing view, taught almost exclusively in nearly every sphere of this author's sojourn among the saints in the American church from coast to coast. It was perceived to be a "given," an inviolable extension of the gospel itself. So what happened? Why this discussion deigning to question such a theory presented as dogma? There are two basic reasons.

After truly and earnestly searching the Scriptures, it became increasingly apparent to this writer that evidence supporting the Pre-trib teaching was slim, and that a countermanding viewpoint was far more persuasive and consistent with the whole of Scripture. The second reason, which is the reason why we dare to discuss it here, is that lurking within this teaching is the potential for dangerous deception that could have serious implications for one's eternal destiny. Be well advised in advance, however, that to admit this, given the fact that so many reputations of the "doctors" of the church are so thoroughly invested in this doctrine, is tantamount to a not-so-civil war. Nevertheless, risking personal reputation in favor of multitudes whose eternal relationship with the Lord is at stake, seems an investment risk worth taking. Please search the Scriptures for yourself. Our purpose here is not to convince you but to alert you to deceptive danger.

First, this author believes in the rapture or "catching up" of the church to meet the Lord. We are to "comfort one another with these words" (I Thess. 4:16-18). The issue here is not *IF* there will be a rapture but *WHEN* that rapture will take place and *WHY* it will take place.

If you believe the church will be raptured or "caught up" to be with the Lord as the Apostle Paul clearly describes, when will that take place? Will it be before, during, or after the seven year period of tribulation? Will it be before, during or after the second 3 ½ year segment known as the "Great Tribulation?" Your answer to these questions has significant spiritual consequences, notwithstanding vociferous protestations to the contrary raised in effort to protect the Pre-trib Rapture teaching.

Second, a brief historical overview might shed a little light, both for those entrenched in the Pre-trib rapture teaching and for those whose eyes may be enlightened as to seductive dangers attendant to it. Though those teaching the Pre-tribulation rapture of the church try to find such teaching throughout church history, a truly honest and impartial student would be hard pressed to validate such a claim with integrity of heart and a straight face. Evidence is slim, at best.

In reality, in about 1830, John Nelson Darby was the first to divide the Second Coming into two stages: Christ's coming *for* His saints before the 7-year tribulation (the rapture), and Christ's coming *with* His saints after the tribulation period. To accomplish this two-part coming, Darby made total distinction between Israel and the Church, contending that the rapture is *imminent* (can occur at any time with no further prophetic events needing to be fulfilled). This viewpoint gained favor in America before World War I and was transformed from theory into virtual dogma by the notes in the vastly popular *Scofield Reference Bible* (1909). It then received popular affirmation as unchallenged "truth" in Hal Lindsey's best-selling *The Late Great Planet Earth* (1970).

Interestingly, one of the foremost promoters of the Pre-trib position actually admitted on *VIEWPOINT*, the author's national radio program, that there is absolutely no passage in the Bible that clearly supports the concept of a Pre-tribulation Rapture. Since that open admission, several other prominent Pre-trib authors have similarly acknowledged the lack of clear Biblical authority to support the doctrine with any degree of Biblical certainty. Why then do they continue so adamantly to believe this teaching? One writer, speaking honestly, declared, "I just choose to believe it."

Why then has the Pre-trib Rapture teaching gleaned such over-whelming support and acceptance in the American church, for many having become dogmatic doctrine? These are the three main reasons: American exceptionalism, historical revisionism and easy believism. We now begin to explore the deceptive dangers lurking with the doctrine.

AMERICAN EXCEPTIONALISM

As Israel was chosen by God, so history has harbored a sense of "chosenness" for America. Even as God ordained the physical descen-dants of Abraham, Isaac and Jacob to display His glory as a covenant people in the earth, so it seems evident that God ordained America, as a covenant people composed of those who would walk as the spiritual descendants of Abraham, to dispense His gospel to the ends of the earth. While Jew and Gentile, Israel and America, have reneged on that cov-enant, there yet remains a profound sense of chosenness. It is out of this historical sense of chosenness that "manifest destiny" was claimed, and hence an inbred claim to *exceptionalism* among the nations.

This inbred sense of exceptionalism now significantly, yet almost surreptitiously, affects and colors our application of the Scriptures as Americans. This is particularly true in the phenomenal receptivity of the Pre-trib Rapture teaching which gained traction in the American church just as the Industrial Revolution took hold, and with America's military strength catapulted America to global pre-eminence. We truly saw ourselves as "exceptional." We even saw ourselves as exceptional to Biblical history. Just as Israel and Judah came to believe God's covenant with Abraham insulated them from Divine Judgment notwithstanding their perpetual waywardness, so American Christians largely see them-selves as somehow excluded from Biblical warnings of judgment despite our nation's rebellion.

The new doctrine of rapture preceding the seven year period of tribulation fit hand-in-glove with our exceptionalist view of ourselves. Despite the fact that both Christ and His apostles, including Paul, warned of end-time persecution and trials, we would delightfully be excluded. We would be "raptured"... removed from the earth... so we would not have to "endure to the end" as Jesus warned. After all, we are Americans. Despite the fact persecution increasingly ravaged the

Church worldwide, we in America need not be prepared, because we will be pre-tribulationally raptured.

HISTORICAL and BIBLICAL REVISIONISM

The Bible invariably throws a "monkey wrench" into the machinery of our fleshly minds. It upsets the neatness of our nuanced rationalizations that purport to give us comfort in beliefs that are not fundamentally true… but we wish they were. We cling to shreds of Scripture that seem to support our pre-conceived notions despite the often overwhelming biblical authority to the contrary. We therefore deftly reach to revise either history, or Scripture…or both, to satisfy the elemental seduction in our souls that incessantly lures us to believe what we want to believe. What does this look like, theologically?

Noah presents a classic nuance. He is used , by many, as a spiritual "numbing agent" so as to render powerful passages of Scripture inert in the minds of those who want to believe what they want to believe. Noah was righteous in his generation, finding grace in the eyes of God. God saved Noah from the deluge that devastated the earth and destroyed mankind. Therefore, it is argued, God will deliver all saints from the destructive ravage of a demonically-driven culture or world. You will not have to experience the wrath of unregenerate man. It sounds good. It has the aura of biblical authority. But, is it true?

Do the saints in China whose leaders are routinely arrested, beaten and tortured believe this? Do the saints in Saudi Arabia or Iran believe this, who carry an automatic death sentence for confession of Christ? It is easy to believe the Pre-tribulation Rapture doctrine in the "land of the free," but not so easy in the "home only of the brave." The prophets and apostles tell the tale, having all suffered outrageous rejection and ultimate death sentences, having not escaped. Neither did the majority of the saints magnified in Hebrews 11 "Hall of Faith" escape the wrath of man.

Perhaps we should remind ourselves, both pastor and people alike, of Peter's loving warning.

Beloved, think it not strange concerning the fiery trial which is to try you, as though some strange thing happened unto you:

But rejoice, insomuch as ye are partakers of Christ's sufferings...
If ye be reproached for the name of Christ, happy are ye; for the
spirit of glory and of God resteth upon you" (I Pet. 4:12-14).

Brethren, we can neither re-write history nor re-write the truth of Scripture to conform to concepts we wish, in the flesh, were true. The first, second and third-century Christians were not raptured to escape the wrath of a pagan Roman empire any more than 21st century followers of Yeshua are guaranteed escape from the escalating wrath of a resurrecting Rome co-opted by Satan to stamp out the residue of the remnant saints, whether Jew or Gentile.

It is God's wrath, and God's wrath alone, from which true saints will be secreted, "for God hath not appointed us to wrath... wherefore comfort yourselves together, and edify one another..." (I Thess. 5:9-11). The wrath of God will be poured out on "the children of disobedience" (Eph. 5:6, Col. 3:6). And we have it on good authority that what the Scriptures refer to as "the wrath of God" will not begin to be poured out until after the mid-point of the seven-year tribulation when "the great day of his wrath is come" (Rev. 6:7). And who shall be able to stand when He appeareth (Mal. 3:2, Rev. 6:17)?

Praise God! Those who walk by grace through faith that worketh by love in true obedience "shall be saved from wrath" (Rom. 5:9).

EASY BELIEVISM

Who, in their natural mind, would not want to believe in a proposition that purports to deliver a believer from end-time persecution and from Satan's vicious wrath expressed through men who hath given themselves over to his control? The avoidance of pain is mankind's natural propensity. Therefore, it takes precious little encouragement... or faith... to believe in a doctrine that promises believers they will be whisked away in a rapture without having to endure anything but the normal problems of life in good times.

It takes little imagination, therefore, to understand why such a teaching would be so readily received, and why it would be presented so prominently in the century that may well precede the Second Coming. It also requires little effort to understand why the Pre-trib Rapture doctrine may be one of the most pernicious deceptions in the church today.

Perhaps you have heard, as have I, pastors and people joking and making light of the problems promised by God in His Word that are coming upon the earth. How many times have we heard in a mocking, joking fashion, "We don't have to worry about that, 'cause we're outa here!"? What has been the collective effect of this seductive sentiment as it has rampantly invaded the mind of the church over the past century? Is it encouraging men and women to "prepare the way of the Lord" in their lives, or is it rather seducing them to spiritual indolence? Is it promoting purity of mind and repentance of heart, or is it promoting a dangerous presumption that one need not prepare to "endure hardship as a good soldier of Jesus Christ" (II Tim. 2:3), because "We're outa here in the rapture"?

A simple and honest look at the decadent moral and spiritual condition of the western church after a century of embracing the Pre-trib rapture doctrine should raise an urgent warning flag to all. The collective consequence of the Pre-trib Rapture teaching, coupled with the common teaching of "Once saved, always saved," has been to effectively insulate professing believers from all of the end-time warnings of Scripture, rendering them moot... and thus meaningless.

Brethren, we must seriously re-assess our commitments on this matter. Deception knocks seductively at the door. And the eternal destiny of many may be laid by our Lord at your door for wilfully persisting in preaching a doctrine whose most respected proponents admit has no specific and clear Biblical authority. The temporal risk you run to your reputation in this life to re-assess and repent of what may well be false teaching, however well intended, will be well-worth the eternal rewards.

Can you believe in the Pre-trib Rapture and be saved? Certainly! But are you and those in your sphere of influence truly preparing to endure should you and they, contrary to your hopeful belief, be forced to face the gut-wrenching spiritual choices that lie ahead? I want to be prepared and prepare those I love and have charge over in my own sphere of ministry to *prepare for the worst, and hope for the best*, persevering in faith until Jesus comes. Deliver us from any doctrine that deceives through *false hope*.

Remember - "Every man that hath this hope in him [Christ's Second Coming] purifieth himself even as he [Christ] is pure (I Jn. 3:3).

Will Mary Plead Your Cause?

The mother of Jesus is gaining considerable press globally. In fact, the growing attraction to the virgin Mary is, in many respects, little short of breathtaking. Why might this be? How might this growing fascination and allegiance to Mary affect our world as we approach the Second Coming of her son and God's "only begotten Son?"

For those raised in the Roman Catholic Church, Mary has commanded cultish reverence ever since the Council of Ephesus in AD 431 sanctioned the Virgin as "Mother of God," allowing creation of icons bearing the image of the Virgin and child. Early representations show Mary as the "Throne of Heaven." Devotion to the Virgin Mary as the "new Eve" lent much to the status of women in the Middle Ages. Proclamations by the Catholic Church venerate the Virgin as "The Queen of Heaven" and as the "Queen of the World."

It should challenge the conscience of every professed believer to know that God, through his prophets, specifically condemned worship or veneration of the "queen of heaven," indicating He "could no longer bear, because of the evil of your doings, and because of the abominations which ye have committed" (Jer. 44:15-27). Yet, despite the dire warnings, the women vowed to continue burning incense to the *queen of heaven*, for which cause God promised to withdraw His name and "watch over them for evil" (Jer. 14:26-27).

Protestants have historically accused Catholics and Eastern Orthodox of "Mariolatry," claiming the extraordinary adoration of the Virgin Mary to be a violation of the Ten Commandments prohibiting worshipful images and false gods. As Catholic history continued, so did pontifical proclamations concerning Mary, none of which have any Biblical foundation. Mary was declared to...

- Be a perpetual virgin;
- Be sinless, having on "Immaculate Conception;"
- Be taken into heaven, without death, by "Assumption" "into heavenly glory, body and soul;"
- Be "Co-Redemptrix" with Christ (Believed by Pope John Paul II but not made infallibly official).

Interestingly, each of these claims contravenes the clear words of the Bible, revealing the Catholic contention that the Pope and the Church magesterium have authority over the very Word of God.

How then do we explain the exploding fascination with the Virgin Mary within the broader reaches of the Protestant faith? Something strange is happening. And why is it happening on the near edge of the Second Coming? Why have Muslims also joined in the rising chorus of veneration? Is trust in Christ no longer sufficient? What additional does Mary have to offer? Is Mary the new harbinger of hope?

The cover story of *Christianity Today* (December 2006), an "official" evangelical protestant publication, was titled "INCENDIARY MARY." The feature article, "The Mary We Never Knew" declared, "On the horizon today is nothing less than a Protestant reclamation of Mary." We should rightly inquire... a reclamation from what?... or a reclamation to what?

The contention of this unusual piece of protestant Mariolatry was not to emphasize that the mother of our Lord was "Blessed among women," therefore "all generations shall call me blessed" (Luke 1:42-48), but rather to exalt her role beyond the clear Biblical revelation. The author called her "subversive," "dangerous" and "radioactive," converting Mary's glorious role as the humble and obedient servant whom God chose to bear the Christ child into a social revolutionary dedicated to bring down the despised Rome so as to restore righteousness.

Mary was given by God a role to bring forth the "Son of righteousness," the "King of kings and Lord of lords," the Savior by whose name alone we must be saved. For that, Mary humbly rejoiced, "from henceforth all generations shall call me blessed" (Luke 1:48). The Scriptures accord her no higher honor nor a more significant calling. Why therefore do we? Why would mankind choose to elevate Mary to "Mother of Mercy," "Mediatrix of all graces," "Queen of Heaven," "Advocate," "Benefactress," and "Our Lady"? Why did Pope John Paul II dedicate Poland, the Roman Church, Russia and the World to Mary rather than to Christ? What authority has Mary been given by God that can be clearly authenticated by Scripture outside the edicts of the Roman Church?

It appears firstly that we choose to relate to Mary rather than to Jesus as Christ, the Anointed One, who alone was "full of grace and truth" (John 1:14). Why? Why does a child run to his mother rather than to his father for comfort? The reality is we do not much trust God the Father to be kind and loving, nor His Son, Jesus as Christ, to be merciful and truly forgiving. We want a woman who will not hold us to the standard of truth nor require us to repent. For this reason alone, Mary's status among professing saints at large is being magnified and will multiply dramatically.

Mary is rapidly becoming a surrogate "Christ." Mankind does not want to relate to a Savior who will "judge the world with righteousness and the people with his truth" (Ps. 96:13, Jn. 16:8). As genuine Biblical faith in Christ wanes, "Mary" will fill the vacuum with her emotive feelings. But it is not the *Mary* of the Scripture. Rather, it is a re-constructed, re-imagined Mary that men will embrace in false hope of salvation. Lamentably, the re-imagined Mary has become a post-modern revised version of the ancient "queen of heaven," seducing untold millions to a false hope.

Though the Catholic and Orthodox churches affectionately affirm Mary, raising her to worshipful status as intermediary between man and Christ, the Bible makes clear such is nothing short of idolatry, "for there is one God, and one mediator between God and man, the man Christ Jesus," the Mashiach, the Holy One of Israel (I Tim. 2:5). Though many Protestants are gravitating toward "The Blessed Evangelical Mary" high-lighted again by *Christianity Today*, December 2003, we must re-assess where God has guided us to put our trust. A false trust provides a false hope, for it is "at the name of Jesus every knee shall bow" (Phil. 2:10), and "there is no other name under heaven given among men, whereby we must be saved" (Acts 4:12).

Consider in closing. A re-imagined, made-over Mary is rapidly emerging to choreograph the world unsuspectingly into the emerging global government. It is a spectacular phenomena to behold. Untold millions have flocked over the last century to far-flung places of the earth to witness purported apparitions of the Virgin Mary. By and through these apparitions, the "Mother of God" usurps the role of Christ, claiming His Biblical attributes in breathtaking blasphemy, according to herself god-hood.

Since citizens of this planet have progressively abandoned the authority of Scripture over this past century, we are now ripe for massive seduction even of the saints through a demonically demonstrated false image of the blessed mother of Jesus who is portrayed as the true mediatrix between God and man and the one who will truly bring peace to the planet. So great has this deception gained dominance, that the Independent Catholic News from Rome, July 3, 2006, gave the following report.

MARY CAN BRING RELIGIONS TOGETHER

An Egyptian Muslim and deputy director of a prominent Italian newspaper has suggested that Mary could be the figure to bring Christians and Muslims together. Mr. Magdi Allam... has launched an appeal... to Muslims in Italy to visit Marian shrines.

The journalist said that he is convinced that the Virgin Mary is a meeting point between Christians and Muslims.

"Mary is a figure present in the Koran, which dedicates an entire chapter to her and mentions her some thirty times. In Muslim countries there are Marian shrines that are the object of veneration and pilgrimage by Christian and Muslim faithful," he said.

Jesus said, "I am the way, the truth, and the life: no man cometh unto the Father by me" (Jer. 14:6). Is Mary an alternative way ... a secondary mediator to whom we can go to circumvent Christ's most exclusive message of genuine hope? Tradition is not the test. Truth must triumph if we are to have true hope. It is time to choose. Respect Mary. Consider her blessed. But do not place your trust in her. There is absolutely no Biblical authority to do so. Horror lies on the other side of a false hope. Jesus Christ alone, the Mashiach, the Holy One of Israel, is our only hope for salvation. He alone is the hope of the Gospel (I Tim. 1:1). Let us together look "for that blessed hope, and the glorious appearing of the great God and our Savior Jesus Christ" (Tit. 2:13). "And every man that hath this hope in him purifieth himself, even as he [Christ] is pure" (I Jn. 3:3).

Chapter Twenty-Three

Daring Thoughts for *Deceptive Times*

~

1. How would you define *false hope*?

2. Is the purpose of salvation that we make a *confession* or that we be *converted*? What is the difference? How does deception lurk in the difference?

3. Is our salvation secure? In what way? If a believer cannot fall away from the faith, why did Jesus, Paul, Peter and John warn of that happening? Can you see the deceptive danger in the commonly taught idea of "eternal security?" Can we really make a confession of faith and live like hell thereafter, without repentance, and be welcomed into the Savior's arms?

4. Why is the word *obey* so despised in the church today?

5. If God is love, will all be saved, even if they refuse to repent? Why do people believe this in spite of the clearly opposite teaching of Scripture?

6. Why do people so easily choose to believe in a Pre-tribulation rapture even though its strongest supporters admit there is no Scripture that directly or clearly supports it? Why do you choose to believe it? Can you see how this teaching can be dangerously deceptive?

7. Why is Mary receiving such growing prominence among religions as we approach Christ's Second Coming? Do you see this as a source of deception, directing trust to a false savior? Will Mary really plead your cause? Can you support your claim with even a single scripture?

A Passion for Purity

"Every man that hath this hope in him
purifieth himself, even as he is pure (I Jn. 3:3).

SEDUCTION IS SEXUAL by nature. Throughout the Scriptures, God uses well-understood sexual and marital analogies to explain spiritual truth. Just as every man desires a sexually pure bride, so God desires a spiritually pure bride to present to Christ, the Messiah, His Anointed One under the holy chuppah of heaven in the presence of a holy God. Satan will therefore exploit every deceptive device to seduce the betrothed, thus betraying Christ the bridegroom.

Successful Seduction

Successful seduction majors on the flesh and our feelings. That is why the seducer's craftiness results in "carnal knowledge." Carnal knowledge is related to fulfillment of sexual or fleshly appetites outside of the legitimacy of marriage. It is that which, in a physical sense, is related to the body or flesh, and in a spiritual sense to that which is worldly, earthly or temporal. How is it that the enemy of our souls is so successful at seduction? It is because we play an active part. We actually have a bent to be bought. It is called the carnal nature or carnal mind, and it is "enmity against God: for it is not subject to the law of God, neither indeed can be. So then they that are in the flesh cannot please God" (Rom. 8:5-8).

"To be carnally minded is death: but to be spiritually minded is life and peace" (Rom. 8:6). "For if ye live after the flesh, ye shall die: but if ye through the Spirit do mortify [put to death] the deeds of the body, ye shall live" (Rom. 8:13). It is the fleshly, carnal nature that we keep alive, that toys with the truth rather than submitting to it, that renders us prime suspects for successful seduction. Seduction almost invariably follows a recognizable pattern. Let's look at it.

The Pattern of Seduction

Just as sexual seduction follows identifiable patterns, so we find with spiritual seduction.

POWER OF SEDUCTION

Seduction is powerful! It is powerful precisely because there is lurking within every man or woman a carnal or fleshly will to be seduced. In the sexual arena, many men and women actually fantasize about seducing or being seduced. That is why pornography and most women's romance novels are popular.

Similarly, in the spiritual arena there is a latent will to be seduced. We would not likely announce it to others, but it lies ready to be tested. Seduction works its powerful magic only on those whose inner character and submission to the Holy Spirit has been made secondary to fulfillment of fleshly desires or "the lust of the flesh." Spiritual weakness renders us susceptible to seduction.

PURPOSE OF SEDUCTION

The purpose of seduction is to allow the seducer to have his or her way with you. We well understand this in the sexual arena, yet somehow convince ourselves we are not really being seduced and hence succumb to the seduction, painfully reaping its delayed consequences. The same is true with spiritual seduction. When we step back to truthfully consider the seductive antics directed to take us down to destruction, it is usually not that difficult to discern the deception. So why then do we yield? We want to. We allow our feelings to overcome our faith. We allow the longing for temporary titillation to overpower our love of the truth and for our bridegroom. The purpose of seduction is to subjugate your faith to your flesh and your feelings.

PATTERN of SEDUCTION

The pattern of seduction is plain. First, the seducer attracts attention to something that speaks to the natural fleshly desires. Second, the seducer or seductress feigns genuine interest in you, not revealing the selfish hidden agenda. Third, you are captivated by your responsive feelings, numbing the faithful witness of the still small voice of God's Spirit. Fourth, you are given an opportunity to equivocate with God's Word, to rationalize a reason why you can allow yourself to submit to the authority of your demanding feelings rather than to the voice of truth of the bridegroom. Fifth, you act on the dictates of your feelings, abdicating your faith, and betraying your Lord, the waiting bridegroom.

PREPARATION for SEDUCTION

It takes preparation to be seduced. The environment must be conducive to compromise. There must be isolation from protective persons. Encroaching darkness, whether physical or spiritual, serves to reduce scrutiny, eliminating the light that would illuminate the contours of compromise. Inhibitions must be lowered. Standards must become relativized. And our wills must be increasingly conformed, not to Christ, but to the ways of the world. The conscience must be gradually seared through rationalized compromise so as to be insensitive to the still small voice of God. The door of decision is left slightly ajar, susceptible to the slightest nudge of the seducer. Satan knows when he can nudge and, in reality, we do too. Our defenses are down. Our vulnerability will strip us of our virginity, whether physically… or spiritually… betraying our betrothed.

PROMISE of SEDUCTION

Seduction always comes with the lure of *promise*. It is the sense of waiting *promise* that creates the allure to ultimately succumb to seduction. In the sexual arena, the anticipated promise may be a sense of feeling loved, being accepted or just pleasurable feelings, however temporal or short-lived they may be. The anticipated promise blinds us to the danger and destruction ahead.

So it is in our spiritual lives. God has given us precious promises, that through these we might escape the seductive corruption that is in the world through lust, but God's promises seem to far off, too illusive, too remote or uncertain to help in our present perceived need or crisis. Unwilling to delay gratification with our beloved... the bridegroom... the lover of our souls, we succumb to the seducer's accomplished schemes to lure us through the lust of the flesh to instant gratification, sacrificing our spiritual purity on the altar of temporal pleasure.

Professing believers will succumb to receiving the Mark of the Beast by the same pattern of seduction that leads them to choose to fornicate before marriage or commit adultery during marriage or justify their divorces and re-marriage when God has clearly spoken. As with the sexual, so with the spiritual. God is seeking a chaste and uncompromising Bride for His only begotten Son. Will He find you?

Now you can more clearly see why we need mercy? It is God's kindness and mercy that leads us to repentance. His grace or enabling power will be sufficient for us to come clean in broken confession and contrition, turning from our compromised and corrupted ways back to the God who woos us with everlasting love. But we cannot continue to yield to the seduction of Satan, the world or our own flesh. Praise God! He has provided a way of victory. We do not have to be seduced. We can live pure in a world of deception.

Living Pure in a World of Deception

Peter makes it plain! "Know this first, that there shall come in the last days scoffers... saying, Where is the promise of his coming," "for... all things continue as they were.... For this they willingly are ignorant" (II Pet. 3:3-5). In plain language, the majority of people on our planet will be willingly deceived, but it need not happen to you. You can live pure in this end-time world that dangles deceptive fruit before us, determined to lure us to dine, thus destroying our souls and leading us to eternal damnation.

Peter makes plain God's divine plan to deliver us from the corruptive power of deception. Here it is in simplicity for all who will heed the call to holiness.

> *His divine power hath given us all things that pertain unto life and godliness, through the knowledge of him [Yeshua, Jesus the Christ] that hath called us to glory and virtue:*
> *Whereby are given to us exceeding great and precious promises: that by these ye might be partakers of the divine nature [not carnal nature], having escaped the corruption that is in the world through lust (II Pet. 1:3-4).*

Our fleshly lust reveals our lack of godly trust. When we do not, either through ignorance or wilfulness, trust God's promises and provision for both life and godliness, we will seek to fill the vacuum of genuine faith with counterfeit or false promises presented by the world, the flesh and the devil. Because, as Jesus warned, "the love of many shall wax cold in these last days (Matt. 24:12), professing believers will abandon the true promises of God in favor of the temporal promises of a global government and global religion promoted by a counterfeit christ and his false prophet. You need not be among them. Peter tells us how to escape.

SEEK THE KNOWLEDGE of GOD

"Grace and peace be multiplied unto you through the knowledge of God, and of Jesus our Lord" (II Pet. 1:2). Notice that God's *grace*, His favor and enabling power, together with His *peace*, God's shalom of security and prosperity, are made available through the "knowledge of God." Notice also that it is not knowledge *about* God but the knowledge *OF* God we must seek. God desires not only that we know about Him but that we actually know Him intimately so that we truly trust Him. Information *about* God puffs us up in pride, whereas the knowledge *OF*

God transforms us into the image of Christ. It is not *religion* but trusting *relationship* God seeks.

God's divine power to overcome and discern deception comes "through the knowledge of him that hath called us to glory and virtue." It is through the "knowledge OF God," not *about* Him, that we are given "all things that pertain unto life and godliness" (II Pet. 1:3). Therefore, we must "Study to show ourselves approved unto God, a workman that needeth not to be ashamed, rightly dividing the word of truth" (II Tim. 2:15).

You and I must personally "study to show ourselves approved." We seek not the approval of men but of God. We cannot rely upon what others say. It is possible to "wrongly" divide the word of truth, leading to deception and compromised destiny. We must learn to study and apply the Word of God so that the entire Old and New Testaments and all component parts thereof are given full meaning, accurately portraying the fulness of God's character as disclosed in the Old Testament and as revealed in Yeshua the Messiah.

GIVE ALL DILIGENCE

As we pursue the "knowledge of God," we are to do so with diligence, but Peter also encourages us to pursue the practical manifestation of this *knowledge of God* with similar diligence, meaning "eagerness, earnestness and haste." It is this diligence in being partakers of the divine nature that protects us from spiritual deception, reducing dramatically our susceptibility to seduction. Seduction is active, and our diligence in Christ must be even more active.

ADD VIRTUE TO FAITH

Words are cheap, aren't they? That is why hypocrisy is rampant. Claiming to be "people of faith" in today's world is nearly meaningless and, in itself, can be and is used deceptively. The word *faith* has now become nothing more than a generic term behind which we can hide whatever beliefs we may have and whatever god we may choose to embrace. Therefore, it becomes increasingly necessary that our lives actively and transparently reflect and display our faith in Christ as "the way, the truth and the life."

The first and most telling manifestation of Christ in our lives is that they be virtuous. Living a life inconsistent from the life of Christ and the commands of Scripture does irreparable harm not only to the witness of our lives but also to the receptivity of others to the gospel. It also opens our lives to increasing deception.

Virtue is moral excellence, in the sexual sense, chastity. Christ wants and demands a virtuous bride, "without spot and blameless" (II Pet. 3:14). Isn't it interesting that in today's world we desire more to be *virtual* than to be *virtuous*? That which is "virtual" is that which only simulates or pretends to be the real thing. We have already seen that while the popular "buzz" is for authenticity, what is desired and promoted in actuality is "synthetic authenticity." The drift to that which is only virtual or synthetic is driven by the spirit of deception. Does genuine Christ-like virtue characterize your life? What would your co-workers say... your neighbors... your spouse... your children... or your Lord?

ADD KNOWLEDGE TO VIRTUE

The word "know" is frequently used in the Bible in a sexual sense and refers to the act of intercourse. A bride can preserve her sexual virtue and yet never really *know* her husband. Similarly, God desires not only that we be morally virtuous but that we *know* Him intimately. We can know much *ABOUT* God without truly *knowing* Him in genuine, mind and heart-synched relationships.

Merely knowing *ABOUT* God is like heresay testimony before a court. It is information gathered from various sources but lacks the personal experience of intimacy that gives credibility to one's life and testimony. It is, in effect, merely *virtual* Christianity that lacks authenticity. Because even the Devil has such *virtual* knowledge (Jam. 2:17-20) without embracing the intimacy of trusting submission displayed in holy obedience, such knowledge ABOUT God merely masquerades as the real, and is disastrously deceptive.

The Apostle Paul yearned to know the Lord intimately. His heart cry was, "That I may know him, and the power of his resurrection, and the fellowship of his sufferings, being made conformable unto his death" (Phil. 3:10). If this is the cry of your heart and the chief pursuit of your life, deception may dance around you but you will not be overly tempted to waltz with it.

ADD TEMPERANCE TO KNOWLEDGE

Temperance in operation is *self control*. It is revealed in a life of moderation characterized by godly control of the mind, will and emotions manifested in our attitudes and behavior. Since temperance or self control is a fruit of the Spirit of God (Gal. 5:22-23), the lack of self control reveals we are not governed by the Holy Spirit but by the flesh, or by demonic spirits. If we are led by the flesh, we are back "under the law" and "shall not inherit the kingdom of God" (Gal. 5:18-21). But if we "walk in the Spirit, we shall not fulfill the lust of the flesh" (Gal. 5:16).

Self control is a behavioral evidence of a converted mind and a re-born spirit. If we yield continually and without true repentance to the "works of the flesh" in our lives (Gal. 6:19-21), we actually "give place to the devil" (Eph. 4:27) and therefore open ourselves to deception. "He that hath no rule over his own spirit is like a city that is broken down, and without walls" (Prov. 25:28). If the walls of your life or mine are broken down, the enemy of our souls has ready access to seduce. Destiny is decided by our decisions. Therefore "be renewed in the spirit of your mind." "Put on the new man... in righteousness and true holiness." "Neither give place to the devil" or your flesh (Eph. 4:22-27).

ADD PATIENCE TO TEMPERANCE

Impatience is a sure test of the absence of trust. When we do not trust God, we will seek other sources in which to place our trust, because "nature abhors a vacuum." Patience requires persistence in pursuing God's promises, resting in His timing. The writer of Hebrews ties *diligence* to *patience*? Show "diligence to the full assurance of hope to the end: That ye be not slothful, but followers of them who **through faith and patience inherit the promises**" (Heb. 6:11-12). "Cast not away your confidence, which hath great recompense of reward. For **ye have need of patience, that, after having done the will of God, ye might receive the promise (Heb. 10:35-36).**

The power of patience in perfecting our faith cannot be overestimated. Impatience often sets us on a dangerous path to deception. "The trying of your faith worketh patience [staying power]. But let patience have its perfect work, that ye may be perfect and entire, wanting nothing" (Jam. 1:3-4). Patience works perfection. Impatience perverts God's perfect plan.

Patience requires endurance. Patience reflects the perfecting of trust in our lives. "Here is the patience of the saints... they that keep the commandments of God, and the faith of Jesus" (Rev. 14:12). Jesus could not have made it clearer... "But he that shall endure unto the end, the same shall be saved" (Matt. 24:13). What is your patience quotient? Will you endure the *Seduction of the Saints*?

ADD GODLINESS TO PATIENCE

Godliness has generally fallen on hard times. True godliness is increasingly mocked in secular society and seldom modeled in the modern church.

A godly person is one who, in great reverence and piety, truly fears the Lord as reflected in both attitude and actions. Interestingly, one of the principle characteristics of the last days is that men will have "a form of godliness, but denying the power thereof." We are advised to "turn away" from those who only mimic rather than model godliness (II Tim. 3:5). They tend to resist the truth, get caught up in a host of lusts, and while ever learning and gaining religious information, are "never able to come to a knowledge of the truth" (II Tim. 3:28).

Purported godliness leads to a perverted gospel. Fidelity in life ways reveals falsity of faith and opens the door to ever-greater deception. Because mere "forms of godliness" will prevail among the vast majority of professing believers the closer we come to the Messiah's Second Coming, "all that will live godly in Christ Jesus shall suffer persecution," just as Yeshua and His apostles did (II Tim. 3:12). But evil men with a pretense of godliness "shall wax worse and worse, deceiving and being deceived" (II Tim. 3:13). Therefore, adding godliness to your faith and life is perhaps the strongest antidote for deception. Remember, "The secret of the Lord is with them that fear him: and he will show them his covenant" (Ps. 25:14).

ADD KINDNESS TO GODLINESS

Why must we add brotherly kindness to godliness? Perhaps affirmative action is required, since we can so easily claim to love God while simultaneously disclaiming or disregarding our brother in Christ. This divided mind and heart opens the door to deception. Those closest to Jesus well understood this dilemma.

The "beloved disciple," John, noted, "If we love one another, God dwelleth in us, and his love is perfected in us." "If a man say, I love God, and hateth his brother, he is a liar: for he that loveth not his brother whom he hath seen, how can he love God whom he hath not seen" (I Jn. 4:12, 20)?

How do we know we truly love our brother in Christ? It is "by keeping his commandments" written on the tablets of our hearts, "and his commandments are not grievous" (I Jn. 5:2-3). Yeshua's brother, James, was blunt: "But be ye doers of the word and not hearers only, deceiving your own selves." "If any man among you seemeth to be religious [godly], and bridleth not his tongue, but deceiveth his own heart, this man's religion is vain" (Jam.1:22, 26). Brotherly kindness is not a feeling but an act of faith unfeigned. Purported faith without brotherly kindness is false, and is perpetuated by self-deception. The fruit always reveals the root.

ADD CHARITY TO KINDNESS

The Greek word translated "charity" in the King James Version is actually "agape" which is the God-kind of love. It is a love beyond feelings or emotions. It reveals itself in selfless sacrifice, requiring nothing in return. It is this dimension of godly love that protects us from deception that always involves an element of self-ishness and self-preservation. When we truly love as Yeshua loved, without regard to self, SELF no more demands the protection that inevitably leads to deception and compromise.

"Seeing ye have purified your souls in obeying the truth through the Spirit unto unfeigned love of the brethren, see that ye love one another with a pure heart fervently" (I Pet. 1:22). "The end of all things is at hand: be ye therefore sober, and watch unto prayer. And **above all things have fervent charity** among yourselves. Use hospitality one to another without grudging" (I Pet. 4:7-8).

GOD'S INCREDIBLE PROMISE

"For if these things be in you, and abound, they make you that ye shall neither be barren nor unfruitful in the knowledge of our Lord Jesus Christ. But he that lacketh these things is blind [deceived]....

"Wherefore the rather, brethren, *give diligence to make your calling and election sure: for if ye do these things, ye shall never fall*" (II Pet. 1:8-10).

Chapter Twenty-Four

Daring Thoughts for *Deceptive Times*

1. Why do you think God used sexual and marital analogies so frequently to describe His relationship to Israel and the Church?

2. Do you see the common pattern of sexual seduction having worked to seduce you spiritually at points in your life? How about right now?

3. Peter tells us how to escape the corruption of deception in an impure world. Are there any of his steps of action that you find particularly needful in your life? Why?

4. Why is patience such a potent spiritual weapon? What is your endurance quotient?

5. What does the fruit of your life reveal about the root in your heart?

6. Why did Peter exhort to "give diligence yo make your calling and election sure?"

7. What changes has the Holy Spirit prompted in your life as a result of reading *Seduction of the Saints*, Living Pure in a World of Deception?

Endnotes

Chapter 1

1. David A. Kaplan and Anna Underwood, "The Iceberg Cometh", *Newsweek*, Nov. 25, 1996, pp. 68-73.
2. Stephen Cox, *Richmond Times Dispatch*, April 15, 2001, p. F3
3. David A. Kaplan and Anna Underwood, *Newsweek*, p. 69
4. Ibid, p. 73
5. Ibid, p. 69.
6. Bob Garner, "Lessons From the Titanic," *Focus on the Family*, April 1997, p. 1-3.
7. Kim Masters, "Glub, Glub, Glub....", *TIME*, Nov. 25, 1996, p. 104.
8. Bob Garner, "Lessons From the Titanic," *Focus on the Family*, p. 2
9. Ibid, p. 3.
10. Graham Tibbetts, "Key That Could Have Saved the Titanic," *Telegraph.co.uk*, August 30, 2007.

Chapter 9

1. "REVEAL...," a report of the Willow Creek Association, August 2007, in which Bill Hybels, founding pastor of the 20,000 member Willow Creek Community Church in South Barrington, Illinois, admitted, "We made a mistake," revealing that the seeker-sensitive "obsession" had failed to produce true disciples as believed.

Chapter 10

1. "Clinton Discusses Equality on Gays," *Richmond Times Dispatch*, November 9, 1997. President Bill Clinton during a speech on November 8, 1997, at a fund-raising dinner for the Human Rights Campaign (HRC), a gay-rights lobby and political action group.

Chapter 11

1. Peter Dazeley, "An Evangelical Rethink on Divorce?", *TIME.com*, November 5, 2007, citing *Christianity Today*, October 2007, cover story, "When To Separate What God Has Joined."
2. Bill Shepson, "Can Christians Be Gay?," *Charisma*, July 2001, pp. 37-44, Cover story.

Chapter 13

1. John Cloud, "Synthetic Authenticity," *TIME*, March 24, 2008, p. 73-74.
2. Thomas Paine, *America's God and Country*, William J. Federer, ed., (Coppell, Texas), FAME Publishing, 1994, p. 490.
3. Richard N. Ostling, "The Church Search," cover story, *TIME*, April 5, 1993, pp. 44-48.

Chapter 14

1. Jerry Adler, "Evolution of a Scientist," *NEWSWEEK*, November 28, 2005, Cover Story, pp. 51-58, p. 54.
2. Ibid, p. 55.
3. Henry Morris, *Steeling the Mind of America*, New Leaf Press, June 1995, p. 205-206.
4. Sarah Cassidy, "World Scientist Unite to Attack Creationism," *The Independent*, Online Edition, June 22, 2006, p. 1.
5. David Rogers, news story posted by National Post and Can West News Service online at www.canada.com, October 24, 2006, p. 6-7 as printed out.
6. Ernst Mayer, "Darwin's Influence on Modern Thought," *Scientific American* (vol. 283, July 2000), p. 83.
7. Richard Levontin, *Review of the Demon-Haunted World*, by Carl Sagan, In *New York Review of Books*, January 9, 1997.
8. Mark Singham, "Teaching and Propaganda," *Physics Today*, (vol. 53, June 2000), p. 54.
9. Julian Huxley, *Essays of a Humanist* (New York: Harper and Row, 1964), p. 222.
10. Ibid.
11. Henry Morris, *Steeling of the Mind of America*, New Leaf Press, June 1995, p. 220-221.
12. *Humanist Manifesto II*, 1973.
13. Ernst Mayer, "Darwin's Influence on Modern Thought," *Scientific American* (vol. 283, July 2000), p. 83.
14. Scott C. Todd, "A View from Kansas on the Evolution Debates," *Nature* (vol. 401, September 30, 1999), p. 423.
15. Will Provine, "No Free Will," in *Catching up with the Vision*, ed. By Margaret W. Rossiter (Chicago: University of Chicago Press, 1999), p. S123.
16. Henry Morris, *Steeling of the Mind of America*, New Leaf Press, June 1995, p. 215.

Chapter 15

1. Ibid, p. 215.
2. Jack Wright Jr., Ph.D., *Freud's War With God* (LaFayette, Louisiana: Huntington House Publishers, 1994), p. 11.
3. Louise S. Idomir, *Psychology-Pied Piper of the New Age* (Oklahoma: Hearthstone Publishing, 1995), p. 44-45.
4. Ibid.
5. Lisa and Ryan Bazler, *Psychology Debunked* (Lake Mary, Florida: Creation House Press, 2002), p. 43-44.

6. Ibid, p. 52-53.

7. "Epicurius," *The Columbia Encyclopedia*, 1963 ed., 2:664.

Chapter 16

1. William J. Federer, *America's God and Country*, (Coppell, Texas; Fame Publishing, 1994), P. 204-205.

2. Ibid.

Chapter 17

1. *World Net Daily*, citing the *Philadelphia Inquirer*, "God-denying buildboard recruits atheists," June 5, 2008.

2. Michael Elliott, "Tony Blair's Leap of Faith," *TIME*, June 9, 2008, p. 33.

3. Pelin Turgut and Nathan Thornburgh, "Postcard: Istanbul, Worshiping with Turkey's Unconventional Minority," *TIME*, June 9, 2008.

4. Lisa Miller, "The Milguepost Manifesto," *NEWSWEEK*, June 2, 2008.

5. *Media Center Cidonkronos*, "Vatican: Pope to reach out to other faiths on Australian visit," May 30, 2008.

6. "If You Preach It, Will They Stay?", *Your Church*, May/June 2008, p. 8.

7. "Christians face arrest for preaching gospel," *World Net Daily*, June 1, 2008.

8. "Quoting Scripture banned in library community room," *World Net Daily*, June 10, 2008.

9. Bob Heye and KATU Web Staff, "Local mom concerned after school drops the Pledge of Allegiance," *Your News TV*, KATU, June 10, 2008, and June 11, 2008.

10. "Government to pastor: Renounce your faith!", *World Net Daily*, June 9, 2008.

11. "District drops John 3:16 ban," *World Net Daily*, May 21, 2008.

12. "Evangelical writers challenged to avoid alienating the included," *Church Executive*, May 14, 2008.

13. Karen Bartlett, "Spirituality for kids: a Kabbalah project supported by Demi Moore," *TIMES Online*, June 5, 2008.

14. Bob Unruh, "Biblical message now criminalized," *World Net Daily*, June 12, 2008.

15. James Macintyre, *The Independent*, (independent.co.uk), May 31, 2008.

16. Gary H. Kah, *The New World Religion* (Noblesville, Indiana. Hope International Publishing, 1998), pp. 199-223.

    Note: Most information in Chapter 17 related to Robert Muller and the U.N. was drawn from this source. This is the only footnote to reflect that, and would best direct the reader to a more detailed exposure on those issues.

17. Steven Waldman, "Jesuit Religious Factoids," *BELIEFNET*, June 23, 2008.

Chapter 18

1. George Bush Sr., Speech on September 11, 1990, in National Archives.

2. Michael White, "Blair says, 'Let us reorder this world'," *The Guardian*, October 3, 2001.

3. Charles Crismier, *Renewing the Soul of America* (Richmond, Virginia; Elijah Books, 2002), p. 351-364.

4. William J. Federer (ed.), *America's God and Country*, (Coppell, Texas, FAME Publishing, Inc., 1994), p. 204-205.

5. Henry Morris, *Steeling the Mind of America* (New Leaf Press, June 1995), p. 218-219.

6. Jeremy Rifkin, "New Europe Shapes Its Version of Dream," *Richmond Times Dispatch*, November 7, 2004, p. E-1, from *The Washington Post*.

7. "The Messiah Factor" - "Der Messias Faktor," *Der Spiegel*, spiegel online, July 2008, cover story.

8. "Who Runs The World? Wrestling for Influence," *The Economist*, internet edition, July 7, 2008, p. 3.

9. Jerome Rifkin, "New Europe Shapes Its Version of Dream," *Richmond Times Dispatch*, November 7, 2004, p. E-1, from *The Washington Post*.

10. Jerome R. Corsi, "Bush OK's 'integration' with European Union," *worldnetdaily.com*, May 8, 2007.

11. Jerome R. Corsi, "7-year plan aligns with Europe's economy," *worldnetdaily.com*, January 16. 2008.

12. Ian Traynor, "Love tops agenda as Sarkozy launches Mediterranean Union," *The Guardian, guardian.co.uk*, July 14, 2008.

13. Benita Ferrero-Waldner, "The Secret of Europe's Success," *Haaretz-Israel News, haaretz.com*, May 9, 2007.

14. Kobi Nachomi, "The Sanhedrin's peace initiative," *ynetnews.com*, May 6, 2007.

15. Steve Watson, Euro Globalists: Anyone Who Resists Eu Is a Terrorist," *New Interviews, prisonplanet.com*, June 18 , 2007.

Chapter 19

1. Gary H. Kay, *The New World Religion* (Noblesville, Indiana: Hope International Publishing, Inc., 1998), p. 199.

2. Ibid, p. 202.

3. Ibid, p. 209.

4. Ibid., p. 203.

5. Ibid, p. 204.

6. Ibid, p. 63.

7. Ibid, p. 65.

8. Ibid, p. 65.

9. Ibid, p. 65.

10. Ibid, p. 206.

11. Ibid, p. 206.

12. Ibid, p. 216.

13. James A. Beverly, "Smorgasborg Spirituality," *Christianity Today*, January 10, 2000, p. 30.

14. "One World Religion on its way?, *worldnetdaily.com*, June 14, 2005.

15. Ibid.

16. John Dart, "Ecumenism's new basis: testimony," *Christian Century*, August 21, 2007, p. 12.

17. Ibid.

18. Ibid, p. 13.

19. Julian Borger, "Moscow signals place in new world order," *Guardian Unlimited, guardian.co.uk*, April 11, 2007.

20. "Putin Calls Russia Defender of Islamic World," *Mos News, mosnews.com*, December 12, 2005.

21. 'Timing not right' for papal visit to Russia," *totalcatholic.com*, July 9, 2008.

22. Malachi Martin, *The Keys of This Blood*, "Forces of the 'New Order.'" (New York, New York; Touchstone, 1990), p. 370-371.

23. Ibid, p. 489-490.

24. "Pope Calls for a new world order," *CNN News* release from VATICAN CITY, January 1, 2004.

25. Deb Richmann, "Bush says US wants partnership with Europe," *BRIETBART.COM*, released from Associated Press, June 12, 2008.

26. Fareed Zakania, "The Post-American World," cover story, *NEWSWEEK.COM*, May 12m 2008, p. 24-31.

27. Ian Traynor, "Love tops agenda as Sarkosy launches Mediterranean Union," *The Guardian, guardian.co.uk*, July 14, 2008.

28. "Union for the Mediterranean," *Wikipedia, widipedia.com, July 14, 2008.*

29. Ian Traynor, "Love tops agenda as Sarkosy launches Mediterranean Union," *The Guardian, guardian.co.uk*, July 14, 2008.

30. Will Durant, *Caesar and Christ, The Story of Civilization Part III* (New York, Simon and Schuster, 1944), p. 618-619.

31. Ibid.

32. Nigel Rogers, *Roman Empire* (New York; Metro Books, Anness Publicity Ltd., 2008), p. 415.

33. Will Durant, *Caesar and Christ*, p. 656.

34. Ibid.

35. Nigel Rogers, *Roman Empire*, p. 13.

36. Alan Franklin, *EU-Final World Empire*, (Oklahoma City, OK; Hearthstone Publishing), pp. 44.

37. "Chief Rabbi Asks Dalai Lama to Help Set Up Religious UN in Jerusalem," *Arutz Sheva, IsraelNationalNews.com*, February 19, 2006.

38. Alan Franklin, *EU-Final World Empire*, pp. 48-50.

39. "Rome," *The Catholic Encyclopedia*, Thomas Nelson, 1976.

40. Ibid.

41. R.W. Southern, "Western Society and the Church of the Middle Ages," Vol. 2, *Pelican History of the Church series,* (Penguin Books, 1970), pp. 24-25.

42. Alan Franklin, *EU - Final World Empire*, pp. 37-38.

43. Ibid, p. 39.

44. "Blair: I'll dedicate the rest of my life to uniting the world's religions," *dailymail. co.uk*, May 29, 2008

45. James Macintyre, "Religion is the new politics...," *The Independent*, May 31, 2008.

46. Michael Elliott, "Tony Blair's Leap of Faith," *TIME*, June 9, 2008.

47. Malcom Moore in Rome, "George W. Bush meets Pope amid claims he might convert to Catholicism," *Telegraph.co.uk*, June 14, 2008.

48. Jim Meyers, "Bush Becoming a Catholic?", *newsmax.com*, June 16, 2008.

49. David Van Brima, "The Global Ambition of Rick Warren," *Time*, August 18, 2008, cover story pp. 37-42.

50. Ruth Gledhill, "Churches back plan to unite under Pope," *timesonline.co.uk*, February 19, 2007.

51. Ibid.

52. Robert Broderich, ed, *The Catholic Encyclopedia,* Thomas Nelson, 1976, pp. 103-104.

53. John A. Hardon, S.J., *Pocket Catholic Dictionary*, Image Books - Doubleday, 1985, p. 99.

54. Dave Hunt, *A Woman Rides the Beast* (Eugene, Oregon; Harvest House, 1994), chapter 6.

Chapter 20

1. Editorial, "Who's Afraid of Fingerprints?", *HAARETZ.com*, August 7, 2008.

2. "Government Okays Bill to Collect Every Citizens Photo and Fingerprint," *HAARETZ.com, August 7, 2008.*

3. Henry Lamb, "The Mark of the Beast," *WorldNetDaily*, January 7, 2006.

4. Justin Davenport, "Tens of Thousands of CCTV Cameras, Yet 80% of Crime Unsolved," *thisislondon.co.uk, September 19, 2007.*

5. "New 'Cell' Chip Being Developed In Israel," *Arutz Sheva, IsraelNationalNews.com*, February 10, 2005.

6. Humphrey Hawksley, "Big Brother is Watching Us All," *BBC News, news.bbc.co.uk*, September 15, 2007.

7. "U.N. to Control Use of Internet?", *World Net Daily, worldnetdaily.com*, February 22, 2005.

8. "Top Secret Group Applies for Patent to I.D. Physical Address of Web Surfers," *World Net Daily, worldnetdaily.com*, September 25, 2005.

9. "FDA Approved Implantable Medical Chip," Associated Press as printed in *Richmond-Times Displatch*, October 14, 2009, p. A2.

10. Christopher S. Bentley, "Who Will Watch the Watchers?", *The New American*, October 4, 2004, pp. 8-15.

11. Sarah Andrews, "Barcelona Boosts E.U.'s Top Supercomputers," *comcast.net*, April 12, 2005.

12. "D.A.R.P.A. Is Funding an Implantable Chip Far More Advanced Than 'Digital Angel'!" M.M.E.A. Multiple Micro Electrode Array Is So Advanced It Can Fulfill Rev. 13:16-18!, *The Cutting Edge*, January 1, 2006.

13. "Brussels planning central database for all fingerprints," *Turkish Weekly, turkishweekly.net*, March 18, 2007.

14. Bernadine Healy M.D., "The Dangerous Art of the Tattoo," *U.S. News and World Report*, August 4-11, 2008, p. 69.

About the Author

FOR A VETERAN TRIAL ATTORNEY to be referred to as "a prophet for our time" is indeed unusual, but many who have heard Charles Crismier's daily radio broadcast, *VIEWPOINT*, believe just that. Now, in *SEDUCTION of the SAINTS*, his words, full of "passion and conviction," provide clear direction to professing believers increasingly drawn into the deceptive ways of the world.

Crismier speaks from an unusual breadth of experience. After nine years as a public schoolteacher, he spent twenty years as a trial attorney, pleading causes before judge and jury. As a pastor's son, also serving in pastoral roles for 25 years, Crismier has been involved with ten distinct Prostestant denominations—both mainline and otherwise, together with other independent and charismatic groups from coast to coast and from North to South—providing an enviable insider's view of American Christianity and life.

Deeply troubled by the direction of the nation and Church he loves, this attorney left his lucrative Southern California law practice in 1992 to form SAVE AMERICA Ministries and was awarded the Valley Forge Freedom Foundation award for his contribution to the cause of "Rebuilding the Foundations of Faith and Freedom." Chuck probes the heart and conscience of our nation and the Church with both a rare combination of insight, directness, urgency and compassion, and a message that "desperately needs to be heard and heeded before it is too late."

From the birthplace of America—Richmond, Virginia—this attorney speaks provocatively and prophetically on daily national radio as "a Voice to the Church," declaring "Vision for the Nation" in America's greatest crisis hour, preparing the way of the Lord for history's final hour.

Charles Crismier can be contacted by writing or calling:

P.O. Box 70879
Richmond, VA 23255
(804) 754-1822
crismier@saveus.org

or through his website at
www.saveus.org